Many of the structural adjustment programmes applied in developing countries and more recently in Eastern Europe have targeted their agricultural sectors, which account for major shares of economic activity and income. Liberalising agricultural trade has major effects on income distribution and hence potentially significant implications for the political economy of reform. These fundamental effects on the organisation of economic activity and the relative positions of different economic sectors remain, however, a neglected issue of policy analysis.

In this volume, derived from a joint conference held by the Centre for Economic Policy Research and the OECD Development Centre in Paris in April 1991, leading international experts explicitly consider such open economy dimensions to structural adjustment. They focus in particular on the relation of domestic to international reforms; the sequencing of trade, sectoral and other reforms; the impact of structural adjustment on infrastructure and investment; the design of policy programmes to stabilise income and agricultural prices in open economies; and the implications for public finance of agricultural reform. They also assess the prospects for the success of trade reform in increasing agricultural competitiveness in world markets, focusing in particular on the circumstances in which the 'small country assumption' is violated and the policy implications of its violation.

Open economies: structural adjustment and agriculture

OECD Development Centre

The OECD Development Centre was established in 1962. Its main activities are research, external relations, in particular with research and training institutes in the world, and the organisation of informal meetings with high-level representatives of Member and non-member countries to discuss economic issues of mutual concern.

In its research activities, the Development Centre seeks to identify issues that will become the subject of growing concern in the near future, and whose implications are of vital interest to both Member and non-member countries. It also seeks to suggest policy directions for dealing with these issues.

The Centre maintains numerous contacts in the field of development and encourages the worldwide exchange of experience and knowledge. It thereby contributes to the flow of information on development and to the bridging of differences between OECD Member and non-member countries in the perception and analysis of problems and policies relating to development and interdependence.

Centre for Economic Policy Research

The Centre for Economic Policy Research is a network of more than 130 Research Fellows, based primarily in European universities. The Centre coordinates its Fellows' research activities and communicates their results to the public and private sectors. CEPR is an entrepreneur, developing research initiatives with the producers, consumers and sponsors of research. Established in 1983, CEPR is already a European economics research organisation with uniquely wide-ranging scope and activities.

CEPR is a registered educational charity. Grants from the Leverhulme Trust, the Esmée Fairbairn Charitable Trust, the Baring Foundation, the Bank of England and Citibank provide institutional finance. The ESRC supports the Centre's dissemination programme and, with the Nuffield Foundation, its programme of research workshops. None of these organisations gives prior review to the Centre's publications nor necessarily endorses the views expressed therein.

The Centre is pluralist and non-partisan, bringing economic research to bear on the analysis of medium- and long-run policy questions. CEPR research may include views on policy, but the Executive Committee of the Centre does not give prior review to its publications and the Centre takes no institutional policy positions. The opinions expressed in this volume are those of the authors and not those of the Centre for Economic Policy Research.

Open economies: structural adjustment and agriculture

Edited by
IAN GOLDIN
and
L. ALAN WINTERS

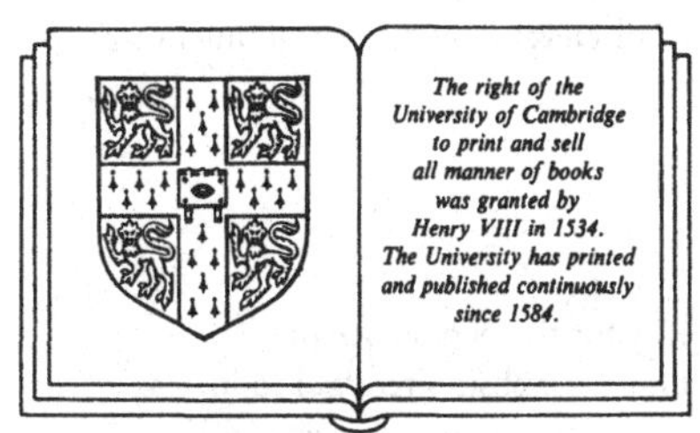

CAMBRIDGE UNIVERSITY PRESS
Cambridge
New York Port Chester Melbourne Sydney

CAMBRIDGE UNIVERSITY PRESS
Cambridge, New York, Melbourne, Madrid, Cape Town, Singapore,
São Paulo, Delhi, Dubai, Tokyo, Mexico City

Cambridge University Press
The Edinburgh Building, Cambridge CB2 8RU, UK

Published in the United States of America by Cambridge University Press, New York

www.cambridge.org
Information on this title: www.cambridge.org/9780521420563

First published 1992

A catalogue record for this publication is available from the British Library

Library of Congress Cataloguing in Publication Data

Open economies: structural adjustment and agriculture/edited by
Ian Goldin and L. Alan Winters.
p. cm.
Papers from a joint conference held by the Centre for Economic Policy Research
and the OECD Development Centre in Paris in April 1991.
Includes bibliographical references and index.
ISBN 0-521-42056-3 (hardback)
1. Produce trade - Government policy - Congresses.
2. Agriculture and state - Congresses.
3. Commercial policy - Congresses.
4. International economic relations - Congresses.
I. Goldin, Ian, 1955-
II. Winters, L. Alan.
III. Centre for Economic Policy Research (Great Britain)
IV. Organisation for Economic Co-operation and Development. Development Centre.
HD9000.6.064 1991
338.1'8 - dc20 91-44688 CIP

ISBN 978-0-521-42056-3 Hardback

Contents

Figures

Tables

Preface

The OECD Development Centre and the Centre for Economic Policy Research share a desire to stimulate economic analysis with policy applications. For developing countries and for Eastern Europe, structural adjustment dominates the policy debate. Nevertheless, key adjustment issues remain poorly understood. This volume arises from the explicit recognition of the need to incorporate an open economy and intersectoral dimension in the formulation of structural adjustment packages.

The book redresses the neglect of intersectoral relations by focusing on agriculture and its interactions with other activities, both domestically and internationally, since agriculture accounts for the major share of employment and income in developing countries.

The study provides a basis for policy perspectives which rest explicitly on the analysis of sectoral, economy-wide and international linkages. It is the outcome of the first collaboration between the CEPR and the OECD. We believe it will enhance understanding of the interdependence of policy reforms, assisting academics and policy makers to face the monumental challenge of transition.

Louis Emmerij
President
OECD Development Centre

Richard Portes
Director
Centre for Economic Policy Research

Acknowledgements

The editors express their gratitude to Louis Emmerij, Richard Portes and Jean Bonvin for their support for this project, to Sandra Lloyd for her excellent administration of the conference on which this volume is based, to Silvia Cornacchia who was rapporteur to the conference, to Kate Millward who administered the preparation of the typescript, and to Barbara Docherty who acted as Production Editor.

The editors also acknowledge with thanks permission from the following to reproduce copyright material.

World Bank, for data in Tables 3.2 and 6.2 and Figures 6.1 and 6.2; and for data in Table 4.2, from *African Economic and Financial Data Base* (1990), in Table 7.1, from T. Akiyama and A. Bowers, 'Supply Response of Cocoa in Major Producing Countries' (1984) and from M. Imran and R. Duncan, 'Optimal Export Taxes for Exporters of Perennial Crops' (1988), and in Table 8A.1, from A. Panagariya and M. Schiff, 'Commodity Exports and Real Income in Africa: A Preliminary Analysis' (1990).

OECD, for data in Table 8A.1, from C. Mabbs-Zeno and B. Krissoff, 'Tropical Beverages in the GATT' (1990), in Table 6.1, from J. C. Barthélemy and C. Morrisson, 'Agricultural Development in Africa and the Supply of Manufactured Goods' (1989), and in Table 13.1, from *Monitoring and Outlook of Agricultural Policies, Markets and Trade* (1988; 1989).

Review of Economics and Statistics, for data in Table 11.6, from R. Anderson and J. Thursby, 'Confidence Intervals for Elasticity Estimators in Translog Models' (1986).

FAO, for data in Figure 6.1.

Bank of Mexico, for data in Table 3.1.

American Journal of Agricultural Economics, for data in Table 7.1, from J. R. Behrman, 'Monopolistic Cocoa Pricing' (1968).

IMF, for data in Tables 12.1–12.4 and in Statistical Appendixes 1 and 2, from *Government Financial Statistics* (various years), and in Table 6.1, from M. E. Bond, 'Agricultural Responses to Price in Sub-Saharan African Countries' (1983).

US Department of Agriculture, for data in Table 13.1, from A. J. Webb, M. Lopez and R. Penn (eds), *Estimates of Producer and Consumer Subsidy Equivalents: Government Intervention in Agriculture 1982–7* (1990).

Commonwealth Secretariat, for data in Table 8A.1, from M. Karunasekera, 'Export Taxes on Primary Products: A Policy Instrument in International Development' (1984).

List of conference participants

F. Gérard Adams (University of Pennsylvania)
Kym Anderson (GATT)
Ronald W. Anderson (Université Catholique de Louvain)
Jean-Paul Azam (Université de Clermont Ferrand and St Antony's College, Oxford)
David Blandford (OECD)
Christopher Bliss (Nuffield College, Oxford, and CEPR)
Jean Bonvin (OECD)
François Bourguignon (Département et Laboratoire d'Economie Théorique et Appliquée, Paris)
Jean-Marc Boussard (Institut National de la Recherche Agronomique)
Colin Bradford (OECD)
Ajay Chhibber (World Bank)
Emil-Maria Claassen (Université de Paris-Dauphine)
Daniel Cohen (Centre d'Etudes Prospectives d'Economie Mathématique Appliquées à la Planification, Paris, and CEPR)
Silvia Cornacchia (OECD)
Shantayanan Devarajan (Harvard University)
Sebastian Edwards (University of California at Los Angeles)
Louis Emmerij (OECD)
David Evans (Institute of Development Studies, Sussex University)
Riccardo Faini (Università di Brescia and CEPR)
Christopher L. Gilbert (Queen Mary and Westfield College, London, and CEPR)
Ian Goldin (OECD)
Christina Hartler (The Industrial Institute for Economic and Social Research, Stockholm)
Walter C. Labys (West Virginia University and Conservatoire National des Arts et Métiers, Paris)
Santiago Levy (Boston University)

Peter Lloyd (Australian National University)
Christian Morrisson (OECD)
Arvind Panagariya (World Bank and University of Maryland)
Richard Portes (CEPR and Birkbeck College, London)
Helmut Reisen (OECD)
Dani Rodrik (Harvard University and CEPR)
Paul Seabright (Churchill College, Cambridge, and CEPR)
Albert Simantov (International Policy Council on Agriculture and Trade)
Kostas Stamoulis (FAO)
Nicholas Stern (Suntori Toyota International Centre for Economics and Related Disciplines, London School of Economics)
Akiko Suwa (Département et Laboratoire d'Economie Théorique et Appliquée, Paris)
Vito Tanzi (IMF)
Dominique van der Mensbrugghe (OECD)
L. Alan Winters (University of Birmingham and CEPR)

1 Introduction: from macro to maize

IAN GOLDIN and L. ALAN WINTERS

1 Introduction

All economies are open. Until recently, however, macroeconomic analysis for development has tended to build from a national rather than an international perspective. Economic analysis has made great strides, and a considerable body of literature is emerging around 'open macroeconomics'. Despite this work, external policy assistance – and not least that associated with structural adjustment – is for the most part insular. The international dimension to structural adjustment has remained a neglected subject of policy analysis.

The relative neglect of the international dimension to structural adjustment is puzzling given the international origins of these policies: namely the 1970s' successive oil price shocks and associated debt accumulation, compounded in the 1980s by high world interest rates, slackening demand and declining commodity prices. 'Openness' became a key consideration as developing countries became more aware of their vulnerability to external developments. Growing external and internal imbalances were compounded by tightening capital markets; starved of private capital and faced by growing disequilibrium, developing countries turned to the multilateral institutions for assistance, which increasingly was offered only on the basis of structural adjustment conditionality.

Adjustment is intrinsic to economic development. Urbanisation, the decline in agriculture's share in economic activity and other structural changes are regarded as indicative of development. 'Structural adjustment', however, refers to the restoration of equilibrium, providing a firmer foundation to withstand further shocks and facilitate development. In the current context, it denotes the set of policies associated most closely with World Bank and International Monetary Fund (IMF) external assistance to developing countries, and which have become conditions for receiving such assistance. Indeed, cross-conditionality, which links reform to other multilateral and bilateral assistance, is now being added. Over 70 developing countries have submitted to adjustment packages, substituting new open economy policy envelopes for the now discredited inward-looking experiments.

Structural adjustment packages aim at establishing a balance between government revenues and expenditures and enhancing competitiveness, in order to promote investment and private enterprise. The means to these ends have been the cutting of government expenditures, notably through the reduction of subsidies, and the liberalisation of domestic markets, prices and trade. The resulting changes in incentives serve fundamentally to alter the organisation of economic activity and the relative position of different economic sectors. These developments remain, however, a neglected issue, which this book aims to address by focusing on agriculture, in the context of open economy analysis and structural adjustment.

Agriculture accounts for around one-third of GDP in low-income developing countries and around 65 per cent of employment. Well over half of the citizens of developing countries depend on rural employment. Agriculture is particularly important to the world's poor, two-thirds of whom are to be found in the countryside, hence agricultural development is necessary for poverty elimination and economic growth. In turn, macroeconomic policies – and particularly those affecting the balance between agriculture and other sectors – are critical determinants of agricultural growth. In many, but not all, developing countries, agriculture has been squeezed by policies which reallocate resources to urban manufacturing and services sectors: producer prices and urban food prices have been held down, overvalued exchange rates have weakened export incentives, and tariff barriers have raised the cost of inputs.

Structural adjustment packages have tended to target these interventions, even though the removal of urban food subsidies has been among the most politically difficult of the reforms. To the extent that relative prices have improved, agriculture should have benefited. The positive effects nevertheless need to be examined in the context of other elements in the adjustment packages. In this volume we identify in particular the open economy dimensions: the question of the relation of domestic to international reforms; the sequencing of trade with sectoral and other reforms; the impact of adjustment on infrastructure and investment; and the global effects of adjustment and the so-called fallacy of composition, by which the simultaneous application of policies to different developing countries may undermine the desired outcome. These are important, but hitherto neglected, issues. In addressing these lacunae, we trust that this volume will provide perspectives which enhance the effectiveness of reform and facilitate development.

This book reports on the proceedings of an international conference held during April 1991 at the OECD in Paris. This introduction provides the analytic and policy context for the volume, and offers a short non-technical summary of the principal conclusions.

2 Open economy analysis

Part One contains chapters by Sebastian Edwards; Santiago Levy and Sweder van Wijnbergen; Shantayanan Devarajan and Dani Rodrik; and François Bourguignon, Christian Morrisson and Akiko Suwa. The papers address the question of the interaction of economy-wide structural reforms and agricultural sector development. Such interactions lie at the heart of structural adjustment, which aims to rebalance the economy intersectorally in order better to cope with the international environment. The natural medium for analysing the interactions between agriculture and the rest of the economy is the open economy general equilibrium model, in which nearly all domestic variables are endogenous and respond to, and in the context of, exogenous international variables. All the chapters in Part One adopt this approach.

Sebastian Edwards (Chapter 2) highlights a number of key open economy issues in a chapter focusing on the sequencing of reforms. He develops an archetypal intertemporal general equilibrium model of a small economy with multiple distortions, and uses this to evaluate the welfare effects of alternative sequencing of reforms. The inclusion of agriculture in the sequencing analysis, the explicit incorporation of labour market distortions, and the addition of the intertemporal dimension extends the existing literature on sequencing. Edwards shows that under certain conditions, a tariff-first sequencing is not an optimal solution and that with an economy-wide minimum wage only in the first period, there are welfare arguments for preferring a capital-market-first liberalisation. The paper emphasises first the extent to which the prevailing distortions (such as those in the labour markets) affect the outcome of the sequencing, and second that rural–urban migration of labour and the reallocation of capital between sectors depend on real exchange rate movements, which constitute the main transmission channel for dynamic and intertemporal effects.

Santiago Levy and Sweder van Wijnbergen in Chapter 3 provide fresh insights into the implications of a North American Free Trade Area. Their applied general equilibrium model of the Mexican economy focuses on agricultural interactions with other sectors and the effect of changing external boundaries. Agriculture is a highly protected sector in the Mexican economy and so liberalisation may be expected to have considerable income and employment effects. The study shows that although there are large potential welfare gains associated with a free trade agreement, the consequences for income distribution within the rural areas, and for relations between agricultural and other economic sectors, is sufficient cause for concern to merit the development of carefully targeted government compensatory schemes. The gradual implementation of the free trade agreement is similarly seen to be preferable on welfare grounds to its sudden introduction, as this dampens the transitional adjustment costs and facilitates adjustment through migration and the rural labour market.

Shantayanan Devarajan and Dani Rodrik in Chapter 4 develop a simple macroeconomic model to explore the relative benefits of fixed and flexible exchange rate regimes for developing countries. Fixed rates have the advantage of imposing a binding commitment to inflate no faster than the reference currency. On the other hand, they imply greater real shocks to the economy and can curtail economic growth by preventing the use of the exchange rate to mitigate the effects of terms of trade changes on output and income. The model takes account of the effect of the choice of exchange rate regime on agents' expectations.

Most sub-Saharan African countries depend heavily on a few primary commodities for their export revenue, and consequently suffer severe terms of trade shocks. The francophone countries of the CFA Zone have maintained fixed parities with the French franc while most other countries have varied their exchange rates at least occasionally. Devarajan and Rodrik calculate the trade-off between inflation and economic growth that would rationalise the CFA countries' adherence to fixed parities and find it implausibly low: a willingness to sacrifice 1 per cent growth of GDP to avoid 1½ per cent inflation! Their conclusion is that, at least over horizons short enough that higher inflation does not directly reduce economic growth, the fixed parity element of the CFA Zone has not been beneficial.[1] Generalising to structural adjustment programmes as a whole, Devarajan and Rodrik's results suggest that some degree of exchange rate flexibility may be desirable for primary producing countries, especially if other mechanisms can be found to ensure macroeconomic stability.

When viewed from the perspective of a relatively small developing country (Mexican GDP is less than 4 per cent of the USA), regional integration such as that envisaged in North America is not dissimilar to global integration. Morocco has recently engaged in considerable opening of its economy, providing a basis for study in Chapter 5 by François Bourguignon, Christian Morrisson and Akiko Suwa. Their applied general equilibrium model tracks the development of the Moroccan economy in the period 1979–87, examining in particular the effects of the major structural reforms. These reforms are shown to have been beneficial to GDP growth and to have improved real farm incomes. Simulations using the CGE model show that where rigidity prevails in the modern sector, both the costs of the crisis and the benefits of structural adjustment tend to be concentrated in the rural sector. Such simulations also show that further tariff reductions would reduce the rural–urban income differential, although reductions in the export taxes would have an unfavourable impact on the rural sector, as phosphate fertiliser prices rose in response to increased external demand.

The chapters of Part One highlight two important policy issues that have not previously received much attention. First, the distribution of income: structural adjustment entails, *inter alia*, changes in relative prices, and from the Stolper–Samuelson theorem and its equivalent in models with specific factors, we know that these feed through into changes, often magnified, in real factor rewards. Changes in factor incomes are important for their influence both on the political economy of reform and on the incidence of poverty. Political economy affects the credibility and sustainability of adjustment packages which, in turn, are increasingly recognised as determinants of packages' success. Poverty, as well as being an important element of political economy, is important on humanitarian grounds and in determining attitudes to risk. The chapters in Part One identify significant changes in income distribution which must be taken into account in any meaningful analysis of structural adjustment.

Second, it is clear from several of the chapters in Part One that migration is a potentially important response to structural adjustment programmes. In some cases this has an international dimension: remittances can be an important source of foreign exchange and cross-border migration can be an important safety-valve for the macroeconomic pressures that often build up under structural adjustment. Mexico and the USA is perhaps the best known example. Internal migration, however, is even more significant. It typically involves transfer between rural and urban areas, but is best thought of as being intersectoral mobility. Levy and van Wijnbergen find that migration is a major determinant of the cost and shape of adjustment to Mexican liberalisation, while Edwards finds that structural adjustment has major implications for labour markets, and vice versa. Modelling mobility and the imperfections of labour markets makes a considerable difference to the analysis of structural adjustment.

3 The small country assumption and trade reform

Part Two of the book brings together the papers by Ajay Chhibber; Arvind Panagariya and Maurice Schiff; and David Evans, Ian Goldin and Dominique van der Mensbrugghe. These papers examine the implications of trade and exchange rate reform from developing countries which are highly dependent on a small number of traditional primary commodity exports. The 'small country assumption' refers to the fact that structural adjustment policies have usually been conceived and applied in a manner which takes world prices and markets as exogenous: countries are price takers on the world markets. In practice, this assumption requires further consideration when a small number of countries account for a large share of the world market, when demand is relatively inelastic, and when the countries concerned are simultaneously being encouraged to undertake similar policy reforms, such as the structural adjustment packages of the 1980s. The focus of Part Two is on international interactions, and the models are constructed accordingly. Panagariya and Schiff in Chapter 7 consider a single commodity; they capture intersectoral aspects of adjustment by means of a simple supply function for this commodity, but model explicitly many supplying countries and the policy responses of governments. Evans, Goldin and van der Mensbrugghe, on the other hand, in Chapter 8 explore domestic intersectoral adjustment in terms of a general equilibrium approach in which policy changes are exogenous. The focus of the analysis is on sub-Saharan Africa, and the policy implications arising from Part Two are particularly relevant to that region.

Chhibber in Chapter 6 addresses two important concerns that have emerged from Africa's experience with World Bank and IMF structural adjustment packages, examining the effective supply response to real exchange rate devaluations and the inflationary pressures associated with nominal devaluations. Evidence marshalled in the paper suggests that real exchange rate devaluations have had positive effects on agricultural supply, although the first-round effects of devaluation result in cost-push inflation. The second-round effects depend on the manner in which the budget deficit is financed, on the extent of external finance and on the export revenue response, which with some notable exceptions – such as that of cocoa – are positive. Devaluation is thus seen as vital to African countries, which suffer from severe exchange rate misalignment.

Panagariya and Schiff develop a model for a single primary commodity of which there are only a few suppliers. The oligopolistic interactions between these suppliers have important implications for trade and welfare, especially when demand is inelastic. Their paper compares equilibria under Nash–Bertrand behaviour, where countries fix export taxes taking other countries' taxes as fixed and given; Nash–Cournot behaviour, where they fix national quotas taking other countries' quotas as given, and Stackelberg behaviour by one or more countries under both tax and quota regimes. Applying their model to the world cocoa market to estimate 10 countries' optimal taxes and quotas, they find that Nash taxes yield lower profits and Nash quotas higher profits than do actual taxes from 1985. Côte d'Ivoire and the non-African producers would increase their taxes from current levels under either Nash regime, but Ghana, Cameroon and Nigeria appear to tax more heavily than is optimal. When Côte d'Ivoire acts as the Stackelberg quantity leader, its profits rise, but both other countries' profits and total profits from cocoa production fall.

Productivity gains in markets such as these can be immiserising for producers as a whole, and Panagariya and Schiff show that this is true for cocoa even when apparently optimal policies are in place. They note, however, that their result does not parallel the traditional case in which optimal policies prevent immiserisation, for the traditional case is based on general equilibrium analysis and ignores other countries' changes in policies as productivity increases. Export cartels have a poor record of success, and there are strong reasons for resisting their establishment, so the appropriate policy conclusion from Panagariya and Schiff's results is that tropical beverage producing countries should diversify their production wherever possible. In this context, it is notable that the World Bank has refused concessionary loans to expand tea, coffee and cocoa production since 1968, whenever an alternative has been available.

Evans, Goldin and van der Mensbrugghe explore the implications for policy reform of relaxing the small country assumption. This results in an apparent fallacy of composition in policy, with particularly important negative consequences for producers of the traditional primary commodity export crops – cocoa, coffee and tea. Countries which are heavily dependent on earnings from these crops face highly inelastic demand for their exports, and in Africa suffer from being among the poorest of the developing countries. The paper begins by developing conceptual arguments on tariff reform. In moving beyond the conceptual debate, it is unique in providing quantitative assessments of the implications of alternative policies, on the basis of simulations using the Rural–Urban North–South (RUNS) model. This is a global applied general equilibrium model, which focuses on agricultural interactions with the rest of the economy, on both a regional and a global level. The analysis suggests that the simultaneous adoption of trade reforms involving reductions in export taxes would have substantial negative implications on export revenues and GDP growth in sub-Saharan Africa. In contrast with present practice, coordinated policy-conditional assistance, such as structural adjustment packages, needs explicitly to take into account the violation of the small country assumption.

The violation of the small country assumption is a major concern for the poor countries producing tropical beverages, but although many commentators use the short-hand term 'fallacy of composition' to refer to the consequences of violation, the problem is only partly one of fallacy. To the extent that a fallacy exists, it is in the analysis of international policy makers, who undermine the advice they offer – to liberalise – by offering it too widely. This problem is essentially an informational one – advice given to Country *A* does not form part of the information set for constructing advice to country *B*.

The serious problem is one of coordination. Panagariya and Schiff analyse Nash solutions to the policy game; their analysis involves a fallacy in the sense that Nash conjectures are inconsistent (at almost all points countries turn out to be mistaken in their conjectures about others' behaviour), but the fundamental problem remains even in models with consistent conjectures such as Stackelberg. If all producers of a particular primary commodity coordinated their export policies, they could almost certainly raise their joint welfare at the expense of the rest of the world.

The policy problem that this observation poses is multi-faceted. First, how could such sets of primary producers maintain cartels? Even with the connivance of consumers, international commodity agreements have found it very difficult to manage production. Second, if such cartel formation were possible, should it be encouraged or permitted? Standard results suggest that free trade would be potentially Pareto superior, but in the absence of international redistribution the relative poverty of certain groups of producer countries might justify at least temporary action – as Evans, Goldin and van der Mensbrugghe argue. Finally there is the question of whether current uncoordinated policies are close to optimal – either for individual countries or globally. The equivalence of import and export taxes in simple models raises the possibility that primary producers' restrictive import regimes render their current export taxes approximately optimal. Two factors suggest that this is unlikely to be the case, however: first the existence of non-traded goods upsets the simple equivalence, and second it is rare that all imports are taxed equally and that all exports will require equal optimal taxes. This suggests that if for some reason, export taxes are warranted, they should be explicit rather than being used to justify a process of import protection.

4 Risk and adjustment

Agricultural markets are risky, and protection from risk is one of the most common arguments advanced for agricultural intervention in both industrial and developing countries. In the former, risk-spreading instruments exist and income levels are such that few risks are life-threatening or even livelihood-threatening.[2] In developing countries, on the other hand, fewer instruments exist and income levels are such that down-side risks can take families very close to, or even below, subsistence levels. This leads to pressure for policy to reduce risks, or at least uncertainty. Many risk-reduction policies are difficult to reconcile with efficiency objectives. Moreover, policies which are successful in that regard can affect consumption and production behaviour, and hence affect mean returns, adversely. Structural adjustment programmes, which frequently aim to make individual decision makers more responsive to the information embodied in world prices, can have major effects on risk; these require analysis both for their direct effect on welfare and for the effects that the changes in behaviour that they induce have on the means of the economic variables of interest. Part Three contains papers by Ronald Anderson and Andrew Powell and by Christopher Gilbert which address these issues.

Anderson and Powell in Chapter 9 ask how the transformation to a market economy in Eastern Europe can be reconciled with a desire for a stable economic environment. Their proposed paradigm is that of multi-market, disequilibrium adjustment, and they evaluate trade tools, public stabilisation on domestic markets, and private risk contracts.

In principle, stabilising border prices by means of variable levies could establish bounds for the fluctuations of domestic prices. For several reasons, however, variable levies are not desirable for Eastern Europe. The implied distortions may be small in any individual market, but they could have a large cumulative effect in the convergence to the new equilibrium. Moreover, since the parameters of such schemes are usually fixed by collective negotiations they could easily be captured by incumbent state enterprises. Finally, variable levies are unlikely to stabilise domestic prices effectively.

Public sector domestic stabilisation works principally through the medium of public storage, but only at the expense of private storage. Two justifications for such schemes are relevant to Eastern Europe: dislocations of the credit markets and high private risk aversion. However, these schemes are flawed because collective management tends to result in a mean bias and because public sector managers are likely to be poor forecasters and poor storage cost minimisers. Finally, market tools – in particular, forward contracts – are shown to avoid many of the problems of impeding the process of transformation in the direction of a new competitive equilibrium. The principal reservation about them is whether they can develop fast enough.

Anderson and Powell conclude by discussing progress towards establishing market-based risk-reduction tools in the grains markets of Poland and Hungary. Hungary has established a genuine forward market, but it is still very small. Poland, on the other hand, has a sizeable scheme, but has allowed it to become subverted into a minimum price guarantee.

Gilbert in Chapter 10 considers the role of forward markets in reducing uncertainty, both in theory and using a simulation model. He considers the incentive for a single producer to hedge his output in an unbiased forward market assuming (1) that all other producers use the cash market or (2) that they all use the forward market. Using a particular set of parameter values Gilbert finds that it always pays an individual producer to hedge in order to reduce the instability of his net income flow and increase his welfare. He also finds, however, that if all producers hedge, all should expect to be worse off than if none did! This classic prisoner's dilemma arises because the ability to hedge encourages producers to expand their output and hence induces a significant fall in the average price received. As in the previous section, Chapter 10 suggests that a general injunction to establish forward markets and allow hedging could harm the people it is designed to support.

5 Government's role

It is now widely recognised that the government's role in structural adjustment amounts to more than just keeping out of the way. Fiscal balance is an important element of a successful macroeconomic programme, and the ability to maintain tax revenue over the adjustment period is critical. In particular, if liberalisation entails the loss of revenue from trade taxes alternatives are necessary. Government revenue is especially significant in that in most developing countries only the government undertakes significant infrastructural investment. A commonly alleged cause of failure in structural adjustment programmes is that stabilisation reduces investment and current maintenance expenditures and thus causes the infrastructure necessary for boosting exports to deteriorate rapidly (from a not very high base) – or in the case of non-traditional exports, not to be developed at all. This disappointment over the abilities of governments to manage adjustment successfully has lead to the underemphasis of these public sector issues over the last decade. The first two Chapters of Part Four, by Riccardo Faini and Vito Tanzi, redress the balance. Each faces problems over the quality and extent of the data available, but each makes substantial progress in analysing a major issue. The third chapter, by Kym Anderson, analyses the political aspects of agricultural policy.

Riccardo Faini in Chapter 11 has provided one of the first estimates of the effect of adjustment on infrastructure and investment. He finds that adjustment programmes appear to be effective in raising agricultural growth, but that this occurs despite the apparent negative correlation between adjustment and investment. The explanation for agriculture's strength is subject to closer analysis, in which it is shown that both price factors and public investment play a significant role in determining the performance of the agricultural sector.

The relationship between adjustment and the level and structure of tax systems is examined in Chapter 12 by Tanzi. The paper draws on the IMF's unique data base to engage in a comparative analysis of the evolution of developing country tax structures over the last decade of adjustment. The results show that in spite of the major structural changes over the decade, the average tax level for the group as a whole remained at around 18 per cent of GDP. In contrast to the accepted wisdom, Africa and Latin America had the highest average tax levels, and also experienced the most significant increases in tax revenues. The paper finds that the share of agriculture, imports and external public debt in GDP explains almost half of the variance in the share of tax in GDP.

In the final Chapter, 13, Anderson considers another role for government – as custodian of policy. Political economy has an important role to play in the analysis of structural adjustment, starting with explaining why economic policy has frequently been so inept that structural adjustment is necessary, and finishing with how to secure the required policy improvements against erosion by antagonistic interested parties. Anderson begins by considering the neoclassical political economy, which considers only domestic factors. This suggests a tendency for 'poor' countries to switch from taxing to subsidising agriculture as their economies develop: richer countries typically have smaller agricultural sectors and proportionately smaller expenditure on food; hence their agricultural policy entails the support of the 'few' by the 'many', and the 'many' do not face very high costs relative to their incomes. All this suggests that protectionism will increase over time. Anderson argues, however, that several international factors are likely to mitigate such effects. For example, US and East European pressures on the European Community to open up its agricultural market and the increased budgetary costs of the Common Agricultural Policy may help the EC to see sense. Recent research on the financial and environmental costs of agricultural protectionism and the potential benefits from its liberalisation may also dissuade policy makers from recourse to protectionism, although there is a danger that farm groups will capture food safety and environmental concerns for protectionist ends. Finally the conditionality of structural adjustment and other lending programmes have, and will probably continue to require, a relatively liberal outlook.

6 Conclusion

Structural adjustment has received much attention from economists during the 1980s. Some have considered its macroeconomic effects while others have explored its effects on trade patterns and comparative advantages. The chapters of this volume have attempted to bridge the gap between these approaches, or at least to provide some of the tools for bridging the gap. They have moved from macro to maize and back again, stressing that, particularly for poor primary-producing countries, meaningful analysis must combine the two perspectives. For example macroeconomic shocks affect agricultural incomes and hence raise important distributional issues, while conversely attitudes to risk and policies to alleviate it have implications for economic growth and investment. Tax regimes have both microeconomic and macroeconomic aspects, as do infrastructural investment programmes. Poor countries typically depend heavily on agriculture, and agriculture is potentially one of the internationally most open of sectors. Hence as structural adjustment programmes seek to influence trade policies, they will almost certainly impinge heavily on agriculture. Moreover, internationalisation introduces dependencies between countries that appear to have received little attention to date in the formulation of programmes.

It is our contention, then, that many of the fundamental issues of structural adjustment revolve around a macro-agriculture-international axis. We have sought to provide a stimulating and provoking introduction to some of these issues. Conference volumes never provide the last word on a subject, but we hope that this one has provided a useful first word on ours.

NOTES

1 They recognise, however, that there may have been other offsetting benefits to CFA Zone membership.

2 The commonest livelihood-threatening risk to industrial country farmers is the threat of removing government support.

Part One
Open economy analysis

2 Sequencing and welfare: labour markets and agriculture

SEBASTIAN EDWARDS

1 Introduction

In the early 1990s the economics profession came to virtual agreement regarding the advantages of economic policies that favour openness and export growth. The decades-old debate regarding inward- vs. outward-orientation seems to have been won by the proponents of outward-oriented policies.[1] The arrival at this quasi-consensus has, however, generated a score of important and pressing questions regarding the actual implementation of outward-oriented policies. Perhaps the questions that have attracted the greatest attention of policy makers and economic analysts are the ones related to the *sequencing* and *speed* of structural reform: In what order should different markets be liberalised? Should a country tackle the inflationary problem before dealing with market-oriented reforms, or should the opposite sequence be pursued? How costly is it to undertake liberalisation reforms if the labour market is still regulated and distorted? What is fascinating is that every day it becomes clearer that these issues are not only of relevance to the developing nations, but that they are increasingly important – crucially vital, we may even argue – for those East European countries currently engaged in reform and restructuring. In fact, it is not an exaggeration to say that in policy circles throughout the world there is a sense of urgency regarding issues of sequencing and speed of reform.

Although questions related to sequencing and speed, such as the ones posed above, are faced every day by policy makers and their advisors, the academic literature on the subject has been sparse and somewhat diffuse. Most of this literature has been rather informal and has concentrated on two broad issues: (1) the evolution of *aggregate* macrovariables such as the current account, interest rates and output; and (2) questions related to the credibility and sustainability of reform.[2]

The traditional literature on the sequencing of reform has concentrated on the order of liberalisation of capital and current accounts. Although there is no generalised consensus on the optimal sequencing of reform, the majority of authors have argued that the opening of the trade account should precede other liberalisation policies.[3] Perhaps the most persuasive argument for this 'trade-first' sequence of reform is that opening the capital account will result in severe macroeconomic destabilisation that could even generate a reversal of the liberalisation process. If the domestic capital market is repressed, and interest rates are below world rates, the relaxation of capital controls will result in capital flight and a balance of payments crisis. If, on the contrary, the domestic financial market has already been reformed, the relaxation of capital controls will tend to result in massive capital *inflows*. These, in turn, will generate a real exchange rate appreciation and a loss of competitiveness that will reduce the chances of a successful trade reform. Recent empirical analyses on the determination of real exchange rates in developing countries have, in fact, provided support to the view that increases in capital inflows have generally resulted in appreciation (Edwards, 1989a).

A number of authors have postulated that in addition to these macroeconomic reasons there are welfare arguments that support the trade-first sequence. For example, Krueger (1984, p. 19) writes:

> Since exchanges of assets are exchanges of capitalised values of income streams, income streams generated by distorted prices are probably the inappropriate ones at which to trade. It would then follow that the capital account liberalisation should not be undertaken unless both current account and domestic financial transactions are already liberalised.

And, according to Frenkel (1983, p. 167):

> When the trade account is opened first the cost of the remaining distortion (i.e., the closed capital account) . . . is likely to be relatively small. On the other hand, when the capital account is opened up first the cost of the remaining distortion (i.e., the closed trade account) . . . is likely to be very large. Thus a comparison of the costs of distortions . . . supports the proposition that the trade account should be opened first.

However, both of these statements, as well as similar ones in the literature, are based on conjectures rather than on formal analyses. The purpose of this paper is *formally* to investigate under what circumstances a welfare criterion indicates that a particular sequencing is preferred to another. This is done by developing an intertemporal framework that focuses on two aspects of the sequencing question previously ignored in (most of) the existing literature: (1) the role of labour market distortions, and (2) the impact of structural reform on the agricultural sector. The explicit incorporation of labour markets into the analysis of the sequencing problem is important for at least three reasons: first, in most developing nations minimum wage legislation and other distortions are quite pervasive;[4] second, from a political perspective the fear of increased unemployment has generally retarded, or even frustrated, reform attempts; and third, labour market distortions are usually difficult to eliminate. This means that from a political economy point of view there will be a tendency to leave the reform of this market until the end of the liberalisation process. An interesting characteristic of labour markets in the developing countries is that the extent of distortions is very different in the manufacturing and agricultural sectors. For instance, in many countries minimum wages either do not cover the agricultural sector or, when they do, their level is significantly lower than in the manufacturing and services sector.[5] This means, then, that structural adjustment reforms will tend to have different effects on agriculture and non-agriculture employment and wages. An additional important characteristic of the agriculture sector is that in a large number of LDCs it is – or has the potential of being – a net exporter. This means, then, that in these nations the export response expected from a trade liberalisation reform will come from this sector.

It is important to state at the outset that the model presented in this paper does not attempt to describe every developing nation, nor is it utterly 'realistic'. Rather, this model should be interpreted as providing a minimal, and yet rigorous, framework for dealing formally with the sequencing issue from a welfare perspective. Some of the specific assumptions, in fact, apply to only a particular type of country, while others are admittedly simplifications. The virtue of the model, however, is that it can be easily manipulated so as to incorporate alternative assumptions. In the rest of the paper I explicitly point out which assumptions are subject to controversy, and discuss ways in which they can be modified.

The rest of the paper is organised as follows. In Section 2, I develop a general intertemporal model of a small open developing economy subject to multiple distortions, that can be used formally to address the issues of sequencing and speed of reform. This model considers the existence of three broadly defined sectors – agriculture, which is considered to be a net exporter; manufacturing, a net importer; and services – and four initial (before reform) distortions. More specifically, it is assumed that imports are subject to an import tariff, that capital flows are restricted, that the services sector is distorted through a consumption tax, and that there is a minimum wage that impacts on the manufacturing and services sector. Section 3 is devoted to comparing the consequences of two specific sequences of reform. The emphasis here is on labour market reaction, the agricultural sector behaviour and economy-wide welfare. Section 4 discusses the model's limitations and considers some extensions, including tariffs on intermediate inputs. Section 5 draws a conclusion.

2 The sequencing of structural reforms: a general welfare approach

The purpose of this section is to develop a general optimising intertemporal model to analyse the most important consequences – and especially the welfare effects – of policies aimed at structurally reforming the economy. The model explicitly considers the existence of multiple distortions, allowing us formally to inquire into the consequences of alternative sequencing scenarios.[6] In this section a general version of the model is presented.[7] In Section 3 the model is manipulated in order to analyse two sequencing scenarios, while in Section 4 some extensions are discussed. In spite of its apparent generality, the model developed in this section provides the minimal structure required formally to analyse sequencing issues from a welfare perspective.

Assume that the country under consideration is a small open economy that faces given world prices of tradable goods and given world interest rates. There are three broadly defined sectors – Agriculture (A), Manufacturing (M) and Services (S) – and two periods, the present (period 1) and the future (period 2). It is assumed that, initially, agriculture is a net exporter and manufacturing a net importer.[8] There is no trade in services, and the market has to clear in every period. In order to simplify the setup of the model, in its general version we assume that there are no intermediate inputs; this assumption, however, is relaxed in Section 4, where the case where agriculture uses imported intermediate goods is analysed in some detail.

This economy is assumed to be subject to four basic distortions. (1) Financial sector regulations that take the form of a tax on borrowing and lending from abroad and, thus, in an interest rate differential between domestic and world interest rates. (2) A minimum wage, which in this version of the model is assumed to cover the manufacturing and services sectors. In this section I assume that this minimum wage is expressed in terms of the agricultural goods; in Section 4, however, we discuss the more general case of nominal wage indexation to a general price index. (3) A consumption tax on services. (4) Tariffs on the importation of manufactures.

Assume that in this economy there are a large number of producers and (identical) consumers, and that perfect competition prevails.[9] We assume that there are three factors of production: labour, capital and natural resources. Initially, and in order to simplify the discussion, we assume that there is no investment; later, however, we discuss how the formal introduction of investment will affect the results.[10]

2.1 The consumers' problem

Consumers maximise utility subject to their intertemporal budget constraint. If the utility function is time-separable, with each subutility function homothetic and identical, the representative consumer problem can be stated as follows:[11]

$$\max V\{u(c_S, c_A, c_M); \quad U(C_S, C_A, C_M)\}$$

subject to:

$$c_A + pc_M + fc_S + \delta(C_A + PC_M + FC_S) \leq \text{Wealth} \tag{1}$$

where lower case letters refer to first-period variables and upper case letters refer to second-period variables. The price of agriculture goods has been taken to be the numeraire (e.g., $p_A = P_A = 1$). V is the intertemporal welfare function: u and U are period 1 and 2 subutility functions. c_A, c_M, c_S, (C_A, C_M and C_S) are consumption of A, M and S in period 1 (2); f and F and p and P are the prices of services and manufacturing relative to agriculture faced by consumers in periods 1 and 2, and are inclusive of the tax on S and the tariff on M. δ is the domestic discount factor equal to $(1 + r)^{-1}$. Since there is a tax on foreign borrowing, the domestic real interest rate r is higher than the world interest rate. The differences between these two rates is given by the tax (σ) on capital movements: $r = r^* + \sigma$. The presence of this tax, then, captures the fact that initially the domestic capital market is regulated and distorted.

Wealth is the discounted sum of consumers' income in both periods. Income, in turn, is given by: (1) income from labour services; (2) income from the renting of capital stock, and of natural resources that consumers own to domestic firms; and (3) income obtained from government transfers. These, in turn, correspond to the government's revenue from tariffs, taxes on non-tradables and capital flows in each period. The solution to the consumers' optimising problem is conveniently summarised by the following intertemporal expenditure function:

$$E = E\{\pi(1,p,f), \quad \delta^* \Pi(1,P,F), V\} \tag{2}$$

where π and Π are exact price indexes for periods 1 and 2. Under the assumptions of homotheticity and separability these price indexes correspond to unit expenditure functions (Svensson and Razin, 1983; Edwards and van Wijnbergen, 1983). Given our assumption of a time-separable utility function, total expenditure in periods 1 and 2 are always substitutes.

2.2 The producers' problem

From the supply side the most important characteristic of this model is the existence of a minimum wage in the manufacturing (import-competing) and services sectors. An elegant way of dealing with the case of sector-specific minimum wages is by introducing an *equilibrium* wage rate differential of the Harris–Todaro (1970) type.[12] In this setup the equilibrium condition is that the wage rate in the agricultural sector is equal to the *expected* wage in the sector protected by the minimum wage. In our case, this means $W_A = E(W_U)$, where W_U is the wage rate in the urban sector and is equal to the minimum wage applicable to manufacturing and services.

Equilibrium under these assumptions of sector-specific minimum wage coverage is depicted by Figure 2.1. Here, total labour used in the manufacturing and services sectors is measured from the right-hand side origin O_M; the wage rate $\bar{W}_M$ is the minimum wage in the importables (manufacturing) and services sectors. Schedule $(L_M + L_S)$ is the demand for labour by the manufacturing and services sectors, while (L_A) is the demand in agriculture. Schedule qq is a rectangular hyperbola known as the Harris–Todaro locus, along which the following equation is satisfied:

$$W_A = \left(\frac{L_M}{L_M + U}\right) W_P \tag{3}$$

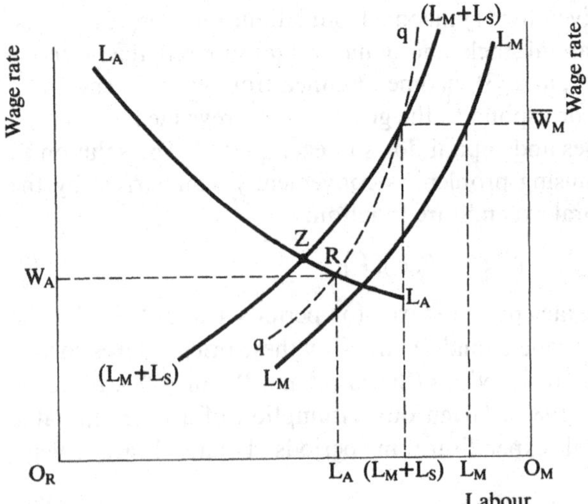

Figure 2.1 Labour market equilibrium with unemployment

where U unemployment and L_M is employment in the M sector. $L_M/(L_M + U)$ is, then, the probability of finding a job in the 'covered' sector. In the absence of a minimum wage, equilibrium is attained at point Z, with full employment of labour resources. With a sectoral minimum wage, however, the intersection of L_A with qq at point R gives the wage rate in the uncovered (no minimum wage) sector, employment in each sector and total unemployment. The distance $O_R L_A$ is total employment in the exportables agricultural sector; the distance $O_M L_M$ is employment in manufacturing; the distance $L_M(L_M + L_S)$ is the initial employment in the covered services sector. Finally, distance $(L_M + L_S) L_A$ is the initial *equilibrium* level of unemployment.

We can formally deal with the case of sector-specific wage rigidity by using two revenue functions – for the covered and uncovered sectors – in each period.[13] For the case of period 1 we can denote them in the following way (remember that lower case letters refer to period 1 variables; of course, for period 2 the case is perfectly analogous):

$$r^c = r^c(1,p,q,l^c); \quad r^u = r^u(1,p,q,l^u) \tag{4}$$

where superscripts c and u refer to covered and uncovered sectors, and where l^c and l^u denote employment in the covered and uncovered sectors, and where q is the price of services faced by *producers*.[14] The employment constraint is given by:

$$l^c + l^u + \mu = l^T \tag{5}$$

where μ is period 1 unemployment and l^T is the total (exogenously given) labour supply in that period.

The wage rate in the covered sector is exogenously set at the minimum level $\bar{w}$. Denoting partial derivative by subindexes we can write:[15]

$$r^c_{l^c} = \bar{w} \tag{6}$$

On the other hand the Harris–Todaro equilibrium condition states that there is a relationship between the wage rate in the covered and uncovered sector:

$$r^u_{l^u} = \psi r^c_{l^c} \tag{7}$$

where $r^u_{l^u} = w^A$ is the wage rate in the uncovered sector, and where

$$\psi = \frac{l^c}{l^T - l^u} \tag{8}$$

Naturally, the assumption of minimum wage coverage made here is a simplification of reality. In most countries, minimum wages cover only a segment of the urban sector and some parts of the agricultural sector. The model can easily be expanded to include that type of labour market configuration. The cost of doing so is that the number of sectors will be doubled, and the algebra will become more cumbersome. However, as the interested reader will readily verify, the main thrust of the analysis presented here will be maintained.

2.3 *Equilibrium*

The complete model is then given by the following set of equations (where subindexes refer to partial derivatives with respect to that variable):

$$\begin{aligned} r^u(1,p,q,l^u) + \delta R^u(1,P,Q,L^u) + r^c(1,p,q,l^c(1,p,q,\bar{w})) \\ + \delta R^c(1,P,Q,L^c(\cdot)) \\ + \text{TRANS} = E(\pi(1,p,f),\delta\Pi(1,P,F),V) \end{aligned} \tag{9}$$

$$\text{TRANS} = \tau^1 r_q + \delta\tau^2 R_Q + bCA + t^1 M^1 + \delta t^2 M^2 \tag{10}$$

$$b = \delta^* - \delta \tag{11}$$

$$CA = R^u + R^c + (\tau^2 R_Q + t^2 M^2) - \Pi E_{\delta\Pi} \tag{12}$$

$$f = q + \tau^1; \quad F = Q + \tau^2 \tag{13}$$

$$r_q^c = E_f \tag{14}$$

$$R_Q^C = E_F \tag{15}$$

$$p = p^* + t^1; \quad P = P^* + t^2 \tag{16}$$

$$M^1 = (E_p - r_p^c); \quad M^2 = (E_P - R_P^C) \tag{17}$$

These nine equations, plus the expressions describing labour market equilibrium (equations (4) through (8)) constitute our intertemporal model of this small distorted economy.

Equation (9) is the intertemporal budget constraint, and says that the present value of income (the left-hand side) has to equal the present value of expenditure (the right-hand side). TRANS is the present value of government transfers to the public and is given by equation (10). Here $\tau^1 r_q^c$ is period 1 tax revenue from the non-tradables' service market (τ^1 is the tax rate in period 1 and r_q^c is the equilibrium quantity produced and consumed in that period); $\delta\tau^2 R_Q^C$ is the present value of the tax on foreign borrowing, where b is the present value of the tax per unit borrowed and is equal to $(\delta^* - \delta)$, and CA is the current account in period 2, which is defined in equation (12) as total income minus expenditure in period 2. This means that, since in this model there is no investment, the current account is equal to savings in each period. Finally, $t^1 M^1$ and $\delta t^2 M^2$ in equation (10) are revenues from import tariffs; t^i is the tariff rate in period

i $(i = 1,2)$ and M^i are imports in period i and are defined in equation (17) as the excess demand for importables in each period. Equation (13) provides the linkage between consumer and producer prices for non-tradables. Equations (14) and (15) state that the non-tradables' goods market has to clear in each period – r_q^c and R_Q^C are quantities produced of these goods, while E_f and E_F are the quantities demanded.

Although the model presented above is quite general and flexible it still has some limitations. In addition to those already pointed out, the most important ones are: (1) the inelastic supply of labour; (2) the absence of intermediate inputs; (3) the presence of only one importable sector; and (4) the minimum wage being fixed in terms of the numeraire good rather than as a function of a (consumption) basket. The relaxation of some of these simplifying assumptions is discussed in Section 4.

2.4 *The welfare effects of structural reform*

The framework presented above can be used to analyse a number of important welfare functions related to the sequencing of structural reform. After manipulating the model, we obtain the following equation that captures the different channels through which structural reforms will affect welfare in this economy (where, as before, subindexes refer to partial derivatives):

$$\begin{aligned} E_V dV = {} & t^1 dM^1 + \delta t^2 dM^2 \\ & + \tau^1 r_{qq}^c dq + \delta\tau^2 R_{QQ}^C dQ \\ & + b dCA + w^A dl^u + \delta W^A dL^u + \bar{w} dl^c + \delta \bar{W} dL^c \\ & + \tau^1 r_{qp}^c dt^1 + \delta\tau^2 R_{QP}^c dt^2 \\ & - \tau^2 R_Q^c db - t^2 M^2 db \\ & + \tau^1 r_{ql}^c dl + \delta\tau^2 R_{QL}^c dL \end{aligned} \qquad (18)$$

Although this is not a reduced form – since many of the right-hand side variables are endogenous – it is a very general and informative equation.[16] In fact, it is possible to derive from it (as special cases) the welfare consequences of many combinations of structural adjustment policies. The first two terms of the right-hand side capture the welfare effects stemming from changes in imports in periods 1 and 2. If as a result of whatever reform we are analysing either M^1 or M^2 increase, we will have welfare gains. These, in turn, will be proportional to the initial distortions. The reason for these welfare gains are intuitively clear: since originally (in the pre-reform period) due to the existence of tariffs, this country was importing 'too little', any policy action that increases imports, moving them closer to the optimum level, will be welfare-enhancing.

The next two terms in equation (18) ($\tau^1 r^c_{qq} dq$ and $\delta\tau^2 R^C_{QQ} dQ$) summarise the welfare consequences of changes in the equilibrium quantities transacted in the non-tradables' (services) sectors. Naturally, these changes operate via changes in the prices of S (or real exchange rate), q and Q. If, for example, a reform raises these prices (e.g., $dq > 0$ and $dQ > 0$) we will have positive social welfare effects (since r_{qq} and R_{QQ} are positive) which will be proportional to the initial distortions in this market.[17] In fact, one of the important properties of this model is that it clearly shows that changes in the relative price of tradables (or real exchange rates) constitute one of the most important channels through which structural adjustment policies will affect welfare. Naturally, when evaluating the effects of a specific reform it will be necessary to evaluate precisely how the reform will affect non-tradable relative prices.

The next term, $bdCA$, captures the welfare consequences of changes in the period 2 current account; if the reform reduces the size of the current account, total welfare will decline. This is because reductions in CA mean that total borrowing will decline, and will thus amplify the pre-existing distortion stemming from the tax on capital mobility: initially this country was borrowing 'too little' and, thus, reductions in borrowing will move it even further away from the first-best. The next four terms ($w^A dl^u + W^A dL^u + \bar{w} dl^c + \delta \bar{W} dL^c$) deal with the labour market and state that if a reform increases employment in the covered and/or uncovered sectors, in either period, social welfare will increase. Naturally, since M^1, M^2, q, Q, CA, l^u, l^c, L^u and L^c are endogenous variables, in order to obtain the exact expressions for these welfare changes we will need to solve the complete model.[18] The reason for this, of course, is that due to the minimum wage, aggregate employment in this economy is too low. Any policy that results in an increase in employment will, thus, result in an increase in social welfare.

The final six terms of equation (15)

$$[\tau r^c_{pq} dt^1 + \delta\tau^2 R^C_{QP} dt^2 - \tau^2 R^C_Q db - t^2 M^2 db + \tau^1 r^c_{ql} dl + \delta\tau^2 R^C_{QL} dL]$$

are indirect terms related to changes in tariffs, taxes and employment which stem from the interaction among the different distortions. Their magnitude, then, will basically depend on the sign of several cross-elasticities. For our purpose, the two terms involving the financial distortion b are particularly important. They state that increases in the tax on borrowing will impact on welfare through changes in the amount of taxes collected in each period. In Section 3 this model is used to perform two exercises on the sequencing of reform. In Section 4 the model is extended to incorporate imported intermediate inputs and investment.

3 The sequencing of reform and the agricultural sector: basic results

In this section I use a variate of the model developed above to analyse the conditions under which the popular recommendation of liberalising the 'trade account first' is appropriate from a strict welfare perspective. I abstract, consequently, from the macroeconomic arguments of McKinnon, Corden and Edwards (1989d). Additionally, I investigate the welfare consequences of reforms that include labour market deregulation.

In order to facilitate the analysis, I assume that the services sector is undistorted ($\tau^1 = \tau^2 = 0$). This means that the three fundamental distortions in this economy are import tariffs, a tax on foreign borrowing and the minimum wage.

3.1 'Tariffs-first' liberalisation sequence

In this subsection we assume that the economy is following the popular 'tariffs-first' sequence, and ask what happens if this policy is altered. More specifically, we investigate how the key variables in the system will react if instead of liberalising trade first, we relax trade and capital market distortions *at the same time*.

The initial conditions in this economy are summarised in Table 2.1. As can be seen, it is assumed that the labour market remains distorted throughout the relevant run, that tariffs are eliminated (or reduced) at the beginning of period 1 and that the distortions on capital controls are eliminated at the very end.[19] In the rest of this section I investigate how (a) agricultural employment, (b) agricultural production, (c) agricultural wages, (d) aggregate unemployment, and (e) total welfare are affected if, starting from the initial conditions in Table 2.1, we (somewhat) relax the extent of capital controls. Formally, this amounts to analysing the way in which these variables react to an increase in the domestic discount factor δ.

Table 2.1 *'Tariffs-first' liberalisation sequence in the presence of labour market distortions*

	Period		
	0	1	2
Manufacturing	Distorted	Undistorted	Undistorted
Labour	Distorted	Distorted	Distorted
Capital	Distorted	Distorted	Undistorted

3.1.1 Agricultural employment, wages and output

A relaxation of capital controls will affect the consumers' rate of discount and, thus, the intertemporal allocation of consumption. This, in turn, will tend to affect agricultural employment and wages in both periods. The mechanism through which this will happen is the following: a reduction in the tax on borrowing σ will make present consumption relatively more attractive, generating an increase in period 1 expenditure and a reduction in period 2 expenditure. Let us first focus on period 1 and assume, for the time being, that labour is the only factor that can move across sectors. A proportion of this period's increase in expenditure will fall on services (non-tradables), provoking an incipient excess demand that will be solved through a higher price of S.[20] This higher price of S (or real exchange rate *appreciation*) will, in turn, result in an increase (an upward shift) in the demand for labour and in higher employment in the services sector. Employment in manufacturing, however, is not affected by this change in policy. Due to the existence of the labour market constraint, the higher employment in services will provoke a reduction in period 1 employment in agriculture.

Formally, and under the assumption that the economy is initially following the 'tariffs-first' sequence of Table 2.1, the effect of an increase in δ on employment in agriculture is given by:

$$\frac{dl^u}{d\delta} = \left\{ r^u_{ll} - \frac{\psi \bar{w}}{(l^T - l^u)} \right\}^{-1} \left(\frac{\psi \bar{w}}{l^c} \right) l^c_q \left(\frac{dq}{d\delta} \right) \tag{19}$$

By convexity of the revenue function $r^u_{ll} < 0$, and thus the first term in the right-hand side is negative; on the other hand, $(\psi \bar{w} / l^c) > 0$; l^c_q is the derivative of employment in the covered sector with respect to the price of services, and under the assumption that capital and natural resources are sector-specific, it is also positive. In fact, with labour mobility only l^c_q is equal to the parallel shift of the demand for labour that results from a change in q. Finally, $(dq/d\delta)$ is the change in the price of services in period 1 generated by the relaxation of the capital distortions, and, as explained above, is positive. Equation (19) as a whole is, then, *negative*, capturing the fact that a liberalisation of capital controls will generate a decline in agriculture employment in period 1. This result is depicted in Figure 2.2, where L'_s is the demand for labour in the S service after the tax on foreign borrowing has been reduced, and where $(L_M + L'_S)$ is the demand for labour in the covered sector after the reform. The new level of employment in the A sector is $O_A L'_A$, lower than $O_A L_A$. Also, as can be seen from Figure 2.2, the wage rate in the uncovered sector A increases after the reform. As is shown below, however, aggregate *unemployment* can go either up or down.

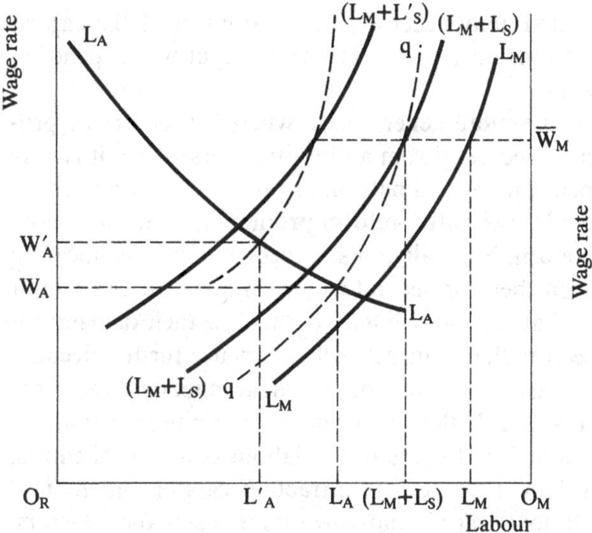

Figure 2.2 The effect of capital controls' liberalisation on employment

A key aspect of equation (19) is that the channel through which the structural reform affects agriculture (and for that matter aggregate employment), is the *real exchange rate*. In fact, if the capital account liberalisation does not impact on the relative price of S ($dq/d\delta = 0$), there will be *no change in period 1 employment*. It is interesting to note that the type of effect discussed here will also take place in the case where there is a *temporary* tariff reform. Indeed, if the public believes that a tariff liberalisation process will be reversed, there will be intertemporal substitution in consumption that will generate the same type of employment effect.

The expression for the change in period 2 agricultural employment is equivalent to equation (19):

$$\frac{dL^u}{d\delta} = \left\{R^u_{LL} - \frac{\psi \bar{W}}{(l^T - l^U)}\right\}^{-1}\left(\frac{\psi \bar{W}}{L^c}\right)L^C_Q\left(\frac{dQ}{d\delta}\right) \tag{20}$$

where all right-hand side terms refer to period 2 and have the same interpretation as in equation (19). The main difference, however, is that it is now not possible to sign ($dQ/d\delta$) unequivocally.[21] This means that while the capital market reform will clearly have a negative impact on period 1 agriculture employment, it can either increase or decrease period 2 agriculture employment.

To the extent that labour is the only mobile factor, agriculture's output will move in the same direction as employment; it will decline in period 1 and will either increase or decline in period 2. If, however, the other factors can be reallocated across sectors, the final effect of the capital market (and other) reforms on employment and output will depend on relative factor intensities.

Let us consider now the more general case where all factors of production can move across sectors. From an intuitive perspective it is easy to see what will happen: capital and natural resources will tend to move out of those sectors with lower after-reform profitability and into those sectors with a higher return. Naturally, this process of factor reallocation will, in turn, have a further (or second-round) impact on the labour market. Those sectors that expand will tend to increase their demand for labour, while those sectors that contract will experience further declines in their level of employment. In terms of our diagrammatical representation in Figures 2.1 and 2.2, the reallocation of capital and natural resources will induce additional shifts in the labour demand schedules: they will shift upward in those sectors attracting capital and natural resources and will shift downward in those sectors releasing these factors. The final effect of this reallocation process on sectoral and aggregate employment will depend on both the direction and the magnitude of these schedules' shifts. In order to find out exactly the nature of this long-run adjustment process, it is useful to turn, once again, to our benchmark model.

In the case of capital market liberalisation, equations (19) and (20) still summarise the employment effects of a relaxation of capital controls under the assumption that all factors are intersectorally mobile. However, the interpretation of the terms l_p^c, l_q, L_P^C and L_Q^C is now rather different and is related to relative factor intensities, which in turn will determine the magnitude shifts of the labour demand schedules discussed above. The exact expressions for each of these terms are:

$$l_p^c = \frac{-r_{pl}^c}{r_{ll}^c}; \quad l_q^c = \frac{-r_{ql}^c}{r_{ll}^c}; \quad L_P^C = \frac{-R_{PL}^C}{R_{LL}^C}; \quad L_Q^C = \frac{-R_{QL}^C}{R_{LL}^C} \tag{21}$$

where r_{ll}^c and R_{LL}^C are the slopes of the marginal products of labour schedules in the covered sector during periods 1 and 2, and are negative. On the other hand, the terms r_{ql}^c, r_{pl}^c, R_{QL}^C and R_{PL}^C are Rybczinski terms. They capture, for example, what will happen to the period 1 output of manufacturing and services (r_p^c and r_q^c respectively) if there is an increase in the labour force (l). Their sign will depend on relative factor intensities, which are difficult to determine in our 3 × 3 model. However, as Leamer (1984) has shown, if services are the most labour-intensive sector – both with respect to capital and with respect to natural resources – r_{ql}^c and R_{QL}^C will be positive. Terms r_{pl}^c and R_{PL}^C, on the other hand, can be either positive or negative. A necessary (although not sufficient) condition for them to be positive is that the manufacturing sector is the second most labour-intensive sector. This means that in the long run the relative factor intensities of the different sectors will be a key determinant of the employment effects of tariff reform. Consequently, those policy makers concerned with the way in which structural reform will impact on the employment–unemployment situation should monitor closely the (relative) factor intensities in the sectors involved.

If we assume that r^c_{pl} and R^C_{PL} are, in fact, positive, then we will obtain the result in which a capital market liberalisation reduces employment in agriculture even in the long run. However, if manufacturing is the least labour-intensive sector (as measured with respect to both of the other factors) R^C_{PL} will be negative. In the rest of the analysis we will indeed assume that the factor intensity configuration is such that r^c_{pl} and R^C_{PL} are positive.

3.1.2 Aggregate unemployment

At the economy-wide level an important question is what happens to aggregate unemployment. We have shown that in period 1 agricultural employment declines; moreover, Figure 2.2 clearly indicates that covered sector employment will increase in period 1 as a result of the relaxation of the capital controls. It is not possible, however, to derive from this figure the net effect of the reform on period 1 unemployment. Formally this net effect will be given by:

$$\frac{d\mu}{d\delta} = -l^c_q\left[\frac{l^c r^u_{ll}/\psi - \bar{w}(\psi - 1)}{l^c r^u_{ll}/\psi - \psi\bar{w}}\right]\frac{dq}{d\delta} \gtrless 0 \qquad (22)$$

Whether this expression is positive or negative will depend on whether $l^c r^u_{ll}/\psi \lesseqgtr \bar{w}(\psi - 1)$. This, of course, means that unless we have more detailed knowledge of the initial conditions prevailing in the economy (including the parameter values) we cannot know whether the acceleration over time of the capital market reform will increase or decrease unemployment.[22] An expression equivalent to equation (21) can be derived for period 2 unemployment.

3.1.3 Sequencing from a welfare perspective

The key question in the current exercise is whether altering the initial (and traditional) sequencing path by moving the capital market reform to the first period will be welfare-enhancing. One way of dealing with this issue is to calculate the optimal value of b, the tax on foreign borrowing. If this turns out to be *positive*, then there will be a welfare criterion that justifies the traditional 'tariffs-first' sequencing suggestion. From equations

(18)–(22) we can calculate the optimal (second-best) tax on foreign borrowing as:

$$\tilde{b} = -\left\{\frac{w^A(dl^u/d\delta) + \bar{w}(dl^c/d\delta) + \delta^*(W^A(dL^u/d\delta) + \bar{W}(dL^c/d\delta))}{(dCA/d\delta) + W^a(dL^U/d\delta) + \bar{W}(dL^c/d\delta)}\right\} \qquad (23)$$

where $(dCA/d\delta)$ is the change in the period 2 current account as a result of the relaxation of capital controls, and is positive.[23]

A simple inspection of the right-hand side of equation (23) clearly shows that we cannot determine *a priori* whether $\tilde{b}$ will be positive. Under some specific constellation of parameters it is possible to generate an optimum positive b, indicating that there are some circumstances where the *tariff-first* sequence will be desirable.[24] This, however, will *not* be the general case. Consider, for example, the case when the labour market distortion is in effect in period 1 only; the optimal tax on borrowing becomes:

$$\tilde{b}' = -\frac{w^A(dl^u/d\delta) + \bar{w}(dl^c/d\delta)}{(dCA/d\delta)} \qquad (22')$$

If we additionally assume that the aggregate effect of the capital market reform on employment will be positive so that $(w^A(dl^u/d\delta) + \bar{w}(dl^c/d\delta)) > 0$,[25] then the optimal tax on capital borrowing is negative! This means that the optimal sequence will not only require that tariffs and capital markets are reformed *simultaneously*, but additionally that foreign borrowing is subsidised! The reason, of course, is that in this case the subsidy on capital inflows will have a positive effect on period 1 employment (partially) offsetting the existing labour market distortion. This result clearly indicates that the timing of labour market reform will have an important effect in determining the appropriate sequence of reform of other sectors.

To summarise, then, this analysis shows that the *welfare-based* arguments in favour of the tariffs-first sequence are not robust to the economy's structure. In fact, we have shown that even in this simple archetypical model, with fairly strong assumptions, the tariffs-first sequence is not always welfare-dominant. What is required to draw *welfare-based* conclusions is to undertake in-depth analysis (preferably at the country-specific level) in order to find out the value of the different coefficients and effects. It is important to note, however, that this does *not* invalidate, in any way, those arguments in favour of a tariffs-first sequence that are based on macroeconomic instability effects.

3.2 Labour market reforms and the sequencing of liberalisation

Most studies that have explicitly incorporated labour market distortions into the analysis of structural reform have assumed that, for political or other reasons, the labour market is the last to be liberalised.[26] Most analyses have therefore assumed, either explicitly or implicitly, a 'labour market-last' sequencing. Although it is indeed possible that political factors will delay the labour market reform, it is still important to investigate the way in which the key variables will react to a relaxation of the minimum wage. In this subsection I use the model of Section 2 to investigate the effects of a reform package that includes as one of its steps the reduction of the minimum wage in period 2. Formally, this amounts to investigating the effects of a fully anticipated future reduction of $\bar{W}$ on the key variables of our system. I assume that the only other policy measure in this package is an early (beginning in period 1) and permanent reduction in import tariffs. Capital controls are assumed to remain in effect throughout the analysis.

A fully anticipated reduction in the period 2 minimum wage will affect the agriculture labour market through a direct channel – the actual change in the wage floor – and through an indirect channel that will operate via changes in the relative price of services, or the real exchange rate. A lower period 2 minimum wage will increase that period's aggregate income and, through consumption smoothing, will result in higher expenditure in periods 1 and 2. This will, in turn, generate higher prices of non-tradables (services) in both periods. Of course, this higher period 1 q will be accompanied by an increase in the demand for labour in services, a decline in agriculture employment in that period, and an increase in agricultural wages. Formally, the change in period 1 agricultural employment will be given by:

$$\frac{dl^u}{d\bar{W}} = \frac{\bar{w}}{(r^u_{ll}(l^T - l^u) - \psi\bar{w})} l^c_q \left(\frac{dq}{d\bar{W}}\right) \tag{24}$$

where under our maintained assumption of factor intensivity $l^c_q > 0$. This equation highlights, once more, the importance of real exchange rate changes as a transmission mechanism. Indeed, it can be seen that if period 1's real exchange rate does not react to a change in *future* minimum wages $(dq/d\bar{W})$, the labour market reform will have *no* effect in today's agriculture (or for that matter any other) employment. What is particularly interesting about this result, then, is that an anticipated labour market deregulation will have an *immediate* negative effect on agriculture employment and output. Since $(dq/d\bar{W}) \geq 0$, from equation (23) it follows that $(dl^u/d\bar{W}) \leq 0$.

A reduction in period 2's minimum wage rate will also affect covered employment in period 1. In this case, the channel will also be the change in the real exchange rate; since the anticipated wage rate reduction will have a positive impact on q, $(dq/d\bar{W}) < 0$, the service sector level of employment in period 1 will increase. It is not possible, however, to know what will happen to aggregate employment.

The effect of a fully anticipated change in the minimum wage on agricultural employment in period 2 is somewhat more complicated. In this case, in addition to the *inter*temporal effects discussed above, there will also be an intratemporal effect. More specifically, employment will also be affected through the period 2 Harris–Todaro equilibrium condition ($W^A = \psi\bar{W}$). Since the policy reform affects $\bar{W}$, the level of unemployment will have to change in order to re-establish labour market equilibrium. Formally, the effect of a change in $\bar{W}$ on period 2 agriculture employment will be given by:

$$\frac{dL^U}{d\bar{W}} = \frac{\bar{W}}{[R^U_{LL}(L^T - L^U) - \psi\bar{W}]} L^C_Q \left(\frac{dQ}{d\bar{W}}\right) + \psi(\eta + 1) \tag{25}$$

where η is the wage demand elasticity of labour in the protected sector, and is negative. The first term on the right-hand side is the indirect employment effect and is equivalent to that in equation (24). The second term, however, captures the change in equilibrium unemployment and can be either positive or negative. If the demand for labour in the protected sector is inelastic $|\eta| < 1$, $\psi(\eta + 1)$ will be positive, and equation (24) as a whole will be positive. This means that in this case a reduction in the protected sector minimum wage will also *reduce* agriculture employment in period 2, and will result in an increase in agriculture wages in that period.

The net effect on period 2 unemployment will be given by:

$$\frac{d\mu^2}{d\bar{W}} = -L^C_Q \frac{dQ}{d\bar{W}}(1 + \phi) - L^C_W - \psi(\eta + 1) \tag{26}$$

$$\text{where } \phi = -\frac{\bar{W}}{[\psi\bar{W} - R^U_{LL}(L^T - L^U)]} < 0$$

Two sufficient conditions for $d\mu^2/d\bar{W}$ to be positive – that is, for a minimum wage reduction to reduce period 2 unemployment – are: (1) $|\phi| > 1$; and (2) $|\eta| > 1$.

4 Extensions: intermediate inputs, investment, and alternative indexation

The basic model presented above can be extended in several directions. However, due to space limitations I sketch only some of the directions in which it can be taken.

4.1 Imported intermediate inputs and the sequencing of tariff reform

One of the simplifying assumptions of the model developed in Section 2 is that production is restricted to final goods. This assumption, however, is not fully satisfactory in a study on structural reforms and the agricultural sector, since in the vast majority of the developing countries agriculture uses important quantities of intermediate goods.

The incorporation of intermediate goods into the analysis requires that we modify the production side of our benchmark model. We now assume an importable intermediate good (only). Assume further that the importation of the intermediate commodity is subject to a tariff t^i; its domestic price is then given by $p^i = p^{*i} + t^i$.[27] Finally, we assume that production of this intermediate good takes place in the 'covered' sector which is subject to a minimum wage.

Formally, in order to incorporate intermediate inputs in our benchmark model it is necessary to distinguish *gross* from *net* output. This is done by defining a new revenue function ρ as the maximum net output (or value-added) that optimizing firms can obtain at given prices and available technology. For period 1 this net revenue function can be written in the following way (an equivalent function can be written for period 2):

$$\rho = \rho(1, p, p^i, q, l^c(\ )) \tag{27}$$

The properties of this 'net output' revenue function ρ are (almost) the same as those of the conventional revenue function. The function is convex and its derivatives with respect to goods' prices are equal to the net output of each good. The derivatives with respect to factors of production, on the other hand, will also give the marginal product of that factor. Finally, our assumption that there are always net imports of the intermediate good implies that the net output of this type of good is negative $\delta p/\delta p^i < 0$.

In terms of the formal model the most important change is that the government transfers equation (10) is now rewritten as follows:

$$\text{TRANS} = \tau^1 \rho^c_q + \delta\tau^2 \Gamma^c_Q + bCA + t^1 M^1 + \delta t^2 M^2 + t^{1i} I^1 + \delta t^{2i} I^2 \tag{10'}$$

where ρ^c and Γ^c are periods 1 and 2 (restricted) net revenue functions; and where I^1 and I^2 are periods 1 and 2 *net* imports of the intermediate good, and are given by:

$$I^1 = -\delta\rho^c/\delta p^i, \quad I^2 = -\delta\Gamma^c/\delta p^i$$

Armed with this extended model, we can explore additional issues, including the welfare consequences of a simultaneous reduction in all import tariffs and specific sequences of tariff reduction.

4.2 *Investment*

The model developed in Section 2 ignores investment. Many times, however, the opening of the capital account results in an increase in direct foreign investment and, thus, in a higher productive capacity in the country. The easiest way to incorporate this into the analysis is to assume that there is an exogenous increase in the stock of capital. To the extent that foreign-owned capital earns its marginal productivity we will face a situation similar to the one developed in Brecher and Diaz-Alejandro (1977) and discussed in detail in Edwards and van Wijnbergen (1983).[28] An alternative, and more elegant, way to deal with investment is explicitly to incorporate an investment function. Assuming that firms maximise their present value, we can depict investment through the following Tobin '*q*' equation:

$$\frac{\delta R_k}{P_k} = 1 \tag{28}$$

where R_k is the (overall) marginal productivity of capital in period 2, and P_k is the price of machines. By combining equation (28) with the basic model in Section 2, we are in a position to investigate how alternative liberalisation reform strategies will affect welfare and other key variables in the economy.

4.3 *Wage indexation*

The analysis in Section 3 and Subsections 4.1 and 4.2 above assumed that the (economy-wide) minimum wage was set in terms of the exportable agricultural good. Although this is a convenient assumption that facilitates the exposition, it may not be a very realistic one. If we assume instead that the minimum wage is fixed in terms of our exact consumption price indices (π and Π), we can write:

$$\frac{w}{\pi} = \text{constant}; \quad \frac{W}{\Pi} = \text{constant}$$

where $\pi = \pi(1,p,f)$ and $\Pi = \Pi(1,P,F)$ were defined in Section 2. A consequence of this modification is that policy reforms that affect the nominal price of manufacturing and/or of services will exert an influence over the nominal wage rate, altering the final equilibrium.

It is easy to see intuitively the way in which the assumption of wage rate indexation will affect labour market adjustment following a trade liberalisation reform. In order to focus the discussion, let us concentrate on the short-run case where factors other than labour are sector-specific. A permanent tariff reduction will directly result in a decline in the nominal prices of manufacturing in both periods (p and P); also, under most circumstances the relative price of non-tradables (f and F) will go down as a result of the tariff reform. These two effects imply that both consumption price indices, π and Π, will also decline. Thus, in order for the *real wage* relative to these indices (π and Π) to remain constant in both periods, the nominal wage will have to go *down* after the tariff liberalisation reform.

5 Concluding remarks

How to liberalise? This is a question that haunts policy makers and that confuses policy advisors. A particularly pressing question refers to the sequencing of reform. Does the order in which markets are reformed affect the outcome of the adjustment package? In this paper I have developed a formal intertemporal framework to investigate how alternative sequencing scenarios affect some key variables. The approach taken here differs from previous work in several respects: first it provides a formal intertemporal model to investigate the welfare effects of reform; second, it explicitly incorporates the role of labour market distortions; and third, it attempts to analyse, in a stylised form, how reform will impact on the agricultural sector.

The main result obtained in Section 3 is that the *welfare-based* arguments in favour of the tariffs-first sequence are not robust to the economy's structure. In fact, we have shown that even in this simple archetypical model, with fairly strong assumptions, the 'tariffs-first' sequence is not always welfare-dominant. As pointed out earlier, what is required to draw *welfare-based* conclusions is to undertake in-depth analysis (preferably at the country-specific level) in order to find out the value of the different coefficients and effects.

The above result should not be interpreted, however, as leading to a completely sceptical view about economists' ability to say more concrete things regarding sequencing. In fact, these results are restricted to the *welfare* perspective, and say nothing regarding the macroeconomic arguments in favour of postponing the opening of the capital account. In fact, I believe that these arguments have a lot of weight; the historical evidence also supports them.

NOTES

I am indebted to Julio Santaella for his assistance. I am grateful to Ian Goldin and Helmut Reisen for their comments. Support from the National Science Foundation, the University of California Pacific Rim Program and the Institute for Policy Reform is gratefully acknowledged.

1 There are, of course, some authors who are still sceptical about liberalisation reforms. See, for example, Taylor (1988) and Banuri (1991).
2 For early discussions on the sequencing issue see McKinnon (1982), Frenkel (1982, 1983) and Edwards (1984). More recent discussions can be found in Corden (1987), Edwards (1989d), and McKinnon (1991).
3 See McKinnon (1982), Corden (1987), Edwards (1984, 1989d).
4 See, for example, ILO (1988).
5 For some interesting data on the Latin American case see, for example, PREALC (1978).
6 Given its intertemporal nature, the model can also be used formally to investigate the important policy question of the appropriate *speed* of liberalisation reforms.
7 The model developed in this paper expands my 1989a working paper in several directions. Perhaps the most important ones are the incorporation of intermediate inputs (Section 4) and the assumption that labour market distortions are market-specific. These assumptions indeed allow us to focus attention on the agricultural sector.
8 This is an important simplification. In many developing nations the agricultural sector is not homogeneous. In fact, we can often find an import competing segment – usually protected through quotas – and an exportable segment. We leave the formalisation of a model with these two agricultural segments for future research.
9 Although formally it is easy to consider the case where many goods are produced, in order to simplify the presentation we focus on the three-goods case.
10 In this type of fully optimising model with constant returns to scale technology, there is a problem with having both minimum wages in both periods and investment. See, for example, Svensson (1984) and the discussion below.
11 An upward-sloping supply of labour can be added into the analysis simply by adding leisure to our utility function (see Edwards, 1989d).
12 In spite of its elegance the Harris–Todaro model has a number of limitations. See, for example, Rosenszweig (1989) and Lindbeck and Snower (1991).
13 Since there now is a wedge between the return to labour in each sector, we cannot use a unique revenue function. We require a revenue function for the covered sector and a different one for the uncovered sector. Naturally, since there is a minimum wage the 'covered' sector has a *restricted* revenue function.

14 Notice that the fact that there is a tax on the non-tradables' market is captured by the inclusion of different prices of non-tradables in the expenditure and revenue functions (f and q, respectively). The difference between producers' and consumers' prices is, of course, given by the tax on non-tradables τ^i:

$$f = q + \tau^1; \quad F = Q + \tau^2$$

15 Remember that an important property of revenue functions is that their partial derivative with respect to a particular factor is equal to the marginal product of that factor. Thus, when evaluated at the actual level of employment, $r^c l^c$ will be equal to the minimum wage rate in the covered sector.

16 See Edwards (1989d) for the reduced-form solution for many of the right-hand side terms.

17 In order to maintain the simplicity of the presentation I have deliberately not solved for the real exchange rate terms dq and dQ. See, however, the discussion in Edwards (1989b) for a detailed analysis of the real exchange rate consequences of different reforms.

18 For the solution of similar – although admittedly simpler – models see Edwards (1989a, 1989b, 1989c).

19 Strictly speaking the interest rate connects periods 1 and 2, and thus appears only once in our two-period model. Still we can interpret this analysis as referring to the case where at the end of period 2 the capital account restrictions have been lifted. In fact, the results discussed here would still be obtained if we use a three-period model.

20 Formally it is not quite so simple, since in addition to the substitution effect described here there will also be an income effect. See Edwards (1989b) for a formal discussion on the effects of capital market reform on the real exchange rate. Formally, however, the final effect will be to generate a real exchange rate appreciation.

21 The reason is that now the income and substitution effects will operate in opposite directions; see Edwards (1989a).

22 This type of result is present in static Harris–Todaro models; see, for example, Edwards (1988).

23 The reason, of course, is that the opening of the capital account will worsen period 1's current account, requiring a larger surplus in period 2 as a way to fulfil the intertemporal budget constraint.

24 The important thing to notice here is that the only rigorous way to evaluate the proposition that a *tariff-first* sequence is welfare superior is by actually introducing an additional distortion into the system. If this is not done, the optimal sequence is trivial: all distortions should be eliminated simultaneously and *now*. Whether the assumption of a distorted labour market is the most appropriate one is subject, however, to debate.

25 This will always be the case if the minimum wage affects every sector in the economy. This result is derived in Edwards and Ostry (1992).

26 See, for example, the discussion in Edwards (1988, 1989d).

27 Another important assumption is that (at prevailing prices) domestic production of good i is not sufficiently large to cover its total (derived) demand. Consequently, at every moment in time the amount imported of commodity i is positive.

28 In this case, in the presence of tariffs an increase in the stock of capital reduces welfare in a country with capital-intensive imports.

REFERENCES

Banuri, Tariq (1991) *Economic Liberalization: No Panacea*, Oxford: Clarendon Press.

Brecher, R. and C. Diaz-Alejandro (1977) 'Tariffs, Foreign Capital, and Immiserizing Growth', *Journal of International Economics*, **7(74)**, November: 317–22.

Corden, W. Max (1987) 'Protection and Liberalization: A Review of Analytical Issues', *IMF Occasional Paper*, **54**, Washington, D.C., August.

Edwards, Sebastian (1984) 'The Order of Liberalization of the External Sector in Developing Countries', *Princeton Essays in International Finance*, **156**, Princeton: Princeton University Press, December.

(1988) 'Terms of Trade, Tariffs and Labour Market Adjustment in Developing Countries', *World Bank Economic Review*, **2**, 165–85.

(1989a) *Real Exchange Rates, Devaluation, and Adjustment: Exchange Rate Policy in Developing Countries*, Cambridge, MA: MIT Press.

(1989b) 'Tariffs, Capital Controls and Equilibrium Real Exchange Rates', *Canadian Journal of Economics*, **22(1)**, February: 79–82.

(1989c) 'Temporary Terms of Trade Disturbances, Real Exchange Rates and the Current Account', *Economica*, **56**.

(1989d) 'On the Sequencing of Structural Reforms in Developing Countries', *NBER Working Paper*, **3138**, October.

Edwards, Sebastian and Jonathan Ostry (1992) 'Capital Controls, the Real Exchange Rate and Welfare', *Oxford Economic Papers*, forthcoming.

Edwards, Sebastian and Sweder van Wijnbergen (1983) 'The Welfare Effects of Trade and Capital Market Liberalization: Consequences of Different Sequencing Scenarios', *NBER Working Paper*, **1245**, December.

Frenkel, Jacob A. (1982) 'The Order of Economic Liberalization: A Comment', in K. Brunner and A.H. Meltzer (eds), *Economic Policy in a World of Change*, Amsterdam: North-Holland.

Frenkel, Jacob A. (1983) 'Remarks on the Southern Cone', *IMF Staff Papers*, **30**, March: 164–73.

Harris, J. and M.P. Todaro (1970) 'Migration, Unemployment and Development: A Two-Sector Analysis', *American Economic Review*, **60(1)**, March: 126–42.

International Labor Office (ILO) (1988) *World Labor Report*, Geneva: ILO.

Krueger, Anne O. (1984) 'Problems of Liberalization', in A. Harberger (ed.), *World Economic Growth*, San Francisco, ICS Press: 403–23.

Leamer, E.E. (1984) *Sources of Comparative Advantage*, Cambridge, MA: MIT Press.

Lindbeck, Assar and Dennis Snower (1991) 'Segmented Labor Markets and Unemployment', *Seminar Paper*, **483**, Institute of International Economic Studies, Stockholm University.

McKinnon, Ronald I. (1982) 'The Order of Economic Liberalization: Lessons From Chile and Argentina', in K. Brunner and A.H. Meltzer (eds), *Economic Policy in a World of Change*, Amsterdam: North-Holland.

McKinnon, Ronald I. (1991) *The Order of Liberalization in Developing Countries*, Baltimore, Johns Hopkins University Press.

PREALC (1978) 'Salarios Minimos en America Latina', *Working Paper*, **18**.

Rozenszweig, Mark (1989) 'Labor Market Adjustment in Poor Countries', in

H. Chenery and T.N. Srinivasan (eds), *Handbook of Development Economics*, vol. I, Amsterdam: North-Holland.

Svensson, Lars E.O. (1984) 'Oil Prices, Welfare and the Trade Balance', *Quarterly Journal of Economics*, **94(4)**, November: 649–72.

Svensson, Lars E.O. and Assaf Razin (1983) 'The Terms of Trade and the Current Account: the Harberger–Laursen–Metzler Effect', *Journal of Political Economy*, **91(1)**, February: 97–125.

Taylor, L. (1988) *Varieties of Stabilization Experience: Towards Sensible Macroeconomics in the Third World*, Oxford: Oxford University Press.

Discussion

HELMUT REISEN

As with a good jazz musician, we have got used to hearing from Sebastian Edwards many variations on a theme. The theme is the sequencing of structural reform. The variation this time in Chapter 2, is a two-period model to explore two previously neglected aspects of the sequencing literature: the role of labour market distortions and the impact of reform on agriculture. Edwards arrives at a very agnostic result (which is also contrary to some of his earlier findings): from a rigorous welfare perspective it does not matter whether you first liberalise trade, dismantle capital controls, or deregulate labour markets. Either this is a very important result which joins those who have stressed political economy considerations, or it merely reflects the failure of Edwards's model to capture some aspects relevant to the sequencing problem. Let me try to explore this second explanation.

Less agnosticism may be produced by modifying Edwards's model in three ways: (1) by giving a more realistic description of the labour market in LDCs, (2) by introducing a richer production function, and (3) by redefining sectors.

First, the labour market. In Edwards's model, for example, financial opening will reduce employment in agriculture. Financial opening in period 1 raises the real exchange rate, here defined as the price of services relative to tradables. Appreciation raises the demand for labour in the service sector and, due to the labour market constraint, reduces employment in agriculture. What do we observe, by contrast, in reality? Search unemployment in the urban informal service sector, disguised low-productivity unemployment in the rural sector, and a tendency of industry to contract as a result of real appreciation. A real appreciation thus results in lower labour demand of industry, which reduces incentives to wait in the informal service sector for formal urban jobs, and hence increases instead of lowering employment in agriculture. Whichever direction the move takes, the labour market constraint in Edwards's model seems hardly binding in LDC reality. Recent research by Oded Stark (1991) also shows that minimum wages and wage differentials may not be the most important determinant of migration. He stresses the intra-family diversification of income risks as an important motive for rural–urban migration. Stark's finding provides an interesting extension for an intertemporal model which would include intersectoral covariance of revenues.

Second, the production function. In the Ricardo–Viner framework employed by Edwards, there is no investment and no change in productivity. This simplification produces results such as that a decline in foreign borrowing will amplify the preexisting (intertemporal) distortion stemming from the tax on capital imports. That finding is, of course, in great contrast to the well-known 'immiserising inflow' proposition by Brecher and Diaz-Alejandro (1977), among others, that a reduction of foreign borrowing raises social welfare in a small tariff-imposing country that remains incompletely specialised and where capital is intersectorally mobile.

With production just linked to labour input and demand, Edwards's model is silent on pre- versus post-reform profitability. Liberalisation and structural reform is intended to raise profitability by moving resources away from uses with low to those with high profitability. Non-perennial agriculture, where fixed costs often matter comparatively less than in industry, is a good candidate for quick increases in profitability after liberalisation. Introducing productivity parameters into Edwards's model is likely to delete a great deal of agnosticism in his conclusion. Productivity parameters will also allow us to compare the social cost of politically feasible but suboptimal sequencings with the social benefits of doing any reform at all.

Third, sectoral disaggregation and factor intensities. Edwards stresses at several times how important the real exchange rate is as a transmission channel for dynamic and intertemporal effects. The importance of the real exchange rate reflects the sectoral structure of the model, which is basically tradables versus non-tradables. Unfortunately, nothing much can be said on *a priori* grounds on the relative factor intensity of tradables and non-tradables. As a general rule, labour-intensive sectors are exportables in industry, informal services in non-tradables, and tropical agriculture; capital-intensive sectors are importables in industry, the formal service sector in non-tradables, and temperate agriculture. At least a six-sector model seems required to arrive at any reliable result on employment effects of different reform sequences.

Finally, less agnosticism with respect to labour market reform will be yielded in models where monetary policy has a role, in particular the discussion of the exchange rate regime. The sequencing literature is very much Southern Cone-inspired. The dismal liberalisation experience of the Southern Cone is largely explained by the active crawling peg of the exchange rate, which induced excessive capital inflows. In Chile, the full indexation of wages to consumer price inflation in the previous year was, in the context of disinflation, bound to result in inertia inflation and, with pegged exchange rates, in real appreciation. In New Zealand recently, financial opening has preceded labour market reform, and exchange rates have been purely floating. Post-reform monetary tightening was thus bound to lead to a Dornbusch-style overshooting of the exchange rate and to a contraction in industry (though not in agriculture). In both Chile and New Zealand, early labour market deregulation would have produced better results for employment and welfare.

NOTE

I have benefited from discussions with Olivier Bouin and Isabelle Joumard.

REFERENCES

Brecher, R. and C. Diaz-Alejandro (1977) 'Tariffs, Foreign Capital, and Immiserizing Growth', *Journal of International Economics*, **7(74)**, November: 317–22.

Stark, O. (1991) *The Migration of Labor*, Cambridge, MA: Basil Blackwell.

3 Agricultural adjustment and the Mexico–USA free trade agreement

SANTIAGO LEVY and
SWEDER van WIJNBERGEN

1 Introduction

On 10 June 1990, the presidents of Mexico and the USA agreed to negotiate a free trade agreement (FTA). Negotiations began in mid-1991, and were expected to be completed within about a year, implementation could start as early as 1993. The FTA would cap major structural reforms undertaken by Mexico over the last few years: trade liberalisation, domestic industrial deregulation and internal financial liberalisation, privatisation of public enterprises, and a successful renegotiation of the external debt.

One of the major issues is trade in agricultural products. Agricultural trade is probably the most distorted of all commodity flows taking place between the two countries. Moreover, agricultural trade intervention cannot be separated from domestic agricultural policies which, in turn, are intricately linked with politically volatile income distribution and labour market problems. This is especially important in Mexico, where land redistribution and agricultural regulation are an essential part of the heritage of the Mexican revolution. Agricultural reform will become necessary if a FTA includes agriculture. But the analysis of agricultural reform has to tackle the complicated interplay between efficiency losses and income distributional objectives underlying current agricultural policies.

Levy and van Wijnbergen (1991a) showed that land distribution and labour markets played an important role in determining the distributional impact of trade liberalisation in maize. Liberalising maize only would probably depress the demand for rural labour. On the other hand, fruit and vegetables, where the USA has trade barriers, is more labour intensive than maize. A comprehensive agreement might thus present less of a problem for rural labour markets than a liberalisation of maize alone.

The incidence of changes in the trade policy is complicated by migration.

Apart from migration to the USA, Mexico has over the past few decades also seen substantial migration to the cities as agriculture lagged behind industry. Without migration, the entire burden of adjustment is likely to fall on rural labour; with migration, some of the incidence is shifted to urban labour.

An analysis of agriculture in the FTA thus requires an explicit treatment of labour markets and migration. We therefore construct an economy-wide model designed to highlight these general equilibrium linkages. Ownership distribution of different types of land (irrigated and rain-fed) is followed with care, as is land allocation to various crops. We also use empirical information to assess substitution possibilities; this is clearly crucial for the incidence questions with which we will be concerned.

Section 2 surveys recent Mexican trade reforms and current Mexican and US trade policy, and places agricultural trade in the context of domestic agricultural policy. Section 3 sketches the model. Section 4 assesses the welfare gains and distributional consequences for Mexico of freeing agricultural trade with the USA. We also discuss the need for, and design of, government adjustment policies. Section 5 offers some concluding remarks.

2 Background

2.1 Mexican–US Trade Policy

Since mid-1985 Mexico has undertaken extensive unilateral liberalisation of merchandise trade. Table 3.1 shows indicators of the liberalisation.

The coverage of import licensing in terms of domestic tradable production is 19.9 per cent, down from 100 per cent in June 1985, export licensing now covers only 17.6 per cent of tradables' production. The maximum tariff is 20 per cent and the production-weighted average tariff 12.5 per cent, about one-fifth and one-half respectively, of their June 1985 values. Trade liberalisation has gone beyond Mexico's commitments to GATT upon accession in 1986.

But barriers still persist. Trade liberalisation has concentrated mostly on manufacturing; Mexican agriculture remains significantly protected. The sectoral make-up of the remaining import quantity restrictions (QRs) is shown in Table 3.2. QRs in agriculture and agro-industry apply mostly to products subject to price controls. The ones of interest to the USA are on grains, oilseeds and dairy products. In the manufacturing sector, QRs apply mainly to sectoral programmes for pharmaceuticals, autos, and auto parts. The QRs on pharmaceutical items will gradually be eliminated over the period to 1993. Removal of import controls in the automotive

Table 3.1 *Trade liberalisation, 1985–90*

	Jun 1985	Dec 1985	Jun 1986	Dec 1986	Jun 1987	Dec 1987	Jun 1988	Nov 1989	Jun 1990
Import licensing[a]	92.2	47.1	46.9	39.8	35.8	25.4	23.2	20.3	19.9
Reference prices[a]	18.7	25.4	19.6	18.7	13.4	0.6	0.0	0.0	0.0
Tariffs – maximum	100.0	100.0	45.0	45.0	40.0	20.0	20.0	20.0	20.0
– average[b]	23.5	28.5	24.0	24.5	22.7	11.8	11.0	12.8	12.5
Export controls[a]	n.a.	n.a.	n.a.	n.a.	n.a.	24.8	23.4	17.9	17.6
Real effective exchange rate[c]	100.0	121.8	134.7	145.2	136.0	128.5	112.6	115.0	113.1

Note:
[a] Percentage coverage of production of tradables; 1986 weights.
[b] Weighted by production of tradables; 1986 weights; excludes 5 per cent surcharge.
[c] Increase in the index represents a depreciation of the peso in real terms.
Source: Bank of Mexico.

Table 3.2 *Sectoral coverage of import QRs, February 1990*

Sector	Coverage of controls (%)	Contribution to total coverage[a]
Agriculture, livestock, forestry and fishing	40.1	7.1
Agro-industrial products	20.1	5.0
Industry	5.1	2.3
Petroleum and derivatives	95.0	5.5
Total	19.9	19.9
Total excluding petroleum	15.3	14.4

Note: [a] Production of tradables, 1986 weights.
Source: World Bank estimates.

sector started in mid-1990 with light trucks and buses; as of 1991, foreign auto makers in Mexico are able to import cars not made in Mexico. Domestic content requirements will be reduced. Only some 300 tariff items (out of a total of 11,949) are subject to the 0 and 5 per cent rates, but they account for nearly one-quarter of imports. Tariffs escalate with stage of processing, and are generally higher than those of the USA.

The USA is relatively open to exports from Mexico. There are QRs on imports of certain Mexican steel, textiles and apparel, broom corn, sugar and cheese. There are marketing orders for many fruits, vegetables and flowers which restrain trade. But Mexico's steel quota under the Voluntary Restraint Agreement (VRA), which is due to expire in March 1992, has been substantially increased in recent years. Mexico's textiles and apparel quotas under the MFA have also been substantially increased. By now, these QRs probably do not restrain trade much, although they may restrain investment to expand trade.

US tariffs are almost all below 10 per cent, and the average is less than half that. About 9 per cent of US imports from Mexico in 1989 entered duty-free under the Generalised System of Preferences (GSP) (and some 200 items were restored to GSP status in early 1990). Another 45 per cent of imports (from the border industries of 'Maquila') entered with duties levied on only the Mexican value-added component. But some of the products where tariffs are higher are of interest to Mexico: high seasonal tariffs apply to fruits and vegetables. Footwear, textiles and apparel are other examples, although the bulk of these items come from the Maquila. Several 'non-trade' measures also restrict bilateral trade: health and sanitary requirements for agricultural products, and emission and safety standards for autos.

Table 3.3 summarizes the main agricultural trade barriers.

Table 3.3 *US–Mexico bilateral trade and trade barriers*

Trade	US imports from Mexico US$2746: mainly coffee, shrimps, cattle, fruit and vegetables	US exports to Mexico US$2628 m: mainly grains and oilseeds
Barriers		
NTBs	QRs on dairy products, sugar and sugar products	QRs on about 60 items, particularly grains and oilseeds
Tariffs	Generally low but high seasonal tariffs on fruit and vegetables	Higher, some 20 per cent
Other	Marketing orders on fruit, vegetables, and flowers Health and sanitary requirements	Health and sanitary requirements

2.2 *Mexican agriculture*

In Mexican agriculture, an import-substituting sector produces basic grains and oilseeds, and an exportable sector fruits, vegetables, sugar, coffee and similar crops. 6 million workers are rural, about one-third of Mexico's labour force. Agriculture contributes 9 per cent of GNP, but is important for distributional reasons: most of the extremely poor are in the rural areas and are engaged in agricultural activities (Levy, 1991).

An FTA in agriculture would have major implications for the Mexican economy. Removing protection to maize would reduce output, and increase the labour supply to the rest of agriculture. Small maize producers would reduce output on their own lands, and increase their participation in the rural labour market since the marginal quality of their land implies that, in the absence of investments in irrigation infrastructure, it probably cannot be used for other crops. Because maize occupies over one-third of the total arable land, and because it is produced by around 2 million small (or 'subsistence') producers, such a change would have large repercussions in the labour market.

But the FTA could give Mexico wide access to the US market for export crops like fruits, vegetables and sugar. Because some of these crops are more labour-intensive than maize, the export expansion could help absorb labour released from maize and other basic grains. But the more labour-intensive export crops like fruits and vegetables require irrigated land, and some of the released land from basic grains will be rain-fed. Second, the expansion of Mexican fruit and vegetable exports could come at the expense of a contraction in US output of these crops. The reduced demand for Mexican migrants in the USA would lower migration incentives, and increase the net supply of Mexican labour to Mexican agriculture.[1]

Further distributional effects would occur through consumer prices. Mexican urban consumers have access to subsidised maize, but the same is not true of rural consumers, since the network of government-operated rural stores fails systematically to reach the rural areas. By lowering maize prices, the FTA would bring direct benefits to landless rural workers and to maize producers who because of their smallholdings and/or low-quality rain-fed land are actually net maize buyers.

3 Model structure

The model used simplifies the urban sector (industry and services), and focuses on income distribution and employment effects within agriculture, on urban–rural migration and on aggregate welfare effects. Levy and van Wijnbergen (1991b) provide full details. Table 3.4 describes trade characteristics and production location.

We make no difference between the skills of urban and rural labour; the labels in Table 3.4 refer to location. Land quality differences are fundamental in Mexican agriculture (Salinas, 1990). To capture this, we distinguish between rain-fed (T1) and irrigated (T2) land. Both types of land combine with rural labour (and intermediate inputs) to produce rural goods, although yields and land–labour ratios for the same crop differ

Table 3.4 *Commodities' characteristics*

Good (1)	Sector (2)	Tradable (3)	Primary factors used (4)
Maize	Rural	Yes	Rural labour, Land
Basic grains	Rural	Yes	Rural labour, Land
Fruits and vegetables	Rural	Yes	Rural labour, Land
Other agricultural produce	Rural	Yes	Rural labour, Land
Livestock	Rural	Yes	Rural labour, Land
Industry	Urban	Yes	Urban labour, Capital
Services	Urban	No	Urban labour, Capital

between types of land. Another important feature of Mexican land-tenure regulations is that land allocated to livestock cannot be transferred to agricultural production (Heath, 1990). We therefore fix exogenously the amount of land devoted to livestock and limit land substitution between the first four rural goods. Finally, we simplify urban production by fixing the capital stock in industry and services.

There are six types of households, classified by ownership of factors of production. Four are in rural areas: landless rural workers, whose only asset is labour; subsistence farmers, who own 2 hectares of rain-fed land, and who work on their own land and participate in the rural labour market; rain-fed farmers, who own the remainder of the rain-fed land and half of the land used for livestock; and owners of irrigated land, who own the irrigated land, and the other half of the livestock land. Neither rain-fed nor irrigated farmers supply labour. Urban workers supply all urban labour, and urban capitalists own the capital stock in industry and services. Landless rural workers and subsistence farmers can migrate to urban areas. This affects the number of these types of households and the numbers of urban workers. There are a fixed number of urban capitalists and owners of rain-fed and irrigated land.

Preferences are described by a nested Cobb–Douglas/CES utility function. An inner CES nest aggregates the five rural goods into a composite rural good, while an outer Cobb–Douglas nest allocates total expenditures between the composite rural good, industry and services. The parameters differ across households. Urban workers, landless rural workers and subsistence farmers all have the same preferences, as do rain-fed and irrigated land owners and urban capitalists. The first group allocates a much larger share of expenditure to rural goods than does the second. Changes in food prices thus have a much larger impact on the first group.

As to technology, production of all seven goods combines intermediate and primary inputs in fixed proportions. Primary inputs produce value-added. For the five rural goods, value-added is produced by rain-fed and irrigated land and rural labour; for the two urban goods, value-added is produced by sector-specific capital and urban labour.

We distinguish *physical* (the actual physical hectares of land allocated to a particular crop) from *effective* land (the amount actually usable. The relationship between the two types of land is:

$$\tilde{T}_j = r_j.T_j^{\phi j} \qquad r_j > 0, \qquad 0 < \phi_j < 1 \tag{1}$$

the ~ denotes effective land; a subscript j refers to the four agricultural goods. Equation (1) shows that as more physical land is applied to a particular crop, the amount of effective land grows less than proportionately. This captures the fact that as more land is allocated to the same crop, the nutrient content of the soil diminishes, while if the same amount were applied to a different crop the pay-off would initially be higher; it thus captures the incentives for crop rotation and other incentives against using all of the land for a single crop. Rain-fed and irrigated land differ in that:

$$\phi 1_i \leq \phi 2_j \qquad \text{for all } j \tag{2}$$

As more irrigated land is allocated to any given crop, diminishing returns set in more slowly than in rain-fed lands.

The use of intermediate inputs in rain-fed and irrigated lands is the same; the value-added production functions are Cobb–Douglas, and exhibit constant returns to scale. Value-added in maize (m) in rain-fed lands is thus:

$$VA1_m = LR1_m^{(1-a1_m)}.T\sim 1_m^{a1_m} = LR1_m^{(1-a1_m)}.\tau 1_m.^{a1_m}T1_m^{\phi 1_m.a1_m} \tag{3}$$

$$= \rho 1_m.LR1_m^{(1-a1_m)}.T1_m^{\lambda 1_m} \tag{3'}$$

$LR1_m$, $T1_m$ are rural labour and rain-fed lands allocated to maize production; $\rho 1_m = r1_m^{a1m}$ and $\lambda 1_m = \phi 1_m.a1_m$. Similar functions apply to the other agricultural products in both types of land. Note that since $0 < \lambda < a < 1$, there will be, for given labour intensity, diminishing returns to physical land. This implies that there need not be full specialisation in agriculture.

Most intermediate inputs are assumed to be used in fixed proportions. However, because there is strong evidence of substitutability between maize and sorghum when used as feedstock in the livestock sector, we allow substitution between maize and other grains into that sector. The technology in the urban areas is simple: fixed intermediate inputs and a Cobb–Douglas value-added function in both industry and services.

The government sets production and consumption taxes and subsidies. Protection to basic grains and to industry is modelled as a production subsidy and an across-the-board consumption tax to all final and intermediate consumers. For maize, a production subsidy and an equal consumption tax (as intermediate and final good) in the rural areas is accompanied by a consumption subsidy in the urban areas. Third, the value-added tax is assumed to apply only in the urban areas, as most transactions in the rural areas escape such taxes.

We include two further forms of government intervention: direct lump-sum transfers to households and rural employment programmes. Recent policy changes in Mexico aim at eliminating general urban food subsidies, replacing them by directly targeted food coupons to the urban poor. Such direct deliveries of food (particularly of maize through a programme labelled 'tortibonos'[2]) are infra-marginal, and thus equivalent to a direct income transfer. Rural employment programmes are important because, through their impact on the rural wage rate, they are one of the few feasible ways of helping the rural poor.

For given taxes and subsidies, domestic prices for tradable goods follow world prices, as we assume domestic goods to be perfect substitutes for world goods, and take world prices to be exogenous. But services are non-traded, so this market, like the markets for rural and urban labour, and rain-fed and irrigated land, is cleared by prices. Our model thus determines factor prices and the real exchange rate. All this leads to:

$$LR^D(P) + L_r^u(P) - LR^0 = 0 \tag{4.1}$$

$$LU^D(P) - L_r^u(P) - LU^0 = 0 \tag{4.2}$$

$$T1^D(P) - T1 = 0 \tag{4.3}$$

$$T2^D(P) - T2 = 0 \tag{4.4}$$

$$qs_s(P) - qd_s(P) = 0 \tag{4.5}$$

P contains the rural and urban wage rates, the rental rates on rain-fed and irrigated land, and the price of services. qs and qd are the vectors of goods' supply and demand, the subscript s refers to services, and the superscript D denotes the market demand for a particular type of labour or land. LR^0 and LU^0 are the initial distribution of the total labour force between the two areas, so that at the initial values of all exogenous variables L_r^u, the stock of migrants is zero.

Migration responds to urban–rural consumption wage differences, and also to other benefits derived from living in a particular area (like the urban 'tortibono' programme). With L_r^u the stock of migrants moving from rural to urban areas, U_r and U_u *per capita* utility of a worker in the rural and urban areas, respectively, and the superscript 0 an initial equilibrium, we get:

$$L_r^u = k[(U_u/U_r)/U_u^0/U_r^0)]^\eta - k; \quad k > 0, \quad \eta \geq 0 \tag{5}$$

η is the elasticity of migration to urban–rural utility differentials.

$(U_u^0 - U_r^0)$ equals the implicit costs of migrating from one area to the other, and is therefore positive in the base run. Second, we take migration costs, measured in utility terms, to be constant. The equilibrium level of migration is that which re-establishes the initial utility differentials.

4 Efficiency and distributional impact of the FTA in agriculture

We first consider the effects of free trade in maize only, and then the impact of the FTA in all agricultural products.

4.1 Free trade in maize

Removing all maize price distortions implies a cut of about one-third in producer prices and rural consumer prices and an increase in urban consumer prices of over 50 per cent.[3] Table 3.5 indicates the welfare effects under various assumptions about government compensation schemes. Columns 1 and 2 bring out the efficiency gains to which liberalising maize trade would lead; columns 3–7 focus on the impact of income distribution, and highlight the need for some form of transitional adjustment scheme.

In columns 1 and 2, the government uses part of the money it saves to make lump-sum transfers (and, for one group, levy lump-sum taxes) so as to bring all households back to their pre-liberalisation *per capita* utility. The resources left over after these compensations (cf. the bottom row) are thus a measure of the pure efficiency gain of liberalising maize, expressed as a percentage of 1989 GDP. The size of these gains is substantial if one bears in mind that the gain is recurrent in all future years, and is due to liberalising trade in one single commodity, maize. Without migration, the gain amounts to almost 0.15 per cent of GDP (about US$310 million per annum).

These already substantial gains are almost doubled once migration is introduced. In this case the welfare gain amounts to almost US$0.6 billion per year! the difference between these two estimates highlights an important second-best aspect: the large urban–rural wage differential implies an inefficient allocation of labour between rural and urban areas, with far

Table 3.5 *Welfare effects of free trade in maize,* per capita *utility as a share of the base case*

	Compensated case; no migration (1)	Compensated case; with migration (2)	No compensation; no migration (3)	No compensation with migration (4)	Rural employment and urban transfer programme; no migration (5)	Rural employment and urban transfer programme; with migration (6)	Urban transfers only; with migration (7)
Subsistence farmers	1.000	1.000	0.918	0.959	0.935	0.975	0.986
Landless rural workers	1.000	1.000	0.932	0.972	0.958	1.000	1.000
Owners of rain-fed land	1.000	1.000	0.981	0.976	0.964	0.952	0.955
Owners of irrigated land	1.000	1.000	1.038	1.035	1.023	1.011	1.015
Urban workers	1.000	1.000	0.989	0.972	1.000	1.000	1.000
Urban capitalists	1.000	1.000	0.994	1.001	0.994	1.004	1.010
Left-over resources (per cent of 1989 GDP)	0.147	0.278	0.829	0.989	0.451	0.217	0.215

too many workers locked in low-productivity rural jobs. Of course, econometric evidence will need to establish that migration is indeed sufficiently sensitive to income differentials fully to restore relative utility levels to pre-policy change levels. Second, the direct resource costs of migration are not taken into account in these calculations.

Of course, the perfect compensation policy assumed in the calculations underlying columns 1 and 2 of Table 3.5 is not feasible in practice: no lump-sum transfer instruments to reach all households are available. Columns 3 and 4 list the welfare gains and losses for various groups in society without any government compensation policy or any handout of the savings the government makes from abolishing its interventions in maize markets. Not surprisingly, additional resources available to the government increase substantially, to almost 1 percentage point of GDP (or almost 2 US$ billion). The per-group welfare measures in columns 3 and 4 should be interpreted with care: they do not yet incorporate the *welfare gains* flowing from any transfer programme or *tax reduction* that the government could undertake. We list these measures because they indicate which groups in society are most in need of assistance.

Within rural areas, Table 3.5 indicates major changes. Landless rural workers lose out in spite of having access to cheaper maize for consumption. This is because rural wages have to fall to absorb in other rural activities the labour released from maize production (Table 3.6). Comparing columns 3 and 4 of Table 3.6 shows that the incidence of this adjustment problem falls almost exclusively on rural workers without migration, but is shifted to a substantial degree to urban workers if migration is brought in. For owners of rain-fed land the reduction in rural wages is not enough to offset the income loss due to lower maize prices. With migration, their welfare loss increases, since they are not users of labour and thus lose out on higher wages. Subsistence farmers are net sellers of maize and thus get hurt twice; hence, their welfare is reduced most (cf. Table 3.5). But since they are net sellers of labour, they do better when there is migration, as in that case rural wages fall less. The clear winners are owners of irrigated land: they gain because of lower wage costs and lose relatively less from lower maize prices since they can more easily switch to more profitable alternatives (mostly fruits and vegetables, see Table 3.7).

In urban areas, the results are less dramatic. Workers are negatively affected by the large increase in urban maize prices and thus lose out unambiguously. Their welfare loss gets magnified when migration is allowed, since this drives down the urban wage. But urban capitalists, with a smaller share of maize in their consumption bundle, are hardly

Table 3.6 *Labour market effects of free trade in maize*

	Compensated case; no migration (1)	Compensated case; with migration (2)	No compensation; no migration (3)	No compensation with migration (4)	Rural employment and urban transfer programme; no migration (5)	Rural employment and urban transfer programme; with migration (6)	Urban transfers only; with migration (7)
Rural product wage[a]	0.929	0.968	0.929	0.968	0.955	0.996	0.996
Rural consumption wage[a]	0.932	0.972	0.932	0.972	0.958	1.000	1.000
Urban product wage[a]	0.994	0.975	0.994	0.975	0.996	0.978	0.965
Urban consumption wage[a]	0.990	0.972	0.990	0.972	0.991	0.975	0.962
Rural–urban migration (000)	0	334.7	0	384.7	0	367.6	647.3
Employment in maize production[a]	0.452	0.429	0.452	0.429	0.433	0.402	0.404
Employment in fruit and vegetables production[a]	1.179	1.105	1.179	1.105	1.113	1.032	1.037
Rural employment programme (000)	0	0	0	0	300.0	300.0	0
Urban transfers[b]	0	0	0	0	0.20	0.60	0.91
Total rural employment[a]	1.000	0.944	1.000	0.944	1.000	0.939	0.892

Note: [a] Fraction of corresponding variable in base case.
[b] Percentage of 1989 GDP.

Table 3.7 *Agricultural output and (net) exports under free trade in maize*

	Compensated case; no migration (1)	Compensated case; with migration (2)	No compensation; no migration (3)	No compensation with migration (4)	Rural employment and urban transfer programme; no migration (5)	Rural employment and urban transfer programme; with migration (6)	Urban transfers only; with migration (7)
Maize output on rain-fed land[a]	0.770	0.758	0.770	0.758	0.753	0.736	0.739
Maize output on irrigated land[a]	0.468	0.447	0.468	0.447	0.447	0.422	0.424
Imports of maize[a]	0.826	0.917	0.826	0.917	0.904	1.018	1.030
Vegetables and fruit output on rain-fed land[a]	1.119	1.083	1.119	1.083	1.079	1.033	1.038
Vegetables and fruit output on irrigated land[a]	1.071	1.053	1.071	1.053	1.047	1.022	1.025
Vegetables and fruit net exports[a]	2.657	2.093	2.657	2.093	1.865	0.918	0.848

Note: [a] Fraction of corresponding variable in base case.

affected at all, and in fact gain a little when, with migration, urban product wages fall.

Table 3.7 shows the effects on agricultural output. Maize production on rain-fed lands falls by about 25 per cent. On irrigated lands, where substitution into alternative crops is easier, the drop is much larger: in excess of 50 per cent in all cases. Not surprisingly, employment in maize production (on both types of land) also falls substantially (Table 3.6). But the net impact on imports is in fact negative as maize consumption goes down even more in response to the more than 50 per cent increase in urban maize prices. On the other hand, output and exports of fruit and vegetables increase, as labour costs fall.

The simulations reported in columns 5–7 of Tables 3.5–3.7 are designed to indicate the extent to which government programmes can alleviate the distributional impact of liberalising trade in maize. The first experiment institutes both a rural employment programme, of about 300,000 workers (or roughly the amount of migration in the no-compensation case), and an infra-marginal transfer programme to urban workers (through the 'tortibono' programme). The second experiment contains the same policy interventions as the first, but allows migration. The last experiment, finally, excludes the rural employment programme, and hence captures the pure incentive effects of the 'tortibono' programme for urban workers. In all three simulations, the transfer programme to urban workers is expanded so as to restore urban workers' utility to their pre-policy change level.

In each case, the costs of these programmes are smaller than the revenue gains triggered by liberalising maize. The programmes can thus be put in place without undermining fiscal policy. Second, the welfare losses of those groups most dependent on the price of labour are in fact substantially reduced or even eliminated. The mechanism behind this result can be seen from Table 3.6: with an urban transfer programme in place to shield urban workers from the effects of higher maize prices, migration to the cities increases by a factor of almost 2 until rural wages are high enough to stem the flow. Thus, through the effects of urban programmes on migration, rural employment programmes and urban transfer programmes are to some extent substitutes.

But perhaps the most important result concerns the contrast between owners of rain-fed and irrigated land. Owners of rain-fed land are worse off. Rural employment programmes and urban transfers fail to reach them directly. More than that, they lose because of them: since they are net users of hired labour, they are negatively affected by the fact that all programmes tighten rural labour markets and higher rural product wages. The welfare loss of rain-fed farmers almost doubles with the various adjustment programmes in place. On the other hand, owners of irrigated land are better off under all scenarios. These results indicate the direction that policies should take to help owners of rain-fed land: use the workers employed under the rural employment programme to improve the productivity of rain-fed lands, possibly through constructing the infrastructure needed for irrigation.

4.2 Free trade in agriculture

In this scenario, existing Mexican tariffs on other grains (in 1989 at a production-weighted average of 10 per cent) are abolished and the USA removes its barriers to Mexican fruit and vegetables exports. These barriers are modelled as a 20 per cent US tariff on the relevant subcategory. The scenario is incomplete because it ignores sugar; improved access to the US sugar market will yield substantial gains for Mexico.

There is a substantial expansion of employment and output in fruit and vegetables production, as one would expect (Tables 3.9 and 3.10). As a consequence, rural wages go down much less than before. Without migration, the welfare gain is larger than in the free-maize case: 0.18 per cent of GDP instead of 0.14 per cent for a total gain of about US$0.4 billion per annum (Table 3.8). Column 2 of Table 3.8 shows that the welfare gains once again increase substantially over the no-migration case, for a total gain of 0.23 per cent of GDP (or US$0.5 billion per annum); but the increase is slightly lower than in the maize-liberalisation case.

The explanation of this at first puzzling result can be seen in Table 3.9. Migration in this case is much smaller, as the fruit and vegetables sector absorbs most of the labour released from maize production. This means that the 'second-best' benefits are correspondingly smaller. Because rural–urban migration is smaller with the FTA in all of agriculture, urban transfer programmes can be much smaller than in the case when only maize is liberalised. As a result, the government is in fact left with substantially higher excess resources in those cases (compare columns 5–7 of Table 3.6 with those of Table 3.9 and with those of Table 3.8) which, as before, can be used for tax reductions and/or investments in irrigation infrastructure. The income distributional shocks to which a liberalisation of trade in maize would lead are considerably softened, although not fully eliminated, when simultaneous access to the US fruit and vegetables markets is gained as part of a comprehensive FTA.

Table 3.8 *Welfare effects of free trade in maize, other grains and fruit and vegetables,* per capita *utility as a share of the base case*

	Compensated case; no migration (1)	Compensated case; with migration (2)	No compensation; no migration (3)	No compensation with migration (4)	Rural employment and urban transfer programme; no migration (5)	Rural employment and urban transfer programme; with migration (6)	Urban transfers only; with migration (7)
Subsistence farmers	1.000	1.000	0.943	0.957	0.959	0.966	0.976
Landless workers	1.000	1.000	0.966	0.981	0.992	1.000	1.000
Owners of rain-fed land	1.000	1.000	0.974	0.972	0.957	0.954	0.958
Owners of irrigated land	1.000	1.000	1.028	1.027	1.011	1.009	1.013
Urban workers	1.000	1.000	0.988	0.981	1.000	1.000	1.000
Urban capitalists	1.000	1.000	0.996	0.998	0.996	0.998	1.005
Left-over resources (per cent of 1989 GDP)	0.184	0.232	0.787	0.846	0.359	0.313	0.318

Table 3.9 *Labour market effects of free trade in maize, other grains and fruit and vegetables*

	Compensated case; no migration (1)	Compensated case; with migration (2)	No compensation; no migration (3)	No compensation with migration (4)	Rural employment and urban transfer programme; no migration (5)	Rural employment and urban transfer programme; with migration (6)	Urban transfers only; with migration (7)
Rural product wage[a]	0.966	0.980	0.966	0.980	0.993	1.000	1.000
Rural consumption wage[a]	0.958	1.000	0.958	1.000	0.966	1.000	1.000
Urban produce wage[a]	0.995	0.988	0.995	0.988	0.997	0.994	0.980
Urban consumption wage[a]	0.988	0.981	0.988	0.981	0.989	0.986	0.973
Rural–urban migration (1000)	0	122.75	0	122.75	0	69.5	345.4
Employment in maize production[a]	0.420	0.411	0.420	0.411	0.398	0.393	0.395
Employment in fruit and vegetables production[a]	1.249	1.221	1.249	1.221	1.180	1.164	1.169
Rural employment programme (1000)	0	0	0	0	300.0	300.0	0
Urban transfers[b]	0	0	0	0	0.25	0.32	0.63
Total rural employment[a]	1.000	0.980	1.000	0.980	1.000	0.988	0.942

Note: [a] Fraction of corresponding variable in base case.
[b] Percentage of 1989 GDP.

Table 3.10 *Agricultural output and (net) exports*

	Compensated case; no migration (1)	Compensated case; with migration (2)	No compensation; no migration (3)	No compensation with migration (4)	Rural employment and urban transfer programme; no migration (5)	Rural employment and urban transfer programme; with migration (6)	Urban transfers only; with migration (7)
Maize output on rain-fed land[a]	0.743	0.739	0.743	0.739	0.727	0.724	0.727
Maize output on irrigated land[a]	0.439	0.432	0.439	0.432	0.419	0.414	0.416
Imports of maize[a]	0.936	0.967	0.936	0.967	1.012	1.033	1.045
Vegetables and fruit output on rain-fed land[a]	1.156	1.142	1.156	1.142	1.114	1.105	1.110
Vegetables and fruit output on irrigated land[a]	1.095	1.088	1.095	1.088	1.070	1.065	1.069
Vegetables and fruit, net exports[a]	4.645	4.438	4.645	4.438	3.822	3.646	3.602

Note: [a] Fraction of corresponding variable in base case.

5 Conclusions

An FTA with the USA will, at least in agriculture, have a major impact on the Mexican economy. We have demonstrated that the potential welfare gains are substantial, but that in the absence of government interventions the gains will be unevenly distributed. But we have also shown a policy package that protects the losers. Moreover, these policies can be fully paid for with the resources freed up by the elimination of protection to agriculture, while still leaving extra resources available.

Second, our results suggest that transitional adjustment problems may be substantial, thus requiring a gradual phasing-in of the FTA. We have indicated that the key mechanism through which the impact of FTA in agriculture will be felt will be via the rural labour market. But rural employment programmes and an extension of the existing programme of infra-marginal food subsidies will substantially soften the impact on labour markets, without preventing the reallocation that is in fact necessary fully to achieve the potential efficiency gains. We highlight in this respect the impact of urban income subsidies on migration – an impact that is in fact desirable given the current degree of overemployment in Mexican agriculture.

But while transitional measures to deal with labour market disturbances can be designed, owners of rain-fed land are more difficult to reach directly. A comprehensive liberalisation of agricultural trade is likely actually to benefit owners of irrigated land, who will profit both from lower labour costs and from increased fruit and vegetables' export opportunities to the USA. But owners of rain-fed land have much lower substitution possibilities, and will thus suffer the most serious losses, as one of their key crops, maize, becomes less valuable. This strongly suggests that ways should be found to direct the rural employment programmes designed to ease labour market adjustment problems towards productivity improvements in rain-fed areas. Rural employment programmes for irrigation infrastructure in rain-fed areas could help the one group that would otherwise be left out, owners of rain-fed land, by raising their productivity. Such a programme, which by its very design would be transitional, would serve also to stimulate in a permanent way the private demand for rural labour, as larger tracts of land became more productive. Such a programme would thus not carry long-term distortionary costs, and would also make it easier to rally support for policies that would lead to substantial aggregate welfare gains. By channelling resources to owners of rain-fed lands through productivity-enhancing investments instead of through protection, the government can protect this group and reap efficiency gains for all.[4]

Different elements in an agricultural FTA are likely to have different impacts on rural labour markets. Liberalising maize prices and trade will release large numbers of rural workers, a substantial part of whom could be absorbed within rural areas if fruit and vegetables export opportunities were opened up in the USA. With such offsetting effects of liberalisation in different areas, a comprehensive approach to the negotiations becomes imperative. Sectoral measures that would seem inconceivable to admit because of their labour market impact may become more palatable if considered in tandem with other measures that tend to soften the labour market impact.

But even a comprehensive approach to agricultural trade, the results suggest, is likely to lead to reallocation of labour from rural to urban areas. This is in fact one of the channels through which efficiency gains will be achieved, since as a result of the current structure of protection the social productivity of labour in rural areas is below that of industrial, urban areas. Once again a comprehensive approach will become necessary; such reallocation will be much easier to bring about if, say, increased direct foreign investment (DFI) shifts out the demand for labour in industrial sectors. This shift could even preclude the need for an extension of infra-marginal food subsidies in the urban areas. Elsewhere we suggest that freeing trade in services and reforming DFI legislation may bring about just that. Only by incorporating these effects can the full impact of the FTA be assessed.

NOTES

This paper is based on 1989 information on trade policies. We thank Hans Binswanger of the World Bank and Rafael del Villar of ITAM and Ian Goldin of the OECD for several helpful discussions, and Neil Roger for his assistance in describing US–Mexican commodity trade. Angel Blanco of the Ministry of Agriculture in Mexico and Hartwig Schafer at the World Bank provided invaluable assistance with data collection. The views expressed in this paper are our own and do not necessarily represent those of the World Bank or the Mexican Government.

1 This latter effect depends on whether one assumes Mexico is a large or a small country in its fruits, sugar and vegetables exports to the USA. If Mexico is a small country, additional Mexican exports to the USA would not influence US prices. There would therefore be no change in the derived demand for labour in US agriculture, and hence no change in the demand for Mexican migrants. If Mexico does influence prices in the USA, further Mexican exports would depress the demand for labour in US agriculture, and hence the demand for migrants. In the rest of this paper we make the first assumption, and leave for further research the impact of the FTA on Mexico–US migration.

2 The 'tortibono' programme delivers 1 kilo of tortillas per day free to any family in the urban areas earning less than two minimum wages. The 1984

Income–Expenditure Survey shows that low-income urban families consume 2 kilos of tortillas per day, so the 'tortibono' programme is an infra-marginal subsidy.

3 The urban consumer subsidy was 37 per cent in 1989; 37 per cent is 58 per cent of (100–37) per cent, the subsidy-inclusive price. The rural price was 47 per cent above the world price in the same year.

4 The challenge to policy makers in this respect is to design some form of commitment mechanism that can convince owners of rain-fed lands that the resources generated by the FTA will in fact be devoted to such productivity-enhancing investments.

REFERENCES

Behrman, J. and A. Deolalikar (1988) 'Health and Nutrition', in H. Chenery and T. N. Srinivasan (eds), *Handbook of Development Economics*, vol. I, Amsterdam: North-Holland.

Feltenstein, A. (1991) 'Oil Prices and Rural Migration: the Dutch Disease Goes South', forthcoming; University of Kansas (mimeo).

Heath, J. (1990) 'Enhancing the Contribution of the Land Reform Sector to Mexican Agricultural Development', Washington, D.C.: World Bank (mimeo).

Levy, S. (1991) 'Poverty Alleviation in Mexico', *PRE Working Paper*, **679**.

Levy, S. and S. van Wijnbergen (1991a) 'Maize and the Mexico–United States Free Trade Agreement', Washington, D.C.: World Bank (mimeo).

(1991b) 'Agriculture in the Mexico–United States Free Trade Agreement', Washington, D.C.: World Bank (mimeo).

Masera Cerutti, O. (1990) *Crisis y Mecanizacion de la Agricultura Campesina*, Mexico City: El Colegio de Mexico.

Nathan Associates, Inc. (1989) *Comermax: A Multimarket Model of Mexico's Agriculture*, Washington, D.C.

Norton, R. and L. Solis (1983) *The Book of Chac: Programming Studies for Mexican Agriculture*, Baltimore: Johns Hopkins University Press.

Salinas de Gortari, R. (1990) 'El Campo Mexicano Ante el Reto de la Modernizacion', *Comercio Exterior*, **40 (9)**: 816–29.

Secretaria de Agricultura y Recursos Hidraulicos (1984) *Annuario Estadistico de la Produccion Agricola Nacional 1984*, Mexico City.

Discussion

DANIEL COHEN

Chapter 3 is an ambitious, and a quite successful, attempt to analyse the economic consequences of the free trade agreement (FTA) between the USA and Mexico for maize, and fruits and other vegetables. In order to do this, the authors decompose the population of Mexico into six categories (subsistence workers, landless workers, owners of rain-fed land, owners of irrigated land, urban workers and urban capitalists) and display in great detail the welfare implications of the trade agreement on each of these segments of the population.

Let us start with the analysis of maize. Maize is a commodity that is subsidised both at the level of the consumer and at the level of the producer. Removing all trade barriers and domestic subsidies consequently hurts both demand and supply, which is a rare combination. In order to get an upper bound to the impact of such a drastic move towards freeing all subsidies, one can readily turn to Table 3.5, column 3, in which the impact on all categories is reported, at a stage when the decision to migrate is not yet taken. One sees that the benefit for the government will amount to about 0.8 per cent of GDP which, for a single commodity, is indeed quite outstanding. In order to analyse the potential Pareto improvements of this measure, Levy and van Wijnbergen then proceed in two stages. They analyse the resources that are freed when the government compensates, in utility terms, all segments of the population: (1) when not taking account of the decision to migrate, (2) when taking account of the decision to migrate.

When migration is assumed away, the net gain for the government is shown in Table 3.5, column (1). It now represents about 0.15 per cent of GDP. This may still look like a large number. However, one should emphasise here that this is a calculation that is performed when assuming that the government has access to lump-sum taxes and subsidies. Since the initial situation was characterised by distortionary taxes and subsidies the 0.15 per cent figure is certainly an upper bound to what the government can actually obtain. If one assumes that terminating a programme of large subsidies allows the government to make one-shot lump-sum payments to the producer that quits but must keep subsidising in a distortionary way the consumer, then one should cut this 0.15 per cent gain by roughly the share that corresponds to the producer's surplus only: this seems to represent less than half the number itself. Now, if more efficient forms of consumers' subsidies exist (as the authors suggest by considering the social programmes that are now being put in place) then this benefit is available anyhow, and should not be reported as part of the net gain that the free trade programme would deliver.

When one turns to the benefits that accrue to the government when migration is taken into account, the net benefit is multiplied by more than 2, and amounts to 0.45 per cent of GDP. This number is obtained by compensating the various segments of the population for their welfare loss and for the cost of migration that some had to bear. The cost of migration itself is obtained by taking the initial difference between the welfare level that was obtained in the countryside and in urban areas. Such a calculation is likely to understate the loss of welfare of a migrant worker. Indeed, the difference between the level of welfares assumes that a migrant immediately gets the average level of welfare that is affordable, say, in the cities. This is obviously valid only if the markets are perfectly competitive. Any (frictional) unemployment will show a different picture: if the migrant worker is last to obtain a job, he leaves an average level welfare (in the countryside) for a *marginal* level in the cities (by calling the 'marginal' level of welfare the level that is obtained by the last entrant in a market). This will mean that the actual cost of migration (before the policy regime change) is actually *less* than what is reported by the initial difference of averages, but – in the case of a large migration – the marginal level of welfare is likely to be (much) lower than what is reported by the average level. And after all, isn't that the main fear of the government: creating unemployed urban workers rather than (inefficient) farmers?

When one turns to the analysis of the fruits and other vegetables story, one finds a description that presents an interesting counterintuitive result. When the gain for the government is assessed before the decision to migrate is taken into account, one finds that it is larger than that which was previously obtained in the maize case. However, when the decision to migrate is taken into account the hierarchy is reversed. What is the origin of this result?

The following mechanism is at work. In the fruit and vegetable story, the equilibrium level of migration is lower than in the maize case (as some of the landless farmers can get a job in the rural areas). As a result, the money value of their new activities is reported as lower; prices are lower in the countryside than in the cities and, because of the cost of migration, neither the law of one price nor purchasing power parity holds. We are consequently back to the same problem as in the maize case: a more thorough approach to the cost of migration and to the arbitrage conditions is needed in order to appraise the empirical magnitude of these discrepancies.

Let me close here my comments by congratulating the authors for an admirable piece of work. They have enlightened the discussion to the best of what economic analysis can deliver. We must now let actual history decide whether the transition to the FTA can indeed be managed in a Pareto improving way.

4 Do the benefits of fixed exchange rates outweigh their costs? The CFA Zone in Africa

SHANTAYANAN DEVARAJAN and DANI RODRIK

A primary reason for structural adjustment in agriculture is the wide fluctuation in the world prices of agricultural commodities, which causes sharp swings in the terms of trade of countries that rely on these commodities for their export earnings. A key instrument in structural adjustment is the exchange rate. How, and whether, this instrument is used, however, depends on the 'rules of the game' – that is, the particular exchange rate regime the country is in. This paper addresses the question of how small, open economies that are subject to sharp swings in their terms of trade should select an appropriate exchange rate regime. We develop a framework to clarify the trade-offs involved, and apply it to the CFA Zone countries in Africa, which have maintained a fixed parity with the French franc since independence.

Thanks to the predominance of a few agricultural products and natural resources in their exports, CFA member countries have suffered frequent shocks in their terms of trade. A flexible exchange rate could have possibly alleviated some of the output costs of these external shocks. On the other hand, a fixed exchange rate has enabled these countries to maintain lower inflation levels than their neighbours. Our framework provides a way of weighing these costs and benefits. Using our model as a guide, we investigate whether their choice of a fixed exchange rate was (and remains) a wise one.

1 The issues

The selection of an appropriate exchange rate regime has aroused considerable academic interest since the 1950s, and the answers provided have changed with academic fashion.[1] Throughout much of the 1950s and 1960s, in line with prevailing wisdom (and practice) in the international monetary system as a whole, developing countries maintained fixed exchange rates. More flexible arrangements began to become commonplace by the late 1960s and 1970s. As the currencies of industrial countries started to float *vis-à-vis* each other after 1971, flexibility became a necessity: pegging to any of the major currencies implied floating against others. During the 1980s, exchange rate flexibility continued to gain ground among developing countries. In particular, many governments experimented with market-based exchange rate regimes, such as auction-based systems, interbank markets, or pure floats.

But by the mid-1980s, the tide had turned. Floating exchange rates began to lose much of their lustre in the eyes of industrial country policy makers. The wide gyrations of the dollar during the 1980s and the short-term volatility of the key currencies eroded confidence in markets' ability to foster adjustment with no (or few) tears. The Europeans linked their currencies tighter, and proposals to limit flexibility became widespread. In many parts of the developing world, exchange rate flexibility became another name for inflation: in Bolivia, Brazil, Argentina, Mexico, Israel and Poland, governments introduced stabilisation programmes based on fixed exchange rates.

There are basically two ways of looking at exchange rates, with divergent implications for desirable exchange rate regimes. Borrowing Corden's (1990) terminology, we can call these the 'real targets' approach and the 'nominal anchor' approach. The real targets school views the exchange rate as an indispensable policy instrument in attaining equilibrium in the 'real' economy, such as in domestic activity, the current account, or the rate of growth. This is the view of the exchange rate embedded in the textbook exposition of the dependent economy model, with its juxtaposition of expenditure-switching (i.e., devaluation) and expenditure-changing (i.e., fiscal policy) as the two independent policies needed to achieve the twin goals of internal and external balance. The real targets approach inevitably leads to an activist, discretionary stance. The exchange rate has to be managed flexibly: the authorities need to respond to external shocks (such as terms of trade changes) or domestic price shocks by undertaking the requisite combination of expenditure-switching (i.e., exchange rate) and expenditure-changing policies to re-attain macroeconomic equilibrium.

Implicit in the real targets approach are two notions: first, that the macroeconomy cannot be relied on to generate on its own the *real* exchange rate changes required by shocks to the system; second, that a nominal devaluation will have real effects (i.e., it will lead to a depreciation of the real exchange rate), at least in the short to medium run. These two notions of how the economy works are encapsulated in the textbook model by the assumption that home-good prices are rigid (upward as well as downward). Putting the two together, we obtain the activist role for the exchange rate called for by the real targets approach.

The alternative, nominal anchor approach is based on a rejection of the efficacy of nominal exchange rate adjustments. The case for this approach can be constructed at several levels. At the simplest level, one can deny the effectiveness of nominal devaluations in achieving real depreciations, thereby denying flexibility of the currency any serious economic purpose. But even if it is granted that nominal exchange rate policy has some power in the short to medium run, it is possible to argue that the inflationary costs are high enough to render it a bad bargain. The pass-through from the exchange rate to domestic prices arises from the openness of the economy and/or from the effective indexing of home-goods prices to the value of the currency. When the pass-through coefficient is below unity but high, nominal exchange rate changes large enough to be 'effective' in the sense of the real targets approach will come at the cost of unacceptable jumps in domestic prices.

A more recent strand of theorising has added a new twist to the nominal anchor approach. The literature spawned by the discovery of rational expectations has stressed that the policy regime in place will shape the way the private sector sets wages and prices in the economy. In a flexible rate regime, domestic price setters will take into account the policy makers' incentive to alter the nominal exchange rate in order to achieve some 'real' objective, an incentive that typically undercuts the price setters' desire to maintain their relative prices. Moreover, any pronouncement that the authorities' discretion over the exchange rate will not be 'abused' is not credible for standard time-inconsistency reasons, as long as the value of the currency can be adjusted at more frequent intervals than wages and domestic prices. The economy will consequently settle at a high rate of inflation, with no guarantee that the authorities will end up any closer to their real targets. In this view, then, exchange rate flexibility has a cost and no benefits. It is better to give up discretion and subscribe to a fixed exchange rate regime, thereby 'anchoring' the domestic price level.[2]

Clearly, both approaches capture some of the reality in developing countries, and neither can be judged right or wrong in the abstract. The weight of arguments on the two sides will depend on the particulars of each case. Here, we will lay out a simple, formal framework which captures the essence of the arguments listed above and provides guidance as to how the weighting of pros and cons can be done explicitly. We will then apply the framework to the African member countries of the CFA Zone. We will ask: knowing what we do about their terms of trade history and their (as well as their neighbours') performance over the last three decades, did their decision to join a currency union with France make sense?

2 The CFA Zone

The CFA Zone consists of thirteen African countries[3] which are divided into two currency unions: the Union Monétaire Ouest Africaine and the members of the Banque des Etats de l'Afrique Centrale. Each union issues its own currency. Since both currencies are the CFA franc, the two unions are referred to jointly as the 'CFA franc Zone', hereafter CFA Zone.

The Zone is an extension of the monetary authority which governed these former French colonies prior to independence. In the late 1950s, the two currency unions were set up, and the newly-independent Francophone countries of Africa were given the option of joining. All but Guinea, Madagascar and Mauritania did so.[4] Membership in the Zone afforded these countries the opportunity to pool their foreign exchange reserves. In addition, the Zone was governed by certain rules which could be interpreted as a means of guiding monetary policy in these fledgling nation-states.[5] First, government borrowing from the Central Bank could not exceed 20 per cent of the previous year's tax receipts. Second, the French government guaranteed the convertibility of the CFA franc. Member countries had to convert 65 per cent of their foreign exchange reserves into French francs and deposit them with the French Treasury. Third, and most relevant to our study, the exchange rate between the French and CFA francs was fixed at 50 CFAF = 1 FF, the rate which had prevailed since 1948. Changes in this parity required the unanimous consent of all Zone members, including France: in other words, the rules of the Zone made a nominal devaluation virtually impossible.

While other aspects of the CFA Zone have changed over the last 30 years, these three rules have remained intact. Several studies have asked whether the rules have led to a difference in the economic performance of Zone members *vis-à-vis* some group of 'comparator' countries. Devarajan and de Melo (1987) showed that CFA countries had a slightly higher growth rate of GDP than their sub-Saharan African (hereafter SSA) counterparts in the period 1960–82. Guillaumont *et al.* (1988) obtained a similar conclusion by examining a richer set of indicators. Both sets of authors attributed the differential performance to the monetary and fiscal discipline engendered by membership in the CFA Zone.

However, in updating their study to include the 1980s, and looking at a broader set of indicators, Devarajan and de Melo (1990) arrived at more equivocal results. While CFA countries continued to enjoy a slightly higher GDP growth rate than their SSA neighbours, this difference was no longer statistically significant for the 1980s. Furthermore, along some other dimensions, the CFA Zone's performance was noticeably worse. CFA countries had lower export growth and investment levels in the 1980s compared with other African countries. When controlling for their size of the external shocks faced by these groups of countries, Devarajan and de Melo found that CFA countries achieved less current account reduction than their SSA neighbours. Moreover, they experienced greater variability in growth than non-CFA countries.[6] On one dimension, however, the CFA countries continued to shine: their average inflation rate was roughly half that of other SSA countries in the 1970s, and one-seventh that of these countries in the 1980s. Furthermore, the degree of inflation reduction between the 1970s and 1980s, controlling for external shocks, was significantly higher in the CFA Zone than outside it.

In sum, both the rules of the CFA Zone and the performance of its members make it an ideal case with which to study the pros and cons of fixed exchange rates. The Zone has maintained a fixed parity with the French franc throughout its history. The relative performance of Zone members *vis-à-vis* their SSA counterparts illustrates the trade-offs involved. On the one hand, Zone members enjoyed lower inflation thanks to the fixed exchange rate regime. On the other, they have apparently been unable to adjust their economies to the large terms of trade shocks of the 1980s, and have experienced greater variability in output. One reason, no doubt, is their inability to use nominal devaluations as an instrument of adjustment. Finally, the comparison between CFA and other SSA countries is especially apt, for the other SSA countries share most of the salient features except the fixed rate with the CFA Zone. They obtained independence at similar times, and are at roughly the same level of development. All are primary producers, as are the CFA members; since they produce similar goods, they had to face the same external shocks as the CFA countries during this period. In short, the other SSA countries provide CFA members with a relatively accurate picture of 'life outside the Zone'. The fact that these two groups of countries are distinguished by exchange rate regime brings us as close to a controlled experiment as economists could hope for.

3 The framework

The experience of the CFA Zone illustrates the main trade-off involved in the choice of exchange rate regimes, as indicated in Section 1: by committing themselves to a fixed rate regime, these countries could anchor their price levels and maintain inflation close to the rate experienced by the country whose currency served as the peg. However, by doing so they lost the ability to adjust to terms of trade shocks. Had they selected a flexible rate regime, they would have been able to limit the damage done to the real economy by the volatility in the world prices of their main imports and exports. That, in turn, would have come at the expense of a higher rate of inflation, as domestic wage and price setters would have lacked the discipline, and domestic monetary authorities the credibility, provided by an irrevocably fixed exchange rate.[7]

Did these countries 'do the right thing' by joining a currency union with France? We will set up a simple model here to provide a partial answer to this question.

Assume that the policy maker is interested in maximising an objective function in which both a nominal and a real variable play a role. The real variable could be the current account, output, or the growth rate. The nominal variable could be the price level or inflation. Since presumably what matters most to policy makers is growth and inflation, we will cast the model in terms of these two variables. We express the objective function in quadratic-loss form:

$$W = -\{(\pi - \pi^*)^2 + \phi(y - y^*)^2\} \tag{1}$$

where W denotes welfare, π is inflation, y is the growth rate, ϕ is the weight attached by the authorities to the real target relative to the nominal one, and π^* and y^* are the policy maker's targets for inflation and growth, respectively (π^* can of course be zero).

A welfare maximum is attained when inflation and growth hit their target levels ($\pi = \pi^*$ and $y = y^*$).[8] The quadratic-loss formulation has well-known problems, chief among which is its symmetric treatment of overshooting and undershooting of targets. But for our purposes, such problems are of secondary importance.

The equilibrium level of growth is determined by two variables, the change in the real exchange rate and the terms of trade:

$$y = \bar{y} + a(e - p) + \beta(\tau - \bar{\tau}) \tag{2}$$

where $\bar{y}$ is the (exogenously given) 'natural' rate of growth, e and p are (log differences in) the exchange rate and the home-good price, respectively, τ is the (log) terms of trade, and $\bar{\tau}$ is the mean level of the (log) terms of trade. The parameters a and β are positive. The terms of trade, τ, is taken to be random, with variance σ^2. Note that $(e - p)$ stands for the percentage change in the real exchange rate.

An equation like (2) follows from expressing the level of output as a function of the level of the real exchange rate and the terms of trade.

To complete the model, we have to specify how domestic prices are determined. We assume that domestic price (or wage) setters are rational and forward-looking, but that they can change their prices less frequently than the authorities can adjust the exchange rate. Domestic prices are therefore set taking into account the government's exchange rate policy, but without actually observing the exchange rate that will prevail. This provides policy makers in principle a temporary leeway in determining the real exchange rate by altering the nominal exchange rate. Further, we assume that terms of trade shocks are revealed *after* domestic prices are set. The timing therefore is as follows:

1 p is set
2 τ is revealed
3 e is set.

We assume that domestic price setters (e.g., urban workers) are rational and forward-looking. In setting their prices, they are concerned both with maintaining their relative prices and with adjusting to shocks. In reduced form, their behaviour can be summarised by expressing the change in domestic prices as follows:

$$p = E(e) + \omega E(\tau - \bar{\tau}) \tag{3}$$

where $E(x)$ stands for the expected value of x. The first term here captures the relative-price motive,[9] while the second captures the desired adjustment in home prices in response to the expected terms of trade shock (ω is a parameter representing the elasticity of the desired adjustment with respect to the shock). Note that p is set *before* τ is revealed, and $E(\tau - \bar{\tau}) = 0$.

Therefore, equation (3) boils down to:

$$p = E(e) \tag{4}$$

Hence, home-goods prices (or, equivalently, wages) increase at the expected rate of nominal depreciation.

Finally, inflation is a weighted average of the increases in the prices of home goods and traded goods:[10]

$$\pi = \mu p + (1 - \mu)e \tag{5}$$

We are now ready to analyse the behaviour of the economy under the two exchange rate regimes.

3.1 Fixed exchange rates

The analysis of this case is very simple. Under fixed exchange rates, the government irrevocably fixes the value of the currency, giving up its discretionary power to alter it. As mentioned above, rational expectations in this context imply $p = E(e)$. Given the inflation target of π^*, then, the optimal policy for the government is to set $e = \pi^*$. This gives:

$$p = E(e) = e = \pi^*$$

That in turn implies that the equilibrium value of the real variable is

$$y = \bar{y} + \beta(\tau - \bar{\tau}) \tag{6}$$

Under this policy regime, then, inflation stays on target while growth fluctuates with the terms of trade.

3.2 *Flexible exchange rates*

Under flexible rates, the government behaves in a discretionary manner and determines the value of e to maximise its objective function as expressed in equation (1). When it does so, it takes home-goods prices (p) as given (as they have been pre-set). Moreover, having observed the terms of trade, it selects an exchange rate that is contingent on the realised value of τ. Substituting equations (2) and (5) into equation (1), we can write the objective function in terms of e, p, and τ:

$$\begin{aligned} W(e,p,\tau) = &-[\mu p + (1-\mu)e - \pi^*]^2 \\ &- \phi[(\bar{y} - y^*) + a(e - p) + \beta(\tau - \bar{\tau})]^2 \end{aligned}$$

Maximising this expression and solving for e yields:

$$\begin{aligned} e = &\{a^2\phi + (1-\mu)^2\}^{-1}\{[a^2\phi - \mu(1-\mu)]p \\ &+ (1-\mu)\pi^* + a\phi(y^* - \bar{y}) - a\phi\beta(\tau - \bar{\tau})\} \end{aligned} \tag{7}$$

Assuming that the policy maker places sufficient weight on the real target (growth) so that $[a^2\phi - \mu(1-\mu)] > 0$, we get the following results:

$$de/d\tau < 0 \tag{7.1}$$

$$1 > de/dp > 0 \tag{7.2}$$

$$de/d\pi^* > 0 \tag{7.3}$$

$$de/d(y^* - \bar{y}) > 0 \tag{7.4}$$

For the ease of exposition, assume an initial equilibrium where $e = p = 0$. The first of these inequalities states that the policy maker will react to terms of trade shocks by a compensatory exchange rate policy; a deterioration in the terms of trade will be met by a depreciation. This is, of course, the main advantage of flexibility in the exchange rate regime. The second result states that an increase in home-goods prices will be accommodated by a depreciation, but only partially. The reason for the partial accommodation is the inflationary cost of depreciation. Third, a reduction in the target value of inflation will call for an appreciation of the currency.

The fourth result links exchange rate policy to the relationship between the government's target for growth and the natural level of growth. When the government has an expansionary motive ($y^* > \bar{y}$), exchange rate policy will have a bias towards depreciation. For the rest of the analysis, we will assume that this is indeed the case. There are two possible justifications for this. First, for many reasons, we could think that the economy's natural rate of growth is suboptimal from a social standpoint. That could be due to pre-existing rigidities in labour markets or to various kinds of distortionary (and unremovable) taxation. The government's desire to push the economy beyond the rate at which the economy would settle on its own would, then, be a well-meaning response to this suboptimality. The second justification is based on a much less benign view. In this view, the bias towards depreciation derives from more dubious motives: gaining political advantage by giving the economy a temporary boost, or allowing inflationary finance of budget deficits.

Under rational expectations, domestic price setters will take into account the government's behaviour, as captured by equation (7). Setting $p = E(e)$ and taking the expectation of equation (7), we can derive the following expression for the expected change in the exchange rate (and therefore the level of home-goods prices):

$$E(e) = p = \pi^* + [a\phi/(1 - \mu)](y^* - \bar{y}) \tag{8}$$

where we have used the fact that $E(\tau - \bar{\tau}) = 0$. This is the rule followed by the private sector in setting p.

Note that home-goods inflation will be higher, the greater the divergence between the target level of growth and its natural level. That is because price setters will want to cover themselves against currency depreciations that erode their relative prices. In turn, the equilibrium level of depreciation of the exchange rate (by plugging equation (8) into equation (7)) will be:

$$\begin{aligned} e = \pi^* &+ [a\phi/(1 - \mu)](y^* - \bar{y}) \\ &- \{a\phi\beta/[a^2\phi + (1 - \mu)^2]\}(\tau - \bar{\tau}) \end{aligned} \tag{9}$$

Note that equation (9) differs from equation (8) by only the last term, which is the terms of trade shock that cannot be anticipated by price setters. Domestic price behaviour therefore fully takes into account the systematic component of exchange rate policy (the part due to the gap between y^* and $\bar{y}$), which implies that the government's expansionary motive creates only inflation and no output gains.

But discretionary policy does buy the economy something, and that is the ability to alter the real exchange rate (and hence smooth output) in the face of unanticipated terms of trade disturbances. This can be seen by solving for the equilibrium level of y:

$$y = \bar{y} + \{(1-\mu)^2/[a^2\phi + (1-\mu)^2]\}\beta(\tau - \bar{\tau}) \tag{10}$$

Since $\{(1-\mu)^2/[a^2\phi + (1-\mu)^2]\} < 1$, exchange rate flexibility enables growth to be less sensitive to fluctuations in the terms of trade than in the fixed exchange rate case (as can be seen by comparing equation (10) with equation (6)).

3.3 *Welfare comparison of the two policy regimes*

Table 4.1 summarises the inflation and growth consequences of the two policy regimes. The fixed exchange rate regime does better on the inflation front (on average), while the flexible rate regime does better on the real side of the economy by reducing the fluctuations in growth rate. The next step is to derive an explicit cost-benefit criterion for choosing between the two.

The appropriate way to this is to take an *ex ante* stand and ask: which of the two regimes provides a higher level of expected welfare, in the light of the structure of the economy, policy preferences of the authorities, and the anticipated pattern of exogenous (in this case terms of trade) shocks? It is possible to answer this question using the results obtained so far. For each policy regime, we can plug the equilibrium outcomes for y and π into the objective function (1), and take the mathematical expectation.

Let us denote expected welfare under the fixed exchange rate regime by EW_f and the corresponding variable under the flexible exchange rate regime by EW_{nf}. Then after some algebra and simplification, the difference between the two can be expressed as:

$$EW_f - EW_{nf} = a^2\phi^2\Delta \tag{11}$$

with

$$\Delta = [(y^* - \bar{y})/(1-\mu)]^2 - \beta^2\sigma^2/[a^2\phi + (1-\mu)^2 \tag{12}$$

We will refer to $(EW_f - EW_{nf})$ as the net benefits of the fixed rate regime. The composite parameter Δ is of ambiguous sign, reflecting the trade-off between the costs and benefits of the two regimes. The first term making up Δ captures the benefit of the fixed rate regime, while the second term represents the cost. A fixed rate is preferable to a flexible rate regime whenever Δ is positive.

Note first that the variance of the terms of trade (σ^2) enters on the cost

Table 4.1 *Inflation and growth: consequences of alternative policy regimes*

	Growth	Inflation
Fixed exchange rate	$\bar{y} + \beta(\tau - \bar{\tau})$	π^*
Flexible exchange rate	$\bar{y} + \{(1-\mu)^2/[a^2\phi + (1-\mu)^2]\} \times \beta(\tau - \bar{\tau})$	$\pi^* + [a\phi/(1-\mu)](y^* - \bar{y}) - \{(1-\mu)a\phi\beta/[a^2\phi + (1-\mu)^2]\}(\tau - \bar{\tau})$

side. That is, the higher is σ^2, the less likely is it that a fixed rate will be preferable to a flexible rate regime. Second, the higher is $(y^* - \bar{y})$ the more likely is it that a fixed exchange rate will be desirable. This follows from the greater temptation of policy makers with expansionary ambitions to inflate the economy (and depreciate the currency). A fixed exchange rate rules out such depreciation, and leaves policy makers better off, *even* when judged by their own welfare criterion. Third, a high β makes flexible rates more desirable – that is, when the real economy is highly susceptible to terms of trade shocks, flexible exchange rates have the edge.[11]

Next, we turn to the effect of ϕ. It can be verified that:

$$d(EW_f - EW_{nf})/d\phi > 0 \quad \text{whenever } \Delta > 0; \quad \text{and}$$
$$d(EW_f - EW_{nf})/d\phi \gtreqless 0$$

In words, when a fixed rate is preferable ($\Delta > 0$), an increase in the weight placed on the real target makes a fixed rate regime even more beneficial. When a flexible rate regime is preferable ($\Delta < 0$), an increase in the weight attached to the real target has ambiguous effects on the net benefits. With respect to Δ itself, we can see from equation (12) that $d\Delta/d\phi$ is unambiguously positive – that is, there must exist a sufficiently high ϕ that a fixed rate regime becomes preferable to a flexible rate one. This may sound paradoxical, because the benefit of a fixed rate regime is lower inflation, not higher growth. But it is an extension of the same logic as previously: when policy makers put a large weight on output relative to inflation, there will be greater temptation to abuse the discretion allowed by flexible exchange rates and a higher inflationary cost. Countries where economic policy is highly politicised, where the central bank lacks autonomy, or where inflation has become chronic and its perceived costs low are all settings where we would expect ϕ and $(y^* - \bar{y})$ to be high.

In the preceding paragraph, we looked at the relationship between ϕ and the choice of policy regimes while holding constant all other parameters, and $(y^* - \bar{y})$ in particular. An alternative approach, and one that we will rely on in our empirical analysis, is to ask how the choice of policy regimes is affected by variations in ϕ, while holding the *inflation differential* between the two regimes constant. From Table 4.1, we can see that the *average* inflation differential under the two regimes is given by:

$$\pi_{nf} - \pi_f = [a\phi/(1 - \mu)](y^* - \bar{y}) \qquad (13)$$

where the subscripts *nf* and *f* once again refer to the flexible and fixed regimes, respectively. This implies

$$[a\phi/(1-\mu)](y^* - \bar{y})^2 = (\pi_{nf} - \pi_f)^2$$

Substituting into equation (11) we get:

$$EW_f - EW_{nf} = (\pi_{nf} - \pi_f)^2 - (a\phi\beta)^2\sigma^2/[a^2\phi + (1-\mu)^2] \qquad (11')$$

It can be shown that the second term on the right-hand side is increasing in ϕ. Thus, holding $(\pi_{nf} - \pi_f)$ constant, $EW_f - EW_{nf}$ is decreasing in ϕ. Therefore, controlling for the inflation differential, an increase in the weight placed on the real target renders fixed rates *less* advantageous. Note that controlling for the inflation differential means in this context adjusting $(y^* - \bar{y})$ *pari passu* with ϕ to maintain the difference between inflation rates fixed (see equation (13)).

We will use the formulation in equation (11′) when we turn to the empirical application to the CFA case. The reason is that we can get a rough handle on the inflation differential under the two regimes by comparing CFA Zone countries with other SSA countries with flexible exchange rates. By contrast, $(y^* - \bar{y})$ is unobservable.

4 The trade-offs: empirical application to the CFA Zone

As we mentioned earlier, there are at least two reasons why a model like that described above is relevant and applicable to the case of the CFA Zone. First, since CFA Zone countries are highly dependent on primary exports, terms of trade shocks are the main exogenous force that buffets their economies: our focus on the terms of trade would therefore appear well placed. Second, the presence of neighbouring countries with similar economic structures but different exchange rate regimes allows us to construct a reasonable counterfactual. In particular, we can derive some ballpark estimates of the inflationary cost of exchange rate flexibility by looking at the experience of these comparator countries.

We proceed as follows. We first note that the choice of a fixed exchange rate regime implies a certain preference for price stability over the real target (or, in the language of the model in Section 3, a particular value of ϕ in the objective function (1)). We then ask: given the evolution of these economies and of their external terms of trade, what does the fact that they joined the CFA Zone say about their revealed, *ex ante* valuation of the output–inflation trade-off? Finally, we compare the range of revealed output–inflation trade-offs we obtain in this manner with what we consider to be 'reasonable' trade-offs.

We proceed by determining the critical level of ϕ at which the policy maker would be *indifferent* between fixed and flexible exchange rate regimes. As discussed in Section 3, it is convenient to work with equation

(11′). Setting this equation equal to zero and solving for ϕ, we obtain the critical value of ϕ, ϕ_c. This critical rate is a function of the inflation differential under fixed and flexible rates $(\pi_{nf} - \pi_f)$, as well as the other parameters of the model. As implied by the earlier discussion, ϕ_c is increasing in the inflation differential and decreasing in σ^2. In words, as the inflation cost of exchange rate flexibility rises, the weight placed on the real target must increase for the policy maker to remain at the same margin of indifference. Conversely, as the terms of trade become more variable, the weight placed on the real target must diminish for continued indifference. Holding everything else constant, a ϕ higher than ϕ_c would imply that a flexible exchange rate regime would be preferable to a fixed rate regime. We now proceed to calculate ϕ_c. We will need empirical estimates of all the other parameters in equation (11′).

To get a handle on $(\pi_{nf} - \pi_f)$, we exploit the structural similarity between the CFA member countries and their neighbours – that is, we use the difference between the average inflation rate inside the CFA Zone and in the rest of SSA as an estimate of $(\pi_{nf} - \pi_f)$. For the GDP deflator, this difference is 15 percentage points (the CFA average rate between 1973 and 1987 was 9 per cent, the non-CFA average 24 per cent). For the consumer price index, the difference is close to 12 percentage points. We use a figure which lies in between these two differences, with a slight bias towards the GDP deflator: 13.8 percentage points.

As for the σ^2 term in equation (11′), this is obtained by taking the (unweighted) average of the variances of the logarithms of the terms of trade of all the CFA countries during 1965–87. The base data and the variances are given in Table 4.2. We also present the levels of σ^2 for various subperiods and individual countries. With the former, we can ask whether the terms of trade have become more volatile so that the decision to fix the exchange rate in 1965 no longer makes sense. With the latter, we calculate the revealed inflation–output trade-offs for individual countries to see if Zone membership continues to be optimal for some countries but not others.

The parameters a, β and μ are difficult to estimate precisely. Hence, we vary them parametrically in our calculations. The parameter a represents the increase in growth for an additional 1 per cent depreciation of the real exchange rate. We vary this from a low of 0.05 to a high of 0.20 in our sensitivity tests. Note that $a = 0.20$ implies that a 10 per cent real depreciation will spur growth – temporarily – by 2 percentage points. The parameter β is the impact of a terms of trade shock on real income. As a first approximation, the direct effect of the shock will be to reduce real income by the share of imports in GDP. Note that this share is also linked to $(1 - \mu)$, the share of tradables in the price index. Under some

Table 4.2 *Terms of trade in the CFA Zone, 1980 = 100*

	BEN	BKF	CMR	CAF	COG	CIV	GAB	MLI	NER	SEN	TGO
1965	132	132	104	123	98	101	59	146	144	133	103
1966	124	144	106	118	93	100	60	146	170	136	100
1967	129	147	109	110	103	98	45	157	154	90	103
1968	131	153	120	118	90	105	33	158	159	112	104
1969	126	147	125	132	89	107	30	171	155	124	103
1970	125	161	119	100	83	106	28	181	157	114	100
1971	108	158	98	92	81	88	29	172	164	106	90
1972	117	155	97	90	71	89	36	169	170	110	86
1973	177	178	114	98	42	96	35	182	150	103	93
1974	116	108	93	86	70	93	70	112	125	128	177
1975	94	94	79	73	64	80	62	101	128	118	145
1976	124	119	117	103	69	115	66	129	134	114	125
1977	152	110	147	115	72	146	64	120	125	113	117
1978	138	107	130	96	67	131	61	130	135	101	99
1979	115	108	104	104	74	118	72	105	122	100	93
1980	100	100	100	100	100	100	100	100	100	100	100
1981	103	89	98	88	106	85	107	93	100	102	102
1982	92	83	96	90	101	87	102	83	104	98	93
1983	95	95	94	89	96	92	95	93	107	99	88
1984	97	95	96	95	97	100	95	93	100	101	92
1985	92	81	92	87	94	96	90	82	99	97	86
1986	67	76	62	85	57	105	56	74	94	86	72
1987	86	88	56	84	64	88	64	85	83	90	77

100 × variance [log(terms of trade)]

Period	BEN	BKF	CMR	CAF	COG	CIV	GAB	MLI	NER	SEN	TGO	CFA average
1965–87	4.10	6.31	4.40	1.99	5.06	1.73	18.30	8.15	4.49	1.44	3.55	5.41
1965–1970	0.38	0.34	0.80	1.71	1.30	0.50	8.57	0.54	0.27	1.55	0.46	1.48
1973–9	3.60	3.54	3.43	1.84	3.17	3.41	5.35	3.29	0.42	0.72	5.13	3.08
1980–87	1.53	0.83	2.49	0.25	3.93	0.54	4.04	0.95	0.14	0.27	1.24	1.47

Source: World Bank (1990).

conditions, the two are equal (see Devarajan, Lewis and Robinson, 1991). We therefore set $1 - \mu = \beta$ in our calculations and vary β from 0.10 to 0.40.

One last step is needed before we can interpret our calculations. It will be convenient to state our results in terms of implied output–inflation trade-offs, rather than in terms of ϕ_c itself. The trade-off can be recovered from ϕ_c by calculating the marginal rate of substitution between π and y along an indifference curve (i.e., holding $dW = 0$). Differentiating the objective function (1):

$$d\pi/dy|_{dW} = 0 = -\phi_c(y^* - \bar{y})/(\pi - \pi^*) \tag{14}$$

This gives us the revealed inflation–output trade-off along the locus on which the country would have been indifferent between a fixed and flexible exchange rate regime. Remember that ϕ_c is the *maximum* ϕ for which fixed rates still make sense (holding the inflation differential and other parameters constant). Therefore the expression $d\pi/dy|_{dW=0}$ answers the following question: what is the *maximum* increase in inflation that the government is revealed to be willing to trade off against a single percentage point increase in growth, given that it has chosen to join the CFA Zone?

In order to map the values of ϕ_c to this inflation–output trade-off, we need to know y, y^*, π and π^* in equation (14). It is reasonable to take as the target level of inflation, $\pi^* = 0$. For the actual level, we take $\pi = 0.08$, which is about the average of CFA countries throughout the post-independence period. The target GDP growth rate (y^*) is taken to be 0.05, which is at the lower end of the range of targets in the (usually optimistic) Five Year Plans of these countries. The actual (y) will be 0.03, which is about the average performance of CFA countries in this period.

Incorporating these assumptions, Table 4.3 presents the revealed inflation–output trade-offs for the countries which chose to join the fixed exchange rate regime. Note that for most values of a and β, the implied trade-off between growth and inflation is exceedingly steep. For example, when $a = 0.15$ and $\beta = 0.25$, $d\pi/dy|_{dW=0}$ is 1.51. The interpretation is that for the decision to join the CFA Zone to have made sense (given these particular values of a and β), member countries should have been willing to tolerate no more than $1\frac{1}{2}$ percentage point increase in inflation for a 1 per cent increase in their average annual GDP growth rate. In other words, the implied preference for price stability over output is extremely high. If they were willing to tolerate a higher inflation rate for this boost in their growth rate, they should not have opted for a fixed exchange rate regime.

The revealed trade-off is even steeper for a country like Gabon, which suffered the largest terms of trade shocks in the CFA Zone (see Table 4.2). This is intuitive. The costs of a fixed exchange rate regime rise with the variance of the terms of trade. For Gabon to have joined the CFA Zone, therefore, it must have had an exceptionally low tolerance for inflation *vis-à-vis* growth (see the central panel of Table 4.3). Likewise, Senegal's trade-off is the least steep, because it enjoyed the lowest variance in its terms of trade (see the bottom panel of Table 4.3).

Table 4.3. *Revealed inflation–growth trade-offs*

Maximum increases in inflation that CFA countries are willing to sustain for a 1 per cent increase in their average annual GDP growth rate, as revealed by their membership in a fixed exchange rate regime, in percentage points

	CFA Zone			
a	0.05	0.10	0.15	0.20
β 0.10	9.71	9.04	8.91	8.86
0.15	4.74	4.15	4.02	3.97
0.20	2.95	2.43	2.31	2.26
0.25	2.08	1.62	1.51	1.47
0.30	1.59	1.18	1.08	1.04
0.35	1.28	0.91	0.82	0.78
0.40	1.07	0.74	0.64	0.61
	Gabon			
a	0.05	0.10	0.15	0.20
β 0.10	3.37	2.83	2.71	2.66
0.15	1.80	1.37	1.26	1.22
0.20	1.19	0.84	0.75	0.71
0.25	0.89	0.59	0.51	0.47
0.30	0.70	0.45	0.37	0.34
0.35	0.58	0.36	0.29	0.26
0.40	0.49	0.30	0.24	0.21
	Senegal			
a	0.05	0.10	0.15	0.20
β 0.10	34.10	33.38	33.24	33.19
0.15	15.67	14.97	14.84	14.79
0.20	9.18	8.53	8.39	8.35
0.25	6.16	5.54	5.41	5.36
0.30	4.50	3.92	3.79	3.74
0.35	3.48	2.94	2.81	2.77
0.40	2.81	2.30	2.18	2.13

Assumptions:
$\pi^* = 0$
$\pi = 0.08$
$y^* = 0.05$
$y = 0.03$

Sensitivity analysis with the inflation differential (not reported here) does not significantly alter the results. For example, raising the inflation differential to its 'high' estimate, 15 percentage points, raises Senegal's trade-off for the intermediate values of a and β (0.15 and 0.25, respectively) to 6.4 percentage points – that is, even if the gain from joining the Zone was an inflation rate that was 15 percentage points lower on average, the Senegalese revealed that they were willing to trade off only 6.4 percentage points of inflation for 1 percentage point increase in their GDP growth rate.

Our impression is that most African policy makers would be willing to trade up to about 10 percentage points of inflation for a 1 percentage point increase in their GDP growth rate – that is, to increase their growth from 3 to 4 per cent per annum on average. Given that most of the numbers in Table 4.3 lie below this figure, it appears that the decision to join the CFA Zone reflects an excessive anti-inflation bias. Put another way, if the future is going to be anything like the past, the CFA Zone countries should perhaps seriously evaluate whether they wish to remain in a fixed exchange rate regime.

5 Concluding remarks

We should stress that we have concentrated here on only some aspects of the costs and benefits of the CFA Zone. We have ignored some important benefits, including the savings obtained by pooling reserves and the attractiveness to foreign investors of a convertible currency. In addition, we have left aside the special relationship with France (and the French Treasury) implied by the existence of the Zone. Depending on one's perspective, the latter consideration can be viewed as either a net gain or a new loss.

Our focus instead has been on the costs of maintaining a fixed exchange rate regime in the context of highly variable external terms of trade. We have attempted to measure the welfare costs arising from the inability to adjust the exchange rate, and to pit these costs against the benefits of lower inflation. The inflation differential between CFA and non-CFA SSA countries has been around 14 percentage points. We attribute this differential to the standard time-consistency problem inherent in discretionary macroeconomic policy. Nonetheless, our highly stylised calculations suggest that fixed exchange rates have been, on the whole, a bad bargain for the CFA member countries. For most of the CFA members, the inflation benefits do not appear to have been large enough to offset the costs on the output side. Under 'reasonable' output–inflation trade-offs, these countries would have been better off having the flexibility to adjust to external shocks.

This conclusion needs one important qualification. Our counterfactual effectively assumes that CFA policy makers would have followed the appropriate exchange rate policies in response to terms of trade shocks, had they had the freedom to do so. In light of experience with exchange rate policy in the rest of SSA, this is perhaps a dubious supposition. Possibly, exchange rate flexibility would have brought only inflation, and no output benefits. However, basing the choice of an exchange rate regime on the assumed incompetence of policy makers does not seem very appropriate either.

NOTES

Dani Rodrik's work was supported by an NBER Olin Fellowship. We thank Jim de Melo for inspiration, and Larry Ball, Emil-Maria Claassen, Alan Winters, and conference participants for comments.

1 See Aghevli *et al.* (1991) for a concise summary of the issues.
2 This is, of course, closely related to the literature on 'rules versus discretion'; see Fischer (1990) for a general survey.
3 The countries are: Benin, Burkina Faso, Cameroon, Central African Republic, Chad, Congo, Côte d'Ivoire, Equatorial Guinea, Gabon, Mali, Niger, Senegal and Togo. Mali left the Zone in 1965 and rejoined in 1984. Equatorial Guinea became a member in 1985.
4 Togo did not join at the outset, but did so after a change of government in 1963.
5 For more detailed descriptions of the institutional arrangements in the CFA Zone, see Bhatia (1985) and Guillaumont and Guillaumont (1984).
6 The unweighted average of the standard deviation of growth for the CFA countries is 7.2 percentage points over the entire 1973–87 period. The comparable average for other SSA countries is 5.4 percentage points.
7 Our approach is somewhat related to that taken in the literature on the insulating properties of fixed and flexible exchange rates in the presence of domestic and external shocks of different kinds (see, for example, Boyer, 1978 and Aizenman and Frenkel, 1985). However, this literature focused on the goal of stabilising output only, and neglected the price discipline argument for fixed rates.
8 With a slight reinterpretation of variables, the model can also be stated in terms of the *levels* of output and prices, rather than their growth rates. We chose the latter because they are the more relevant variables for policy.
9 There is actually a slight conceptual problem here. Since p and e stand for the *changes* in the exchange rate and home prices, the relative-price motive is stated in proportional, rather than absolute, form. This implies that price setters let bygones be bygones, and do not attempt to make up for previous losses (or gains). Tracking these dynamic effects would complicate the model considerably.
10 Note that inflation has no direct effect on the equilibrium growth rate (equation (2)). Of course, in the long run, persistent inflation will undermine

economic activity and growth, which is one of the reasons why inflation is included separately in the objective function (1).

11 β is likely to be large in economies that are very open. Openness therefore increases the desirability of flexibility in exchange rates. This is at odds with the usual conclusion drawn in the literature on optimum currency areas, wherein greater openness is taken to imply less latitude in manipulating the real exchange rate through changes in the nominal rate, making flexibility less desirable.

REFERENCES

Aghevli, Bijan, Mohsin Khan and Peter Montiel (1991) 'Exchange Rate Policy in Developing Countries: Some Analytical Issues', *IMF Occasional Paper*, **78**, Washington, D.C.: IMF.

Aizenman, Joshua and Jacob Frenkel (1985) 'Optimal Wage Indexation, Foreign Exchange Intervention, and Monetary Policy', *American Economic Review*, **75**, June: 402–23.

Bhatia, R. (1985) 'The West African Monetary Union: An Analytical Survey', *IMF Occasional Paper*, **35**, Washington, D.C.: IMF.

Boyer, R. (1978) 'Optimal Foreign Exchange Market Intervention', *Journal of Political Economy*, December: 1045–55.

Corden, W. Max (1990) 'Exchange Rate Policy in Developing Countries', *PRE Working Paper*, **412**, April, Washington, D.C.: World Bank.

Devarajan, Shantayanan and Jaime de Melo (1987) 'Evaluating Participation in African Monetary Unions: A Statistical Analysis of the CFA Zones', *World Development*, **15**(4): 483–96.

Devarajan, Shantayanan and Jaime de Melo (1990) 'Membership in the CFA Zone: Odyssean Journey or Trojan Horse?', *PPR Working Paper*, **482**, August, Washington, D.C.: World Bank.

Devarajan, Shantayanan, Jeffrey D. Lewis and Sherman Robinson (1991) 'External Shocks and the Equilibrium Real Exchange Rate', unpublished paper.

Fischer, Stanley (1990) 'Rules Versus Discretion in Monetary Policy', in B.M. Friedman and F.H. Hahn (eds), *Handbook of Monetary Economics*, vol. II, Amsterdam: North-Holland.

Guillaumont, P. and S. Guillaumont (1984) *Zone Franc et Développement Africain*, Paris: Economica.

Guillaumont, P., S. Guillaumont and P. Plane (1988) 'Participating in African Monetary Unions: An Alternative Evaluation', *World Development*, **16(5)**: 569–76.

World Bank (1990) *African Economic and Financial Data Base*, International Economics Department, Washington, D.C.: World Bank.

Discussion

EMIL-MARIA CLAASSEN

1 Introduction

The overwhelming majority of developing countries pursue pegged arrangements, either to a single currency (the US dollar or the French franc) or to a currency basket (see Aghevli and Montiel, 1991). However, there is an increasing trend towards more flexible arrangements: during 1976–89, the proportion of countries relying on a managed float more than doubled to one-third of all developing countries.

The technique that Devarajan and Rodrik use in Chapter 4 is a cost–benefit analysis analogous to that of Giavazzi and Giovannini (1987) (and of many other authors) who questioned what would be the costs and benefits of European countries joining the European Monetary System (EMS). The benefits of a fixed (but adjustable) exchange rate regime consist of lower inflation rates, and the costs potential output losses.

Devarajan and Rodrik compare the African member countries of the French franc Zone (FFZ) with their neighbours who pursue a flexible arrangement; they think that the comparison of these two exchange rate regimes 'brings us as close to a controlled experiment as economists could hope for'. I am not at all in agreement with this statement. In Chapter 6 in this volume Ajay Chhibber compares the FFZ model with three alternative African exchange rates: fixed-but-adjusting exchange rates (as Zimbabwe, Malawi and Kenya), fixed-but-adjusting exchange rates with parallel markets (as Ghana, Nigeria, Tanzania and Zambia), and dual exchange rates (Algeria and Ethiopia). All three alternative systems practise heavy exchange controls while the CFA franc is fully convertible with respect to the French franc.

In my view, there are two main differences between the CFA model and the neighbouring exchange rate regimes. On the one hand, there is the issue of exchange controls, with the consequence of parallel markets being black or officially tolerated. This kind of regime is certainly not the model which the African member countries of the FFZ should strive for. On the other hand, exchange rates are either fixed-fixed or fixed-but-adjustable. It is on the latter alternative that I shall concentrate my remarks.

I shall begin with the issue of real 'shocks' under alternative exchange rate regimes. According to Devarajan and Rodrik the main advantage of flexibility in the exchange rate regime (I limit the term 'flexibility' for the

FFZ to the notion of adjustability) is a depreciation as a 'shock absorber' for a deterioration in the terms of trade. This is one possible and important real 'shock' for the African countries which are predominantly exporters of primary products. However, there is still another important real 'shock' for the FFZ which is rather a long-run accumulation of steady increases in the relative price of non-tradables over decades within growing industrialised countries. If developing countries with *per capita* low income have pegged to one of them over decades (like the member countries of the FFZ), their currencies should follow a gradual and steady real depreciation. However, this gradual real depreciation did not take place via a lower inflation rate for the FFZ and the consequence was an overvalued CFA franc (see Section 1). The ultimate reason for the overvaluation is linked to the monetary adjustment mechanism of the FFZ which apparently did not function during the 1980s (see Section 2). The final Section 3 is devoted to the policy-oriented issue whether the FFZ still has an option between devaluation (adjustability) and the present policy of deflation which has pushed many member countries into painful adjustment costs and, in particular, into the neighbourhood of a financial crisis.

2 An 'island of price stability', but an overvalued currency

All French governments have pointed with pleasure and pride to the FFZ as the 'island of price stability' within the African continent, a statement which has been valid at least since the mid-1970s. From that time onward the inflation rate lay systematically below the average inflation rate of the African continent. Furthermore, during the 1980s it was generally below the French inflation rate although, significantly, it had exceeded that rate during the 1970s. Since the second half of the 1980s French monetary policy has become increasingly disciplined, with the consequence that while the direct monetary anchor of the CFA franc remained the French franc, the indirect anchor became increasingly the Deutschmark. This was to the benefit of the FFZ.

Devarajan and Rodrik are concerned with the deterioration of the terms of trade. If the exchange rate is adjustable, a devaluation of the domestic currency will be less harmful for the tradables sector than will the maintenance of fixed rates. This is a cost of the FFZ. However, the causes of the decline of output in many member countries of the FFZ are not linked to the specific exchange rate regime (fixed versus adjustable), but to the underlying policies. Even within the FFZ the harmful effects of a deterioration in the terms of trade could be partially met by restrictive monetary policies reducing the inflation rate of non-tradables compared with the inflation rate of tradables. Only the latter is determied exogenously by the French economy; the monetary anchor implies only a synchronised path of the inflation rates of tradables.

The disastrous economic performance of many member countries of the FFZ started with the considerable improvement in the terms of trade during the mid-1970s. The spectacular price boom in commodities prices set off vast expansionary macro-policies which continued even when world commodity prices returned to their original level. The subsequent budget and current account deficits had to be financed mainly by external borrowing. When the limits of external indebtedness and in the volume of international reserves were attained, structural adjustment programmes had to be introduced.[1]

This sequence of events has occurred in many developing countries independently of their underlying exchange rate regimes, but for the resulting structural adjustment process it makes a lot of difference whether the exchange rate regime is fixed-fixed or fixed-but-adjustable. In this context, the costs of the FFZ exceed those of an adjustable exchange rate regime.

There is still another real 'shock' on which Devarajan and Rodrik remain silent and which may be absorbed more easily in an adjustable exchange rate regime than in a fixed one: the long-run change in the real exchange rate between developing and industrialised countries over several decades. There has been a tendency over time for the relative prices of non-tradables (which are labour-intensive) to rise in rich countries such as France: on the other hand, technical progress is more important in tradables than in non-tradables while on the other, the income elasticity of the demand for non-tradables exceeds unity. If this is not true of developing countries, given their surplus labour, and if developing and industrial countries have identical tradable good inflation, then overall inflation in France should not exceed that in Africa. That did not happen with the FFZ during 1970–85, which suggests a continuing trend towards overvaluation in the FFZ.

3 The disregard of the rules of monetary adjustment

The monetary adjustment mechanism of the FFZ is that of any other system of fixed exchange rates. An expansionary monetary policy is 'punished' by a balance of payments deficit which, through the subsequent loss of international reserves, eventually induces a policy reversal. Although these textbook rules were institutionalised within the FFZ, they were not applied in the crisis years of the 1980s. High monetary growth over the 1970s and early 1980s reduced the ratio of external assets to the monetary base below 20 per cent, at which point restrictive monetary policy is mandated. In fact, however, monetary growth remained positive until 1988, even though external assets were negative after 1979 (negative assets represent the accumulation of debt to the French Treasury). This indiscipline was markedly worse within the occidental zone (UMOA, i.e. the Union Monétaire Ouest Africaine) than in the central zone (BEAC, i.e. the Banque des Etats de l'Afrique Centrale).

4 Deflation versus devaluation

According to Devarajan and Rodrik the benefits of fixed exchange rates for the FFZ consist of low inflation rates compared with other African countries. However, as we have argued above, the inflation rate of FFZ should have been systematically lower than the French one, but was not. Lower inflation could have been brought about through monetary adjustment, but was not until 1987, when international reserves were exhausted.

For structural adjustment policies – and, in particular for the adjustment of the real exchange rate – the underlying exchange rate makes a big difference, as Devarajan and Rodrik show. Under a fixed exchange rate regime, adjustment consists of a painful process of deflation, whereas under flexible rates it could be achieved by a devaluation.

Figure 4D.1 represents the Australian model of a dependent economy. The *TT* and *NN* schedules are the equilibrium conditions in the markets for tradables (*T*) and non-tradables (*N*), respectively. Their slope depends exclusively on the relative price $q = P_T/P_N$. The goods are assumed to be gross substitutes. For a given real income, the demand for tradables and non-tradables depends also on the volume of absorption and of real cash balances. The *MM* schedule illustrates the equilibrium condition of the money market for a given money supply. *MM* implies a certain equilibrium value for the general price level which is compatible with various combinations of P_T and P_N.

The initial situation is characterised by the thick lines, with a macroeconomic disequilibrium at point *A*. There is an internal equilibrium (the economy is at the intersection point of the *NN* and *MM* schedules) accompanied by an external disequilibrium in terms of a trade balance deficit. If the trade deficit is unsustainable stabilisation policies are required which consist of expenditure-reducing and expenditure-switching policies. There are two possible ways to realise the required real depreciation to q_1. The first method is to devalue by the exchange rate E_1/E_0. The change in the relative price comes about by an increase in P_T and a decrease in P_N which is necessary in order to maintain the price level stability indicated by the *MM* schedule. This will result in equilibrium *B*.

The second method consists of maintaining the parity and inducing a decline in the price level of non-tradable goods (point *C*). A deflationary monetary policy has to be pursued which shifts the *MM* schedule to the position MM_1. Since the slope of the *NN–TT* system is dependent only on relative prices, NN_1–TT_1 must shift downward along the Oq_1 line towards NN_2–TT_2.

A final remark concerns the trade balance. Under certain circumstances, a heavily indebted developing country does not only need an equilibrium of the trade balance, but a surplus in order to service its debt. In that case, a further reduction in absorption and a further real depreciation are indispensable. These cases are indicated by points D_1 and D_2 in Figure 4D.1.

To summarise, there are two methods to realise a real depreciation: either by a nominal devaluations or by a restrictive monetary policy which reduces the absolute price level of non-tradable goods. The inflationary implications made by Devarajan and Rodrik with respect to fixed exchange rates have to be slightly modified in the case of a necessary change in the real exchange rate: a real depreciation necessitates a deflationary impulse and a real appreciation an inflationary impulse. The policy makers of the FFZ have opted for the method of deflation since

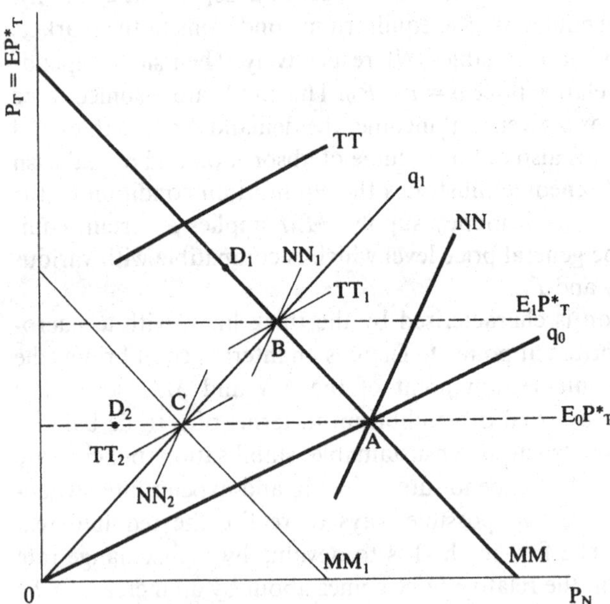

Figure 4D.1 Stabilisation policy with nominal devaluation

1988 and as a result have come close to causing a collapse of the financial system.

Several factors have contributed to such a nascent financial crisis. Despite the various structural adjustment programmes budget deficits still exist and have somehow to be financed. Credit from central banks is limited to 20 per cent of last year's tax revenues, but the statutes of the FFZ have not regulated the access of governments to the credit granted by commercial banks – which are, by the way, mostly in public ownership. Public enterprises and Treasuries have become the main clients of banks such that there is practically a total crowding-out of credit for the private sector. Since the bank credit volume also has its limits, various governments have imposed 'forced credits' by accumulating payments arrears with enterprises, peasants (who produce the agricultural exports) and commercial banks. In addition to this financial paralysis central banks have pursued negative monetary growth rates since 1988. Finally there is the rising capital flight in terms of CFA bank notes, which land increasingly on the desk of the Banque de France since there is still full convertibility. Devaluation would have been less painful.

5 Concluding remarks

Since the OECD–CEPR conference dealt mainly with the agricultural issue, my final remarks concern the agricultural sector not only of the FFZ but of sub-Saharan Africa as a whole. The 1980s were lost years for Africa. The IMF's stabilisation policies and the World Bank's structural adjustment policies had no particular success. The nucleus of the African development problem has for decades arisen from the neglect of the agricultural sector in which 75–80 per cent of the population is still living. The political power continues to remain in the 'industrial' sector (i.e., in the cities). Whether pseudo-democracies or dictatorships, all regimes must obtain the favour of the urban population in order to remain in power. The rural sector is without relevance for the consolidation of political power, and as a result *per capita* production has fallen steadily for thirty years. Exchange rate policies and structural adjustment policies should be guided principally by the future economic welfare of the rural sector. Otherwise, the structural adjustment policies for the 1990s will have no better results than those of the 1980s.

NOTE

1 Cameroon, which hoarded so much of its oil revenues, provides an exception to this pattern.

REFERENCES

Aghevli, B.B. and P.J. Montiel (1991) 'Exchange Rate Policies in Developing Countries', in E.M. Claassen (ed.), *Exchange Rate Policies of Developing and Post-Socialist Countries*, San Francisco, ICS Press.

Chhibber, Ajay (1992) 'Exchange Reforms, Supply Response, and Inflation in Africa', Chapter 6 in this volume.

Giavazzi, F. and A. Giovannini (1987) 'Models of the EMS: Is Europe a Greater Deutschmark Area?', in R. Bryant and R. Portes (eds), *Global Macroeconomics: Policy Confllict and Cooperation*, London: Macmillan, pp. 237–76.

Kravis, Irving B. (1986) 'The Three Faces of the International Comparison Project', *Research Observer* (January).

Kravis, Irving B. and Robert E. Lipsey (1983) *Toward an Explanation of National Price Levels*, Princeton Studies in International Finance, **52**, November.

5 Adjustment and the rural sector: a counterfactual analysis of Morocco

FRANCOIS BOURGUIGNON,
CHRISTIAN MORRISSON and
AKIKO SUWA

1 Introduction

Structural adjustment is usually seen as merely a macroeconomic problem because of its strong link to stabilisation which deals with the full restoration of internal as well as external equilibrium. But the aim of structural adjustment is larger: it is meant to place the economy on a new efficient path. These reforms will affect socioeconomic groups differently. Some groups may even block the adjustment process. In Morocco, for instance, three major upheavals of middle-class urban workers took place after the beginning of the adjustment period (in 1977), and succeeded twice in stopping the process. Political sustainability is obviously an important constraint on adjustment, but there also are good reasons to follow the fate of socioeconomic groups with less immediate political power. For adjustment to be objectively successful in the long run, it is important that no permanent damage be caused to human capital through an increase in absolute poverty and a worsening of health or education conditions in groups which, although politically weak, may in fact represent the majority of the population.

The present paper focuses on the effects of the adjustment process in Morocco upon rural workers and the agricultural sector. The former represent approximately 70 per cent of the labour force and they are responsible for 20 per cent of the GDP. In the perspective of adjustment, there are three reasons why this group may be important. First, it is clear from the previous figures that poverty largely concentrates in this group, and that it is there that the social cost of adjustment may be the heaviest. Second, by supplying food to the rest of the economy, rural workers and peasants have a direct impact on urban wages, and therefore on the macroeconomics of adjustment – it may be recalled in this respect that the social upheavals in Morocco were linked to the abolition of food subsidies in cities. In that respect, Morocco is not atypical when compared to adjustment experiences in countries like Côte d'Ivoire, Tunisia or Venezuela where the same type of urban middle-class upheavals caused by increases in the relative price of foodstuffs took place. Third, the Moroccan agricultural sector has some export potential, and may thus directly contribute to the structural adjustment of the economy.

The basic objective of the present paper is to examine the effects that the structural adjustment process in Morocco had – or might have had if fully implemented – on the rural sector and its relationship with the rest of the economy. This is done through a counterfactual analysis based on a general equilibrium approach which extends previous work conducted at the OECD Development Centre in its research Programme on 'Adjustment and Income Distribution' and at the World Bank.[1] However, instead of the predominantly macro approach followed in that project, we focus on the more 'structural', or microeconomic-oriented measures that were included in the initial adjustment package.[2] We analyse in some detail the likely effects of the most important measures included in the Structural Adjustment Loans (SAL) agreement signed between Morocco and the World Bank in 1985 and which concern financial and trade liberalisations.

The paper is organised as follows. Section 2 offers a brief summary of the recent evolution of the Moroccan economy, concentrating upon the macroeconomic stabilisation policies which have actually been implemented, their effects and the measures in the 1985 SAL agreement. The model used for the simulation of the effects of these measures is briefly sketched in Section 3. Simulations are analysed in Section 4 under alternative sets of assumptions concerning the 'closure rules' of the Moroccan economy. The first set intends to replicate short-run conditions where some markets adjust imperfectly, whereas the second set aims to replicate medium- to long-run effects where all markets are taken to be fully flexible. The lessons to be learned from these simulations about the effect of structural adjustment upon the rural sector or developing economies are summarised in the concluding section 5.

2 Disequilibrium and adjustment in Morocco

2.1 Unbalanced growth: 1976–83

As in some other developing countries, unbalanced growth in Morocco largely resulted from a 'Dutch disease' phenomenon after a sudden increase in the price of phosphate in 1974. As the main beneficiary of the revenue surplus, the government embarked on an ambitious spending programme. Typically of the Dutch disease, prices increased faster for non-tradable than for tradable goods, and production switched from exports to domestic demand. When the export boom abruptly ended in 1976 with a 47 per cent fall of phosphate prices, the government was not able to cut spending. The resulting budget deficit amounted to 17 per cent of GDP, and a drastic reallocation of resources was called for.

After 1976, fiscal revenues remained at practically the same level as current expenditures, so that public capital expenditures were financed by borrowing from abroad. The government attempted twice to adjust. In 1978, a first adjustment programme included a civil servants' wage freeze, a rise in tax rates and a cut in public investment. But several exogenous factors interrupted the application of the programme in 1979: the second oil shock, bad crops due to a drought, and a social uprising. The second attempt at adjustment took place in October 1980 with a three-year programme approved by the IMF. A reduction in food subsidies was part of this. However, this led to a 50 per cent increase in food prices and to violent riots in Casablanca in the spring of 1981. In addition, the external environment and weather were unfavourable (drought, revaluation of the US dollar). The stabilisation programme was thus cancelled again in 1981.

Morocco's growth between 1976 and 1983 was therefore achieved at the expense of widening imbalances. Over that period, the budget deficit varied between 10 and 17 per cent of GDP, and the current account deficit between 8 and 16 per cent of GDP. The latter deficit was financed by foreign borrowing. The foreign debt rose from $2.3 billion in 1976 to $11.2 billion in 1983. The debt service–exports ratio reached 45 per cent in 1982. In 1983, foreign exchange reserves were exhausted and the government had to resort to a drastic rationing of imports. The resulting crisis led to a new negotiation with the IMF and the World Bank and to a new adjustment programme.

2.2 *The 1983 adjustment programme*

The adjustment programme involved two sets of measures: on the one hand, measures to reduce aggregate demand sharply (as defined in the standby agreement with the IMF signed in September 1983); on the other, medium-run supply-oriented measures included in the two SAL agreements signed with the World Bank in March 1984 and July 1985.

The agreement with the IMF included the following measures:

- reducing food subsidies: sugar, oil and flour prices went up by 30 per cent, 52 per cent and 87 per cent respectively between 1982 and 1985; other food subsidies (butter, milk, high-quality flour) were fully eliminated

- bringing the fiscal deficit down to 7 per cent of GDP (from 14 per cent in 1982): in particular, real public investment fell by half between 1983 and 1986
- limiting public sector recruitment
- slowing down the annual growth rate of domestic credit from 20 to 15 per cent.
- finally, reducing the current account deficit through a series of devaluations: the real effective exchange rate depreciated by 23 per cent between 1982 and 1986.

On the supply side, the SAL agreements signed with the World Bank included measures to reform the financial sector, to liberalise external trade and financial and tax reforms.

Measures to liberalise trade were the most significant component of the package. To promote exports, export taxes (except on mining products) were eliminated and all export licensing requirements were lifted. Agricultural exports were to be encouraged by abolishing the monopoly of the State marketing board. On the import side, the system of high tariffs and quantitative restrictions (QRs) was lifted. The share of goods the import of which was strictly prohibited or required a prior licence fell from 100 per cent in March 1983 to 37 per cent in February 1986, when all QRs were eliminated. The maximum tariff rate was limited to 60 per cent in July 1984 and to 45 per cent at the beginning of 1986 (instead of 200 per cent in 1983). The average nominal rate consequently went down from 36 per cent in 1983 to 23 per cent in 1986.

Other measures were meant to improve the efficiency of the tax system and to stimulate savings and production. Sales taxes were replaced by a value-added tax (VAT) after 1 April 1986. An ambitious financial reform was to be undertaken in order to foster savings and make credit allocation more efficient. This implied in particular that nominal interest rates were raised so that real rates, which were negative in 1982–3, became positive. Agricultural output was encouraged by systematic increases in producer prices. Price distortions were limited by a 40 per cent reduction in fertiliser subsidies, an increase in the water supply fee, and an improvement in crop collection. The private sector was permitted to sell fertilisers, to produce or to buy seeds, activities that were previously under a public monopoly.

Manufacturing incentives included the liberalisation of some prices (controls were completely lifted for 60 products) and the introduction of a new investment code. The possibility of faster depreciation was eliminated, which resulted in a significant increase in the cost of capital.

Several attempts were also made at improving the efficiency of the public sector, which included settling payment arrears and reforming the relationship between State enterprises and the government.

2.3 *The impact of the adjustment programme*

As of 1988, the results of the programme can be summarised in three points:

- satisfactory growth performance, although this was partly due to favourable exogenous factors
- a reduction in the fiscal deficit, that was in fact more apparent than real
- a significant reduction of the external deficit, thanks to the growth of exports and, possibly, the liberalisation of trade.

Contrary to the experience of other countries, the negative impact of adjustment on growth was limited. After a slowing down in 1984 to 1.7 per cent, GDP growth resumed at 4.2 per cent in 1985 and 6.7 per cent in 1986. But what this performance actually shows is the strong dependence of a country where one-quarter of the GDP comes from agriculture on an exogenous factor – namely, the climate. Favourable rains produced a boom in agriculture over 1985–6.[3] It is clear that without this favourable climate, GDP would have grown by less than 2.5 per cent, resulting in a small decrease in GDP *per capita*. On the contrary, a drought occurred in the fall of 1986 and hit the spring crops: GDP fell by 2.5 per cent in 1987 before a sharp recovery in 1988. No common trend is apparent in the other sectors. The building sector was severely affected by the drop in public investment: its output fell by 5 per cent on average in 1984–5. Manufacturing output stagnated over 1984–5 before a slight recovery in 1986.

The adjustment programme coincided with a significant reduction in the budget deficit. In terms of effective payments, the latter fell from 14 per cent of GDP in 1982 to 4.2 per cent of GDP in 1988. However, the outcome is quite different in terms of actual spending. From that perspective, the deficit remained stable between 1982 and 1985, thus implying growing payment arrears by the government (4 per cent of GDP in 1985). This situation changed after 1986, when both expenditure commitments and disbursements were controlled.

The adjustment programme was an undeniable success in reducing the current account balance, from a deficit of 12.7 per cent of GDP in 1982 to a slight surplus in 1986, despite a lower degree of protection. This resulted from the outstanding export growth stimulated by the adjustment programme. Between 1982 and 1985, exports went up from 24 per cent to 33 per cent of GDP. The devaluation policy led to dramatic progress in three export areas: fertilisers and phosphoric acid, consumer goods (textiles, clothing, footwear) where sales doubled, and tourism where revenues increased by 145 per cent in three years.

How did the rural sector fare during those years? Because of the recovery over the drought years, output growth was impressive: 62 per cent for cereals between 1983 and 1985–7, 37 per cent for leguminous crops. As the standard of living of small farmers depended mainly on these crops, it went up significantly over that period. On the export side, the output of citrus fruits went up slightly, and that of early vegetables increased by 24 per cent (over the same period as before). As mentioned above, climatic factors explain part of this success and that of the overall increase of agricultural output (33 per cent from 1982 to 1986), as well as the temporary decline (−23 per cent in 1987). However, some measures included in the adjustment programme – such as higher production prices, the liberalisation of internal trade in some agricultural inputs and some crops, as well as the effect of the successive devaluations on the price of agricultural exports such as early vegetables, citrus fruits and fish – also played an important role. This is confirmed by the evolution of agricultural exports: overall, their share in GDP rose from 3.7 to 5.1 per cent between 1982 and 1987.

Whereas the real income of wage-earners in the modern sector decreased during the adjustment period, labour productivity increased in agriculture (+7 per cent between 1982 and 1986), so that the mean real income of farmers was higher in 1986–7 than before adjustment. Home production of various crops went up, whereas the terms of trade of both cereals and leguminous plants were maintained despite the growth in production. On the other hand, given the economic link between small farmers and agricultural workers, the latter group also benefited from the general progress being made in the agricultural sector over that period.

3 A disaggregated simulation model applied to Morocco

The model used in the counterfactual analysis of some of the preceding measures integrates a standard CGE model and fully-fledged macroeconomic closures. Special emphasis has been given to the financial sector. A full description of the 'maquette'[4] can be found in Bourguignon, Branson and de Melo (1989a and 1989b). Here, we merely sketch its main characteristics.

The Moroccan economy has been divided into six sectors and six socioeconomic groups. The six sectors are: primary exports (phosphates, 6 per cent of GDP), agriculture (15 per cent), light industry (20 per cent), heavy industry (16 per cent), services (32 per cent), and informal urban activities (11 per cent). The socioeconomic groups are: capitalists, big farmers, small farmers, modern workers, agricultural workers, and informal workers. Capitalists own the factor specific to primary exports and most capital in other sectors. Agents operate in four types of market: goods and services, labour, money (or domestic bonds), and foreign exchange. The clearing of all these markets under alternative specifications, or 'closures', defines the equilibrium of the economy during a year.

In the goods market, adjustment is either: (1) a non-competitive mark-up pricing rule with quantity adjustment through changes in capacity utilisation; or (2) a competitive Walrasian price adjustment. The first option is open only to the modern sectors of the economy, and both closures are used in the simulations below. Agriculture and the urban informal sector are always assumed to be Walrasian.

Households provide three types of labour: agricultural, urban modern and urban informal. Wages are determined in labour markets – one market for each type of labour – under the following specifications; (1) full wage flexibility; or (2) nominal or real wage rigidity. The first specification is used for agricultural labour and the second for the modern urban sector. Urban informal workers' income is taken to be the *per capita* revenue in the informal sector. Civil servants' wage is exogenous.

Together with the alternative assumptions about the markets for goods and services, these clearing mechanisms imply that the maquette can be operated under regimes that range from full 'Keynesian' to full 'Walrasian'. In the applications below, the main closure is a hybrid between a 'Keynesian' (in the modern sectors) and a 'Walrasian' (in agriculture and informal sectors) closure. We also experiment with a full 'Walrasian' closure indicative of long-run movements.

The model comprises four types of assets: money, domestic and foreign bonds, and equities or physical capital. Households' portfolio allocation results from arbitraging between these assets. As a short cut to modelling the equity market, we assume that firms' financing requirements are partly and directly met by the change in households' non-financial assets. The remaining requirements are met by new domestic or foreign loans.

The domestic credit market is directly affected by the budget balance of the government, and how it is financed. Fiscal revenues come from various taxes. Government spending includes subsidies to exports of specific sectors, transfers to households, civil servants' wages, the debt service, investment and current expenditures. The difference may be financed by borrowing from the domestic financial market (bonds[5]), from abroad, or from the Central Bank (money creation).

The maquette is equipped to deal with various market-clearing assumptions on the money and the domestic bond markets. In the Moroccan case, the following closures are used: (1) competitive determination of the rate of interest on the credit market; (2) credit rationing with an exogenous ceiling on the interest rate and an allocation of credit to productive sectors proportional to capital stocks; and (3) no formal foreign exchange control. The arbitrage elasticity between domestic and foreign bonds is allowed to vary across experiments, reflecting alternative assumptions on capital mobility.

In the foreign exchange market, three closures can be used: (1) fixed nominal or pegged real exchange rate: government foreign borrowing is then endogenous; (2) flexible exchange rate: government foreign borrowing is then exogenous; (3) import rationing; government foreign borrowing is exogenous as in (2), but the official exchange rate is fixed and importers pay a premium on imports.

Table 5.1 *Elasticities and key exogenous growth rates*

Households	Firms
Labour supply growth (%)	Technology
Average growth: 2.5	Elasticity of substitution in production function (Cobb–Douglas): 1
Capitalists and big farmers' population growth: 1	
Small farmers' population growth: 1.5	0 < Technical progress < 3%
	Depreciation: 4%
Consumption	
0.34 < expenditure elasticity < 1.30	Portfolio
1.25 < Frisch parameter < 2	Sales elasticity of working capital: 0.5
Capital gain effect on consumption: 10%	Domestic/foreign loans elasticity: 5
Portfolio	
Money demand:	
Semi-elasticity with respect to interest rate: 2	Foreign trade (price elasticities)
Income elasticity: 0.6	Export demand elasticity ≈ 8
Arbitrage between physical and financial savings:	0.6 < Import demand elasticity < 1.5
Physical/financial saving elasticity: 1	
Average share of physical saving: 0.93	
Arbitrage between domestic and foreign assets:	
Domestic/foreign bonds elasticity: 5	
0.45 < average domestic share of total financial wealth < 1	

Ranges are given when elasticities differ or growth rates differ across sectors or household groups.

The dynamics of the model correspond to a sequence of 'temporary' equilibria. These equilibria are linked to each other through changes in capital stocks, population and technology.[6] Capital changes in each sector through depreciation and investment. Productivity growth is exogenous – although it is influenced by public investment – as are expectations about inflation and devaluation. The overall rate of demographic growth is exogenous, but the breakdown of the population into socioeconomic groups results from an endogenous Harris–Todaro-like migration mechanism.

In the base run, closures have been set according to the features of the Moroccan economy during the period under analysis (1980–6):[7] mark-up pricing, quantity adjustments, nominal wage rigidities in the modern sector, fixed nominal exchange rate with import rationing in 1983–4, fixed interest rate and credit rationing, limited capital mobility. The basic elasticities and exogenous growth rates are summarised in Table 5.1. The comparison of the base run predictions and the actual values of a few macroeconomic aggregates depicted in Figures 5.1–5.3 shows that the model tracks relatively well the actual evolution of the Moroccan economy during the early 1980s.

As the main events during the 1983–6 period correspond to the crisis

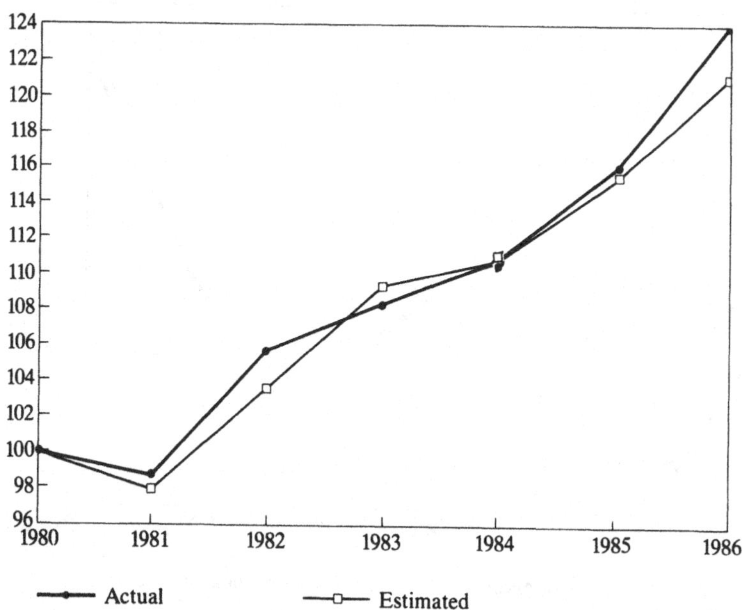

Figure 5.1 Base run simulation: GDP

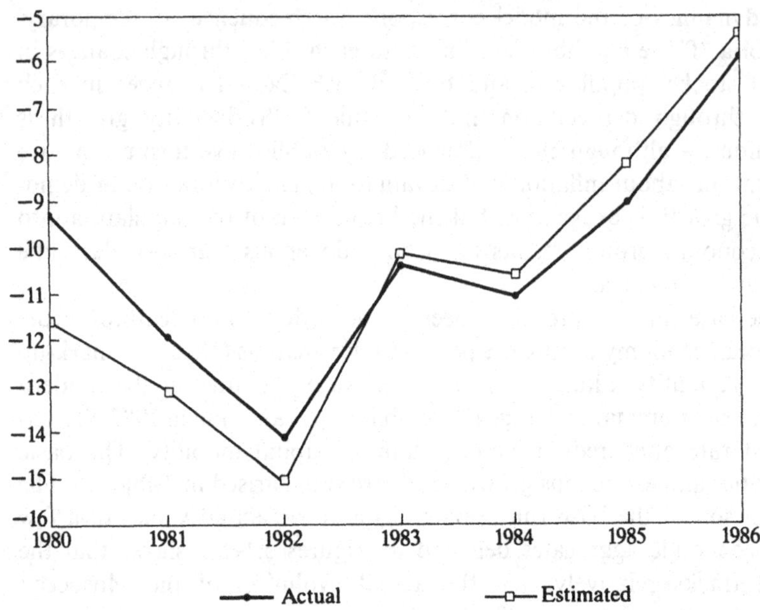

Figure 5.2 Fiscal deficit

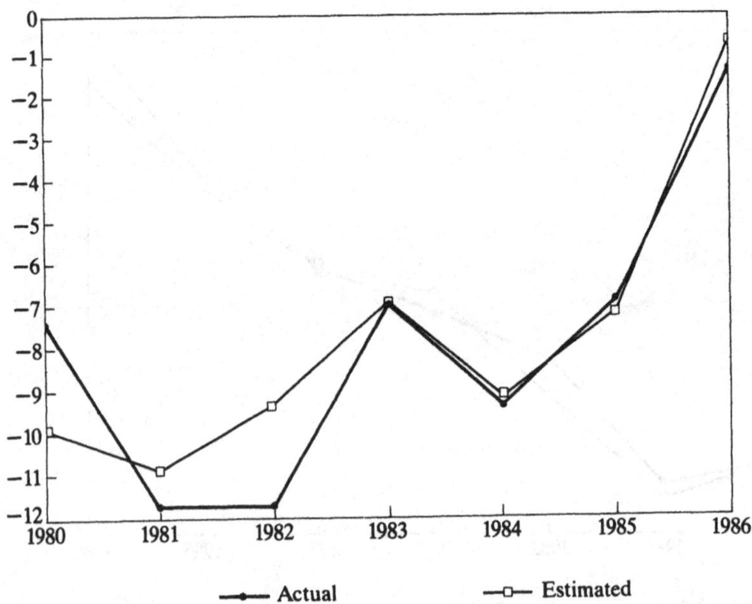

Figure 5.3 Current account

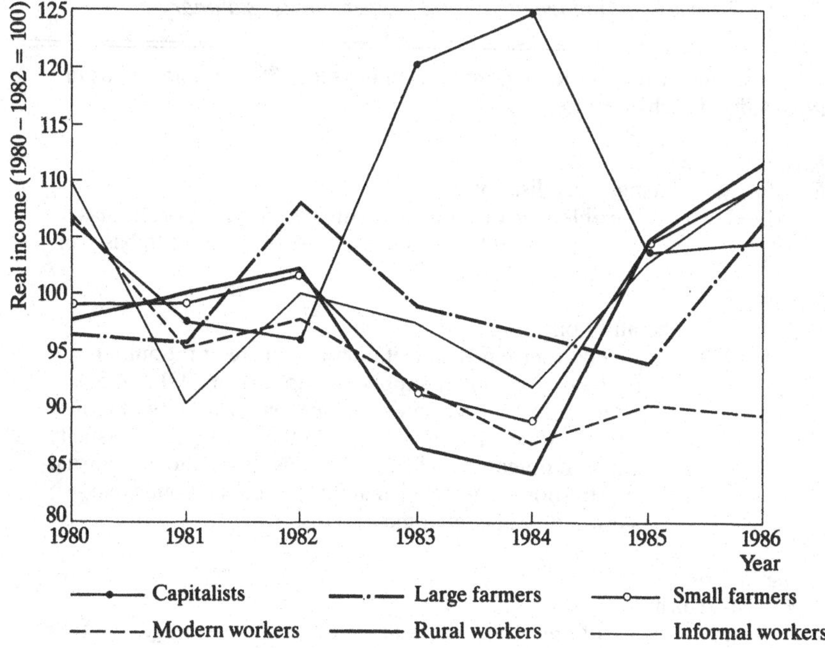

Figure 5.4 Real income, 1980–6

and the adjustment period, the base run of the model may be used to assess more precisely than incomplete available statistics how the various socioeconomic groups fared during that period. It may be seen in Figure 5.4 that, after six years, the rural sector was the main beneficiary, even though it had been the most affected by the 1983 crisis. In 1985–6, the real income of agricultural workers, small and large farmers was above its value in 1980, whereas it was the opposite for modern workers and the owners of capital. However, it is also the case that the drop in real income corresponding to the bottom of the crisis in 1983 was much more pronounced for the rural sector than for the other socioeconomic groups. This is to be explained mostly by rigidities of prices in the modern sector, and rigidities of the exchange rate. The latter indirectly transferred the burden of the short-run adjustment of the current account – that is, the contraction of demand – on to the agricultural sector.

4 Simulation of the reforms included in the 1985–6 SAL

This section reports on two sets of simulations (Table 5.2). One set consists of progressive financial market reforms, starting from the

Table 5.2 *Financial and trade reforms' experiments: summary*[1]

E–1: base run Credit rationing, interest ceiling set to 8%, import quotas in 1983–4, fixed exchange rate.

Financial Reforms

E–2: foreign exchange liberalisation

(E − 1) + Flexible exchange rate and elimination of import quotas. (Public foreign borrowing is exogenous and set to base run value.)

E–3: financial liberalisation

(E − 2) + Freely determined rate of interest (no credit rationing). Reduction of money supply growth: 0% in 1981 and 5% afterwards. Increase in the interest semi-elasticity of money demand (from 2 to 6). Increase in the substitution elasticity between domestic and foreign bonds (from 5 to 20). Partial substitution of money demand for domestic bonds. No sterilisation of capital movements.

Trade Reforms

E–4: tariff reform

(E − 2) + Tariff uniformisation and lowering of the average rate from 19 to 14.5%.

E–5: reduction in export tax rates

(E − 2) + Reduction of export tax.[2]

[1] All changes begin in 1981 and last until 1986.

[2] Change in tax rate is computed so as to keep the same tax revenue changes as in (E–4).

adoption of a floating exchange rate and leading to the liberalisation of the domestic credit market and the opening up of the capital account to private capital movements. The other set deals with a trade reform involving the tariffs, a lowering of the average duty rate and a reduction in export taxes. All simulations are run under two alternative closure rules. The former (c#1) intends to replicate short-run rigidities. Prices and wages are rigid in the modern sector of the economy, so that most market clearing is done through quantity adjustments; full competition on both product and labour markets is assumed to hold in the agricultural sector. In the second closure (c#2) prices and wages are fully flexible in all sectors of the economy. It thus is more appropriate for long-run evaluation.

Of course, all SAL measures are additional to the more macroeconomic aspects of adjustments in Morocco which have been briefly reviewed in the preceding sections – that is, the reduction in public expenditures, the various devaluations of the currency, and the monetary tightening. All these measures are included in the base run. A full evaluation of the adjustment-stabilisation package adopted by Morocco would thus require additional simulation work, with some assumptions about what the adjustment process would have been had the Moroccan authorities decided not to follow the recommendations of the IMF and the World Bank.[8]

If fully implemented, all the preceding measures would necessarily lead to some changes in the current account and in the net indebtedness of the country. As it would make little sense to compare the evolution of the economy in situations where the country borrowed different amounts from abroad, a closure rule had to be selected which would lead to a constant borrowing policy by the government. The rule selected is that foreign public borrowing is constrained to be, in all simulations and for every year, at the level actually observed. As the move toward a flexible exchange rate system is one of the simulations we wanted to consider, the simplest way to meet the foreign borrowing constraint at each point of time was to keep the exchange rate flexible throughout all the remaining simulations.

4.1 Liberalising the foreign exchange market

During 1983–4 additional import rationing was imposed by the Moroccan government as a way of meeting the foreign payment constraint while avoiding a drastic devaluation. Import quotas were present before (and to a lesser extent afterwards), but their actual effect on foreign trade was much weaker than during those crisis years.[9] The effects of abolishing import quotas and adopting a flexible exchange rate system were thus felt only during 1983–4.

Replacing import rationing by a further devaluation of the currency in order to meet the foreign exchange constraint has major effects with the rigidity closure c#1 (Table 5.3). Exporters benefit from higher domestic currency prices for their product. The resulting increase in exports permits a faster growth of GDP, since more goods can be imported while satisfying the foreign payment constraint. Accordingly, GDP grew by 3 per cent on average in 1983 and 1984, whereas exports increased by 13 per cent, thanks to a 6 per cent additional devaluation. Because the current account now adjusted on both the export and the import sides, the additional exports due to the replacement of import quotas by a devaluation also permitted larger imports of investment goods than before. However, the period was too short to see the subsequent effects on growth.

Table 5.3 *Simulated effects of the foreign exchange liberalisation, absolute (a) or relative (r) deviation from base run, per cent*

	1983	1984	1986
Volume of GDP (r) c#1	2.4	3.6	−0.1
c#2	0.7	1.7	0.6
Exchange rate (nominal) (r) c#1	2.5	4.7	0.0
c#2	3.3	5.5	0.0
Exchange rate (real) (r) c#1	5.3	8.6	0.0
c#2	4.8	7.6	0.4
Inflation (CPI index) (r) c#1	−2.6	−3.6	0.0
c#2	−1.3	−2.0	−0.4
Volume of exports (r) c#1	9.7	17.2	0.4
c#2	7.7	14.4	3.0
Volume of imports (r) c#1	8.8	12.8	−0.6
c#2	6.7	10.9	1.3
Agricultural terms of trade (r) c#1	0.9	2.3	0.4
c#2	−5.1	−6.3	2.6
Rural/urban real income[1] (r) c#1	0.3	0.9	3.2
c#2	−6.1	−8.0	7.2
Urban unemployment (a) c#1	−1.0	−1.2	0.3
Theil index (r) c#1	−10.3	−15.7	−0.9
c#2	−10.5	−17.1	−2.3
Poverty (headcount) (a) c#1	−1.5	−2.4	−0.1
c#2	−0.1	−1.9	−1.3
Share of agriculture in GDP (a) c#1	−0.3	−0.4	0.2
c#2	−1.4	−2.1	0.5

[1] Real urban income corresponds to modern workers' real earnings corrected by the unemployment rate.

The social effects of using devaluation rather than import rationing to equilibrate the balance of payments are impressive. Inequality goes down considerably, and poverty falls quite significantly. The first effect was essentially due to our base run assumption that the rents associated with import rationing were appropriated by the 'capitalists' class. With closure c#1 the drop in poverty is due to the increase in the overall level of activity in the economy, to the resulting fall in urban unemployment, and also to the significant increase in the relative real income of peasants and rural workers. That rural households benefit more than others from the switch to a flexible exchange rate in the case of fix-price closure is easy to understand: the push in exports due to the devaluation of the currency affects both the agricultural and the manufacturing sectors – and to a lesser extent primary exports (phosphates). Given the assumptions of the base run, however, there is some excess capacity at fixed prices in the latter whereas there is full employment in the former. Output increase in the modern sector thus lowers unemployment whereas prices remain approximately constant. In the agricultural sector, the rise in exports, and the rise in the demand coming from the modern sector of the economy pushes food prices (and, more generally, the agricultural terms of trade) up. This has a positive effect on the real income of rural households, and a negative effect on that of urban households, which somewhat compensates the positive effect due to the drop in unemployment.

Switching to the closure rule c#2 where all prices are flexible in the modern sector and full employment holds rather drastically modifies these results. It is still the case that the substitution of import quotas by a real devaluation has positive effects on the whole economy, including a drop in inequality and poverty. However, the rural sector is now negatively affected. This is because it is not any more the only sector where price flexibility allows it to take advantage of the devaluation. Other sectors producing exportable goods are now in the same position, and given export elasticities they are in some sense more successful on foreign markets than the rural sector. The price flexibility advantage held by the rural sector in the base run has simply disappeared.

Note that the possible effects of permanent import quotas could be readily inferred from the present experiment. From the base run and additional simulations, one can calculate that the import rationing implemented in 1983–4 was equivalent to a reduction of imports of approximately 15 per cent. If some estimate were available for permanent quotas, their effect could be estimated through proportional corrections of the preceding figures.

4.2 Financial liberalisation

As may be seen from Table 5.2, there are several steps in the simulation of the liberalisation of financial markets. The first is to free the interest rate and to abolish credit rationing. Such a measure could have two kinds of effects. On one hand, the free allocation of investment funds across sectors may become more efficient. On the other, the resulting increase in the creditor rate of interest may have two effects. First, it may directly increase savings.[10] Second, a higher domestic interest rate may induce a reallocation of households' and firms' portfolios from foreign to domestic assets, and thus some repatriation of capital. The second step in the financial liberalisation consists of developing an attractive domestic financial market. It is therefore assumed that households demand less money and more bonds, and also that their demand for money becomes more elastic with respect to the domestic rate of interest. To be consistent, the initial money supply and its rate of growth are reduced so that a larger share of the budget deficit is financed by bonds at the initial level of interest rates. The normal consequence of such a reform would be to ensure more stability of the domestic interest rate, and larger multiplier price or output effects of fiscal policy or exogenous changes in demand.[11] The last piece of liberalisation consists of increasing capital mobility between Morocco and the rest of the world – that is, the elasticity of substitution between domestic and foreign assets.[12] As foreign interest rates are higher than Moroccan ones for 1981, 1983, 1984 (and, to a lesser extent, 1985), increased capital mobility leads to substantial capital outflows during those years, a slower growth of the money supply, and a smaller gap between domestic and foreign interest rates. The opposite occurs in 1982 and 1986.

The dominant effects of this set of reforms are unambiguously those which result from the increase in capital mobility and make the Moroccan economy closely follow the movements of the foreign interest rates (Table 5.4). In the fix-price c#1 case, the opening of the capital market in 1981 leads to an outflow of private capital, which raises the domestic interest rate, accelerates the nominal and real devaluation, and increases the rate of inflation. Private investment is negatively affected, and despite the positive effect on demand of the real devaluation, GDP goes down slightly in the c#1 Keynesian closure (GDP remains approximately constant at a lower general price level in c#2). Not surprisingly, through the devaluation and the resulting increase in the relative price of exported agricultural commodities, the effect on the rural sector of opening the capital market is quite impressive. In comparison with the base run, the agricultural terms of trade improve by almost 10 per centage points, whereas the real income of all rural socioeconomic groups – large farmers, small farmers and landless workers – increases both in absolute and in relative terms (more than 15 per cent in comparison with modern workers). If 1981 is taken as an example, the isolation (or the low degree of development) of the Moroccan capital market negated important benefits that would have accrued to the rural sector. The conclusion would have been the opposite if one had had 1986 conditions, as an open capital market would have meant a lower domestic interest rate, an investment-led expansion, and a re-evaluation of the domestic currency in comparison with the preceding simulation.

Table 5.4 *Simulated effects of the financial liberalisation, absolute (a) or relative (r) deviation from base run, per cent*

	1981	1983	1986
Volume of GDP (r) c#1	−1.2	3.4	6.2
c#2	0.1	0.4	−0.8
Exchange rate (nominal) (r) c#1	20.3	15.8	2.8
c#2	10.2	10.8	0.0
Exchange rate (real) (r) c#1	7.6	7.7	−4.0
c#2	8.3	4.2	−11.0
Inflation (CPI index) (r) c#1	11.4	7.5	8.2
c#2	1.9	6.5	12.3
Real domestic interest rate (a) c#1	3.7	2.1	−0.3
c#2	2.0	1.2	0.5
Foreign interest rate (level)	15.2	10.7	7.3
Agricultural terms of trade (r) c#1	8.1	6.5	4.8
c#2	8.7	−6.9	−15.8
Rural/urban real income (r) c#1	17.8	9.6	−2.2
c#2	15.8	−3.2	−20.7
Investment (r) c#1	−19.4	5.4	68.3
c#2	−10.7	9.4	46.9
Theil index (r) c#1	−3.9	−10.5	10.2
c#2	−0.7	−10.4	5.2
Poverty (headcount) (a) c#1	0.6	−2.2	−2.9
c#2	1.4	−0.9	1.5
Share of agriculture in GDP (a) c#1	1.9	0.8	0.0
c#2	2.0	−1.5	−3.7

Whether Morocco would have fared better with a more highly integrated capital market during the early 1980s, and whether it will do better in the future if that measure is enforced, is difficult to gauge on the basis of this simulation. A financial reform of the type considered here is not really a 'policy measure' like a fiscal contraction or a monetary expansion. It rather corresponds to a change in the macroeconomic 'closure' of the economy – and, therefore, in the likely effects of traditional policy instruments like fiscal and monetary tools. Thus, excepting the case where the abolition of credit rationing would directly benefit agriculture, it is only indirectly that the rural sector will be affected by such a reform.

The preceding simulation shows that a financial reform of the type considered for Morocco may have a significant effect on the rural sector of the economy only inasmuch as it affects the real exchange rate. It is well known since Mundell and Fleming (Mundell, 1963) that moving from a fixed exchange rate system with capital controls to a flexible rate and free capital movements makes monetary policy strongly effective through its direct impact on the exchange rate. If fully implemented, the financial reform considered in the SAL agreement would thus make the rural sector much more sensitive to the macroeconomic policy than it was in a system of fixed exchange rates, credit rationing and foreign exchange control.

4.3 Trade reforms

The first simulation undertaken under this heading deals with tariff reform. Following World Bank recommendations, the average effective tariff rate is brought down, from 19 per cent in the base run to 14 per cent during the simulation period, and made uniform, at that rate, across sectors. It is assumed that the foreign payment constraint is binding and that the resulting changes in the current account are met through changes in the exchange rate; the reference experiment is thus E–2.

With the Keynesian c#1 closure, the drop in tariffs initially increases imports and depresses domestic production through substitution effects. The resulting deterioration of the current account is compensated by a faster real devaluation of the currency (3–4 per cent). This real devaluation in turn increases exports and the overall level of effective demand, overcompensating the initial depressive effect of tariff reductions and pushing up GDP. As may be seen from Table 5.5, however, this is obtained at the cost of an increased budget deficit – met through crowding out private investments – because the rise in GDP is not enough to compensate for the initial loss in tariff revenues.

The effect of the tariff reform upon the rural sector is positive overall: its share of GDP is maintained at its initial level, whereas its terms of trade slightly appreciate. Note, though, that the rural–urban income differential deteriorates in favour of modern workers. Given that agriculture is initially the sector most protected from foreign competition, it is also the most severely hit by the drop and the uniformisation of tariff rates. That it does not fare so badly with the Keynesian closure rule c#1 is to be explained, as before, essentially by the real devaluation and the export-led GDP expansion (in the non-agricultural sector) entailed by the tariff reform and the resulting small appreciation of the agricultural terms of trade. These effects overcompensate the initially negative impact of the reform on agriculture.

Things are slightly different with the flex-price closure c#2. Because of

Table 5.5 *Simulated effects of the tariff reform, absolute (a) or relative (r) deviation from E–2, per cent*

	1981	1983	1986
Volume of GDP (r) c#1	0.6	0.4	1.8
c#2	0.6	0.2	−0.1
Exchange rate (nominal) (r) c#1	2.8	3.3	1.4
c#2	2.8	2.4	2.1
Exchange rate (real) (r) c#1	3.3	3.9	2.0
c#2	3.5	3.1	1.5
Volume of exports (r) c#1	7.5	8.0	3.7
c#2	7.2	7.8	4.2
Volume of imports (r) c#1	3.3	3.1	5.5
c#2	3.3	2.9	2.3
Volume of private consumption (r) c#1	1.6	1.5	2.4
c#2	1.7	1.3	1.0
Volume of investment (r) c#1	−5.6	−10.3	5.1
c#2	−3.7	−9.8	−10.8
Budget deficit/GDP (a) c#1	1.5	1.6	0.8
c#2	1.8	2.0	1.3
Agricultural terms of trade (r) c#1	0.9	0.9	1.3
c#2	−0.8	0.5	−0.1
Share of agriculture in GDP (a) c#1	0.0	0.1	−0.2
c#2	−0.4	0.0	−0.4
Theil index (r) c#1	−1.1	−0.4	0.8
c#2	−0.5	−0.4	0.0
Poverty (headcount) (a) c#1	−1.1	−0.8	−1.0
c#2	−0.7	−1.1	−0.9
Rural/Urban real income (r) c#1	−0.9	0.6	−3.7
c#2	−1.8	−2.0	−2.4

price and wage rigidities in the modern sector, the c#1 results refer more to the short than to the long run. However, since agriculture is initially the most protected sector, it may be expected to be negatively affected by the reform when the economy is at full equilibrium. In effect, the simulations performed under the assumption of full price and wage flexibility in all the sectors of the economy show a small relative decline of the agricultural sector in GDP, and a slight worsening in the relative (but a constant absolute) real income of the rural socioeconomic groups in the popu-

Table 5.6 *Simulated effects of a drop in export tax rates, absolute (a) or relative (r) deviation from E–2, per cent*

	1981	1982	1984	1986
Volume of GDP (r) c#1	0.4	0.5	0.0	0.6
c#2	0.6	0.5	0.8	0.8
Exchange rate (nominal) (r) c#1	−2.8	−2.7	−2.5	−2.9
c#2	−0.9	−1.7	−1.4	−2.0
Exchange rate (real) (r) c#1	−2.1	−2.1	−2.6	−3.6
c#2	−0.3	−1.3	−0.9	−1.4
Volume of exports (r) c#1	1.6	1.3	−1.6	−1.7
c#2	2.1	0.7	0.4	0.4
Volume of imports (r) c#1	0.7	0.6	0.4	−0.9
c#2	0.6	0.6	0.8	0.5
Volume of private consumption (r) c#1	0.9	0.6	0.7	0.6
c#2	0.4	0.4	0.7	1.0
Volume of investment (r) c#1	−2.2	−0.2	0.0	−5.3
c#2	1.0	1.1	3.4	0.5
Budget deficit/GDP (a) c#1	0.5	0.0	−0.3	0.8
c#2	0.0	−0.3	−0.4	−0.1
Agricultural terms of trade (r) c#1	−2.5	−2.8	−6.0	−5.8
c#2	−1.2	−1.0	−1.4	−1.2
Share of agriculture in GDP (a) c#1	−0.7	−0.8	−1.3	−1.3
c#2	−0.4	−0.4	−0.7	−0.6
Theil index (r) c#1	2.6	2.7	5.1	5.4
c#2	2.5	2.7	3.7	2.8
Poverty (headcount) (a) c#1	0.0	0.2	0.8	0.7
c#2	0.2	0.0	0.0	0.3
Rural/Urban real income (r) c#1	0.0	2.5	−1.6	−1.1
c#2	0.0	0.0	−0.8	2.7

lation. Not surprisingly, modern urban workers are then the main beneficiaries of the tariff reform.[13]

The export tax reform bears only on the primary export sector (a 10 per cent tax rebate) – that is, the phosphate sector in Morocco (Table 5.6). Indeed, there would be no point checking that reducing export taxes or introducing export subsidies in agriculture favours the rural sector. On the other hand, handling the phosphate sector in Morocco as if it were fully private (and thus price-responsive) is somewhat misleading, since that sector is essentially administered by the State. This experiment must therefore be taken as only indicative of the possible effects of freeing trade in a primary export sector without many backward or forward links with the rest of the economy. Such a situation is not uncommon in developing countries, although the supply price elasticity of such primary exports may be smaller than that which is postulated in the present model.

With both closures, the increase in primary exports due to the drop in the tax rate is somewhat unfavourable to the rural sector. The reason is initially the same as before. The initial gain in exports brings a real appreciation of the currency, which reduces exports and increases imports. This process is clearly detrimental to agriculture as well as to other tradable goods other than primary exports, and it mitigates somewhat the initial push on primary exports. Although, in the Keynesian closure, a positive multiplier effect somewhat compensates (initially) the previous effect (GDP changes with closure c#2 result only from index problems since full employment holds), it remains the case that the agricultural terms of trade as well as the share of agriculture in GDP fall. These effects are somewhat limited at the beginning of the simulation period because foreign export prices are assumed to be low. They are more pronounced in 1985–6 when the (exogenous) terms of trade of primary exports improve by some 30 per cent. We note, on the other hand, that these effects are less pronounced with closure c#2 because price and wage flexibility in the modern sector permit a more even spread of the effects of the tax change. Note also that, in both cases, the rural–urban income differential is virtually not affected. This is because this differential is defined on modern workers and small farmers, and the change in the primary export tax rate benefits capitalists more than workers in the urban sector – hence the slight increase in income inequality.

The reason why the agricultural sector is negatively affected by a fall in the primary export tax rate in the case of Morocco is first of all that both sectors are competing against each other very indirectly; indeed, the situation would be quite different if primary exports were relying on the same type of labour or land as agriculture.

5 Conclusions

Several conclusions about the fate of the rural sector in a typical process of stabilization and structural adjustment arise from the above counterfactual analysis of the Moroccan experience. First, it is worth stressing that the macroeconomic closure of the economy matters very greatly. In a typical developing economy where the modern sector is rather rigid, the burden of a crisis and the benefits from a successful adjustment tend to concentrate upon the rural sector because of their sector's inherent flexibility. Things would not necessarily be the same if there were more flexibility in the modern sector of the economy; in that case, modern and rural sectors would compete for the advantages of the adjustment process. Agriculture would then benefit less than under a fixed-price closure in the modern sector.

Second, relative prices are obviously what matters in determining the sectoral bias of adjustment. All measures which may change internal relative prices therefore also discriminate across sectors or socioeconomic groups. This is true of trade reforms which change internal prices through a modification of import tariff duties or export tax rates. But, more significantly, this is also true of any macroeconomic or structural policy that affects the real exchange rate. As seen above, general policies meant to change the framework of the economy – like switching from a fixed to a flexible exchange rate regime, modifying monetary policy, reforming the internal financial markets, or increasing capital mobility with the rest of the world – all have powerful, and certainly unexpected, effects on the rural sector. More than this, our experiments show that, in the short and the medium run, such distributional effects may largely dominate general equilibrium effects stemming from standard reforms in trade policies or in the tax system, on which the standard literature tends to focus. This impact should be taken into account when implementing more targeted measures.

NOTES

This work draws on a previous paper presented at the conference on Adjustment Policies (Manchester, September 1990), a part of which appears in Chapter 8 of P. Mosley *et al.* (1991). Partial support for this paper was received from World Bank (RPO 675–18). The views are those of the authors not those of their respective affiliations. We have benefited greatly from the comments of Jaime de Melo and thank Shlantayanan Devarajan and Ian Goldin for their reflections on this chapter.

1 See the synthesis and summary of that programme in the forthcoming symposium issue of *World Development* edited by Bourguignon, de Melo and Morrisson and the forthcoming OECD publication by Morrisson and Bourguignon. Further developments of the model, originally due to Bourguignon, Branson and de Melo, used in the Côte d'Ivoire and Morocco studies in that programme have been made at the World Bank – see, in particular, Bourguignon, de Melo and Suwa (1991a) and (1991b).
2 A thorough analysis of the macroeconomic package implemented from 1983 onwards, including its structural and distributional consequences, is provided by Morrisson (1989). A short summary is given in Section 2.

3 It is fair to say that this growth is also explained by the abnormally low levels of production observed in the previous years after the 1981 drought.

4 This term may be more appropriate than that of 'model' because of the extreme flexibility that has been built in and which allows for applications to a large variety of countries and institutional setting. This maquette considerably enlarges the scope of the usual CGE models, as described, for instance, in Dervis, de Melo and Robinson (1982). More recent attempts at introducing the financial and monetary sector in a CGE framework also include Fargeix, de Janvry and Sadoulet (1989) and Lora (1989). Developments of CGE in that direction are surveyed in Robinson (1989).

5 In the case of Morocco, there formally were no government bonds markets prior to the financial reform in 1985. However, time deposits in banks were statutorily used to finance the public budget, which is somewhat equivalent to a system of bonds.

6 Note that the model is not truly dynamic, in the sense that agents do not optimise intertemporally. For more recent attempts at developing such dynamic models, see, for instance, Manne and Preckel (1985); Auerbach and Kotlikoff (1987); Goulder and Eichengreen (1989); Mercenier and de Souza (1990).

7 A complete description of the calibration method is found in Morrisson (1989).

8 Some simulations along that line may be found in Morrisson (1989).

9 To what extent those quantitative constraints on imports were actually binding before 1983 is ambiguous.

10 Savings in the model is modelled in the usual Keynesian fashion with a zero interest rate elasticity. However, an increase in the creditor rate produces a negative wealth effect on consumption which corresponds to increased savings.

11 In a IS–LM framework, the LM curve has become flatter.

12 It must be kept in mind that in a country like Morocco (where emigrant workers' remittances represent approximately 5 per cent of GDP), control of capital movements cannot be fully effective. 'Compensation' practices, whereby residents export capital by short-cutting wage remittances from abroad, are widespread. This is the reason why the calibration assumptions selected for the base run allowed for limited capital mobility, despite the quite restrictive official foreign exchange controls in Morocco.

13 Note that the previous effects would be stronger in the absence of the crowding-out effect on investment due to the increase in the budget deficit, which remains present even with full price and wage rigidities. This is because this effect tends to slow capital accumulation in agricultural capital-intensive sectors.

REFERENCES

Auerbach, A. and L. Kotlikoff (1987) *Dynamic Fiscal Policy*, Cambridge: Cambridge University Press.

Bourguignon, F., W. Branson and J. de Melo (1989a) 'Macroeconomic Adjustment and Income Distribution: a Macro–Micro Simulation Model', *OECD Technical Paper*, **11**.

(1989b) 'Adjustment and Income Distribution: a Counterfactual Analysis', *NBER Working Paper*, **2943**.

Bourguignon, F., J. de Melo and A. Suwa (1991a) 'Distributional Effects of Adjustment Policies: Simulations for Two Archetypes Economies', *World Bank Economic Review*, May.

(1991b) 'Adjustment and Equity With Alternative Programs' (mimeo).

Dervis, K., J. de Melo and S. Robinson (1982) *General Equilibrium Models for Development Policy*, Cambridge: Cambridge University Press.

Fargeix, A, A. de Janvry and E. Sadoulet (1989) 'Economic, Welfare, and Political Consequences of Stabilization Policies: an Analysis for Equador and Latin America', monograph prepared for the OECD Development centre, Paris.

Goulder, L. and B. Eichengreen (1989) 'Trade Liberalization in General Equilibrium: Intertemporal and Inter-industry Effects', *NBER Working Paper*, **2814**.

Heller, P. *et al.* (1988) 'The Implication of Fund-supported Adjustment Programs for Poverty', *IMF Occasional Paper*, May.

Lora, E. (1989) 'Real and Financial Interaction in a Computable General Equilibrium Model for Colombia' (mimeo).

Manne, A. and P. Preckel (1985) 'A Three Region Intertemporal Model of Energy, International Trade and Capital Flows', *Mathematical Programming Study*, **23**: 56–74.

Mateus, A. (1988) 'Growth and Equity: the 1980–1985 Moroccan Adjustment Process (mimeo).

Mercenier, J. and M. Sampaio de Souza (1990) 'Structural Adjustment and Growth in a Highly Indebted Economy: Brazil' (mimeo)

Morrisson, C. (1989) 'Adjustment et distribution des revenus: application d'un modèle macro–micro au Maroc', *OECD Technical Paper*, **7**.

Mosley, P., J. Harrigan and J. Toye (eds) (1991) *Aid and Power: the World Bank and Policy-based Lending*, vol. 2. London, Routledge: 150–200.

Mundell, R. A. (1963) 'Capital Mobility and Stabilization Policy Under Fixed and Flexible Exchange Rates', *Canadian Journal of Economics and Political Science*, November.

Robinson, S. (1989) 'Computable General Equilibrium Models of Developing Countries: Stretching the Neo-Classical Paradigm', Berkeley: University of California (mimeo).

World Bank (1987) 'Morocco: the Impact of Liberalization on Trade and Industrial Adjustment', Washington, D.C.: World Bank.

World Bank (Country Economics Department) (1988) 'Adjustment Lending: An Evaluation of Ten Years of Experience', *Policy and Research Series*, **1**, Washington, D.C.: World Bank.

Discussion

SHANTAYANAN DEVARAJAN

Chapter 5 is yet another in the series applying the now famous 'maquette' – originally developed by Bourguignon, Branson and de Melo – to Morocco. Having seen most of the previous papers, I could not help feeling a sense of '*déjà vu*' in reading this one. Nevertheless, the framework is so rich that you learn something new every time it is applied. In discussion Chapter 2, Helmut Reisen likens Sebastian Edwards to a jazz musician, playing variations on a theme; in that vein, the Bourguignon–Branson–de Melo model is like a Mozart concerto.

The model is a multi-sector, multi-household, computable general equilibrium (CGE) model with some monetary elements. As it has been documented elsewhere, the authors do not dwell on the model's features in this paper; instead, they describe Morocco's adjustment experience and then highlight the impact of their counterfactual experiments on the rural sector. Their basic conclusions are: (1) that the functional distribution of income depends critically on changes in relative prices; and (2) that the changes in relative prices, in turn, depend on the particular closure rule chosen. These conclusions are reminiscent of the early work on CGE models applied to income distribution (Adelman and Robinson, 1979; Taylor *et al.*, 1980). However, these early authors never looked at structural adjustment policies. The contribution of Bourguignon *et al.* here is to examine specific adjustment policies (trade liberalisation, interest rate liberalisation, etc.) in a distributionally-sensitive model. It is, however, reassuring that their conclusions about relative prices and closure rules are no different from those of the early authors on the subject.

The paper contains a myriad of experiments and a lot of numbers are thrown at the reader. Instead of going through them one by one, I will describe the four salient mechanisms which drive the results of the model. In describing each of them, I will also make some comments on the paper.

1 In all of the experiment results, the authors describe the impact of a particular shock on the growth of GDP. Yet, this is a model with exogenous total factor supplies and total factor productivity growth; hence, the total GDP growth rate is exogenous to the model. Any variations in this growth rate, then, is due to composition effects. These, in turn, will depend on which numeraire is used. For example, in Figure 5D.1, consider a shock which changes the relative price of non-tradables to

tradables from (P_N/P_T) to $(P_N/P_T)'$. This changes the production mix of the economy. Whether it increases or decreases, GDP, however, depends on whether we are measuring GDP on the T-axis or the N-axis, as Figure 5D.1 shows.

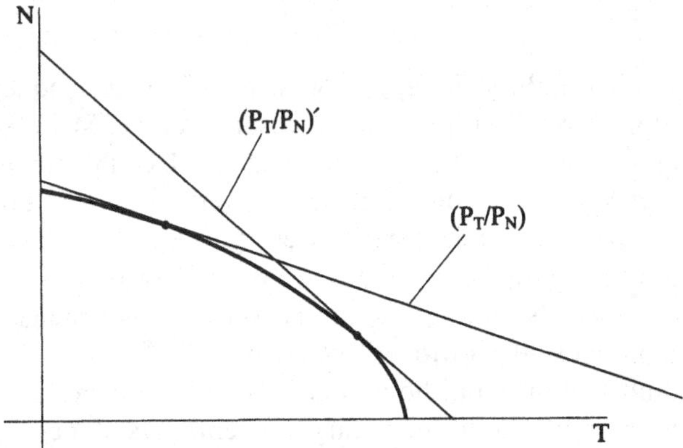

Figure 5D.1 The effect of relative price changes on GDP

The one exception of this mechanism is the experiments with unemployment and fixed prices (closure c#1 in Chapter 5). In this case, the economy is inside the production possibility frontier and 'growth' results from increased employment (i.e., from Keynesian multiplier effects). It is hardly surprising, therefore, that the growth effects are much greater under c#2 than under c#1. However, it is perhaps misleading to call these outcomes 'growth'. After all, Keynesian multiplier effects are static and cannot be sustained for very long (because eventually the economy hits a resource constraint).

2 The authors state, correctly, that many of their results are driven by their choice of closure rule. The rule they choose is one in which foreign savings is fixed exogenously. Given the *ex post* identity between investment and savings, this implies that the level of investment in the economy will be sensitive to variations in private and public savings:

$$I = S^P + S^G + S^F$$

Note that government savings, S^G, is equal to revenues minus government current expenditure. Experiments involving trade liberalisation in Morocco result in a drop in government revenues. Both in the model and in the real world, these tariff reductions are not replaced by lump-sum taxes. The drop in tariff revenues thus results in a decline in investment, given the closure rule described above. This has two implications for how we interpret the results of the model. First, the drop in investment leads to a shift in the production mix of the economy away from investment goods in favour of consumer goods. If the latter has a higher value-added coefficient than the former, there will be an increase in GDP, again due to composition effects. Second, investment is typically a non-tradable-intensive good (construction is a major component). Therefore, the shift away from investment goods leads to a decline in demand for non-tradables, bidding down their price, and accentuating the real exchange rate depreciation triggered by the tariff liberalisation. Note that if, instead, investment had been fixed and foreign savings had been adjusting, the reverse would have happened. The drop in government savings would have required more foreign savings (to hit the same investment target), causing the real exchange rate to appreciate.

3 Trade liberalisation in Morocco involves more than reducing tariff rates; it includes eliminating quantitative restrictions on imports as well. If there were import quotas initially, some assumption must be made about who was receiving the rent from these quotas. Then, when the quotas are eliminated, the income-distributional effects are driven by which group loses these rents. For example, the urban capitalists consistently lose from trade liberalisation in the present paper because they are the ones assumed to be receiving the quota rents. My only question here (which is often asked of my own work as well) is: do you need a sophisticated, general equilibrium model to tell you that?

4 My final comment has to do with the treatment of the labour market. The authors assume there is classical unemployment in the manufacturing sector and full employment in the agricultural sector (see Figure 5D.2). The implication is that increases in demand will lead to output increases in the former and wage increases in the latter. However, they obtain the result that trade liberalisation has a greater effect on output in the agricultural than in the manufacturing sector, and they attribute this difference to the rigidity of the wage in the manufacturing sector. Both my intuition and my experience with such models tell me that it should be the reverse: because of the rigidity of the wage in the manufacturing sector, we would expect greater output responses than in the agricultural sector. In particular, if the manufacturing wage is fixed with respect to the domestic price level, say, a real depreciation will necessarily lower the real wage in that sector, increasing labour demand and output.

Before concluding, I would like to mention some features, not captured in the present model, which are nevertheless important in discussing the

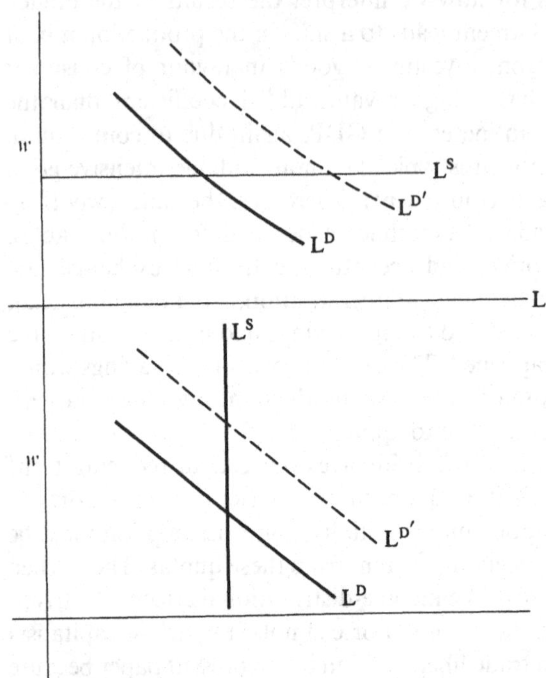

Figure 5D.2 The implications of alternative labour market specifications

general issue of income distribution and adjustment in Morocco. First, I would imagine that the agricultural sector is characterised by informal capital markets (like the *tontines* of West Africa), whose functioning is crucial to the outcome of any financial liberalisation. Some recent work by Timothy Besley and Stephen Coate (1991) attempts to formalise these markets in a manner which, possibly permits their inclusion in CGE models. Second, the role of infrastructure is surely critical in determining rural incomes. Farmers' access to markets through roads, bridges, etc. often makes a bigger difference than the prices they receive. Third, all of the income distribution results in the paper refer to distribution across sectors (e.g., rural versus urban.) Very little is said about what happens to distribution *within* sectors. Yet, as some work by Martin Revallion (Revallion and Huppi, 1991) on Indonesia shows, the within-group distribution could go in the opposite direction from that across groups.

In sum, this paper is a useful contribution to the growing literature on income distribution and structural adjustment. The authors' use of a CGE model is entirely appropriate, given their emphasis on counterfactual analysis. I would encourage them, however, to present their results in such a way that we can more easily see which are determined endogenously by the model and which are the results of specific assumptions made in it. In addition, they may wish to speculate on which features of the Moroccan economy they would have highlighted to answer the question at hand if they were starting from scratch, rather than with a time-tested, well-established model.

REFERENCES

Adelman, Irma and Sherman Robinson (1979) *Income Distribution Policy in Developing Countries*, Stanford: Stanford University Press.

Besley, Timothy and Stephen Coate (1991) 'The Economics of ROSCAs', Woodrow Wilson School of Public and International Affairs, Princeton University, unpublished.

Revallion, Martin and Monika Huppi (1991) 'Measuring Changes in Poverty: A Methodological Case Study of Indonesia During an Adjustment Period', *World Bank Economic Review*, **5(1)**, January: 57–84.

Taylor, Frank, Edmar Bacha, Eliana Cardoso and Frank Lysy (1980) *Models of Growth and Distribution for Brazil*, London: Oxford University Press.

Part Two
The small country assumption and trade reform

6 Exchange reforms, supply response, and inflation in Africa

AJAY CHHIBBER

1 Introduction

A central element of reform programmes in sub-Saharan Africa (SSA) has been the realignment of exchange rates. Other than in the CFA Zone the extent of exchange rate reforms has been very widespread in Africa. Almost every country in SSA outside the CFA Zone has undergone substantial exchange rate devaluation. During the period 1984–9 exchange rate reforms were undertaken in 18 countries in the continent. Of these 10 countries experienced devaluations of 10 per cent or more each year from 1984 to 1989.[1] It is alleged that the introduction of such programmes has led to cost-push inflation. Without sufficient supply response (and export response) these devaluations have had little positive real effects, while generating higher inflation.[2] Concern over the inflationary consequences of reform and the lack of supply response have led several countries to delay, and in a few cases to abort, reform programmes. The relatively low inflation in the CFA Zone countries in Africa has lent credence to these arguments. It is widely believed that the fixed exchange rate for the CFA Zone countries has been an important factor in their low inflation rates (see Chapter 4 for an explanation of the CFA Zone's genesis).

This paper focuses on the issue of the inflationary consequences of exchange rate reforms and accompanying price liberalisation. The paper reports on the major findings of a research project carried out at the World Bank on this subject, and places these findings in the context of existing literature on the subject. The paper does not go into other important issues related to the pace of the exchange rate reforms, the politics of reform, and questions dealing with the distributional consequences of reform. These are all important and interesting questions, and have been dealt with quite adequately elsewhere.[3]

The paper presents evidence which concludes that export and supply elasticities are no lower in Africa than in other region in the world: if anything, correctly estimated elasticities appear to be higher than those estimated elsewhere. The paper also presents evidence that the concern with the potential negative effects on world prices of contemporaneous devaluations is short-sighted from a welfare and revenue objective. In effect, the large and persistent overvaluation of the real exchange rate has allowed Asian producers (in the case of cocoa) to enter and in some commodities (palm oil) to dominate world trade. With a realistic exchange rate policy this trend is beginning to be reversed, but will obviously require other supporting actions to be more effective.

The paper acknowledges that, at first glance, the evidence appears to suggest a strong correlation between exchange rate regimes and inflation. Countries with floating exchange rates (or auction systems) appear to have experienced higher inflation. On the other hand, countries with fixed exchange rates have typically faced lower inflation. A careful analysis, however, indicates that the story is more complex. In countries such as Ghana, Uganda, Sierra Leone and Zambia, the high inflation was prevalent prior to the exchange reforms and was prevalent through periods when the exchange rate was fixed. The high inflation rendered the official exchange rate more or less irrelevant, and parallel markets emerged. The level of the official exchange rate was important for accounting purposes, but was irrelevant in affecting behaviour which was driven by the true price of foreign exchange – the parallel exchange rate. Detailed analysis of the Ghanaian exchange reforms shows that adjusting the official exchange rate may actually have lowered inflation by reducing fiscal deficits. The underlying cause of inflation was the high fiscal deficits, which were financed primarily through monetary creation. Careful analysis with simulations of a model on Zimbabwe show that the effect of devaluation on inflation depends more on the fiscal response, and not so much on the size of the export response. The lower and stable inflation in countries with pegged exchange rates, such as those of the CFA Zone, also has its genesis in the underlying monetary and financial arrangements, rather than in the fixed exchange rate.

2 Exchange rate and incentive reforms and supply response

It is now commonly believed, although not with too much empirical backing, that the real sector response to exchange rate reforms in Africa has been low.[4] A closer examination of the evidence shows that this extreme export pessimism is not justified. Using data from the period 1965–82 Balassa (1989) finds that a 1 per cent change in the real exchange rate is associated with a 0.8 to 1 per cent change in the ratio of exports to output in SSA countries. Moreover, contrary to what is generally believed, Balassa finds that the response of the export–output ratio to the real exchange rate changes for SSA is higher than for other parts of the world. Evidence on export shares also argues against the strong export pessimism position. Figure 6.1 presents evidence on SSA's share in world commodity exports. The results show that Africa's share in world exports had declined sharply for a number of commodities in the 1970s. However, in the 1980s this decline has been reversed (or at least slowed down) for a number of commodities. This halt in the decline of Africa's export shares in the 1980s has not been given sufficient attention.[5]

Three caveats to these results should be borne in mind. The first is that the observed increase in exports (or a slow-down in their decline) may simply be due to a switch from the parallel to the legal channel for exports. However, the reported data is for the region as a whole, so an increase in recorded exports in one country should be counterbalanced, at least partially, by a decline in the recorded exports of another country in the region. The second caveat is that the increase in exports comes mainly from a shift in production from food to cash crops. The response of total agricultural production to exchange rate and price changes is small, so that the only way in which cash crop exports and production can increase is through a decline in non-cash crop production.[6] The third caveat is that while each country is a price taker in the world market, the accumulated export response of a number of developing countries undertaking contemporaneous devaluations can produce a perverse terms of trade effect which reduces export revenues for each country. Let us examine each of these arguments in turn.

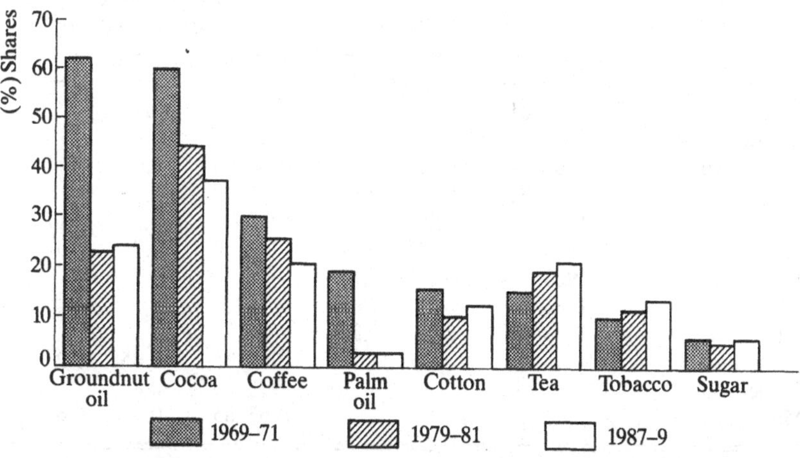

Figure 6.1 Sub-Saharan Africa's share in world commodity exports: selected items

There exists a substantial body of evidence for countries in SSA which shows that the response of single-crop output to price incentives is high.[7] The results on the single-crop supply elasticities demonstrate that farmers in SSA behave as rational producers much like farmers elsewhere in the world: they allocate resources between commodities on the basis of price incentives. But it is not enough to show that the single-crop supply elasticities are high, the crucial parameter is the aggregate supply elasticity. If the aggregate elasticity is low the increase in export crop response must come at the expense of non-export crops. This limited evidence on the aggregate supply elasticity for SSA countries is presented in Table 6.1 and is drawn from Bond (1983) and Berthélemy and Morrisson (1989). The supply response estimates in the Bond study are generally lower than in the Berthélemy and Morrisson study; the latter is interesting and innovative, in that it attempts to model the disequilibrium in the market for goods and the input supply market. Controlling for the availability of manufactured goods through various specifications in that study leads to estimated aggregate price elasticities which are fairly high and certainly comparable to those obtained in other parts of the world.[8]

Another concern is that a set of contemporaneous devaluations would generate export expansion in each country, which could be counterpro-

Table 6.1 *Estimates of aggregate supply response in agriculture: sub-Saharan Africa*

Country	Period	Estimate	Period	Estimate
	Bond (1983)		Berthélemy and Morrisson (1989)	
Ghana	1963–81	0.20 – 0.34*	1963–85	0.76*
Kenya	1963–81	0.10 – 0.16*	1961–85	0.2
Côte d'Ivoire	1963–81	0.13 – 0.13	1962–86	0.6
Liberia	1963–81	0.10 – 0.11		
Madagascar	1963–81	0.10 – 0.14	1963–85	0.09 – 0.17
Senegal	1963–81	0.54 – 0.54	1962–84	0.7 – 1.0*
Tanzania	1963–81	0.15 – 0.15		
Uganda	1963–81	0.05 – 0.07		
Burkina Faso	1963–81	0.22 – 0.24		
Cameroon			1962–85	0.05 – 0.2
Cameroon			1975–85	0.8
Mali			1963–85	0.5 – 0.6*

Note: * Statistically significant at 10 per cent level of significance.

ductive for all countries taken together.[9] This issue remains unresolved, especially in the context of a mono-primary-commodity exporter which faces limited prospects for market expansion, and where the shift into manufactured exports is not easily forthcoming. Panagariya and Schiff (1991) examine this issue for 9 cocoa producers. They show that lowering tax rates (or lowering exchange rate overvaluation) can lead to lower combined export revenues for all cocoa producers, with some winners and some losers. This result is, however, subject to certain qualifications. First, it applies to only one product, cocoa, where the share of SSA countries in world trade is relatively high, and second it may apply only in the short run. In a more recent paper de Rosa and Greene (1991) examine this issue for a number of products – specifically cocoa, coffee, tea, cotton, sugar and groundnuts. Their evidence[10] shows that while the world price declines the revenue effect is positive in the short run for all commodities except cocoa. In the long run, when one takes into account the reaction of non-SSA producers to a decline in the world price, the revenue impact is positive even for cocoa, although the improvement is small.

In fact, over time, the large overvaluation of exchange rates in SSA has allowed the entry of Asian producers such as Malaysia and Indonesia into primary product markets which cannot easily be reversed. The recovery by African producers of their market shares will require more than exchange rate policies. In addition, supply-side policies to improve productivity and restore infrastructure are going to be necessary. Export marketing is also going to be important. Moreover, without increases in manufacturing exports, export markets for SSA will remain limited. But for this to happen, and for some recovery in primary commodity exports, the evidence presented here shows that a realistic exchange rate is a key first step.

3 Exchange rates and inflation

Section 2 has presented evidence which shows the positive effects of real exchange rate depreciation on export and supply response. The question of how one brings about a real exchange rate depreciation must still be addressed. If the consequence of rapid nominal devaluation is high inflation, then achieving a particular level of real exchange rate depreciation will be highly inflationary.[11] While few African countries have experienced the triple-digit inflation often observed in Latin America,[12] the average inflation rate has increased markedly, sometimes five-fold in many countries (see Figure 6.2 and Table 6.2) consequences of this inflation can be harsh, more so because few African countries have

Table 6.2 *Inflation in sub-Saharan Africa, 1975–89, average annual*

	1980–9	1975–89	Highest
Recorded			
Industrial Countries	5.0	6.4	
Asia	7.9	7.3	
Sub-Saharan Africa	17.2	16.7	
More than 20 per cent			
Ghana	43.7	52.2	122.9
Sierra Leone	63.7	43.9	178.7
Somalia*	41.1	32.9	91.2
Sudan*	33.1	25.1	64.7
Tanzania*	30.5	24.1	35.3
Uganda	104.6	-	238.1
Zaire	58.8	62.1	101.0
Zambia*	30.8	24.5	55.6
Between 10–20 per cent			
Botswana	10.5	11.0	16.4
Burundi	7.6	10.1	36.6
Gambia	17.9	15.1	56.7
Kenya	10.4	11.3	20.4
Lesotho	13.6	13.9	18.0
Madagascar*	17.2	14.3	31.8
Malawi	16.6	-	33.9
Mauritius	7.6	10.8	42.0
Nigeria	20.5	18.9	40.9
Swaziland*	13.9	13.7	20.8
Zimbabwe	13.5	12.3	23.1
Under 10 per cent			
Burkina Faso	4.1	6.4	30.0
Cameroon*	9.4	9.8	17.2
C. Afr. Rep.**	3.9	-	14.6
Congo*	8.0	8.5	17.4
Côte d'Ivoire*	5.3	9.5	27.4
Djibouti	4.2	-	18.1
Ethiopia	4.3	8.3	28.5
Gabon*	7.7	9.8	28.4
Liberia*	4.3	6.1	19.5
Niger	2.4	6.7	23.5
Rwanda	4.4	6.8	31.1
Senegal	6.5	6.6	31.7
Togo	4.0	6.3	22.5

Note: * For these countries averages are for 1980-8 and 1975–88.
** For these countries averages are for 1981–9.

Source: World Bank data.

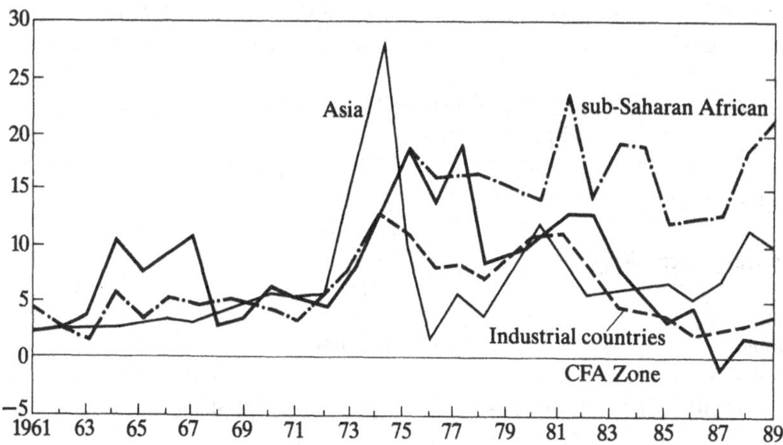

Figure 6.2 Inflation in sub-Saharan Africa

the institutions to manage inflation either through indexation or through safety net programmes. Moreover, with persistently high inflation there is the danger that inflation may become self-generating because of changing expectations about future inflation.[15]

4 Exchange rates and inflation: a framework for analysis

We begin with a general framework for analysing inflation. The framework incorporates cost-push and monetarist features, and it builds in the implications of price controls – both selective and general. We then examine the implications of the four prototype policy regimes alluded to in the introduction, and show that these are special cases of the general framework. We have classified African countries into these four prototypes in Table 6.3. Overall inflation is a weighted average of inflation in traded goods prices (*pt*), non-traded goods prices (*pn*), and controlled-price goods (*pc*).

$$\hat{p} = a1\,\hat{p}t + a2\,\hat{p}n + (1 - a1 - a2)\,\hat{p}c \qquad (1)$$

where $0 < a1$ and $a2 < 1$

When the economy is subject to widespread price controls $a1$ and $a2$ are close to zero and domestic inflation reflects a governments decision to change controlled prices. The wedge between *pc* (the controlled prices) and free prices reflects price distortions in the system. For traded goods, the domestic inflation is equal to the change in the foreign price plus the change in the nomimal exchange rate.[14]

$$\hat{p}t = \hat{p}f + \hat{e} \qquad (2)$$

Table 6.3 *Classification of macro-policy regimes in sub-Saharan Africa*[1]

Type I–Fixed exchange rates; open capital account; no (or very few) price controls

Benin	Equatorial Guinea
Burkina Faso	Gabon
Cameroon	Lesotho
Central African Republic	Mali
Chad	Niger
Comoros	Senegal
Congo	Swaziland
Côte d'Ivoire	Togo

Type II–Fixed-but-adjusting exchange rates, closed capital accounts; selective price controls

Burundi
Cape Verde
Kenya
Mauritius
Rwanda
Seychelles
Zimbabwe

Type III–Dual/multiple exchange rates; closed capital accounts; selective price controls

Gambia	São Tome and Principé
Ghana	Somalia
Guinea	Sudan
Guinea–Bissau	Tanzania
Madagascar	Uganda
Malawi	Zaire
Nigeria	Zambia

Type IV–Dual/multiple exchange rates; closed capital accounts; widespread price controls

Angola[2]
Ethiopia
Mozambique[2]

Note: [1] It should be noted that in no African country do we observe a combination of open capital account with adjusting exchange rates as in Indonesia, which allowed Indonesia stable and low inflation. I am grateful to J.-P. Azam for pointing this out.

[2] It is important to point out that countries such as Angola and Mozambique have extensive price controls, but are unable to enforce them.

For non-traded goods we use a standard mark-up model.[15] The mark-up is applied to unit labour costs (*wc*) and the cost of imported inputs (*mc*).

$$pn = (1 + mu)f(mc, wc) \tag{3}$$

Instead of using a fixed mark-up (mu) as is commonly assumed, we make the change in the mark-up a function of excess demand in the system. The excess demand is not directly measurable. In economies in which financial instruments are not well developed and substitution between money and other financial assets is small, a good proxy for excess demand is excess real money balances, defined as the excess real money supply over real money demand (*EMB*).[16] Using a quadratic cost function we get the following simplified mark-up equation for inflation in non-traded goods:

$$\hat{pn} = b1\,EMB + b2\hat{mc} + b3\,\hat{wc} \tag{4}$$

where $b2 + b3 < 1, b1 > 0$

Changes in import costs are the sum of changes in foreign prices and the exchange rate.

$$\hat{mc} = \hat{pf} + \hat{e} \tag{5}$$

$$EMB = \log(M/p) - \log(Md/p) \tag{6}$$

$$= \hat{p} + \log(M/p - 1) - \log(Md/p) \tag{7}$$

The money demand function is specified as:

$$\log Md/p = do + d1 \log y + d2i + d3\hat{pe} \tag{8}$$

Combining equations (1)–(8) we get the overall inflation equation

$$\hat{p} = f1\,(\hat{pf} + \hat{e}) + f2\,\hat{wc} + f3\log(M/p - 1) + f4i + f5\hat{pe} + f6\hat{pc} + f7\log y \tag{9}$$

This general model adequately identifies the basic sources of inflation in the African context. These can be categorised as: imported inflation ($\hat{pf}$), inflation due to the cost-push effect of devaluation (ê), wage-push inflation ($\hat{wc}$), demand-pull inflation (*EMB*), and inflation arising from the control and subsequent decontrol of prices ($\hat{pc}$). We turn now to the four prototype policy regimes that were identified earlier, to see how this general framework is modified under each of them.

Type I: Pegged exchange rate: open capital account

This is the CFA Zone model, the exchange rate is fixed at one-fiftieth the value of the French franc. The exchange rate is therefore fixed only in relation to the French franc, but obviously varies with respect to other currencies. There are no significant price controls. Each individual country has no effective control on monetary policy. Economic policy in the CFA Zone is managed in the two sub-zones, each with a central bank – the BCEAO and the BEAC. The money supply is not an effective policy variable because of the open capital account.[17]

In this policy framework the underlying or base inflation is equal to the French inflation rate. Temporary deviations around this base inflation rate can come from several factors such as droughts, wage-push, or because of differences in pass-through of imported inflation to non-traded goods prices. But over the long run, inflation converges to the French inflation rate. This is confirmed in the study of inflation in CFA Zone countries by Honohan (1990a). Honohan also looks at the effect of domestic credit policy on money supply in four CFA Zone countries, and confirms that in three of them domestic credit policy has no lasting effect on money supply. This is to be expected given the open capital account in these countries and the statutory freedom of capital movements between France and the CFA Zone members. Membership in the CFA Zone therefore ensures low inflation, as there is very little imported cost-push inflation and checks on monetary policy are provided by membership in the monetary union.

Type II: fixed-but-adjusting exchange rates, closed capital account, selective price controls

This policy regime is typically found in economies such as Kenya and Zimbabwe.[18] The exchange rate is fixed but subject to discrete devaluations, but is temporarily misaligned. However, the misalignment is never large enough for the system to spill over into large parallel markets. The capital account is closed; as a result, government expenditure and credit policies affect the money supply. There are selective price controls, applied to particular commodities to protect the poor and the urban working class, but the controls are not widespread.

In this system, the diagnosis of inflation is complex. It can come from any of the four sources in our general model. There is the cost-push inflation from discrete devaluations. Demand-pull inflation is prevalent when there is excess demand in the system created by excessive credit expansion in the economy, typically to finance unsustainable budget deficits. Note that while we classify the devaluation-generated inflation as cost-push, the reasons for it are often excess demand in the system which spills over into balance of payments problems requiring corrective devaluation. This inflation is temporarily suppressed by import controls, but is then released by the devaluation.

Selective price controls also keep inflation temporarily in check. When price controls are applied directly to private traders they are generally not enforceable. If they are enforced they typically reduce private profit margins and discourage future investment. Price controls are better enforced when applied to products produced or distributed by a state enterprise (e.g., utilities, transport agencies and public food distribution agencies). The cost of these controls are higher deficits of these state agencies, which must then be financed by transfers from the state budget. The financing of these higher budgets creates inflationary pressures. When controlled prices deviate widely from market prices their readjustment creates inflation.

A detailed analysis of inflation in Zimbabwe by Chhibber *et al.* (1989) brings out some of these elements. The inflation equations from the Zimbabwe study are shown in Table 6.4. These confirm that the diagnosis of inflation in Type II economies is complex. Separate equations are also presented for the high-income and low-income consumers. These show that the causes of inflationary pressures in the two cases vary. As one would expect, in the case of high-income consumers the effect of selective price controls[19] is non-existent, whereas in the case of low-income consumers changes in selective price controls matter a great deal.

The pass-through effect of cost-push inflation from a devaluation is small (coefficient of 0.14, equation 1, Table 6.4), considering that the import–GDP ratio is over 25 per cent of GDP. This low pass-through may be unique to Zimbabwe because of its relatively well developed industrial sector and a capital goods sector which allows for greater substitution possibilities when import prices rise. The effect is reduced further when price control variables are introduced (coefficient 0.08, equation 2, Table 6.4). This indicates that the government cushions the effects on the poor of imported inflation for consumer goods also. The study of Killick and Mwega (1989) also shows similar results, with significant effects on Kenyan inflation from monetary growth and import price change and negative effects due to output growth. The pass-through effect of import prices is about 0.20, again somewhat lower than the share of imports in GDP which is around 25 per cent of GDP. Because inflation has been typically low, lagged inflationary expectations are not important. In both the Kenya and Zimbabwe studies, the lagged inflation term was insignificant.

Type III: dual/multiple exchange rates, closed capital account, selective price controls

Ghana, Nigeria, Tanzania and Zambia are typical examples of this policy regime. The exchange rate is fixed but is adjusted through discrete

Table 6.4 *Zimbabwe inflation equations, 1965–88*

Equation		Constant	$\hat{e} + \hat{p}f$	$\hat{w}P$	log (M/P − 1)	log y	i	Cf	Cs	R^{-2}	D.W.
1 Overall inflation	$\hat{p}$	0.8312 (1.55)	0.1402 (2.42)	0.3483 (2.58)	0.0818 (1.94)	−0.1482 (2.21)	0.83 (3.42)			0.79	1.99
2 Overall inflation	$\hat{p}$	0.5150 (1.83)	0.0781 (1.83)	0.2738 (3.01)	0.1213 (4.15)	−0.1819 (3.82)	0.73 (3.86)	−0.3713 (2.38)	−0.1584 (1.78)	0.91	2.48
3 Low-income	$\hat{P}L$	0.4118 (1.09)	0.0929 (1.88)	0.1473 (1.21)	0.1489 (3.76)	−0.1898 (2.82)	0.83 (3.28)	−0.8505 (3.11)	−0.3443 (2.85)	0.89	2.83
4 High-income	$\hat{P}H$	0.8135 (2.15)	0.0693 (1.40)	0.3912 (4.25)	0.0984 (3.25)	−0.1541 (3.39)	0.84 (3.33)	−0.0962 (0.81)	0.0214 (0.23)	0.89	2.19

Note: All equations were estimated with two-stage least squares, using TSP. The instrument used were changed in import prices, lagged nominal interest rates, lagged real money balances, lagged money growth, lagged inflation, lagged log GDP, fiscal deficit as a share of GDP, Cf, Cs, and the lagged difference between real wages and productivity growth.

$\hat{e} + \hat{p}f$ = Change in import prices in Zimbabwe
M/P − 1 = M2 deflated by lagged CPI
y = Real GDP
i = 6-month deposit interest rate
Cf = Difference between food inflation for low-income versus high-income
Cs = Difference between service inflation for low-income versus high-inflation
$\hat{w}P$ = Change in unit labour cost

devaluations. However, in the past severe misalignment of the exchange rate has led to the emergence of a large parallel market for foreign exchange. The capital account is closed, but there is illegal movement of assets through the parallel market. There are selective price controls, but these are not enforceable because of parallel markets in goods and services.

Excess demand spills over into higher inflation as well as into the parallel market, it therefore affects the exchange rate premium. The official exchange rate affects the parallel market exchange rate in two ways. On the supply side, an overvalued exchange rate induces exporters to sell in the parallel market and increases the supply of foreign exchange in that market. On the demand side, a more overvalued official exchange rate increases the demand for imports. As this demand cannot be met in the official market it spills over into the parallel market, where it leads to a higher parallel exchange rate and widening exchange premia. Interest rate policy also matters, as it affects the portfolio choice between holding domestic currency and foreign assets. The only channel to acquire foreign assets is through the parallel market for foreign exchange. Widening interest rate differentials increase the preference for foreign assets, this leads to a higher demand for foreign exchange in the parallel market, and widening exchange premia.

The results for the inflation equations for Ghana are presented in Table 6.5.[20] As the size of the parallel markets grows, the cost of foreign exchange increasingly reflects the parallel exchange rate. In terms of our general model the exchange rate (*e*) becomes a weighted average of the official exchange rate (*eo*) and the parallel exchange rate (*ep*). The inflation equation becomes:

$$\hat{p} = (w\hat{c},\ EMB,\ e\hat{w} + \hat{p}f,\ \hat{p}c) \tag{10}$$
$$e\hat{w} = s.\hat{e}o + (1 - s)e\hat{p}$$

where $0 < s < 1$, is the share of foreign exchange transactions in the official account.

In the extreme, the official exchange rate has little relevance in the market. It simply becomes an accounting price in government transactions with its own agencies, in debt service calculations and in customs duty calculations. Domestic prices increasingly reflect the shadow cost of foreign exchange, which is the parallel market exchange rate; $s = 0$. Grid tests reported in Chhibber and Shafik (1990) confirm, that this was the case in Ghana.

Table 6.5 *Ghana inflation equations, 1965–88*

Equation	Constant	$\hat{e}o + \hat{p}f$	$\hat{e}p + \hat{p}f$	log (M/P – 1)	log y	i	$\hat{p}_{-1}$	X_1^2	D.W.
1	14.3193 (2.07)	0.2909 (2.03)		0.4036 (3.80)	– 1.5513 (2.30)	0.0390 (2.97)	0.3209 (2.17)	22.62	1.80
2	8.8233 (1.97)		0.1639 (4.52)	0.3566 (6.90)	– 1.0049 (2.32)	0.0258 (3.25)	0.5872 (5.22)	69.60	1.39
3	9.1805 (1.80)	0.0691 (0.39)	0.1474 (1.60)	0.3832 (5.31)	– 1.0533 (2.12)	0.0281 (2.86)	0.5596 (3.32)	42.74	1.35

Note: All equations were estimated by two-stage least squares, using PGCIVE. The instrument used were lagged values of inflation, output, money supply, interest rates, import prices at the official parallel market exchange rates, and the parallel market premium.

êo = Change in the official exchange rate (Cedis/$US)
êp = Change in the parallel market exchange rate (Cedis/$US)
p̂f = Change in the foreign price index in $US
M = Money supply (M2)
y = Real GDP
i = Six-month deposit rate
P_{-1} = Lagged inflation

Type IV: dual/multiple exchange rate: closed capital account, widespread price controls

The last prototype we examine is the economy subject to widespread controls. The exchange rate is typically fixed. The capital account is closed. There are demand pressures in the system arising from high fiscal deficits, but these do not translate into inflation because of price controls. There are widespread shortages in the system so that the 'true' inflation is much higher than observed inflation. There may be a parallel market, but this market remains small because the system is able to enforce price controls. There is very little private ownership and most assets, including fixed assets, are owned by the government or state agencies. The private sector is allowed to hold domestic foreign assets. The system leads typically to institutionalised accumulation of financial assets. Real money holdings rise since incomes cannot be translated into consumption, leading to forced savings. This pattern has been observed in a large number of socialist countries.

5 The devaluation–inflation interaction and supply response

The evidence in Section 4 showed that inflation was low only in Type I or Type IV countries, although for very different reasons. These are two extreme cases. In the first case we have an open capital account, a fixed exchange rate and no independent monetary policy. This is the policy regime in the CFA Zone. In the second case we have complete price controls. But it is clear that this is usually unsustainable and the unravelling of price controls generally involves significant economic (and often political) change because of a release of repressed inflation; moreover, 'true' or virtual inflation is much higher than recorded inflation, reflecting unmet demand. What does the evidence from the empirical studies tell us about the link between devaluation and inflation?

First, there is no doubt that there is a direct cost-push effect from exchange rates to domestic prices. This is confirmed by the studies on Ghana and Zimbabwe. The first-round pass-through effect of exchange rate changes on domestic prices is lower when there is a substantial domestic capacity to produce goods which can substitute for imports. It is also lower when the government does not allow the full pass-through with price controls and subsidies. This is the case in Zimbabwe, where both factors lead to a very small first-round effect of exchange rate changes on domestic inflation. In the extreme case where there are complete price controls there is no effect of exchange rate changes on domestic prices.

The concerns reflected in the ECA (1990) report on the effects of devaluation on inflation are examined with a simulation exercise on the Zimbabwe model reported in Table 6.6. The effects of exchange rate changes on domestic inflation are examined under alternate assumptions about export response and the share of monetary financing of the budget. The simulations show that in Zimbabwe under normal circumstances about a third of the devaluation would get wiped out by inflation (Case 1). Note that the full effect of a devaluation on inflation is larger than the first-round effect, because the budget deficit increases with a devaluation. The higher budget deficit leads through monetary financing to higher inflation, how much inflation depends on the share of the budget deficit financed by money creation. In the case of Zimbabwe, the net effect of a 10 per cent increase in the rate of devaluation is an increase in inflation by 3.33 per cent.

Table 6.6 *Devaluation, inflation and the real exchange rate (RER) under alternative assumptions*

Simulation	Cumulative devaluation of 27.5% at the rate of 5% per annum: Inflation	RER depreciation
SI: Real exports to RER s-run elasticity 0.3 l-run elasticity 1.0	9.0	18.5
SII: Real exports to RER s-run elasticity 0.1 l-run elasticity 1.0	10.0	17.5
SIII: Real exports to RER s-run elasticity 0.1 l-run elasticity 1.0 50% of budget deficit financed by borrowing from Central Bank (instead of about 25% in (SI) and SII))	16.0	11.5
SIV: Real exports to RER s-run elasticity 0.1 l-run elasticity 1.0 50% of budget deficit financed by borrowing from Central Bank (instead of about 25% in (SI) and (SII)) Slower revenue adjustment to inflation	27.5	0.0

In the extreme when the supply response of exports is low in the short run (elasticity 0.1), and 50 per cent of the budget is financed by monetary creation (Case IV) the devaluation gets wiped out completely.[21] There is no effect on the real exchange rate. A 10 per cent increase in the rate of devaluation would lead to a 10 per cent increase in the inflation rate. The high share of monetary financing of the budget deficit is quite common in Africa, the domestic bond markets being inadequately developed for the government to borrow in the domestic market. The ECA critique therefore needs to be taken seriously.

On the other hand, in Ghana the devaluation led to an improvement in the fiscal deficit, and as a result a declining rate of inflation. Both theory as well as simulations with the Ghana model reported in Chhibber and Shafik (1990) show that a slower official devaluation would have meant a higher rate of inflation, as well as a more depreciated parallel exchange rate. The fiscal deficit improved, as mentioned earlier, because devaluation resulted in a higher domestic currency equivalent in foreign aid and a reduction in exchange subsidies to importers. The key role of foreign aid in the funding of Ghana's exchange reforms came through its impact in improving the government's fiscal position.

The Ghana case also shows that once the misalignment of the exchange rate had gone very far, and there was a very wide differential between the official and parallel exchange rate, there was very little choice but to devalue. Consumer and producer prices already reflected the parallel market exchange rate, the official devaluation was just the formalisation of the status quo. This was confirmed by careful econometric tests in the Ghana study. The devaluation of the official exchange rate therefore had no direct cost-push effect. This is true also of a large number of countries in the Type III category in Africa where the extent of misalignment is so large that reforms without devaluation are unlikely to be successful. Large parallel markets are prevalent. In these cases managed official devaluation leads to lower inflation if – and only if – the budget improves with the official devaluation.

One important conclusion that can be drawn from these studies is that there is no unique relationship between devaluation and inflation. In the first round there is always a positive cost-push effect of a devaluation on inflation. This is confirmed by almost all studies of inflation in Africa, the exceptions are countries with complete price controls, but here we see a build-up of repressed inflation. But the subsequent and overall effect of devaluation on inflation depends on the impact of the devaluation on the budget, the adequacy of external funding of the programme and the export response. Carefully managed exchange reforms therefore remain the only vehicle to correct exchange rate misalignment. The ECA concern that the impact of nominal devaluation on real devaluation is small is a possibility, only if supporting fiscal policies are not in place.

NOTES

The paper does not represent the views of the World Bank. Thanks to Jean-Paul Azam and Ian Goldin for their comments on earlier versions of this paper.

1 For evidence see Oyejide (1990) and de Rosa and Greene (1991).

2 The most recent criticism has come from the ECA (Economic Commission for Africa). The issue of the external versus internal causes of Africa's poor export and growth performance is discussed analytically as well as empirically in Mkandawire (1989) and Ndulu (1990).

3 See, for example, Herbst (1990), Hansen (1987), and Callaghy (1989).

4 The IMF *World Economic Outlook* for 1990 provides evidence on the real effective exchange rate by region. This evidence shows that the extent of real exchange rate depreciation has been the highest for the Africa region relative to Latin America, the Middle East and Asia. The real effective exchange rate index in 1990 had declined to 54 (1980 = 100). The critique against exchange rate reforms has come from different sources. See for example ECA (1990) and Faini and de Melo (1990).

5 The link between exchange rate overvaluation and decline in export shares is very evident in the case of SSA and has been documented in WDR (1986). It should be stated that market shares could be changing for reasons other than exchange rate changes. The author is grateful to Ian Goldin for making this point.

6 There is straightforward link between real farm prices and the real exchange rate. The change in the real farm price is equal to the change in the nominal protection ratio plus the change in the external terms of trade and the change in the real exchange rate (PPP).

7 These results are summarized in Helleiner (1985) and Oyejide (1990).

8 For these estimates see Chhibber *et al.* (1989). The studies presented in that survey show that the provision of public infrastructure is also an important constraint on aggregate supply response. There are no careful econometric studies in the African context which have tested this, although there is anecdotal evidence suggesting that infrastructure constraints have hindered the development of markets. Mkandawire (1989) discusses the issue of infrastructural bottlenecks to agricultural growth.

9 This issue has been addressed in a broader context by Lewis (1980), Cline (1982), and Balassa (1988).

10 Based on a model of production, consumption and world trade of primary commodities in Koester, Schaefer and Valdes (1989).

11 See for example, Guillaumont and Guillaumont (1989).

12 One exception is Uganda, where a combination of civil war, drought and mismanagement has led to triple-digit inflation since 1985. Triple-digit inflation has also occasionally been observed in Ghana, Sierra Leone and Zaire. The inflation rates used in this study refer to recorded CPI inflation. In some cases, unrecorded inflation has been much higher. We will discuss this issue in later sections of the paper.

13 For a survey of issues dealing with initial inflation, see Kiguel and Liviatian (1988), Blejer and Cheasty (1988). Countries with inflation over 20 per cent in the 1980s are, for example, Ghana, Sudan, Sierra Leone, Somalia, Tanzania, Uganda, Zaire and Zambia. The recorded inflation often greatly underestimates true inflation in the system. This is especially true of countries with extensive price controls.

14 This should strictly also include changes in the trade regime. For the sake of simplification we ignore those generally discrete changes.

15 Bruno (1978) and Gordon (1975). 'Non-traded goods' refer both to goods that it is not feasible to trade, such as land, and goods that are *de facto* non-tradables, such as those subject to non-tariff barriers.

16 We follow Khan (1980), who argues that in developing countries the substitution between money and goods is far more important than that between money and other financial assets.

17 For a more detailed description of the monetary arguments in the CFA Zone, see Bhatia (1985) and Honohan (1990b).

18 For a good description and analysis of Kenya's monetary and exchange rate policy, see Killick and Mwega (1989). For Zimbabwe, see Chhibber *et al.* (1989).

19 In the case of Zimbabwe, we specify *Cf* and *Cs* (defined in Table 6.4) as proxies for $\hat{p}c$.

20 The model in Chhibber and Shafik (1990) endogenises the exchange rate premium between the parallel and the official exchange rate.

21 It should be recognised that the effect of changing the export elasticity in this particular case has a very small effect on the impact of devaluation on inflation.

REFERENCES

Balassa, B. (1988) 'The Adding Up Problem', *PRE Working Paper*, **30**, Washington, D.C.: World Bank.

(1989) 'Incentive Problems in Sub-Saharan Africa', *New Directions in the World Economy, Essay 8*, London: Macmillan.

Berthélemy, J. C. and C. Morrisson (1989) 'Agricultural Development in Africa and the Supply of Manufactured Goods', *OECD Development Centre Studies*, Paris: OECD.

Bhatia, R. J. (1985) 'The Western African Monetary Union: An Analytical Review', *IMF Occasional Paper*, **35**, Washington, D.C.: IMF.

Blejer, Mario and A. Cheasty (1988) 'High Inflation and Heterodox Stabilization and Fiscal Policy', *World Development*, **16(8)**: 867–81.

Bond, M. E. (1983) 'Agricultural Responses to Prices in Sub-Saharan African Countries', *IMF Staff Paper*, **30(4)**, December: 703–26.

Bruno, Michel (1978) 'Exchange Rates, Import Costs and Wage–Price Dynamics', *Journal of Political Economy*, **86**, June: 379–404.

Callaghy, T. M. (1989) 'Towards State Capability and Embedded Liberalism in the Third World: Lessons for Adjustment', in J. M. Nelson (ed.), *Fragile Coalitions: The Politics of Economic Adjustment*, New Brunswick and Oxford: Oxford University.

Chhibber, A. (1988) 'The Aggregate Supply Response in Agriculture: A Survey', in S. Commander (ed.), *Structural Adjustment in Agriculture: Theory and Practice in Africa and Latin America*, London: James Curry.

Chhibber, A. and N. Shafik (1990) 'Exchange Reform, Parallel Markets and Inflation in Africa: The Case of Ghana', *PRE Working Paper*, **427**, Washington, D.C.: World Bank.

Chhibber *et al.* (1989) 'Inflation, Price Controls, and Fiscal Adjustment in Zimbabwe, *PRE Working Paper*, **192**, Washington, D.C.: World Bank.

Cline, W. R. (1982) 'Can the East Asia Model of Development be Generalised?', *World Development*, **10(2)**: 81–90.

Darrat, A. F. (1986) 'Money, Inflation, and Causality in the North African Countries: An Empirical Investigation', *Journal of Macroeconomics*, **8**: 87–103.

De Rosa, D. and J. Greene (1991) 'Will Contemporaneous Devaluations Hurt Exports from Sub-Saharan Africa?', *Finance and Development*, March.

Devarajan, S. and J. de Melo (1990) 'Membership in the CFA Zone: Odyssean Journey or Trojan Horse?', *PPR Working Paper*, **482**, Washington, D.C.: World Bank.

Dornbusch, R. *et al.* (1983) 'The Black Market for Dollars in Brazil', *Quarterly Journal of Economics*, February: 25–40.

ECA (1990) *African Alternative Framework to Structural Adjustment Programmes for Socio-Economic Recovery and Transformation*, Economic Commssion for Africa, Addis Ababa: United Nations.

Faini, R. and J. de Melo (1990) 'Adjustment, Investment and the Real Exchange Rate in Developing Countries', *Economic Policy*, **11**: 492–519.

Gordon, R. (1975) 'Alternative Responses of Policy to External Supply Shocks', *Brookings Papers on Economic Activity*, **1**: 184:204.

Greene, Joshua (1989) 'Inflation in African Countries: General Issues and Effect on the Financial Sector', *IMF Research Paper*, Washington, D.C.: IMF.

Guillaumont, P. and S. Guillaumont (1989) 'The Social Consequences of Adjustment in Africa as a Function of the Exchange Rate Policy', paper presented to the World Bank Conference on African Economic Issues, June.

Hansen, E. (1987) 'The State and Popular Struggles in Ghana, 1982–1986', in P. A. Nyong'o (ed.), *Popular Struggles for Democracy in Africa*, New York: UN University.

Helleiner, G. K. (1985) 'Smallholder Decision Making: Tropical African Experience', in L. G. Reynolds (ed.), *Agriculture in Development Theory*, New Haven: Yale University Press.

Herbst, J. (1990) 'Exchange Reforms in Ghana: Strategy and Tactics', Princeton: Princeton University (mimeo).

Honohan, Patrick (1990a) 'Price and Monetary Convergence in Currency Unions: The Franc and Rand Zones', *PRE Working Paper*, **WPS 390**, Washington, D.C.: World Bank.

Honohan, Patrick (1990b) 'Monetary Cooperation in the CFA Zone', *PRE Working Paper*, **WPS 389**, Washington, D.C.: World Bank.

Horton, Susan and J. McClaren (1989) 'Supply Constraints in the Tanzanian Economy: Simulation Results from a Macroeconomic Model', *Journal of Political Modelling*, **4**.

Khan, M. S. (1980) 'Monetary Shocks and the Dynamics of Inflation', *IMF Staff Papers*, **27(2)**.

Kiguel, Miguel and N. Liviatian (1988) 'Inflationary Rigidities and Orthodox

Stabilization Policies: Lessons from Latin America', *World Bank Economic Review*, September.
Killick, Anthony and Francis Mwega (1989) 'Monetary Policy in Kenya', Nairobi (mimeo).
Koester, U., H. Schaefer and A. Valdes (1989) 'External Demand Constraints for Agricultural Exports: An Impediment to Structural Adjustment Policies in Sub-Saharan African Countries?', *Food Policy*, **14**, August.
Lewis, W. A. (1980) 'The Slowing Down of the Engine of Growth', The Nobel Lecture, *American Economic Review*, **70(4)**: 555–64.
London, A. (1989) 'Money, Inflation and Adjustment Policy in Africa: Some Further Evidence', *African Development Review*, **1**: 87–111.
Macedo, J. B. de (1984) 'Collective Pegging to a Single Currency: The West African Monetary Union', in S. Edwards and L. Ahmed (eds), *Economic Adjustment and Exchange Rates in Developing Countries*, Chicago: Chicago University Press.
Mkandawire, T. (1989) 'Structural Adjustment and Agrarian Crises in Africa: a Research Agenda', *CODESRIA Working Paper*, **2/89**, Dakar, Senegal.
Ndulu, B. (1990) 'Growth and Adjustment in Sub-Saharan Africa', in A. Chhibber and S. Fischer (eds), *Analytics of Economic Reform, in Sub-Saharan Africa*, Washington, D.C.: World Bank.
Oyejide, T. A. (1990) 'Supply Response in the Context of Structural Adjustment in Sub-Saharan Africa', Africa Economics Research Consortium, *Special Paper*, **1**.
Panagariya, A. and M. Schiff (1991) 'Commodity Exports and Real Incomes in Africa: A Preliminary Analysis', in A. Chhibber and S. Fischer (eds), *Analytics of Economic Reform in Sub-Saharan Africa*, Washington, D.C.: World Bank.
Rocha, R. (1989) 'The Black Market Premium in Algeria', Washington, D.C.: World Bank (mimeo).
Rwegasira, D. (1979) 'Inflation and Economic Development: Some Lessons from the Tanzanian Experience', in K. S. Kim *et al.* (eds), *Papers on the Political Economy of Tanzania*, Nairobi: Heinemann: 28–49.
WDR (1986) *World Development Report 1986*, Washington, D.C.: World Bank.

Discussion

JEAN-PAUL AZAM

1 Introduction

Chapter 6 makes some valuable contributions to the debate on devaluation and exchange reform in sub-Saharan Africa, focusing on their impact on agriculture. Section 2 is devoted to the supply response of agriculture to devaluation, assuming that nominal devaluation leads to real devaluation. Sections 3–5, where most new insights are found, focuses on the inflationary impact of devaluation. The main conclusion is that the devaluation depends on the control regime prevailing in the economy, and on the accompanying policy package.

2 Devaluation and supply response

Chhibber criticises first the arguments dismissing devaluation on the ground that it prompts poor supply response, as the available evidence shows large response of exports to real devaluation. But a perverse response of imports is possible, perhaps due to the aid boom which often follows an exchange reform. Second, econometric evidence shows that the elasticity of aggregate agricultural response is positive, so that the response of export crops is not obtained at the expense of subsistence crops. Lastly, the evidence cited shows that, when many primary commodities' exporters devalue simultaneously, boosting their joint exports, the world price of this commodity may fall. But the elasticities are such that export revenues increase in spite of this. Hence, the 'adding up' problem does not arise.

3 Devaluation and inflation

Fears have been raised that the numerous devaluations of the 1980s might pull Africa into a 'Latin American' type of inflationary environment. The questions arise whether inflation can offset nominal devaluation so that no real devaluation occurs, and if the size of the nominal devaluation needed to effect a real devaluation, and the ensuing inflation, is affordable. This is important because in Africa there are few nominal rigidities, needed to make devaluation effective in most textbook models, except in repressed economies with enforced price controls.

Chhibber tackles this issue using (1) a simple encompassing model for analysing the different cases, and (2) a typology of four types of economies, differing by the extent of state control on the markets for foreign exchange (fixed exchange rate, control of capital flows) and for goods (price controls, parallel markets). In Africa, there is no economy with fixed but adjusting exchange rate, open capital account, and no price control. The combination exists in a large LDC economy with a reputation of wise macroeconomic management like Indonesia. In the cases presented here, exchange rate adjustability comes with capital controls. Only the CFA Zone countries (and the Rand Zone ones) afford an open capital account, because of exchange rate credibility, pooled foreign reserves, and automatic balance of payments support by France.

Chhibber draws attention to the different inflationary impact of devaluation, with different transmission channels, in the three remaining groups of countries. The case of the relatively open economies (Kenya, Zimbabwe, etc.) is complex, and the pass-through elasticity of devaluation into inflation seems rather weak. In fact, the control regime prevailing in Kenya is far from liberal (Bevan, Collier and Gunning, 1990). The remaining two cases are particularly interesting.

4 The parallel market economies

The analysis of this economy type is mostly based on Ghana, which Chhibber has studied elsewhere (Chhibber and Shafik, 1990). Like Azam and Besley (1989a) he observes that the price level reflects the parallel market exchange rate, and not the official one. He then concludes that an official devaluation has a limited impact on the price level, assuming that the parallel market premium buffers this shock. But it can be transmitted to the parallel market rate, and hence the price level, by two channels: (1) the devaluation may prompt a capital outflow by fuelling expectations of further depreciation; (2) it will divert the flow of exports from the parallel segment to the official one, and the flow of imports in the opposite direction.

Depreciation on the parallel market will follow either of these moves, unless structural changes are adopted to reduce the premium, like unification of the foreign exchange market, liberalisation of imports, aid-induced increased availability of foreign exchange, etc. Such changes dampen the inflationary influence of an official devaluation. In the case of Ghana, the inflationary impact of the main devaluation was offset by two events: (1) the active population increased by about 20 per cent when 1.3 million migrants returned, expelled from Nigeria. For property rights reasons, they went into food production, rather than cocoa, with a strong impact on food supply and, hence, a negative impact on prices; (2) imports of consumer goods increased massively by the end of 1984, with the IMF/World Bank, supported Economic Recovery Programme (Azam and Besley, 1989b).

Such events did not occur in Madagascar, where three massive devaluations totalling 75 per cent were needed between 1982 and 1985 to create any impact at all on the real exchange rate. Further massive devaluations were needed in 1987; the resulting inflation substantially destroyed the purchasing power of monetary assets, eventually depressing aggregate demand, and thus bringing about real devaluation in this economy without much nominal anchor. The social consequences were dismal, particularly for the groups whose survival depended on precautionary cash balances.

5 The repressed economies

Similarly, devaluation in the repressed economies, where price controls are enforced, aims at the significant destruction of real money balances. Parallel markets, fiercely combated by the police, are not developed enough there for 'venting excess demand' (Azam and Besley, 1991). Widespread shortages lead to the accumulation of massive cash balances, and deter cash-crop production. Peasants do not want to earn money any more, when they own cash balances worth more than what they can spend. Thus, peasants return to subsistence, as shown in the case of Mozambique by Azam and Faucher (1988).

Then, one may face an implosive spiral where import compression leads to shortage, which results in a fall in cash-crop production and exports, and hence in further import compression as the government runs short of foreign currency. Devaluation is then required to stop the implosion, allowing the massive price increases for the products and the consumer goods which are needed for wiping out the monetary overhang (Azam and Faucher, 1988). This is what the IMF and the World Bank did in Mozambique, with the help of the French CCCE who funded imports of consumer goods, to relieve the shortages.

6 Conclusion

Chhibber has made an important contribution by showing the complexity of the relationship between devaluation, inflation, and supply response. His typology helps to dismiss the simple idea that a unique model could be applied everywhere on these issues. I hope it will stimulate further studies capturing the specificity of the different control regimes existing in Africa.

REFERENCES

Azam, J.-P. and T. J. Besley (1989a) 'General Equilibrium With Parallel Markets for Goods and Foreign Exchange', *World Development*, **17**: 1921–30.

(1989b) 'The Case of Ghana', in J.-P. Azam, T. J. Besley, J. Maton, D. Bevan, P. Collier and P. Horsnell, *The Supply of Manufactured Goods and Agricultural Development (Ghana, Rwanda, Tanzania)*, *Development Centre Papers*, Paris: OECD.

(1991) 'Peasant Supply Response Under Rationing: the Role of the Food Sector', *European Journal of Political Economy*, forthcoming.

Azam, J.-P. and J. J. Faucher (1988) 'The Case of Mozambique', in J. C. Berthélemy, J.-P. Azam and J. J. Faucher, *The Supply of Manufactured Goods and*

Agricultural Development (Madagascar, Mozambique), *Development Centre Papers*, Paris: OECD.

Bevan, D., P. Collier and J. W. Gunning (1990) *Controlled Open Economies*, Oxford: Clarendon Press.

Chhibber, A. and N. Shafik (1990) 'Exchange Reform, Parallel Markets and Inflation in Africa: The Case of Ghana', *PRE Working Paper*, **427**, Washington, D.C.: World Bank.

7 Taxes versus quotas: the case of cocoa exports

ARVIND PANAGARIYA and MAURICE SCHIFF

1 Introduction

This paper is part of an ongoing research effort aimed at analysing the interactions among commodity exports, real incomes and trade policies. We are particularly interested in evaluating the concern that efficiency or policy-induced changes in the supply of exports of primary commodities may lead to such a large decline in the prices of the latter that export revenues and incomes of the exporting countries actually decline.[1] The commodities in question include cocoa, coffee, and tea.

The possibility of income and revenue loss arises principally because the world demand for primary commodities is relatively inelastic. The natural instrument the exporting countries can employ to counteract this problem is trade policy. In doing so, one must, however, recognize that since the exporting countries are neither *small* nor *monopolies* in the world markets, their policies are interdependent. Because the conventional trade models rely on one of these two extremes, they fail to capture the interdependence of policies central to the problem under consideration.

In our recent work, we have analysed in detail the implications of interdependence among countries when the policy instrument is an export tax. In Panagariya and Schiff (1991a), we derive Nash optimum taxes in a 10-country model of the world cocoa market. In our simulations, we find that compared to the initial equilibrium, tax competition implicit in Nash behaviour leads to a loss in real income for 8 out of 9 exporting countries.[2] In Panagariya and Schiff (1991b), we compare income and revenue-maximizing Nash taxes. A key result in this paper is that under plausible circumstances, revenue-maximizing Nash taxes can yield higher levels of income than income-maximizing Nash taxes. For example, in the symmetric case, income-maximizing Nash taxes are lower than income-maximizing cooperative taxes and generate a lower level of income than them. Because revenue-maximizing Nash taxes are larger than income-maximizing Nash taxes, they are likely to be closer to the income-maximizing cooperative taxes.

In the present paper, we continue this line of research and focus on the implications of quantitative restrictions. We derive the equilibrium which will result if exporting countries set their export quotas optimally, taking the quantities of exports of other countries as given. We compare this equilibrium with the one which obtains when countries use export taxes as the policy instrument. We also perform a number of simulations, assuming that countries choose their export quotas optimally in the Nash–Cournot fashion.

We may note at the outset that the equivalence between export quotas and export taxes discussed in the standard trade theory literature (e.g., Bhagwati, 1969) will break down in the present context. We know from the recent literature on oligopoly and trade (e.g., Eaton and Grossman, 1986) that the equilibria based on price and quantity games exhibit very different properties. The essential point in the present context is that, starting at a given initial quantity of the rival's exports, the excess demand curve facing a country is more elastic when the rival imposes an export tax rather than an export quota.[3]

In Section 2, we present a simple demand and supply model and, borrowing from the literature on oligopoly and trade, draw a contrast between equilibria under Nash–Bertrand and Nash–Cournot behaviour. In the former case, countries choose their export taxes optimally, taking the other countries' tax rates as given. In the latter case, they choose export quotas optimally. We also compare the effects of a movement to Stackelberg behaviour by one or more countries under the tax and quota games. Finally, we employ the model to provide an interpretation of the fallacy of composition in the present case.

In Section 3, we apply the model to the world cocoa market and derive numerically the optimal taxes and quotas under various behavioural assumptions; we find that the fallacy of composition takes a bigger bite under the Bertrand than under the Cournot game. Implicit tax rates under the quota game are substantially higher than under the tax game. The associated profits are also higher under the quota game. Our simulations for a productivity increase show that it is possible for growth to result in an overall decline in income, even if countries choose their taxes or quotas optimally.

In Section 4, we discuss some important limitations of our paper, and suggest directions for future research. A summary and conclusions are provided in Section 5.

2 The model

We employ a simple demand–supply model. All functions are assumed to have a linear form. The world demand is represented by

$$Q = A - BP \qquad A, B > 0 \tag{1}$$

where P is the price paid by buyers in the world market. Quantity supplied by country i is written

$$q_1 = a_i + b_i p_i \qquad i = 1, 2, \ldots \tag{2}$$

where p_i is the price received by sellers. Note that we denote the variables and parameters on the supply side by lower case letters. The difference between P and p_i is accounted for by a quota premium. We denote the quota premium in country i as a proportion of the world price by e_i. Thus,

$$p_i = (1 - e_i)P \qquad i = 1, 2, \ldots n \tag{3}$$

We assume that the government captures the quota premium through either a competitive auction of export licences, an explicit tax at rate e_i, or by marketing the product itself.

The excess demand facing country j may be written

$$\begin{aligned} Q_j &= Q - \sum_{i \neq j} q_i \qquad i, j = 1, 2, \ldots n \\ &= \left(A - \sum_{i \neq j} q_i\right) - BP \\ &\equiv A_j - BP \end{aligned} \tag{4}$$

Note that A_j in the last equality is a function of the sum of the total quantity supplied by country j's rivals and hence, in the absence of quotas, of the world price.

We assume that exporters do not consume the good and importers do not produce it. This assumption is valid for cocoa. Each country behaves like a Cournot oligopolist. That is to say, each country maximises its profits taking the exports of the other countries as given. Equation (4) therefore represents the perceived demand curve of country j. The corresponding marginal revenue may be written

$$MR_j = \tfrac{1}{B}(A_j - 2Q_j) \qquad j = 1, 2, \ldots n \tag{5}$$

The marginal cost of production is given by equation (2). Thus,

$$MC_j = p_j = \frac{1}{b_j}(q_j - a_j) \qquad j = 1, 2, \ldots n \tag{6}$$

At a profit-maximising equilibrium, we have $MR_j = MC_j$ and $Q_j = q_j$. The latter equality simply says that the quantity demanded must equal quantity supplied for country j. Making use of these equalities, equations (5) and (6) lead to

$$q_j = \frac{b_j A_j + a_j B}{2b_j + B} \qquad j = 1, \ldots n \qquad (7)$$

Embedded in equation (7) are n linear equations in $q_1, \ldots q_n$. We can solve these equations for the n equilibrium quantities. Once we have these quantities, equations (1)–(3) can be used to obtain P, p_i and e_i. This is the approach taken in the simulations presented in Section 3.

The model outlined above is a standard Nash–Cournot model. We do not therefore, need to provide an elaborate discussion of its properties. However, it is useful to state briefly some of the properties relevant to the specific problem in which we are interested. For this purpose, we concentrate on the duopoly case.

From equation (7), it is clear that the reaction functions will be linear in the (q_1, q_2) space in the duopoly case. In the symmetric case, we have $a_1 = a_2 \equiv a$ and $b_1 = b_2 \equiv b$ and the equilibrium is characterised by $q_1 = q_2$. In Figure 7.1 point C, lying on the 45° line (not shown) through the origin, represents the Cournot equilibrium.

The isoprofit curves for country 1 will be strictly concave to the horizontal axis with a slope equal to 0 at the point where they intersect the reaction curve, R_1R_1 (see Eaton and Grossman, 1986). Intuitively, for a given value of q_2, the corresponding point on R_1R_1 gives the country's best response. Holding q_2 fixed, if the country moves away in either direction from this best-response output, its profits decline. In order to restore profits to the original level, we must reduce q_2 as this will lead to a higher world price. Hence, the isoprofit curves must be flat at the point of intersection with R_1R_1.

As we move down R_1R_1, profits of country 1 rise. This movement is associated with lower values of q_2 and hence increased market power for country 1. Indeed, at $q_2 = 0$, country 1 becomes the monopolist in the market. Two isoprofit curves, labelled $\pi_1^C \pi_1^C$ and $\pi_1^S \pi_1^S$, are shown in Figure 7.1.

Country 2's isoprofit curves (not shown in Figure 7.1) are strictly concave to the vertical axis and have a slope equal to infinity at the points of intersection with R_2R_2. Country 2's profits rise as we move up R_2R_2. At point M_2 where $q_1 = 0$, country 2 becomes the monopolist in the world market.

As noted earlier, Cournot equilibrium is given by point C in Figure 7.1. We know from oligopoly literature that one of the two countries could improve its profits position by behaving as a Stackelberg leader. If

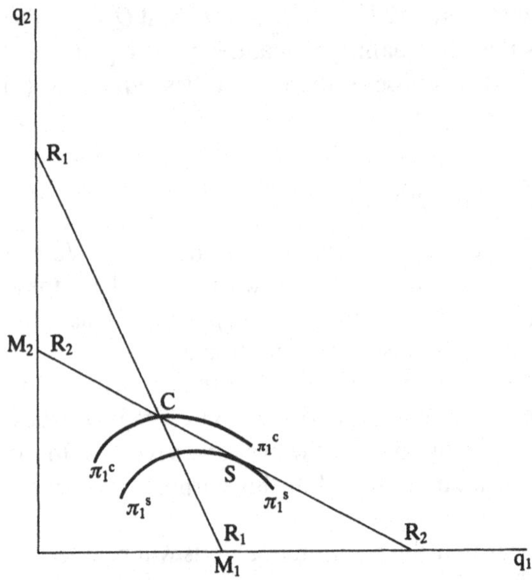

Figure 7.1 Cournot and Stackelberg equilibria

country 1 is to behave as the leader, it will thus export at point *S*. As expected, its profits will be higher, and the follower's profits lower, at *S* than at *C*.

This result is robust to at least two modifications. First, if the countries are of a different size, Stackelberg equilibrium continues to be superior for the leader and inferior for the follower. For example, an increase in a_1 shifts R_1R_1 to the right in a parallel fashion, but does not change the qualitative relationship between Cournot and Stackelberg equilibria.

Second, addition of more countries leaves the above result unchanged. If there are *n* countries and one of them acts as a Stackelberg leader, profits and output of that country are thus higher, and those of the other countries, lower, than at Cournot equilibrium. Essentially, as a Cournot player, each country ignores the fact that an expansion of output by it causes the competitors to contract their output. This pessimistic view leads the country to produce too little relative to Stackelberg equilibrium where it does take into account the rivals' response.

An interesting exception to the above result may arise when we allow a *group* of countries to act as Stackelberg leaders. In the linear, symmetric case, if there are 3 players in all and 2 of them jointly become leaders, they thus produce less than when they act independently as Cournot players. In this case, Stackelberg equilibrium yields a higher profit than Cournot equilibrium, even for the follower. This result can be explained in two steps. In the first, suppose the two countries act jointly as a single Nash player. Their combined output in this case will be less than when they act independently. In the second step, we let the two countries act jointly as Stackelberg leader. This leads to an expansion of output. But this expansion is less than the contraction in the first step. The net effect of turning the two countries from independent Nash players to joint Stackelberg leader is thus a contraction of output. This allows the third country to expand its output and profits.[4]

These results contrast sharply with the results obtained from Bertrand competition. As discussed in Panagariya and Schiff (1991b) in detail, if countries base their decisions taking each other's export taxes as given, reaction functions in the tax rates space are positively sloped. Contrary to the situation depicted in Figure 7.1, an increased restriction on exports via a higher export tax by the rival thus causes a country to raise its own export tax. In this setting, it is easy to show that Stackelberg equilibrium is associated with a greater restriction on exports by both the leader and the follower, even in a two-player game. More interestingly, in the symmetric case, at a Stackelberg equilibrium, profits of the follower are larger than those of the leader! This is because starting from Nash equilibrium, the follower increases his tax by less, and hence has a larger market share than the leader. The results cannot be obtained when countries choose export quotas strategically.

Another subtle but interesting difference between the two policy instruments is that with taxes, Stackelberg equilibrium is more restrictive than Nash equilibrium, while with quotas the opposite is true. With taxes, the world price at Stackelberg equilibrium is thus higher than at Nash equilibrium. But with quotas, the world price is lower at Stackelberg equilibrium than at Nash equilibrium. This is because in Figure 7.1, the increase in the leader's output at S relative to C is larger than the reduction in the output of the follower. Hence, joint profits are lower under Stackelberg than under Nash when countries choose quotas strategically, with losses to the follower larger than the gains to the leader.

Before we proceed to the simulation results of the cocoa market, we find it useful to provide an interpretation of the fallacy of composition with the help of Figure 7.2, which is a modification of Figure 7.1. We know that the joint profits of the two countries will be maximized somewhere on the segment OC of the 45° line. Essentially, the output of each country must be less at the joint profit-maximizing equilibrium than at Cournot equilibrium, C. Let J represent the point of joint profit-maximisation. Suppose now that the current exports of the two countries happen to be at point A. From A, each country can increase its profits by expanding

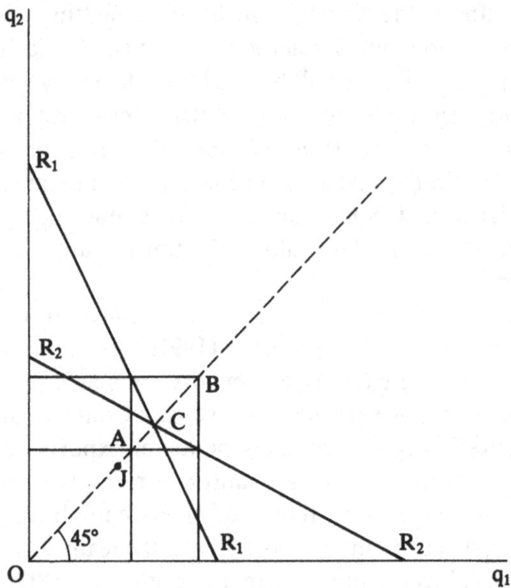

Figure 7.2 Independent actions and the fallacy of composition

exports towards its reaction function provided the other country keeps its exports at the level indicated by *A*. However, if *both* countries expand their exports, they will find themselves at point *B* and make *less* profits than at *A*. This is the essence of the fallacy of composition.

A final related point to note is that in the example shown in Figure 7.2, if the countries are initially at *B* and move simultaneously, assuming that the other country will maintain its current output, both countries will *reduce* their exports and *increase* their profits. To the extent that an equilibrium is reached only at *C* and not *J*, however, an element of the fallacy of composition remains. That is to say that even at the Nash-Cournot equilibrium countries wind up exporting too much relative to their joint profit-maximisation levels.

3 Simulation results

We note at the outset that there are important empirical and theoretical limitations of the simulations reported below. Although we will discuss these limitations in detail in Section 4, we wish to caution at the outset that the results reported below should be considered tentative.

Table 7.1 provides the information on the initial equilibrium. The columns (1)–(5) with numbers are self-explanatory.[5] The columns (6) and

Table 7.1 *Basic data on the initial equilibrium*

	Output (000 MT) (1)	Output share (%) (2)	Export tax[a] (%) (3)	Domestic price ($US/MT) (4)	Elasticity[b] (5)	Slope[c] (6)	Intercept (000 MT) (7)
Côte d'Ivoire	585	35.8	25.1	1550	1.15	0.434	− 87.7
Ghana	219	13.4	70.0	621	0.71	0.250	63.5
Cameroon	118	7.2	40.0	1242	1.81	0.172	− 95.6
Nigeria	110	6.7	50.0	1035	0.45	0.048	60.5
Malaysia	125	7.7	0.0	2070	3.00	0.181	− 250.0
Indonesia	32	2.0	0.0	2070	3.00	0.046	− 64.0
Oceania	30	1.8	0.0	2070	3.00	0.043	− 60.0
Ecuador	85	5.2	0.0	2070	0.28	0.011	61.2
Brazil	329	20.1	20.0	1656	0.58	0.115	138.2

[a] The non-zero export tax rates are from Imran and Duncan (1988) Table 7, p. 21 and refer to 1982 and 1983 (for Brazil).

[b] The long-run elasticities for Brazil, Côte d'Ivoire and Malaysia were obtained from Akiyama and Bowers (1984) p. 25. They apply to 10-year periods, using the highest production levels to obtain those values. We assume that the elasticities of Indonesia and Oceania are equal to that of Malaysia. The other elasticities are from Behrman (1968).

[c] The slope is the change in metric tons for a 1 $US change in the domestic producer price.

(7) are derived from the output, price and elasticity. The elasticities were estimated by their authors assuming constant elasticity functions. We linearised these functions around the price and quantity shown in Table 7.1 and applied the elasticity estimates to obtain the slope and intercept shown in columns (6) and (7). The elasticity of demand in the world market used in the simulations is 0.4. Given the price and quantity in 1986, this yields an intercept of 12286.3 metric tons and a slope of − 315.6 metric tons per US dollar.

The elasticities in Table 7.1 are diverse, and require some explanation. For traditional, long-established producers such as Brazil, Côte d'Ivoire, Ghana and Nigeria elasticities are low, while for more recent entrants such as Malaysia and Indonesia they are high. This may be because traditional producers have only limited possibilities with respect to substitution into and out of other crops. In addition, for output expansion, these countries do not have suitable land available at the margin. By contrast, Malaysia and Indonesia have been able to take advantage of vast amounts of suitable virgin land. We hope to shed more light on this issue in our future work, where we will attempt a careful estimation of supply elasticities using flexible functional forms.

Using the information in Table 7.1, we can calculate what we call the 'Actual' equilibrium. By virtue of the calibration procedure, this equilibrium is the same as that in Table 7.1. In Table 7.2, we show the profits associated with this equilibrium in column 4. These profits include the producers' surplus and tax revenues. Table 7.2 also provides the output and profits if all restrictions on exports are removed (i.e., if the marginal cost is equated to the world price). Not surprisingly, a total removal of export restrictions lowers the world price (from $2070 to $1562 per metric ton) and benefits the importers of cocoa. In principle, countries which tax exports too heavily can experience an improvement in welfare by a movement to free trade, but this does not happen in our simulations. Only Ghana, which taxed exports in 1982 at the rate of 70 per cent of the *world* price, experiences more or less no change in profits. All other countries experience significant losses from a movement to the free trade equilibrium.

In Tables 7.3–7.5, we present several simulations. These include:

1. Each country takes the export taxes of its competitors as given and chooses its own tax rate optimally. This is referred to as Nash (T) game in Tables 7.3–7.5, and was analysed in detail in Panagariya and Schiff (1991a).
2. Each country takes the export quantities of the competitors as given, and chooses its own export optimally. This is referred to as Nash (Q) game in Tables 7.3–7.5.

Table 7.2 *Initial results with actual taxes and free trade. World price ($US/MT): actual 2070, free trade 1562*

	Tax rates (%)	Output (000MT)		Profit[1] (million $US)	
Country	actual (1)	actual (2)	free trade (3)	actual (4)	free trade (5)
Côte d'Ivoire	25.1	585	590	698	401
Ghana	70.0	219	454	405	404
Cameroon	40.0	118	171	138	86
Nigeria	50.0	110	134	202	152
Africa		1032	1349	1443	1043
Malaysia	0.0	125	33	43	3
Indonesia	0.0	32	8	11	0.7
Oceania	0.0	30	7	11	0.6
Ecuador	0.0	85	78	151	109
Brazil	20.0	329	318	523	356
World		1633	1793	2182	1512.3

Note: [1] Profit is defined to include producers' surplus and government revenue. Actual profits are derived by assuming that the calibrated demand and supply curves are true demand and supply curves. These profits will be different in general from actual observed profits (inclusive of tax revenues).

3. The largest exporter, Côte d'Ivoire, is Stackelberg leader and the other countries are followers. The countries choose export quantities and play what we call Stackelberg (Q) game in Tables 7.3–7.5.
4. Ghana's supply curve shifts to the right by 100,000 metric tons. We simulate the effects of this change both under initial quotas and Nash tax and quantity games.
5. Malaysia's supply curve shifts to the right by 100,000 metric tons. As in 4, we simulate effects of this change both under initial export quotas and Nash tax and quantity games.

In the following, we discuss each of these simulations in detail and where relevant compare them to each other or to the initial equilibrium.

3.1 *The Nash tax game*

In this simulation, each country chooses its export tax optimally, taking the taxes of other countries as given. As shown in columns (1) and (2) of Table 7.3, the changes from the initial equilibrium are rather dramatic.

Table 7.3 *Actual, Nash and Stackelberg equilibrium*

Actual: A; Nash Tax Game: Nash (T); Nash Quantity Game: Nash (Q); Stackelberg Quantity Game: S(Q)

	Tax rates (%)				Output (000 MT)				Profit (million $US)				Revenue (million $US)			
Country	A (1)	Nash (T) (2)	Nash (Q) (3)	S(Q) (4)	A (1)	Nash (T) (2)	Nash (Q) (3)	S(Q) (4)	A (1)	Nash (T) (2)	Nash (Q) (3)	S(Q) (4)	A (1)	Nash (T) (2)	Nash (Q) (3)	S(Q) (4)
Côte d'Ivoire	25.1	25.2	52.7	29.5	585	490	371	539	698	496	595	659	304	220	436	324
Ghana	70.0	19.5	49.3	49.7	219	421	347	321	405	493	614	523	318	146	382	326
Cameroon	40.0	8.2	26.4	25.6	118	184	186	165	138	125	210	165	98	27	109	86
Nigeria	50.0	5.7	20.5	21.2	110	139	144	136	202	182	247	218	114	14	66	59
Africa					1032	1234	1048	1161	1443	1296	1666	1565	834	407	993	795
Malaysia	0.0	2.8	13.9	11.9	125	63	98	76	43	14	57	35	0	3.2	30	19
Indonesia	0.0	0.7	4.8	4.1	32	17	34	26	11	3.4	16	10	0	0.2	3.6	2.2
Oceania	0.0	0.6	4.5	3.8	30	16	32	25	11	3.2	15	9	0	0.2	3.2	1.9
Ecuador	0.0	3.2	11.8	12.6	85	80	83	81	151	126	164	148	0	4.6	22	20.7
Brazil	20.0	13.4	41.1	42.4	329	315	289	274	523	424	547	480	136	75	266	237
World					1633	1725	1584	1643	2182	1866.6	2465	2247	970	490.2	1317.8	1075.8

Note: World price ($US/MT).
Actual = 2070
Nash (T) = 1779
Nash (Q) = 2233
S(Q) = 2046

Table 7.4 *Effects of increasing Ghana's supply by 100,000 MT at various equilibria*

Actual: A; Nash Tax Game: Nash (T); Nash Quantity Game: Nash (Q)

Country	Tax rates (%)			Output (000 MT)			Profit (million $US)			Revenue (million $US)		
	A (1)	Nash (T) (2)	Nash (Q) (3)	A (1)	Nash (T) (2)	Nash (Q) (3)	A (1)	Nash (T) (2)	Nash (Q) (3)	A (1)	Nash (T) (2)	Nash (Q) (3)
Côte d'Ivoire	25.1	25.3	52.6	560	470	361	642	460	565	280	205	414
Ghana	70.0	23.5	57.5	313	492	395	579	631	755	437	200	496
Cameroon	40.0	8.1	26.2	109	175	180	121	114	197	87	24	103
Nigeria	50.0	5.8	20.6	107	137	142	191	173	239	107	14	64
Africa				1089	1274	1078	1533	1378	1756	911	443	1077
Malaysia	0	2.5	13.4	111	53	92	34	10	50	0	2.3	27
Indonesia	0	0.6	4.6	28	15	32	8.3	2.5	14	0	0.2	3.2
Oceania	0	0.6	4.3	26	14	30	7.7	2.3	13	0	0.1	2.8
Ecuador	0	3.3	12.0	83	79	82	144	122	159	0	4.6	22
Brazil	20.0	13.7	41.5	322	309	285	495	405	528	128	73	258
World				1659	1744	1599	2222	1919.8	2520	1039	523.2	1390

Note: World Price ($US/MT).

Actual = 1993
Nash (T) = 1722
Nash (Q) = 2182

Table 7.5 *Effects of increasing Malaysia's supply by 100,000 MT at various equilibria*

Actual: A; Nash Tax Game: Nash (T); Nash Quantity Game: Nash (Q)

Country	Tax rates (%)			Output (000 MT)			Profit (million $US)			Revenue (million $US)		
	A (1)	Nash (T) (2)	Nash (Q) (3)	A (1)	Nash (T) (2)	Nash (Q) (3)	A (1)	Nash (T) (2)	Nash (Q) (3)	A (1)	Nash (T) (2)	Nash (Q) (3)
Côte d'Ivoire	25.1	25.2	52.6	560	470	360	642	457	561	280	203	411
Ghana	70.0	19.7	49.4	213	408	338	380	463	585	297	138	364
Cameroon	40.0	8.1	26.1	109	174	179	121	113	195	87	24	102
Nigeria	50.0	5.8	20.7	107	136	142	191	172	238	107	14	64
Africa				989	1188	1019	1334	1205	1579	771	379	941
Malaysia	0	6.6	22.6	211	140	155	123	70	142	0	16	76
Indonesia	0	0.6	4.6	28	14	31	8.3	2.4	14	0	0.1	3.1
Oceania	0	0.6	4.3	26	13	29	7.7	2.2	13	0	0.1	2.8
Ecuador	0	3.3	12.0	83	79	82	144	121	159	0	4.5	21.5
Brazil	20.0	13.7	41.5	322	309	284	495	404	525	128	73	257
World				1659	1743	1600	2112	1804.6	2432	899	472.7	1301.4

Note: World Price ($US/MT).

Actual = 1993
Nash (T) = 1717
Nash (Q) = 2174

With the exception of the countries with 0 initial tax and Côte d'Ivoire, Nash taxes for all countries are substantially below the actual levels. For Ghana, Cameroon and Nigeria, the ratio of actual to Nash taxes is especially high at 3, 5 and 8, respectively. Under Nash behaviour, countries ignore the fact that a tax reduction by them leads the competitors to do the same and, as a result, act aggressively to capture a larger share of the market. Given a relatively steep world demand curve, this behaviour is accompanied by a sharp decline in the price and only a limited expansion of the quantity sold. The decline in the price from the initial equilibrium is thus 14.1 per cent while the increase in quantity is only 5.6 per cent.

The effects of these changes in taxes, the world price and total quantity are reflected in the changes in real incomes defined as the tax revenue plus producers' surplus and referred to as 'Profit' in Tables 7.2–7.5. Of the 9 countries, only Ghana's real income (profit) is higher in the Nash tax equilibrium than initially. All the other countries experience a lower profit! Africa as a whole also experiences a lower profit in the Nash tax equilibrium than initially.

Several African countries and Africa as a whole do gain in terms of output share. The total African output rises by 19.6 per cent, yielding a 71.5 per cent share in the world market. The latter is higher than the corresponding share at the initial equilibrium by 8.3 percentage points. Ghana makes the biggest gain in output: from 219,000 MT to 347,000 MT. This 58 per cent increase in output is the result of reduction in the tax rate from 70 per cent to 19.5 per cent, and the fact that Ghana enjoys a cost advantage relative to its competitors.

Tax revenues for Ecuador, Malaysia, Indonesia and Oceania are 0 in the initial equilibrium due to no taxation. For these countries, revenues in the Nash tax equilibrium are obviously higher. For all the remaining countries revenues decline, however, due to a reduction in the tax rate and limited expansion of quantity. It is striking that even Ghana, which gains substantially in terms of output expansion, loses on account of tax revenue.

3.2 *Export quotas: The Nash quantity game*

Next, we consider the case when the countries play a Nash-Cournot game and set export quotas optimally, taking the competitors' export quotas as given. The result in this case, shown in columns numbered 3 in Table 7.3, stands in sharp contrast to those in the previous case. Most importantly, countries are far more restrictive under the quota game than under the tax game. Remarkably, all countries except Côte d'Ivoire experience a higher real income (profits) in this case than at the initial equilibrium.

It is most interesting to compare the equilibria based on the tax and quota games. Broadly speaking, the Nash tax outcome is less restrictive and Nash quantity outcome more restrictive than the initial equilibrium. In terms of Figure 7.2, assuming symmetry, we can imagine that the initial equilibrium corresponds to *B*, the Nash tax outcome to a point farther out along *OB* and the Nash quantity outcome to *C*.

Comparing columns (2) and (3) under the heading 'Tax Rates' in Table 7.3, we note that the implicit tax rates under the quota game are consistently higher than those under the tax game. This result is related to the earlier observation (due to Eaton and Grossman, 1986) that in considering tax reductions under the tax game countries are 'too optimistic', while in considering output expansion under the quota game they are 'too pessimistic'. In the former case, a tax reduction by a country is matched by rivals, but this is ignored by the country. In the latter case, rivals respond to a quantity expansion by quantity *reduction*, and the country ignores it while choosing its own optimal level of exports.

As expected, the largest exporters – Côte d'Ivoire and Ghana – are most restrictive under both tax and quantity games. Compared to the initial tax rate, Côte d'Ivoire's tax rate is approximately the same under the Nash tax game but twice as high under the quantity game. In each case, its output is lower than the initial output. In the former case, the country loses market share due to tax competition, especially to Ghana. In the latter case, it also loses the market due to a very high implicit export tax of its own.

The restrictive effect under the quota game is so strong that the world price *rises* by 7.9 per cent relative to its level in the initial equilibrium. This price increase is the result of a greater exploitation of monopoly power by the exporting countries. Combined profits of the countries rise by 13 per cent. Compared to Nash tax equilibrium, the increase in profits is even larger (32.1 per cent). Interestingly, the quantity game equilibrium is associated with higher profits for every country than the tax game equilibrium.

Tax revenues follow the same essential pattern as profits. The major exception is Nigeria which experiences a decline in revenues under both games relative to the initial equilibrium. This is due to the fact that Nigeria's initial tax rate at 50 per cent seems to be aimed primarily at raising revenue regardless of real income considerations.

3.3 The Stackelberg quantity game

In columns numbered (4) in Table 7.3, we show the outcome under the assumption that Côte d'Ivoire acts as a Stackelberg leader in a quantity game. The main result here is that Côte d'Ivoire benefits, relative to the Nash quantity game, at the expense of all other countries. Côte d'Ivoire's exports expand by more than the combined contraction of exports by the followers. The world price falls relative to the Nash quantity game and Côte d'Ivoire's profits rise. Profits of the followers decline across the board.

We may note that these results are qualitatively different from those obtained in a Stackelberg tax game. In this latter case, both the leader and followers increase restriction on exports, and are better off relative to the Nash tax game in terms of profits.

3.4 A shift in Ghana's supply curve

In Table 7.4, we report the effects of a parallel, rightward shift of 100,000 MT in Ghana's supply curve under various assumptions about trade policy. Differences among the various cases within this set of simulations are similar to those in the original case (Table 7.3). Therefore, we do not discuss this comparison; instead, we focus on a comparison of each case with the corresponding case in Table 7.3 (i.e., on the comparative static effect under each equilibrium concept).

Under no tax policy response (i.e., keeping the tax rates at their initial level), the shift benefits Ghana and hurts all the other countries. This is as expected, since the shift represents an exogenous productivity increase in Ghana, and is associated with a decline in the world price of cocoa. Interestingly, the overall gain in profits is only 1.8 per cent; a substantial part of Ghana's gains is offset by losses in other countries.

Under Nash tax equilibrium, the story is more or less similar, in that Ghana continues to gain while other countries lose. The world price declines, but by much smaller magnitude than under actual taxes, as a result, the percentage gain in total profits is larger. However, if we compare the post-shock *levels* of profits under actual and Nash taxes (Table 7.4, bottom line, columns (1) and (2), we find that profits are lower in the latter case. The shift in Ghana's supply curve is accompanied by an increase in optimal Nash taxes in most (but not all) countries. Interestingly, the tax rates in Cameroon, Malaysia, and Indonesia thus decline slightly.

Finally, the results under the Nash quantity game follow a similar pattern. Ghana's profits increase, while those of the other countries decline. Overall profits rise, although by a very small amount.

3.5 A shift in Malaysia's supply curve

The effects of a shift in Malaysia'a supply curve are shown in Table 7.5. In the case of existing taxes, the effects are identical to those in the previous simulation for all countries except Ghana and Malaysia. World profits are lower in the present case than when Ghana's supply curve shifts. The reason is that in the present case a high cost producer, Malaysia, expands output while in the other case a low cost producer, Ghana, expands output.

Perhaps the most interesting result in the present case is that the increase in Malaysia's productivity leads to a *decline* in the total profits under all regimes. In spite of the fact that countries adjust the taxes and quantities optimally, they thus fail to escape a decline in their combined real incomes.

4 Limitations and future directions

We now describe some of the limitations of our analysis which future research must attempt to overcome. We consider first the empirical limitations, and then the theoretical issues.

Information on which our simulations are based does not relate to a single year. For example, elasticity estimates have been drawn from various studies and do not relate to the same time period. Prices and quantities which form the basis of the initial, calibrated equilibrium relate to 1986 while tax rates are from the year 1982 (1983 in the case of Brazil). The simulations also suffer from the limitation that the demand and supply functions are assumed to be linear. In models of oligopoly, results may be more sensitive to functional forms than in models based on perfect competition. In particular, along a linear demand curve, the elasticity of demand declines with price. This property does not hold in general and under plausible circumstances, the opposite may happen. In this eventuality, some of the qualitative conclusions discussed in Section 2 may not hold. In future work, we plan to base our simulations on a more careful econometric analysis allowing for flexible functional forms.

On the theoretical front, it is of utmost importance to recognise the implications of the partial equilibrium nature of our analysis. The partial equilibrium framework, employed in a large number of recent simulation studies of optimal policies for oligopoly industries, relies on the assumption that the sector under study is not sufficiently large to affect the prices in the rest of the economy. However, if the sector is large enough to warrant the analysis of optimal policies, it is likely to be large enough to influence the rest of the economy. This means that the general equilibrium aspects of the present problem, and presumably of the various oligopoly studies, could potentially be important.

The key problem which deserves emphasising is that if the rest of the economy is distorted, moving one sector *in isolation* towards its partial equilibrium optimum is not necessarily welfare-improving. The most serious implication of this point for our analysis is that within the standard Walrasian model with balanced trade, restrictions on imports act as substitutes for restrictions on exports via the Lerner Symmetry theorem. Indeed, if import restrictions are sufficiently high and the Lerner Symmetry holds, it may be optimal to impose no restrictions on exports, or even to subsidise them.

This point raises the natural question as to whether the current levels of import restrictions in some of the cocoa exporting countries are sufficiently high that these countries will benefit from further reductions in export taxes, even if such reductions are carried out by all of them jointly. Given the high levels of import restrictions in many of these countries, this may seem highly plausible. Yet, the example of the International Coffee Agreement (ICA) suggests that the issue is more complicated. Despite the fact that some of the coffee exporting countries have had a highly restrictive import regime, the conventional wisdom is that the ICA was beneficial for coffee exporting countries. Indeed, the general consensus appears to be that the ICA resulted in substantial transfers in real incomes from coffee importing to coffee exporting countries.

A resolution of these conflicting observations may lie in the possibility that the assumptions required for the validity of the Lerner Symmetry theorem fail to obtain in reality. The theorem requires that the trade balance be fixed exogenously, and is derived from a model in which the nominal exchange rate plays no role even in the presence of non-traded goods. If the trade balance is endogenous and is affected by nominal devaluation, however, the symmetry will break down. A 10 per cent devaluation is equivalent to a 10 per cent import tariff combined with a 10 per cent export subsidy. If the Lerner Symmetry theorem is valid, the tax and subsidy should neutralise each other, implying neutrality of the exchange rate. Yet, in most practical situations, it is difficult to imagine that the nominal exchange rate has no effect on the economy.

If one believes that the exchange rate matters, an import tariff is likely to have a smaller effect on exports than an equivalent export tax. The reason is that in the former case, resources will be drawn out of the non-tradable as well as the exportable sector. By contrast, in the latter case, the exportable sector will lose resources to the importable as well as the non-tradable sector. This point somewhat blunts the force of the Lerner Symmetry argument, but the broader proposition that general equilibrium effects may be important for our analysis remains valid. Future research must take this factor into account.

5 Conclusions

We now turn back to the results of our paper. We have compared the implications of optimal Nash taxes and quotas in a setting when two or more countries compete against each other in the world market. We have found that the outcome under taxes is less restrictive than under quotas. However, profits of the countries are higher under quotas than those under taxes. In the simulations undertaken for the world cocoa market, we find that for most countries, optimal Nash taxes yield lower profits and optimal Nash quotas yield higher profits than the initial taxes or quotas. We have also seen that if one of the countries becomes a Stackelberg leader, its profits rise and those of the others fall. The rise in the former's profit is lower, however, than the decline in the latter's profits. Total profits thus decline. Finally, we have found that even if countries choose taxes or quotas optimally, growth in a country can lead to a decline in the combined real income of the exporting countries.

In conclusion, we note that the simulations in this paper cast doubt on the hypothesis, advanced frequently by analysts, that a market characterised by five or more players can be regarded as approximately perfectly competitive. If this hypothesis were valid for policy formulation in the cocoa market, the optimal export taxes would be approximately zero. Our results indicate, however, that the outcome of the 9 country game is far from the zero-tax solution. The optimal taxes exceed 10 per cent for the largest producers (Côte d'Ivoire, Ghana and Brazil) in the Nash tax game and in all countries except Indonesia and Oceania in the Nash and Stackelberg quantity games.

NOTES

This paper is part of the World Bank research project, 'Commodity Exports and Real Incomes in Africa' (RPO 676–70). We thank François Bourguignon, Jaime de Melo, Peter Lloyd, Nicholas Stern and Alan Winters for helpful comments and Lili Liu for excellent research assistance. The findings, interpretations, and conclusions in this paper are entirely those of the authors. They do not necessarily represent the views of the World Bank, its Executive Directors or the countries they represent.

1 See Panagariya and Schiff (1991a) for a documentation of the concerns raised recently. Earlier concerns on these lines had led the World Bank in 1968 to adopt guidelines which severely restricted lending for projects aimed at output expansion of the commodities in question.

2 As noted in the paper, this and other findings are to be viewed as preliminary. The simulations are based on rough and ready estimates of demand and supply. A more thorough econometric analysis is planned for the future.

3 We may also note in passing that the nature of our problem is different from

that in the conventional retaliation literature *à la* Johnson (1954), Rodriguez (1974) and Tower (1975). In our paper, two or more countries impose restrictions on goods going to the rest of the world. By contrast, in the literature just cited, two countries restrict exports to *each other*.

4 In the general case with *n* players, the outcome depends on the number of players who jointly become Stackelberg leaders *relative* to those who remain Nash followers.

5 Some small producers, other than the 9 appearing in Table 7.1, have been excluded from the analysis. The implicit assumption is that their supply is fixed and does not respond to the world prices.

REFERENCES

Akiyama, T. and A. Bowers (1984) 'Supply Response of Cocoa in Major Producing Countries', *Division Working Paper, 1984–3*, Commodities Studies and Projection Division, EPD, Washington, D.C.: World Bank.

Behrman, J.R. (1968) 'Monopolistic Cocoa Pricing', *American Journal of Agricultural Economics*, **50**: 702–19.

Bhagwati, J. N. (1969) 'On the Equivalence of Tariffs and Quotas', Chapter 9 in J. N. Bhagwati, *Trade, Tariffs and Growth*, Cambridge, MA: MIT Press.

Brander, J. and B. Spencer (1985) 'Export Subsidies and International Market Share Rivalry', *Journal of International Economics*, **18**: 83–100.

Dixit, A. K. (1984) 'International Trade Policy for Oligopolistic Industries', *Economic Journal*, **94**, Supplement: 1–16.

Eaton, J. and G. M. Grossman (1986) 'Optimal Trade and Industrial Policy Under Oligopoly', *Quarterly Journal of Economics*, **101**, May: 383–406.

Imran, M. and R. Duncan (1988) 'Optimal Export Taxes for Exporters of Perennial Crops', *Division Working Paper*, **10**, International Commodity Markets Division, Washington, D.C.: World Bank.

Johnson, H. G. (1954) 'Optimum Tariffs and Retaliation', *Review of Economic Studies*, **21**: 142–53.

Panagariya, A. and M. Schiff (1991a) 'Commodity Exports and Real Incomes in Africa: A Preliminary Analysis', in A. Chhibber and S. Fischer (eds), *Analytics of Economic Reform in Sub-Saharan Africa*, Washington, D.C.: World Bank.

Panagariya, A. and M. Schiff (1991b) 'Commodity Exports: A Theory of Optimum and Revenue-Maximizing Trade Taxes in a Multi-Country Framework', Washington, D.C.: World Bank, CECTP (mimeo).

Rodriguez, C. A. (1974) 'The Non-equivalence of Tariffs and Quotas Under Retaliation', *Journal of International Economics*, **4**.

Tower, E. (1975) 'The Optimum Quota and Retaliation', *Review of Economic Studies*, **42**: 623–30.

Discussion

PETER LLOYD

In Chapter 7, the world cocoa market is treated by the authors as an oligopoly with nine players/countries. The alternative forms of the market considered are the Nash tax game (in which countries fix export taxes, taking the tax levels of other countries as given and unchanging), the Nash quota game (in which countries fix national quotas, taking the quota levels of other countries as given) and Stackelberg quantity leadership with the Côte d'Ivoire, which supplies about one-third of the world's supply, as the Stackelberg leader. These three game forms give different quantities traded and profits traded for each of the nine countries. However, they can be summarised by considering the aggregate 'profits' for all nine countries. They are – in descending order of aggregate profits – Nash quantity, Stackelberg quantity and Nash tax. This is consistent with the theory. We know that the Nash quantity must rank – from the point of view of the supplying countries – above the Nash tax solution because the aggregate quantity supplied is less. This follows in turn because the reaction curves in quantity space are negatively sloped (and thus one country reacts to a greater quantity supplied by others by *reducing* its quantity), whereas the reaction curves in price space are positively sloped (and one country reacts to a greater quantity (lower tax) supplied by others by *increasing* its quantity (lowering its tax)). We know, too, that a Stackelberg quantity leadership will increase the profits of the Stackelberg leader compared to the Nash quantity solution and reduce the profits of the others collectively, and it turns out that the aggregate quantity supplied is greater under the Stackelberg quantity game.

All this is fine analysis. But how does it compare with reality? In the real world the real or actual aggregate profits are greater than the Nash tax but less than the Stackelberg quantity and Nash quantity solutions. This suggests there is a moderate use of market power by the real world cocoa producers. It also turns out that the individual country outputs (and profits) are substantially different than under any of the three games. This is quite worrying as it raises the question of the relevance of any of these games if, in the real world, the players play quite differently. We should try to find out the rules of the real world game and forget the other games, except perhaps using some for reference.

I shall now comment on some particulars of the model and analysis. First, I question some of the details of the oligopoly characterisation. It assumes the cocoa supplies are homogeneous. Is this true, approximately at least? (It is certainly not true of coffee, for example, and even less true of tea.) Ten or nine is a large number of players in an oligopoly, except perhaps for some form of leadership game.

On a positive note, the assumption that an exporting country does not consume the commodity is useful. It means that an increase in the export price benefits *all* residents of the country concerned. This follows – unlike the usual case of a price rise which has some gainers and some losers – because all households are on the same side of the market (see Lloyd and Schweinberger, 1990 for an analysis of trade where households are considered as implicit net suppliers or demanders of a commodity). A fallacy of composition is noted under which both of two suppliers can gain if they do not behave as Nash quantity oligopolists from an initial point. One can regard any oligopoly solution as a fallacy of composition since the joint maximum cooperative solution reveals the collective inefficiency of individual country strategies.

I confess that all this game theory makes me uneasy. It ignores the fundamental facts that the supplying countries may gain by restricting supplies but the importing countries must lose, and their losses are greater than the gains, so the world as a whole loses. This kind of strategy is just the opposite of what we are searching for as a basis of the rules of international trade. And countries tend to exaggerate their monopoly power, in the longer run, supply restrictions will encourage new country suppliers or the substitution at the margin from other commodities. What is the long-run substitutability for cocoa or tea or coffee of other beverages and substitutes in other end uses such as carob or other confectionary? On this point, too, the Lerner Symmetry Theorem states that, for one country, an import tax has the same effects as an export tax. This theorem can be extended to multiple imports and exports and non-traded goods. Even if exact symmetry does not hold, severely restrictive import regimes contract the export sector. Most of the cocoa exporting countries restrict imports, so their attempts to use their monopoly power are greater than their restrictions of exports of cocoa alone. We should be encouraging them to liberalise their trade, improve their competitiveness, and develop new exports, not to try to exploit their trading partners.

REFERENCE

Lloyd, P. J. and A. G. Schweinberger (1990) 'Indices of Welfare for the Economy and Households in Distorted Open Economies', Department of Economics, University of Melbourne, *Research Paper*, **273**, September.

8 Trade reform and the small country assumption

DAVID EVANS, IAN GOLDIN and
DOMINIQUE van der MENSBRUGGHE

1 Introduction

This paper is concerned with the consequences of policy-conditional adjustment assistance being applied simultaneously to several developing countries. Is there a contradiction between individual actions and group outcomes, often referred to as the fallacy of composition in policy discussions? How important is it likely to be empirically? If it is empirically relevant, how can adjustment policies best be adjusted to take weaknesses in the small country assumption into account?

1.1 Trade and protectionism

The contrast between the trade policies of developing countries and those of OECD member countries is increasingly stark. Whereas a growing number of developing countries are engaged in fundamental trade reform, OECD protectionism has increased in the 1980s.[1] The extent of protection is particularly evident in agriculture, where the costs of distortions in 1990 reached a record $300bn.[2]

Many developing countries have not embraced trade liberalisation willingly. The burden of debt has nevertheless constrained their choice and – with the withering of commercial bank lending – increased their reliance on multilateral and bilateral agencies whose lending has increasingly been associated with reform conditionality. The extent of outside pressure should not, however, be exaggerated: developing countries are learning some of the lessons of their failed development (and those of Eastern Europe), and are now a more receptive audience to the benefits of freer trade. Nevertheless, strong reservations remain. This paper focuses on a key concern for the tropical product exporters: the small country assumption, and the possibility of a fallacy of composition in policy advice.[3]

1.2 The fallacy of composition

Different branches of economics have long been concerned with phenomena where the elasticity of demand for one seller is greater than for the market as a whole. And, in development economics, a long-running debate has centred on the extent to which reforms undertaken by one country may be rendered ineffective if similar reforms are undertaken by others.[4] While much of the recent debate has focused on manufacturing exports from developing countries, analysis of the 'small country assumption' suggests that the adverse terms of trade consequences of export expansion may be an awkward, but appropriate, concern for developing countries heavily dependent on primary commodity exports. Our interest is in the possible consequences for developing countries of a removal of the small country assumption from the design of structural adjustment and trade reform.[5]

If successful, trade policy reform with structural adjustment may lead to increased traditional and non-traditional exports, as well as to more efficient import substitution. However, in the case of traditional primary exports, there is some evidence that the policies may induce comparative static welfare loss because of the fallacy of composition. For example, Karunasekera (1984), identified eight primary commodities for which this was possible – coffee, cocoa, tea, bananas, bauxite, copper, tin and tropical timber. Similarly, Koester *et al.* (1990), found that African cocoa and coffee exporters will not gain by expanding production of those crops, while Panagariya and Schiff (1990b) explore the implications of the argument in the context of strategic behaviour.

The evidence suggests that the countries which would suffer the strongest terms of trade effects of developing country trade reform are precisely those poor, typically sub-Saharan, countries which have the weakest trade performance.[6] Trade reforms by these countries, to the extent that they mirror those of their principal competitors, may not improve their position. The case may therefore be made, on redistributive grounds, of allowing some of the costs of trade policy reform to fall on better off countries.

Despite the mass of empirical work on the relationship between trade policy and economic performance, the evidence regarding the effects of policy reform is inconclusive.[7] In part, this reflects the difficulties of comparative historical analysis, both because it is difficult to measure trade policy variables and to measure their independent influence on growth, and because the contemporary nature of the recent reforms mean that the full consequences have yet to be realised. The use of available modelling techniques provides an opportunity to explore the consequences of policy choices outside the range of historical experience.

1.3 Outline of the paper

Section 2 explores the conceptual relationship between myopic, Nash equilibrium and optimal export tax prices and revenues when the fallacy of composition holds. It then examines the consequences of exchange rate devaluation for the equilibrium prices and export taxes in each case. This provides the background for a brief review of the consequences of the fallacy of composition in a growth context and for protected tropical product commodities.

Section 3 provides an empirical estimation of the effects of different reform scenarios, using a computable general equilibrium model. The section provides a brief introduction to the Rural–Urban North–South (RUNS) applied general equilibrium growth model currently being developed at the OECD Development Centre, and presents the results of simulations exploring the reform of labour markets and export tax instruments, both of which tend to be included in structural adjustment programmes. The policy implications and conclusions are explored in Section 4.

2 Conceptual issues

2.1 Some background

Adverse terms of trade movements are usually welfare-reducing in a static context. It is often implied in the Prebisch–Singer tradition that this static result carries over to the context of economic growth. However, with factor input growth, adverse terms of trade movements can be associated with output growth, which can be either welfare-improving or welfare-worsening. In both cases, a single country can do something about its 'terms of trade problem' only when it has independent market power – that is, when the small country assumption does not hold and a single country has an imperfectly elastic demand curve for one or more of its export products.

The analysis of welfare- and revenue-maximising export taxes in the literature, when a single country faces a less than perfectly elastic demand curve for its exports, has usually been carried out within a two-country general equilibrium context (Johnson, 1950–1; Tower, 1977). In policy terms, however, although export taxes have been recognised as one of the very few cases where optimal intervention requires a trade tax, optimal export taxes have in practice not been recommended for two reasons. First, because of the free-rider problem when two or more countries face a less than perfectly elastic demand schedule for a homogeneous product (so that other producers will benefit when taxes are raised). Second, because within the context of a cosmopolitan rule-based international trading system, there is no place for the long-run legitimisation of the collective monopoly power of one country or group of countries over another, even if the free-rider problems associated with cooperative solutions can be overcome.

The cosmopolitan view was easier to sustain in the context of rapidly growing world trade. However, when there is a group of countries with market power and export taxes on their chief export crops which are also some of the poorest in the world (for example, cocoa producers), the cosmopolitan view may be challenged from a poverty-focused perspective.[8] In the context of slower growth of world output and trade, the status of policy recommendations regarding trade policy reform in structural adjustment programmes requires further analysis.[9] Should the costs of trade policy reform which raise welfare be borne by the countries in question in this case? Could the Bretton Woods institutions overcome the free-rider problems involved in taking into account the combined monopoly power of such poor producing countries when designing policy-conditional structural adjustment assistance? Could this be done without undermining a rule-based world trading system?

In their recent analysis of the sequencing of trade policy liberalisation, Michaely, Papageorgiou and Choksi (1991, vol. 7) make an argument for the use of selective incentives where trade liberalisation has employment implications, to allow a longer period for adjustment in larger and labour-intensive industries. We suggest here that the argument should be extended to include the selective retention of some level of export taxes where the chief exporting countries individually face a substantially less than perfectly elastic demand curve for exports, where collective action in reducing existing levels of export taxes could have significant welfare costs, and where the countries concerned are poor. The argument is particularly pertinent when the policy conditionality driving the export tax reform is from the Bretton Woods institutions whose job it is to assist in the financing of both stabilisation and structural adjustment. If it is in the long-run interest of a cosmopolitan rule-based world trading system to remove export taxes, even when welfare-reducing for the poorer countries concerned, there appears to be an argument for a slower rate of reduction of export taxes and other trade policy instruments, whilst other policies are reformed. There may also be a case for additional adjustment assistance to offset the costs of early trade policy reforms, or for export tax reduction to be carried out only in the context of renewed growth in the world economy and multilateral trade policy reform. Usually, the negotiating 'chips' in multilateral trade negotiations are tariff reductions, which are widely believed by trade economists to be welfare-enhancing even if carried out unilaterally. When multilateral trade policy reform is clearly welfare-reducing for some of the poorer countries involved, surely there is a case for some offsetting transfers, finance or market access? For the tree crops, the removal of tariff escalation facing processed exports would be an obvious offsetting trade policy reform.

The extension of the earlier literature on optimum export taxes to include strategic behaviour has only just begun (see Panagariya and Schiff, 1990a, 1990b and Chapter 7 in this volume). This new literature uses a partial equilibrium framework because a general equilibrium approach is said to be analytically intractable, especially if growth is also considered. However, a first exploration of the general equilibrium issues in an empirical context is carried out in Section 3 of this paper, where the RUNS growth model is described and some preliminary results are reported for tropical beverages, focusing mainly on coffee and cocoa.

In its present formulation, the RUNS model has an endogenously specified behavioural mechanism governing agricultural export taxes, whereby the target variable is farm-gate prices in each country or country block; there is no behavioural mechanism to incorporate strategic behaviour. What is done in the preliminary results reported is to explore the model implications for growth and the terms of trade for two types of overall structural adjustment shocks: changes in the degree of wage flexibility – to simulate a drop in the real wage and a lowering of the urban–rural real wage differential – and changes in trade policies – for a subgroup of developing countries which encompasses the main producers of tropical beverages or tree crops. These groups of countries are shocked with an across-the-board change in the export taxes on their tree crops with and without wage policy changes, followed by a policy shock where only one of the country groups pursues policy changes. To understand the model results reported, the next two subsections review the optimal tax arguments in the context of cooperative and strategic behaviour, paying particular attention to the relationship between actual export tax revenues and the optimal welfare and revenue taxes.

2.2 *Optimum export taxes and actual behaviour*

Panagariya and Schiff (1990a, 1990b) examine the problem of optimum and revenue-maximising export taxes in the context of a 3-country partial equilibrium model with myopic, Nash and cooperative behavioural assumptions. The competitive outcome always leads to a higher level of output than either of the cooperative taxing outcomes, and the cooperative revenue-maximising tax is always higher than the profit-maximising tax.[10] The welfare outcomes of the Nash revenue and Nash profit-maximising solutions cannot be uniquely ranked; for higher elasticities of supply, the Nash revenue-maximising tax has the higher welfare, but for lower elasticities of supply, the Nash profit-maximising solution has the higher welfare outcome.

If one of the countries has a real exchange rate depreciation, this is equivalent to a downward shift in the country's (and the world's) supply curve. The optimum taxes will increase, as will the Nash profit and Nash revenue taxes, but the rankings of the optimum cooperative profit- and revenue-maximising taxes will not change.[11]

Similarly, on account of the Lerner Symmetry condition, the introduction of tariff or other forms of protection of import competing production will lead to an appreciation of the real exchange rate, an upward shift in the export supply curve and a lowering of the optimal export taxes. In a general equilibrium context, exploitation of a country's monopoly power in trade can be achieved either through export taxes, import protection, or some combination of both.

Exploration of the implications of strategic behaviour by export taxing governments in the producer countries of tropical beverages is very much in its infancy. It is too early to tell how closely the pattern of actual export taxes matches that predicted by the Panagariya and Schiff multi-commodity model of strategic behaviour of the governments of cocoa producing countries. For present purposes, it is sufficient to draw on their work, developed in a partial equilibrium context, to understand the implications of exogenously imposed patterns of export tax changes on applied general equilibrium growth models such as RUNS. These implications can now be drawn together.

1 When a group of countries has monopoly power in its export market, lowering their export taxes below the cooperative optimal levels can lower export tax revenue. The lower export taxes will be associated with higher domestic prices and higher levels of output of the exported product, lower profits – and, when domestic consumption of the export product is small – lower levels of welfare. In a growth context, the lower profits in export production may lead to a lower level of investment and lower growth. Moreover, if the loss of export tax revenue lowers total savings (public and private) because of redistributive and budgetary effects, there can be additional adverse growth consequences.
2 One country, or group of countries, acting alone in lowering its export tax will lower the optimal tax structure for the remaining countries. In the absence of retaliation, lower export taxes for the single country or

subgroup of countries may or may not be revenue- or profit-enhancing. The outcome will depend on the relationship between existing tax structures and the optimal tax for the subgroup of countries acting alone, given the tax levels of the remaining countries. The effects on growth will follow from the revenue and profit effects discussed above.

3 The removal of other distortions such as tariff protection or exchange rate overvaluation, leading to an exchange rate depreciation, will tend to increase the level of the optimal export tax structure. By themselves, the removal of other distortions may be revenue- and welfare-enhancing or reducing, depending on whether the changes move the economy closer to or away from the optimal export taxes. The growth effects following the removal of other distortions will depend critically on the effects of the changes on gross savings, as noted above.

4 The removal of export taxes will be welfare-enhancing for the world economy as a whole.

These results are drawn on in interpreting the initial set of policy shocks reported for the RUNS model in Section 3.

3 Empirical estimates

3.1 The RUNS model

The Rural–Urban North–South (RUNS) model is a global applied equilibrium model, with a focus on agriculture. RUNS was initially developed in the early 1980s and was used, among other things, to inform the projections in various World Bank *World Development Reports.* Since its adoption by the OECD Development Centre it is being developed further for analysis of the interaction of international and national policy reforms.[12]

The model specification is summarised in Appendix 2 and has been well documented elsewhere by Burniaux and van der Mensbrugghe (1990). RUNS models the flows between the developed and developing regions, and between the agricultural and other sectors within the different regions. It is recursive and currently solves through to 2002, permitting the analysis of both short- and medium-term effects, transition costs, factor accumulation, and supply and demand trends. The model does not have forward-looking expectations, and is not monetised. Investment is driven by savings and the allocation of investment depends on current profitability; in the urban sectors, there is full capital mobility but in the rural sectors, returns to investment in each period are maximised so that the investment structure will gradually change over time, reflecting the relative scarcity of capital in relation to other rural factors.

Rural aggregate supply functions are derived from Cobb-Douglas production functions, disposable income is allocated via the Extended Linear Expenditure System (ELES) and labour migration is modelled in the Harris-Todaro tradition. Urban production is modelled using a Leontief specification for intermediate inputs and a constant elasticity of substitution (CES) function for aggregating labour and capital. Urban consumption is modelled in a manner similar to rural consumption (via the ELES), but with different income and price elasticities. Government revenue derives from direct taxes in the urban and rural sectors, plus a share of income from foreign trade, dependent on the taxes and tariffs which are introduced in the form of price wedges.[13]

Domestic agricultural prices are formed using a price transmission equation whereby domestic prices are a function both of domestic non-agricultural prices and of world prices. The pass-through coefficients governing the influence of world prices on domestic agricultural prices have been estimated using historical data. This mechanism generates endogenous price wedges, so that domestic prices may diverge from world prices as a function of the pass-through coefficient. Note that in practice this means that the endogenously specified price wedges quickly settle down to roughly constant values in model solutions from 1993.[14]

Unemployment is generated by having a semi-rigid real wage, where the real wage is a function of a fixed real wage and the equilibrium wage. In the agricultural goods markets, world prices are solved to clear world markets. Prices of other goods are determined competitively nationally and internationally, with imperfect substitution between domestic and import sources of supply, specified by Armington elasticities, governing the extent of pass-through between world and domestic markets. Macro closure is achieved by assuming that the balance of payments equals exogenous capital flows in each period; implicitly the real exchange rate is the equilibrating mechanism.

3.2 *Adapting the RUNS model to explore structural adjustment and export tax policy issues*

The tree crop supply and demand elasticities used in the RUNS model are discussed and compared with those used in other studies in Appendix 1. As a first attempt to use the RUNS model to explore structural adjustment issues, a base run scenario was developed which was consistent with current World Bank macro growth and foreign capital flows projections, and with wage inflexibility which roughly reproduces the base levels of unemployment. Two types of shocks were then considered. The first was designed to simulate the effects of changing the degree of wage flexibility on the real exchange rate and growth, and the second to simulate the effects of changes in the price wedges affecting tree crop exports for varying combinations of the major tree crop exporters.

Within the RUNS model, as already indicated, there is no explicit exchange rate variable or monetary instrument. This means that it is not possible to model the effects of a deviation of the actual real exchange rate from its equilibrium value, as frequently occurs when there is macro-economic disequilibrium. However, the RUNS model can capture the effects of varying degrees of wage rigidity on the equilibrium real exchange rate and on growth. In the Armington world of universal but imperfect tradability in non-agricultural commodities, these is no real exchange rate as conventionally defined, the ratio of the price of non-tradables to tradables. However, it is possible to define an Armington world counterpart to the conventional definition by measuring the relationship between domestic prices and the prices of imports.[15] To shock the model with a change in export taxes levied by tropical beverages producers (tree crops in RUNS terminology), the 1993 price wedges for these commodities were cut by 25 per cent from the 1990 level with full pass-through of world price changes starting in 1993. This is done in varying combinations with the other policy shocks. Finally, in order to explore the consequences of one country (or group of countries) cutting export taxes, the final policy shock lowers all African tree crop export taxes by 25 per cent after 1993.

Table 8.1 *The base run and policy shocks*

Base Run: Underlying World Bank projections of growth and capital flows to 2002; labour market rigidities roughly reproduce base year rates of unemployment; constant export taxes from 1993.

Shock I: Base run plus more flexible urban employment in Africa, Latin America, Mediterranean and Low-Income Other Asia from 1993.

Shock II: Base run plus 25 per cent cut in tree crop export taxes in Africa, Latin America, Mediterranean and Low-Income Other Asia from 1993.

Shock III: I and II combined.

Shock IV Base run plus 25 per cent cut in tree crop export taxes in Africa only from 1993.

Shock IVB: Sensitivity test with both base run comparator and policy shock IV calculated with cocoa and coffee supply elasticities in Africa doubled.

The characteristics of the base run and the five different policy shocks considered are reported in Table 8.1.

Table 8.2. *Key results for countries subject to policy shocks*

	% p.a.	% change in level 2002				
	Base	(I)	(II)	(III)	(IV)	(IVB)
GDP (deflated by consumption price index)						
Africa	4.10	4.29	−0.94	3.87	−0.60	−0.51
Low-Income Asia	4.07	2.63	0.03	2.65	−0.01	−0.01
Brazil	3.96	12.79	−0.39	12.49	−0.04	−0.19
Latin America	3.41	12.00	−0.35	11.76	−0.10	−0.17
OECD	2.75	0.04	0.05	0.80	0.01	0.01
World	3.19	1.13	0.00	1.13	0.00	−0.01
TRADE VOLUME (imports + exports)						
Africa	4.51	4.98	−0.75	4.54	−0.45	−0.11
Low-Income Asia	6.36	7.14	0.09	7.21	0.02	0.02
Brazil	4.62	11.17	0.23	11.47	0.03	−0.02
Latin America	3.44	9.10	−0.09	9.11	−0.05	−0.10
OECD	3.07	0.30	0.04	0.33	0.01	0.01
World	3.91	0.94	0.02	0.96	0.00	0.00
RURAL–URBAN PARITY						
Africa		−3.41	2.28	−4.00	3.00	2.76
Low-Income Asia		−1.36	0.08	−1.24	−0.10	−0.10
Brazil		−2.81	1.22	−2.59	0.83	−0.27
Latin America		−3.43	0.69	−2.70	−0.01	0.04
TERMS OF TRADE (excluding oil)						
Africa		−2.57	−0.61	−3.63	0.24	0.10
Low-Income Asia		−2.78	−0.07	−2.96	−0.07	−0.05
Brazil		−3.79	−0.85	−4.54	−0.30	−0.41
Latin America		−4.12	−0.49	−4.61	−0.13	−0.18
WORLD PRICES						
Coffee		0.42	−13.76	−12.80	−2.98	−3.79
Cocoa		0.07	−13.52	−9.12	−7.10	−10.90
Tea		1.82	−5.49	−8.06	−1.33	−1.38
REAL EXCHANGE RATES (ratio domestic price importables to price imports)						
Africa		−3.11	0.43	−3.36	0.65	0.61
Low-Income Asia		−3.04	0.05	−3.01	−0.02	−0.02
Brazil		−5.44	−0.18	−5.58	−0.11	−0.10
Latin America		−5.52	−0.01	−5.58	−0.02	−0.05

Table 8.2 (*cont.*)

	% p.a. Base	% change in level 2002 (I)	(II)	(III)	(IV)	(IVB)
TREE CROP NET TRADE ($billion 1985)						
Africa		0.06	0.37	−0.25	0.60	0.99
Low-Income Asia		0.00	0.09	0.08	−0.01	−0.01
Brazil		−0.05	0.41	−0.06	−0.06	−0.15
Latin America		−0.07	0.31	−0.07	−0.07	−0.15
TREE CROP TAX REVENUE ($billion 1985)						
Africa		0.03	−0.93	−0.35	−0.74	−0.68
Low-Income Asia		0.01	0.00	−0.01	−0.01	−0.01
Brazil		0.02	−0.65	−0.63	−0.14	−0.21
Latin America		−0.02	−0.45	−0.47	−0.11	−0.17

3.3 *The empirical results*

The essential results of the base run and for the policy shock simulations are set out in Table 8.2. The key results for the present set of policy shock simulations for the main producers of coffee and cocoa crops are set out as a percentage change in the 2002 level for each of the variables considered. The reported results include GDP growth rates, trade volume, rural and urban incomes and factor prices, country or block terms of trade, world prices of tree crops, real exchange rates, tree crop net trade, and tree crop tax income.[16] The latter results are reported in terms of change in levels measured in $ billion (1985).

Overall world GDP growth to 2002 is 3.2 per cent p.a. and world trade growth is 3.9 per cent in the base run. The effects of the policy shocks considered are presented as deviations from the base run for each of the policy simulations.

The results of the first policy experiment are shown in column (I) of Table 8.2. The pattern of the marked increase in GDP and trade volumes from the elimination of labour market distortions in this policy simulation reflects the higher initial levels of measured unemployment in Brazil and the rest of Latin America. For Africa, Brazil and the rest of Latin America, where the growth stimulus is greatest, there are relatively large adjustments in the overall terms of trade and the real exchange rate accompanying increased labour market flexibility. Whilst the accuracy of the base projections of unemployment and the feasibility of eliminating labour market distortions must be heavily qualified, it is interesting to note from simulation (I) that the effect on tree crops of sharply increased growth in the countries shocked is relatively small. There are many other possibilities for adjustment to the higher growth outside of the tropical beverages, the export tax and terms of trade effects of increased growth in the main supplying countries for coffee and cocoa are minor.

Policy Shock (II) was designed to throw light on the revenue and welfare implications of cutting tree crop export taxes in a growth context in the longer run. The 25 per cent cut in the 1993 price wedge for tree crops was not applied to India and China, as the analysis focuses on the major producers of coffee and cocoa. In the case of the latter crops, there is a sharp decline in world prices, tax revenues and GDP for the major producing countries.[17] The cut in tree crop export tax revenue p.a. for the countries shown in Table 8.2 is $2.0bn (1985 prices) by the year 2002, compared with the base run, of which $0.9bn is in Africa and $1.1bn in Brazil and the rest of Latin America. The largest percentage impact on GDP is in Africa, Brazil and the rest of Latin America, which have a 0.94 per cent, 0.39 per cent and 0.35 per cent drop in GDP by the year 2002, respectively, compared with the base run.

If the GDP effects for the rest of Latin America and Africa were traced back to the major producing countries within these country groups, the percentage fall in GDP would be very much higher. In absolute terms the changes in GDP are large – for Africa, Brazil and the rest of Latin America, the fall is $5.8bn whilst Low-Income Asia and the Mediterranean gain is $0.4bn leaving a net GDP loss of $5.4bn. These orders of magnitude of the effects of a collective export tax cut for coffee and cocoa on tax revenue and GDP are also large in relation to total Official Development Assistance (ODA) to developing countries of around $40bn p.a. at the end of the 1980s.

How much of the effects of the policy shocks arises from static efficiency gains, and how much from the longer-run growth effects? In the present formulation of the RUNS model it is not possible to make an accurate separation of these effects, since investment is endogenously determined and will exert some influence on current levels of output. However, some indication of the comparative static effects is given by the comparison of the orders of magnitude of the effects in 1993, the first year of their policy shocks, compared with the final year considered, 2002. Thus, in the case of policy shock (I), about 75 per cent of the relative GDP effect occurs in Africa in the initial year, and 40–50 per cent of the relative GDP effect occurs in the remaining countries in the initial year. For policy shock (II), roughly 50–60 per cent of the relative GDP effect occurs in the first year in Africa, Brazil and Latin America, and almost all of the terms of trade effect happens in that year as well. In other words, the 25 per cent cut in export taxes in 1993 leads to an initial decline in GDP of between 0.20 and 0.45 per cent in the main producing countries and a terms of trade decline for coffee and cocoa of 12–13 per cent. Thereafter, the growth effects contribute little to a further decline in coffee and cocoa prices but, in the absence of offsetting taxes to recoup lost government revenue, the additional loss of GDP after 9 years of growth is of a similar amount to the initial effects.

There are obviously many ways in which countries may offset the negative effects of an across-the-board cut in export taxes. One of these is considered in policy shock (III), which combines shock (I), the removal of labour market imperfections, with the cut in export taxes considered in shock (II). In so far as shock (I) is possible and realistic, the results for shock (III) show that the negative effects of the export tax cut can be offset by faster growth arising from policy changes in the countries concerned. Other alternatives, such as an increase in transfers from developed countries during some transition period, trade policy reform in the developed countries affecting the processing of tree crops, or faster developed country growth, have yet to be explored.

The final policy shock considered is a 25 per cent cut in tree crop export taxes for Africa alone, reported as policy shock (IV). Potentially, it would be possible for African tree crop shares in world trade to increase enough for such a policy to be welfare-enhancing. However, as the results in Table 8.2 show, negative effects on African growth and export tax revenue are more than half the declines which were estimated for policy shock (II). A 25 per cent cut in tree crop export taxes for Africa alone would lead to a GDP loss of $1.86bn and a loss of export tax revenue of $0.6bn, measured in 1985 prices, after 9 years of growth with roughly half of these losses occurring in the first year. Note also that the other tree crop producing areas have GDP losses as a result of the fall in African export taxes, illustrating the converse of the free-rider problem of individual or subgroup action in raising export taxes.

Two final sets of calculations were made. First, it may be legitimately argued that the econometric estimates of the supply elasticities used and reported in Appendix 1 are too low. It should be recalled that, in the context of an applied general equilibrium growth model, the relevant elasticities are the short-run estimates; the model itself, through investment, allows for a long-run supply response. As a sensitivity check, the supply elasticities for coffee and cocoa for Africa were doubled in size and shock (IV) was re-run with the larger elasticities and an appropriately adjusted base simulation, reported as shock (IVB) in the last column of Table 8.2. In effect, the size of the short-run elasticities used in shock (IVB) are similar to the econometrically estimated long-run supply elasticities which can be found in the literature. A comparison of shock (IV) and (IVB) shows that the results with higher supply elasticities are very similar, suggesting that the key results obtained in this paper are not sensitive to the supply elasticities used. However, note that, because of market share effects, the losses for Brazil and the rest of Latin America are sharply increased in shock (IVB) compared with shock (IV).

4 Conclusions

The results of this paper remain preliminary and tentative. In Section 1 we argued that the design of the appropriate trade and adjustment policies is not fully understood. This makes the case for an empirically-driven approach, and for the use of models which are able to capture dynamic behavioural relations.

The policy simulations using the RUNS model obtained so far suggest that the order of magnitude of the annual tax revenue and GDP loss arising from a 25 per cent across-the-board cut of tree crop export taxes is very substantial for the crops considered; the immediate GDP losses for this policy change alone amount to over 5 per cent of total ODA to developing countries. These results need further refinement and extension, but the overall orders of magnitude are unlikely to change.

The results suggest that, in contrast with present practice, coordinated policy-conditional assistance needs explicitly to take into account the removal of the small country assumption. The fallacy of composition issue is a valid concern for policy makers in tree crop exporting developing countries. Stabilisation could be provided through continued use of trade policy instruments, such as export taxes, and this could enhance the possibility of success of other adjustment instruments. For these countries, there may well be a case for special and differential treatment, allowing for a slower rate of reform of selective trade interventions during a transition period. Alternatively, the tree crop producers might wish to argue for some compensation for reforms which are in the general interest, either through additional ODA, or through trade policy reform in developed countries in downstream processing of tree crop products. The key is to ensure that the legitimate concerns of developing countries are met, without eroding the wider commitment to freer trade, including reductions in OECD protectionism.

Appendix 1: The elasticities used for tree crops

In so far as the empirical results from the RUNS model have a bearing on the policy consequences of the fallacy of composition as it affects the tropical beverages, it is important that the supply and demand elasticities used for tree crops in RUNS are roughly in conformity with the range of estimates obtained econometrically from other studies, and are in line with the values used in other tree crop modelling exercises. Table 8A.1 summarises the RUNS elasticities and those used in some other studies.

Not all of the elasticities shown in Table 8A.1 are comparable; for example, the price elasticities from the Panagariya and Schiff (1990a, 1990b) study on cocoa are country-based, whereas the RUNS values are for total world exports. However, the country-level price elasticities implied by the export shares in RUNS for cocoa are somewhat higher than the values used by Panagariya and Schiff (1990a, 1990b). On the other side, the RUNS price elasticities of demand are somewhat lower than assumed by Mabbs-Zeno and Krissoff (1990) for cocoa and tea.

Table 8A.1 *Empirical estimates of demand and supply elasticities for exports*

	Demand		Supply
	Price	Income	
Coffee			
Karunasekera (1984, Annex Table 2)	−0.15 to −0.31		0.33 to 1.28
Mabbs-Zeno and Krissoff (1990: 188)	−0.3		n.a.
RUNS	−0.33	0.6	0.35
Cocoa			
Karunasekera (1984, Annex Table 2)	−0.11 to −0.33		0.34 to 1.0
Mabbs-Zeno and Krissoff (1990: 188)	−0.7		n.a.
Panagariya and Schiff (1990a, Table 1)	−0.28 to −3.0[a]		
RUNS	−0.27	0.6	0.35 to 0.37
Tea			
Karunasekera (1984, Annex Table 2)	−0.2 to −0.5		0.16 to 0.72
Mabbs-Zeno and Krissoff (1990: 188)	−0.6		n.a.
RUNS	−0.14	0.5	0.24 to 0.39

[a] Country based estimates rather than world.
n.a. Not available.

Overall, the price elasticities of demand used in RUNS are close to the range of estimates found in the Karunasekera (1984) survey. On the supply elasticities, the RUNS values are near the low end of the range found by Karunasekera, which is to be expected since the relevant econometrically estimated supply elasticities used in RUNS are short-run; the long-run supply elasticities are implicit in the model solutions. The use of lower-bound estimates of supply elasticities in RUNS can also be justified in the light of the recent discussions of the role of non-price factors affecting export supply (see Lipton, 1987).[18] Given that the supply and demand elasticities for tree crops used in the RUNS model are roughly in the range used in other studies, the main role of RUNS is to provide a systematic background of general equilibrium effects associated with the policy shocks examined.

Appendix 2: RUNS model overview

The RUNS model (Rural–Urban, North–South Model)[19] is intended to analyse some key linkages, specifically rural–urban and developed–developing region linkages. Its geographic scope encompasses the world. At present, RUNS has 15 regions. The 10 developing regions have been categorised as follows: Africa, China, India, Brazil, Latin America, Low and Upper Income Asia, Low and Upper Income Oil Exporting Countries, and the Mediterranean. The developed regions are the European Economic Community, the European Free Trade Area, Japan, the USA, and food exporting countries (Australia, Canada and New Zealand). RUNS also has a reduced-form regional model which comprises the rest of the world (Eastern Europe, the USSR, and Indochina).

Each of the 15 regions comprising the bulk of the RUNS model is modelled with an identical structure which will be described below. The data and parameter values are region-specific. The model is dynamic with a time span of 17 years in seven steps. The base year is 1985 and the model solves for 1986, 1987, 1990, 1993, 1996, 1999 and 2002. The dynamic nature of the model permits the analysis of both short- and medium-term effects, transition costs, factor accumulation, and supply and demand trends. The model does not have forward-looking expectations, nor is it monetised in any sense. Investment is strictly driven by savings and the allocation of investment depends only on current prices and profits.

The regional models are organised around the rural–urban dichotomy. The rural sector produces only agricultural commodities and income in rural households is derived from agricultural production. The urban sector produces manufactured commodities and services. Urban households derive income from urban production. The commodity scope covers 14 agricultural products and 5 urban products.[20]

Production in the rural sector

Production data for separate agricultural products are limited. For this reason, RUNS uses a system of separable multi-input/multi-output production functions to characterise agricultural production. The choice of outputs depends on the price of the output and the price of the aggregate input. Aggregate supply functions are constant elasticity functions based on Cobb-Douglas production functions and have the general form:

$$S_i = (1 + \gamma_i)^t \, a_i \left(\frac{PP_i}{P_i} - c_i \right)^{\beta_i}$$

where S is supply, PP is the producer price, P is the price of the aggregate input, γ is a supply trend, and a, c, and β are parameters. Optimisation requires that marginal revenue product equals marginal cost, and inversion of the supply function leads to the optimal level of the aggregate input. In general we have $R_i = f(PP_i/p,\ S_i)$ where R is demanded for aggregate input. Due to the nature of the base data, it is not possible to identify the production structure for each agricultural commodity. Agricultural production is divided into two distinct sectors, crop production and livestock production. The aggregate input for the crop sector is simply the sum over the aggregate input for each of the crop subsectors: $R_c = \Sigma\, R_i$.

The next stage in optimisation is the splitting of the aggregate composite resource in the crop sector. Part of the input is modelled as strictly fixed coefficients. This is essentially seed input, feed input for draught cattle, and urban inputs (manufactures, energy, and services). The urban inputs are further split into domestic and imported goods, following the Armington framework in which domestic and imported goods in the same sector are assumed to be imperfect substitutes.[21] The residual input is a composite which is split according to a constant elasticity of substitution (CES) aggregation function. This composite is composed of fertilizers, a composite of land + tractors, and a composite composed of labour + irrigated land + draught cattle. These three composite inputs are imperfect substitutes. They characterise the essential production structure where the intensity of land, labour and chemicals use will depend on their relative prices.

The treatment of the livestock sector is similar but the production structure is different. Seed, feed, and urban inputs are likewise fixed coefficients, except for the three important feed grains: wheat, coarse grains, and oils. The residual input is therefore a composite aggregate of wheat, coarse grains, oils, and the land + tractors composite. This treatment reflects the substitution between intensive meat production based on feed input, and range-fed meat production based on the extensive use of lands.

The supply of cattle, land, and tractors depends on previous investments. Investment in the key agricultural factors is also disaggregated via a CES function which depends on the current price of the various components. The level of total rural investment is equal to the level of rural savings, less any share of rural savings which flows to the urban sector.

Agricultural products are perfect substitutes around the world; there is no differentiation depending on origin. Domestic prices, however, reflect domestic agricultural policies and are not necessarily equal to world prices. Agricultural policies are represented in three ways. First, they are reflected in the price wedge between domestic and world prices. Second, they are reflected by sectoral transmission coefficients; the coefficient measures the degree to which changes in the world prices are passed through to domestic prices. The third policy is an input subsidy to farmers which directly influences the supply decision.

Domestic agricultural prices are modelled as a weighted sum of current and lagged world prices and a domestic price index. The weights have been estimated for each sector from data provided by the Food and Agriculture Organisation. These weights reflect the historical agricultural policies of each region. The basis of these policies varies from region to region. In Europe, the policies have essentially been used to maintain incomes in the farm sector. Domestic prices have been kept higher than world prices via a variety of programmes which to a large extent isolate the European farmer from changes in world prices. In many developing regions, agricultural prices are below world prices, reflecting policies to ensure low food prices for the politically volatile urban sector. This type of policy is normally detrimental to the rural sector as it has unfavourable consequences on the rural–urban terms of trade and, in the long run, it distorts the efficient allocation of resources.

Rural households

Rural households derive their income from returns on the factors of production used in agricultural production plus any surplus over input costs. Disposable income is allocated to the different consumption goods via the Extended Linear Expenditure System (ELES), which leads to the following general equation for consumption:

$$C_i = \theta_i + \mu_i \, (Yd - \Sigma p_j \theta_j) \, / \, p_i$$

where C is consumption, Yd is disposable income, p is consumer price, and μ and θ are parameters.[22] Consumption is the sum of two components, a constant θ_i which is often interpreted as the subsistence minima, and a variable part which is a share of disposable income after total expenditures on the subsistence minima, sometimes referred to as discretionary income.[23] There are two additional levels of nesting in consumer demand for final urban goods. The first level is the Armington assumption which assumes imperfect substitution between goods produced domestically and imports. The next and final level is the allocation of the import aggregate across the different regions of the model – i.e., this assumes that the same import good is not a perfect substitute across regions.

Rural savings also derives from the ELES.

$$S = \mu_s \, (Yd - \Sigma p_j \theta_j)$$

where S is savings and μ_s is the share of discretionary income which is saved. (Note that $\Sigma \mu_i + \mu_s = 1$.) Rural savings may be augmented by a share of foreign aid flows.

Labour supply

Both the total labour supply and the urban labour supply grow at the same exogenously determined rate. There is also a flow of rural labour towards the urban sector which is modelled in the Harris-Todaro tradition. The level of migration is essentially a function of the ratio of *per capita* incomes in the rural and urban sectors. The unemployment effect is taken into account indirectly in the calculation of urban income. The model also incorporates a 'magnet' effect: even if there is strict parity in incomes, migration will occur due to the assumed attraction of living in an urban area. Growth in rural labour is the residual of the growth in total labour supply and urban labour supply.

Urban production

Urban production occurs along the rather classic lines of many computable general equilibrium (CGE) models.[24] A Leontief specification is used for intermediate inputs. Substitution is possible between imports and domestic intermediates. A CES aggregate is used for the factors of production, of which there are two, capital and labour. A constant returns to scale technology is assumed in the urban sector, so producer prices depend only on factor costs. Total domestic output is the sum of total domestic demand plus exports. Exports and domestic goods are assumed to be perfect substitutes. At all levels of demand for urban products, the Armington assumption is used. The degree of substitutability differs across commodity groups.

The aggregate capital stock is exogenous in each period. It is equal to the depreciated level of the previous period's stock plus any additional investments. As stated above, urban labour supply grows exogenously, but is augmented by a contemporaneous migration component.

Urban households

Urban households derive their income from production in the urban sector. They may obtain additional income from trade policies and unemployment compensation. Urban consumption is modelled similar to rural consumption (i.e., by the ELES), but with different income and price elasticities.

Urban investment is equal to urban savings, augmented by a share of rural savings, government savings, and a share of foreign aid flows. Demand for urban investment goods is a fixed coefficient function of total real investment.

The government sector

Government revenue derives from direct taxes in the rural and urban sectors, plus a share of income from foreign trade. Income from foreign trade is generated from the price wedge between the domestic and world price of agricultural commodities (it may be positive or negative, depending on the level of the price wedge and whether the region is a net importer or exporter). The level of government expenditures grows as a function of the growth rate of GDP. Sectoral expenditures are determined by a fixed coefficient function. The government purchases products only from the urban sector. Government savings is determined by the difference between revenues and expenditures.

Equilibrium equations and model closure

In the rural sector there are two key equilibrium prices. The first is the equilibrium price for the composite input of fertilizers + (land + tractors) + (irrigation + labour + cattle). The second is the equilibrium price for the composite factor tractors + land. The other equilibrium prices are calculated as residuals.

In the urban sector there is one key equilibrating price, the price of the composite factor labour + capital. This price will be a function of the nominal wage and the rental rate. The rental rate on capital always clears the capital market, where in any given period aggregate capital supply is fixed and aggregate demand for capital is derived from the aggregate CES value added function (via cost minimisation).

Semi-rigidity of the real wage is a key structural feature in the RUNS model, reflecting a common view of the operation of labour markets in many developing countries. The model can simulate both full flexibility and total rigidity of the real wage. Neither, however, appears to capture the whole story. In almost all regions, medium- and long-term unemployment (and/or underemployment) is an economic reality. Total rigidity is also too strong an assumption. The RUNS model assumes an intermediate position where the real wage is calculated as a weighted average of the equilibrium real wage and a sticky real wage. The weights are essentially 'guesstimates', but can easily be varied for sensitivity analysis.

The equilibrium real wage is equal to the real wage which would clear the labour market assuming the actual labour supply. This is not the true 'general' equilibrium real wage for two reasons. The urban labour supply itself is endogenous due to the migration component. Second, the true equilibrium real wage depends on interactions across all other markets whose equilibria are likely to be different under full employment. Unemployment will tend to decrease the actual real wage, since the equilibrium real wage will be below the actual real wage. The influence of unemployment on the real wage will depend on the value of the weighting factor in the wage equation.

In the goods market, world agricultural prices are solved so as to clear world markets.[25] For each region, macro closure is achieved by assuming that the balance of payments must equal exogenous foreign capital flows in each period. This is a key equilibrating mechanism. A growth in imports requires a growth in exports which can be achieved only by a devaluation of the real exchange rate. The real exchange rate is the equilibrating variable in each region.

World trade

World trade in the agricultural sectors is straightforward. Within each sector, agricultural goods are assumed to be perfect substitutes. Only the net trade of each country is accounted for. World trade in the urban sector goods is different. Demand for a good occurs at several levels. At the first level, an agent desires a certain level of a composite good. At the next level, the composite good is divided between a domestic and an imported good. In the final level in the decision structure, the imported good is allocated according to the region of origin.

NOTES

The authors are grateful to Christopher Bliss, Shanta Devarajan, Sebastian Edwards, Santiago Levy, Peter Lloyd, Nick Stern and Alan Winters for their helpful comments and to David Naude for research assistance. David Evans is Senior Fellow at the Institute for Development Studies, University of Sussex; Ian Goldin is Head of Programme and Dominique van der Mensbrugghe economist at the OECD Development Centre. The views expressed are those of the authors alone.

1 For evidence of developing country trade reform see: World Bank (1990, Table 4); World Bank (1988, Chapter 3); UNCTAD (1990).

2 See OECD (1991); Goldin and Knudsen (1990).

3 Often the substance of economic analysis is about differences between individual and collective outcomes. The phrase 'fallacy of composition' is used in policy discussions to refer to the failure of policy analysis to identify situations in which individual and collective interests diverge.

4 Milestones in the debate include: Prebisch (1950) and Singer (1950), whose export pessimism was challenged by Krueger (1961), Balassa (1971) and Bhagwati (1978a, 1978b). Lewis (1980) countered the optimistic challenge in the light of the apparent slowing of OECD growth, arguing that it would be better for developing countries to promote South–South trade, while Cline (1982) showed that without increases in market access to developed markets, developing countries could not hope to emulate the dynamic Asian economies. Riedel (1984, 1988) and Balassa (1987) countered that there was no correlation between developing country exports and OECD rates of growth, and that with effective price and exchange rate policies, international demand no longer represents a significant constraint on developing country export growth, but this view has recently been challenged by Faini *et al.* (1990).

5 World Bank and IMF adjustment programmes generally make small country assumptions. See, for example, Michaely (1986), Krueger (1978), Goldstein (1986), Thomas and Nash (1990), World Bank (1988, 1990) and World Bank and UNDP (1989). Note that the small country assumption is an extreme case of the elasticity proposition by which the elasticity of demand for one seller is much greater than for the market as a whole.

6 See Koester *et al.* (1990); and UNCTAD (1989).

7 See Evans (1991).

8 For documentation of the collapse of tropical product commodity prices in the 1980s, see UNCTAD (1989, Annex Table 4).

9 See, for example, Bateman *et al.* (1990), which recommends the removal of cocoa export taxes in Ghana.

10 Note that in the absence of domestic consumption of the exportable, the profit-maximising tax is also welfare-maximising.

11 For some types of non-linear demand curves, it is possible for the optimal taxes to decrease. However, the result in the text will hold for the linear and for the constant own-price elasticities implied by the ELES used in the RUNS model.

12 The World Bank has simultaneously renewed its commitment to the RUNS model, which is now being used in the context of the World Bank's 'Long-Term Prospects' and other projections. The development of the model is a collaborative effort between the OECD Development Centre and the World Bank, with development work centred at the OECD under the direction of Ian Goldin.

13 In the present formulation of the RUNS model, half of the export tax revenue is allocated to rural households and half to government revenue. For non-agricultural sectors, there are no trade tax wedges: it is implicitly assumed that all trade taxes are included in household savings and are transferred to government to finance investment expenditure through the gross savings–investment balance relationship.

14 Note that the estimated 1993 price wedges are based on projections of past pricing behaviour. In so far as some countries have already changed export tax policy since the 1985 base period, the results reported capture the effects of some reforms which may already have taken place.

15 For a discussion of indexes relating to the real exchange rate calculated on the export and the import side, see Devarajan *et al.* (1991). In the RUNS model, there is a perfect elasticity of transformation between production for domestic and export markets so that tax-inclusive domestic and export prices are the same, and only the import-side real exchange rate index is relevant.

16 In its present formulation of post-simulation analysis, Hicksian Equivalent Variations and a disaggregation of sources of welfare gain or loss is not undertaken. This facility is being developed for future RUNS simulations.

17 For Low Income Asia and the Mediterranean (not represented in Table 8.2), there is a slight improvement in GDP. This occurs because there are export subsidies on tree crop exports in the Mediterranean, and no taxes on exports of cocoa from Low Income Asia.

18 Our supply elasticities are derived by the International Trade Division of the World Bank.

19 For a full description of the RUNS model, see Burniaux and van der Mensbrugghe (1990).

20 The agricultural goods are wheat, rice, coarse grains, sugar, meats, coffee, cocoa, tea, oils, dairy, other food products, wool, cotton, other non-food products. The urban products are manufactured goods, energy, services, equipment, and fertilisers.

21 See Armington (1969).

22 See Deaton and Muellbauer (1980) for a derivation of some of the properties of the ELES consumption system.

23 Note that in either estimating or calibrating the parameters, there is nothing which guarantees the parameter θ to be positive.

24 For a detailed description of classical CGE models for developing economies see Dervis *et al.* (1982).

25 Computationally, supply and demand from all regions are aggregated and the equilibrium world price is solved via a *tatônnement* procedure.

REFERENCES

Armington, P. (1969) 'A Theory of Demand for Products Distinguished by Place of Production', *IMF Staff Papers*, **16**: 159–78.

Balassa, B. (1971) *The Structure of Production in Developing Countries*, Baltimore, Johns Hopkins University Press.

(1987) 'The Adding-Up Problem' (mimeo); *PRE Working Paper*, **30**, Washington, D.C.: World Bank (1989).

Banuri, T. (1991) *Economic Liberalization: No Panacea*, Oxford: Clarendon Press.

Bateman, M. J. *et al.* (1990) 'Ghana's Cocoa Pricing Policy', *Working Paper*, **WPS 429**, Washington, D.C.: World Bank.

Bhagwati, J. N. (1978a) *Anatomy and Consequences of Exchange Control Regimes*, Cambridge, MA: Ballinger/NBER.

(1978b) *Foreign Trade Regimes and Economic Development: Anatomy and Consequences of Exchange Control Regimes*, Cambridge, MA: Ballinger/NBER.

(1988) 'Export-promoting Trade Strategy: Issues and Evidence', *World Bank Research Observer*, **3(1)**: 27–57.

Burniaux, J. M. and D. van der Mensbrugghe (1990) 'The RUNS Model: A Rural–Urban North–South General Equilibrium Model for Agriculture Policy Analysis', *Technical Paper*, **33**, Paris: OECD Development Centre.

Burniaux, J. M., F. Delorme, I. Lienert, and J. Martin (1990) 'WALRAS – A Multi-Sector Multi-Country Applied General Equilibrium for Quantifying the Economy-Wide Effects of Agricultural Policies', *OECD Economic Studies*, **13**: 69–102

Cline, W. (1982) 'Can the East Asian Model of Development be Generalised?', *World Development*, **10(2)**: 81–90.

Cornia, A. C., R. Jolly and F. Stewart, (eds) (1987) *Adjustment with a Human Face: Protecting the Vulnerable and Promoting Growth*, Oxford: Oxford University Press.

Deaton, A. and J. Muellbauer (1980) *Economics and Consumer Behavior*, Cambridge: Cambridge University Press.

De Melo, J. and S. Robinson (1989) 'Product Differentiation and Treatment of Foreign Trade in Computable General Equilibrium Models of Small Economies', *Journal of International Economics*, **27**: 47–67.

Dervis, K., J. de Melo and S. Robinson (1982) *General Equilibrium Models for Developing Policy*, Cambridge: Cambridge University Press.

Devarajan, S. *et al.* (1991) 'External Shocks, Purchasing Power Parity, and the Equilibrium Real Exchange Rate', Department of Agricultural and Resource Economics, University of California, Berkeley, *Working Paper*, **611**.

Edwards, S. (1989) *Real Exchange Rates, Devaluation, and Adjustment: Exchange Rate Policy in Developing Countries*, Cambridge, MA: MIT Press.

Evans, H. D. (1989a) *Comparative Advantage and Growth: Trade and Development in Theory and Practice*, Hemel Hempstead: Harvester–Wheatsheaf.

(1989b) 'Alternative Perspectives on Trade and Development', Chapter 24 in H. Chenery and T. N. Srinivasan (eds), *Handbook of Development Economics*, vol. II, Amsterdam: North-Holland.

(1991) 'Visible and Invisible Hands in Trade Policy Reform', in C. Colclough and J. Manor (eds), *States or Markets? Neo-liberalism and the Development Policy Debate*, Oxford: Oxford University Press.

Faini, R., F. Clavijo and A. Senhadji-Semlali (1990) 'The Fallacy of Composition Argument: Does Demand Matter for LDCs' Manufacturing Exports?' (mimeo).

General Agreement on Tariffs and Trade (GATT) (1986–90) *International Trade Year Book*, Geneva: GATT.

Godfrey, M. (1985) 'Trade and Exchange Rate Policy', *IDS Bulletin*, July: 31–8.

Goldin, I. and O. Knudsen (eds) (1990) *Agricultural Trade Liberalization: Implications for Developing Countries*, Paris and Washington, D.C.: OECD and World Bank.

Goldstein, M. (1986) 'The Global Effects of Fund-Supported Adjustment Programs', *IMF Occasional Paper*, **42**, Washington, D.C.: IMF.

Harrigan, J. and P. Mosley (1991) 'Evaluation of the Impact of World Bank Structural Adjustment Lending 1980–87', *Journal of Development Studies*, **27(3)** April.

Harris, J. and M. Todaro (1970) 'Migration, Unemployment and Development: A Two-Sector Analysis', *American Economic Review*, **60(1)** (March): 126–42.

Johnson, H. G. (1950–1) 'Optimum Welfare and Maximum Revenue Tariffs', *Review of Economic Studies*, **19**: 28–36.

Karunasekera, M. (1984) 'Export Taxes on Primary Products: A Policy Instrument in International Development', *Commonwealth Economic Papers*, **19**, London: Commonwealth Secretariat.

Koester, U., H. Schafer and A. Valdes (1990) *Demand-Side Constraints and Structural Adjustment in Sub-Saharan African Countries*, Washington, D.C.: IFPRI.

Krueger, A. O. (1961) 'Export Prospects and Economic Growth', *Economic Journal*, June: 436–42.

(1978) *Foreign Trade Regimes and Economic Development: Liberalization Attempts and Consequences*, Cambridge, MA: Ballinger for the NBER.

Lewis, W. A. (1980) 'The Slowing Down of the Engine of Growth', The Nobel Lecture, *American Economic Review*, **70(4)**: 555–64.

Lipton, M. (1987) 'Limits of Price Policy for Agriculture: Which Way for the World Bank?', *Development Policy Review*, **5**: 197–215.

Mabbs-Zeno, C. and B. Krissoff (1990) 'Tropical Beverages in the GATT' in Goldin and Knudsen (1990).

Michaely, M. (1986) 'The Timing and Sequencing of Trade Policy Reform', in A. M. Choksi and D. Papageorgiou (eds), *Economic Liberalization in Developing Countries*, Oxford: Blackwell.

Michaely, M., D. Papageorgiou and A. Choksi (eds) (1990, 1991) *Liberalizing Foreign Trade in Developing Countries* (7 vols), Oxford: Blackwell.

Organisation for Economic Cooperation and Development (OECD) (1991) *Agricultural Policies, Markets and Trade: Monitoring and Outlook 1991*, Paris: OECD.

Panagariya, A. and M. Schiff (1990a) 'Commodity Exports and Real Income in Africa: A Preliminary Analysis', paper prepared for the World Bank Africa Economic Issues Conference (Nairobi, 4–7 June).

Panagariya, A. and M. Schiff (1990b) 'Optimum and Revenue Maximising Trade Taxes in a Multicountry Framework', Washington, D.C.: World Bank (mimeo).

Prebisch, R. (1950) *The Economic Development of Latin America and its Principal Problems*, New York: United Nations.

Riedel, J. (1984) 'Trade as the Engine of Growth in Developing Countries, Revisited', *Economic Journal*, **94(373)** March: 56–73.

(1988) 'The Demand for LDC Exports of Manufacturers: Estimates from Hong Kong', *Economic Journal*, **98(389)** March: 138–48.

Salvatore, D. and T. Hatchet (1991) 'Inward and Outward Oriented Trade Strategies', *Journal of Development Studies*, **37(3)**: 1–25.

Singer, H. W. (1950) 'The Distribution of Gains between Investing and Borrowing Countries', *American Economic Review*, **40(2)**: 473–85.

Stewart, F. (1984) 'Recent Theories of International Trade: Some Implications for the South', in H. Kierskowski (ed.), *Monopolistic Competition and International Trade*, Oxford: Oxford University Press.

Syrquin, M. and H. B. Chenery (1989) 'Patterns of Development 1950 to 1983', *Discussion Papers*, **41**, Washington, D.C.: World Bank.

Thomas, V. and J. Nash (1990) 'Trade Policy Reform: Recent Evidence From Theory and Practice', Washington, D.C.: World Bank (mimeo).

Thomas, V., K. Martin and J. Nash (1990) 'Lessons in Trade Policy Reform', *Policy and Research Series*, **10**, Washington, D.C.: World Bank.

Tower, E. (1977) 'Ranking the Optimum Tariff and the Maximum Revenue Tariff', *Journal of International Economics*, **7**: 73–9.

UNCTAD (1989, 1990) *Trade and Development Report*, Geneva: United Nations.

Van der Mensbrugghe, D., J. Martin and J. M. Burniaux (1990) 'How Robust are the WALRAS Results?', *OECD Economic Studies*, **13**: 173–204.

World Bank (1983, 1987) *World Development Report*, New York: Oxford University Press.

World Bank (1988) 'Adjustment Lending: An Evaluation of Ten Years of Experience', Country Economics Department, *Policy and Research Series*, **1**, Washington, D.C.: World Bank.

World Bank and UNDP (1989) *Africa's Adjustment and Growth in the 1980s*, Washington, D.C.: World Bank.

World Bank (1990) 'Adjustment Lending Policies for Sustainable Growth', Country Economics Department, *Policy and Research Series*, **14**, Washington, D.C.: World Bank.

Discussion

CHRISTOPHER BLISS

The authors of Chapter 8 address the problem of the 'fallacy of composition', which arises when trade expanding reforms which would be good for the individual country acting alone are undertaken by many countries. The result of the summed actions for many countries may be a decline in the terms of trade such that all the countries would be better off by not implementing the reforms. For the authors the export of tropical products from sub-Saharan Africa is the case in point; export tax agreements are examined as a possible answer to the fallacy of composition problem, and the results illustrated by output from the RUNS model.

The 'fallacy of composition' is an old idea. Nicholas Stern long ago expressed to me the fear that by encouraging small countries to treat border prices as constants, the Little–Mirrlees method might trap those who used it into neglecting the effect of the general application of the approach on the future time path of those prices. In the case which he had in mind, tea farming might look good in many small countries if one assumed a continuation of present tea prices which the expansion of tea farming would not support.

The authors note that the evidence from cross-section studies of a connection between trade-expanding structural adjustment and enhanced economic growth is far from unqualified, although the old ways of import substitution and inward-looking policy are so discredited in the developing countries that nowadays OECD countries could learn some lessons in trade liberalisation from their developing trade partners.

Cross-section studies are notoriously difficult ground on which to verify intuitively plausible relationships. With consumption studies, for example, the relation which emerges from a cross-section may not be that which applies over time. Investigations of structural reform are typically part cross-section, part intertemporal, as growth rates are compared. Growth rates are attractive statistics since they are pure numbers easily compared across countries. It is not clear, however, that theory predicts more rapid long-run growth as a consequence of reform. Countries implement reforms at different dates and with varying energy; hence a comparison of growth rates at the end of some period is at best an imperfect test.

Theoretical cost-benefit analysis would maintain that predictions for future prices should be as good as possible and never consist simply of the extrapolation of present prices into the future. The fallacy of composition point reminds us that there is a game theory side to the accurate prediction of future prices. The Nash equilibrium case mentioned in Chapter 8 is presumably the Nash solution to the common knowledge game of several smallish countries, which embodies accurate prediction, and also terms of trade deterioration, but much less than would occur with static expectations. A too easy assumption of common knowledge and Nash equilibrium sometimes worries game theorists, but as usual it is hard to find an alternative procedure.

Note, however, that cooperative export taxes are not simply an alternative to the non-cooperative Nash game, as proposed by the authors. Schemes which promote the exchange of information may themselves be valuable if they help to move all parties towards a Nash equilibrium from the direction of static expectation adjustment. Otherwise the case for export taxes is the same as the case for any export cartel and the problems also familiar. If the members are poor sub-Saharan countries and the scheme works, it would be ungracious to oppose it. Yet experience teaches that export cartels lead to many difficulties of outside competition, insider cheating, distributional problems and fiscal distortion, so *caveat emptor*.

In the longer term, the unfavourable terms of trade prognosis, if correct, indicates that the comparative advantage of tropical countries does not lie in the wholesale expansion of their traditional exports. This is unsurprising if one considers that distorted policy has long ago suppressed the expression of much underlying comparative advantage. Strong comparative advantage in certain tropical products may have asserted itself despite distorted policy, but this does not imply a scope for large-scale and general expansion.

I remain sceptical whether the tropical countries would be well-advised to try to promote joint export taxation schemes. The principle may be good but the practical consequences are quite unpredictable, and the costs of failure can be severe.

Part Three
Risk and adjustment

---

9 Markets, stabilisation and structural adjustment in Eastern European agriculture

RONALD W. ANDERSON and
ANDREW POWELL

1 Introduction

In this paper we consider issues arising in the development of a market economy in Eastern Europe, with particular reference to agriculture. The central question addressed is: to what extent is it possible to achieve the transformation from a planned economy to a market economy while satisfying a desire for a stable economic environment?

It is frequently stated that there are currently large uncertainties facing Eastern Europe. For instance, the future of the USSR, the major trading partner of all of the countries in the region, is a significant, exogenous source of uncertainty. Moreover, there are crucial uncertainties relating to the adjustment *within* the countries of the region. How will the proposed privatisation plans proceed? Where will true comparative advantages lie?

In many cases, changes are likely to arise in the form of discrete shocks rather than smooth processes and changes are likely to be permanent, not temporary. For instance, a collapse in the USSR, if it does occur, may be sudden. Changes in exchange rates are likely to be discrete, permanent devaluations. Changes in the trade regime, opening these economies to increased Western imports, are also likely to be in the form of discrete and permanent shocks.

In the face of these uncertainties, there is an understandable tendency for enterprises and individuals to seek stability. This is particularly marked in agriculture.[1] The plea for greater stability has often been in the form of a call for state interventions. Indeed, one way of satisfying the desire for stability is simply to stop the process of liberalising the economy. However, such a clear-cut policy reversal is generally rejected, while at the same time it is suggested that a government can intervene to eliminate excessive instability. The problem with this approach is to define a coherent framework for distinguishing unacceptable changes from those that are necessary, or even desirable.[2]

One perspective on the process of change in Eastern Europe is as a disequilibrium adjustment. The starting point was a set of production and consumption patterns that did not constitute a competitive equilibrium. Evidence for this comes in the form of the pervasive taxes and transfers and the numerous forms of rationing during the period of central planning. The system of administered prices and quantitative controls prevented any tendency to converge to the competitive equilibrium. Price liberalisation, and the elimination of many subsidies, will allow markets to adjust to find a more market-based equilibrium.

While this characterisation may be too stark or simplistic, it places the emphasis on the disequilibrium adjustment that must proceed simultaneously in many sectors. Given this perspective, the problem of establishing even the basic parameters of the uncertainty represents a daunting task. For example, what is the long-run average price about which plans and perhaps stabilisation programmes could be made? What are the areas of a country's comparative advantage? These difficult questions are rendered even more difficult in the context of liberalising economies. In fact, from the perspective of anticipating new equilibria, it is even worse than our analogy suggests. For not only do we face liberalised markets but also state enterprises are being privatised and the legal–accounting framework is changing. Consequently, the economic agents, their objectives and the array of exchange goods are all in the process of change.

This is the environment where it is hoped to find a response to the strong and growing calls for economic policies to reduce uncertainties. The issue is how this can be done without inhibiting constructive change.

In this paper we focus on three possible approaches to reducing uncertainty within the context of the liberalised economies of Eastern Europe:

* trade tools
* domestic market stabilisation programmes
* market-based risk contracts.

There have been some attempts to compare these tools.[3] Generally, past analytical comparisons have been made in the context of smoothing or hedging around some long-run equilibrium. In contrast, we start from the perspective of adjustment to a new equilibrium as we have outlined it above. There are thus two set of issues that need to be considered when evaluating an instrument in the context of Eastern Europe. One is the potential effectiveness of achieving some given goal for stabilisation. The second is the implication of using the tool for the adjustment to a new equilibrium.

In Section 2, 3 and 4 we examine these three categories of tools.

Throughout the paper, we consider the market for grains as an important example of an agricultural market undergoing liberalisation. In Section 5 we briefly compare the stabilisation tools within Hungary and Poland, again concentrating on grains. These countries are similar to the extent that they both have important agricultural economies and have both taken important steps towards adopting market economies, but they also offer interesting contrasts. Poland has followed a radical course with a swift liberalisation programme, whereas Hungary has adopted a more gradual approach. Nevertheless, Budapest boasts the first futures market in the region. In Section 6 we present a brief conclusion.

2 Stabilisation by trade tools

The basic idea of these tools is to stabilise border prices through a progressive system of border taxes and subsidies. Generally, such schemes are called *variable levies* systems. There are a great many different variants, depending whether they apply to imports, exports or both, whether they are symmetric or asymmetric, and how the tax–subsidy rate is calculated with respect to world price and some more stable reference price.

As an illustration, consider the case of levies applied to exports. Such schemes are quite widely employed in developing countries.[4] They can be represented by the expression,

$$E = W - L$$

where E is the price received for exports, W is the world price and L is the export levy.

In a symmetric system,

$$L = A(W - R)$$

where R is the reference price of the system and A is a parameter. For a progressive system, $A > 0$. In that case, when the world price exceeds the reference price, the levy is an export tax (i.e., $L > 0$). If the world price is below the reference, exports are subsidised ($L < 0$).

The parameter A determines the relative weight of the reference price in the determination of the export price and the degree of stabilisation. When R is fixed, the export price is entirely stabilised by setting $A = 1$. Note that, with R fixed, a greater degree of smoothing of the export price is obtained only at the expense of increased volatility of tax receipts. In an asymmetric system,

$$L = A \max (W - R, 0)$$

That is, only taxes are taken.

Enforcement of the system inevitably involves conferring a degree of monopoly power for exports on some institution. The precise forms that this takes seem to be as many as there are individual cases.[5] Indeed, the systems appear to have as much to do with an implicit definition of property rights as a technique to manage risk. For example, in the case of African export marketing boards there appears to be a strong element of transferring a surplus from the nominal owners of the resources to the state.[6] In other cases (e.g., coffee in Colombia), the system appears to be more neutral from the producer perspective, with income smoothing over periods of low world prices.

A variable levy to stabilise import prices is analogous. Once again symmetric and asymmetric case can be defined, the asymmetric case where the government, on behalf of consumers, has written put options for domestic producers with a strike equal to the reference price.

Although there may be little difficulty conceptually with these schemes, we believe they may be costly and inappropriate in the context of the disequilibrium adjustment of Eastern Europe. The taxes and subsidies involved are distortionary, and will involve an efficiency loss, they will tend to preserve current trading patterns. However, they are surely a poor reflection of comparative advantage both before and after liberalisation. By maintaining the *status quo*, they will seriously undermine the process of adjustment towards a competitive equilibrium. This will constitute an example of the spectre of cumulative distortions which although appearing individually small nevertheless lead to an equilibrium that is far from optimal.

It is sometimes argued that efficiency costs will be small since no permanent deviation from long-run world price is intended. Even assuming that a variable levies system is mean-neutral, a fundamental objection remains.[7] Stabilising at the long-term mean will lead producers to equate marginal costs with long-term price rather than the short-term price, as required for efficiency. To argue that these are small costs implies that supply and demand curves are inelastic, however, there is no serious empirical evidence to support this contention with Eastern Europe. Furthermore, if world commodity prices are stationary at all, the rate of mean reversion is very low indeed. This means that a wedge between the world price and the long-term mean must persist for a very long time, and routinely beyond the horizon of a single crop year. If distorted prices are allowed to affect decisions about acreage cultivated, varieties planted, and level of chemical treatments employed, the effect on supply will clearly be non-trivial.

Beyond these problems it must be recognised that past experience shows that variable levies are generally not mean-neutral even over relatively long horizons of 10 years or more.[8] Thus in our view, the desirability of variable levies systems should then be viewed as essentially an issue about the assertion of property rights. The important parameters of these systems (A, R, etc.) tend to be negotiated collectively. Bargaining theory leads us to expect that the results will vary significantly across cases as a reflection of political coalition formation, rather than as an aggregation of risk preferences.[9]

This issue is related to the question of whether the system parameters should be set by rules rather than by discretion. In many systems (e.g., the EC's CAP, Sweden's variable levy system, Colombia's coffee trade regime, etc.) the reference price is determined by a committee including producer representatives who often base off producer costs. Within Eastern Europe, where traditionally price formation has been on an historical cost-plus basis, there will be a strong tendency for this pricing mechanism to prevail. However, historical costs in this context are poor indicators of marginal (or even average) costs. And even if they were accurate, stabilisation around, say, average costs would hinder adjustment by delaying exit from sectors which should contract and entrance into sectors which should expand.

In the light of these considerations, economists often recommend that variable levies be designed around a rule that will not be changed on the basis of political convenience.[10] This advice appears to be usually, but not always, ignored. The exceptions are a number of systems that are based on moving averages of historical prices. However, as we have seen, there are also problems with these types of rules. These problems are generic to moving average schemes, whether they are used to formulate variable levies or for domestic market stabilisation measures as discussed in Section 3.

We have argued above that changes in Eastern Europe may take the form of discrete shocks and may be permanent in nature: i.e., the generation process for prices will (a) be non-stationary and (b) exhibit discrete jumps. Even if this is not the case, there is considerable recent evidence for international commodity prices to have exactly these characteristics.[11] this is true of oil, metals and agricultural commodities. Agricultural commodities do exhibit a greater component of cyclical variation, due to seasonal factors, but also suffer from sharp jumps in prices, and reversion towards long-run means tends to be weak.[12]

Non-stationarities and jumps create significant problems for moving average-type rules. An alternative is to adopt a partial adjustment technique with the same average lag. Relative to the partial adjustment technique adopting a moving average rule may yield a higher degree of stabilisation but at a significant extra cost.[13] The cost is in terms of an increased maximum amount of resources required to run the scheme, these problems occur because the moving average takes a longer time to adjust to the new mean than the partial adjustment. In short, the danger is that moving average schemes tend to preserve the status quo. This is especially evident when there are sharp jumps in the process generating prices.

3 Public stabilisation through domestic markets

We now turn to forms of market intervention that will specifically aim at stabilising domestic prices. There are a great variety of possible schemes, and some have already been proposed for Eastern Europe. They are relevant to the extent that trade barriers or transport costs can support deviations from world prices.

The essence of all schemes is for a public authority to purchase at a time when demand is thought to be inadequate and sell when demand is excessive. In turn, this implies the maintenance of a buffer stock, and hence the assumption is that the good is storable.

Buffer stock programmes have been subjected to repeated economic analyses and have been criticised on a number of grounds. They are flawed if the underlying market demand or supply is non-stationary (Townsend, 1977), they are vulnerable to speculative attacks (Salant, 1983) and they can result in both high direct costs and serious efficiency losses (Knudsen and Nash, 1990). These criticisms are convincing and relevant to the context of Eastern Europe. For example, we have argued above that shocks are likely to be frequent and permanent and hence non-stationarities problematic. However, there are other aspects on which we wish to focus here.

The hallmark of a buffer stock operation is the public supply of storage. This should be seen as competing with private storage. As in other economic activities, if the supply of private storage is inadequate due to certain externalities then public intervention may be justified. Whether the correct form of intervention is the direct supply of storage is a second important question.

Private merchandising firms store to arbitrage over time, and by doing so stabilise prices. If left to private decisions, goods will be stored when expected price rises outstrip the costs of storage where costs are composed of physical storage costs (including deterioration and insurance against loss), credit, and the risk premium.[14]

Past practice in Eastern Europe was for the state to announce the price for important agricultural goods for the year: in other words, expected price rises were zero over the year and with no incentive to store it was not surprising that private institutions ready to fulfil this role did not become well developed. There is a serious possibility that the managers of any buffer fund will tend to carry over this practice, which will have an extremely discouraging effect on the development of private markets. Indeed, the objective of a state agency to stabilise prices is in direct contradiction to the objective of developing private merchandising in this context.

On the other hand, there are problems for the development of private storage, for example, there are numerous signs of credit rationing. However, externalities in the credit market may not justify public supply of storage. For example, ensuring a supply of credit at reasonable rates of interest may then be a better solution. Further, the problem of access to credit is linked to the problem of risk.

If the perceived riskiness of storage is high (due to a high price variance) then the cost of credit will rise, and the amount of storage will diminish. Also, the risk premium required will increase, further lowering the amount of private storage required. In turn, this implies a higher price variance, as there is a reduced effect of storage to lower price fluctuations: that is, instability breeds more instability, and this externality may justify storage by a less risk averse public entity.[15]

This is a potentially legitimate argument. However, an alternative solution is to create risk-shifting or insurance contracts such as futures contracts which we discuss in Section 4. By reducing uncertainty, futures can mitigate problems in the credit market, reduce the cost of borrowing, allow credit markets to operate more smoothly, increase storage and thus reduce price variability, further increasing storage.

4 Market tools for risk management

In this section we consider the development of market-based tools for risk management in the context of the disequilibrium adjustment taking place in Eastern Europe. A first strategy to reduce uncertainty that a farm or processing firm can take is through diversification. There is, however, frequently a trade-off between increased diversification and economies of scale. In other words, if price risk can be reduced then there may be efficiency gains from specialisation, in any event, diversification may not allow the degree of risk reduction desirable. We shall consider more sophisticated techniques for risk-shifting – specifically, forwards, futures and options contracts, the principal risk management contracts that allow agents to shift risk in agriculture.

An option gives the holder the right, but not the obligation, to buy (in the case of a call option) to sell (in the case of a put option) a quantity of the commodity at a specified price (the strike) during a certain period.

Although options provide attractive hedges for farmers, as illustrated by the repeated calls by producers for guaranteed minimum prices, the problem is that there are no natural sellers of such options. This need not be a problem if there are liquid physical or futures markets for the commodity, then, options can be hedged by standard techniques.[16] Thus in Eastern Europe it is natural to think about the creation of liquid forwards and futures before thinking about the creation of options markets.

A forward contract is simply a standard merchandising contract calling for the delivery of the good at a later date, generally, no money changes hands until delivery occurs. One problem with these contracts is that of default risk: if prices rise, the seller has an incentive to default; if they fall, the buyer will be tempted to default. This problem is dealt with by enquiring about the credit worthiness of your counterparty, by requiring a collateral, or by adding a third-party credit guarantee.

Experience has shown that there are important benefits in developing standardised and formalised forward trading. Through standardisation, it is easy to arrange for secondary trading. For example, a producer who initially sells a good forward may find an attractive alternative use of the good. To pursue it, he will need to buy back his forward contract. If there is a regular flow of sellers and buyers of the same formal contract, recontracting is easy. This liquidity of the contract means that more and more participants will want to concentrate their trading in a particular contract, if so, this liquid contract will draw upon a large pool of information about supply and demand.

One route to a liquid forward market is for a large dealer (or dealers) to become market maker(s). This involves the dealer standing ready to buy or sell standard amounts at announced prices. Liquid dealer-operated forward markets exist in gold bullion, Brent oil, protein feedstuffs and foreign exchange. This last market is the biggest and deepest market in the world.

Futures markets are an alternative means of achieving a liquid market for deferred delivery contracts. The essence of futures contracting is a system of payments known as margins, which are designed to control for default risks. Margins are normally arranged through an exchange or associated clearing house. In general, an initial margin is paid by both buyer and seller as the deal is struck and then buyer and seller pay or receive a variation margin depending on price movements. On most exchanges, this margin is calculated on a daily basis such that buyer and seller receive their winnings, or post their losses, on a futures transaction each day.

In what follows, our arguments apply to both futures or standardised forward contracts. For brevity, we shall refer simply to futures. It is generally recognised that futures markets serve two purposes. The first function is that of price discovery. Futures markets allow agents (producers, consumers, traders and speculators) to make transactions based on their expectations. Hence futures prices reflect the market's view as to the likely course of future events.

Futures prices often become a standard reference for making plans and engaging in transactions. Producers will tend to produce more of the crop whose futures price is relatively high at the time of planting. Or merchandisers will negotiate the price of a cash transaction in relation to the futures price. Indeed, this practice can become highly developed; for many goods it is common to sign forward merchandising contracts with the price quoted as a specified basis above or below a futures price selected as a reference.

In Eastern Europe one of the signs of the underdeveloped nature of the market system is that it is often difficult to discern prices for a given good, or whether prices are tending to rise or fall. Consequently, a viable futures market will fill an informational void and, for that reason alone, will make a very positive contribution to market development.

The second function of a futures market is risk-shifting or hedging. A farmer or other commodity producer can sell a proportion of the harvest forward using futures contracts in order to gain more certainty about future incomes. However, this does not necessarily imply that incomes, year to year, are stabilised. Indeed, if commodity prices exhibit non-stationarity then we would not expect incomes to be stable. However, incomes will be more certain. In other words, futures may not stabilise incomes, but they may reduce uncertainty.

In our view, there is a third role for futures of particular importance in the context of Eastern Europe. We believe that such instruments can serve to reduce barriers to entry, increase competition and hence aid in the development of market economies. Consider the activities of grain purchase, sorting and trading. In some countries (e.g., Hungary and Poland) state grain companies are being privatised on a regional basis. This gives each regional grain company a high degree of monopsony power, especially as the limited storage capacity and processing facilities tend to be concentrated in their hands. A considerable responsibility is then placed on the threat of entry to ensure that this monopsony power is not abused.

A considerable deterrent to entry is risk, especially as most potential entrants are likely be relatively poor in terms of capital. Futures markets can reduce the risk involved in grain trading and facilitate entry into these activities. In this sense futures markets are pro-competitive. By reducing uncertainty, they can enhance the growth of competition. We view this role of futures as an extremely important one in the context of Eastern Europe during the current phase of market development.

For many agricultural commodities and in many countries, futures markets are regarded as an important and normal component of the merchandising system. However, some tend to view futures markets as rather marginal institutions. In part, this view may stem from the experience of interventionist agricultural systems, such as the EC's CAP, where the need for private risk management instruments is severely reduced. It may also stem from perceived problems in the operation of futures.

We do not wish to deny the existence of problems such as (a) the complexity of the instruments, (b) inadequate credit or banking, (c) the potential for abusive trading practices, (d) an inadequate legal environment or (e) inflation. However, we do feel that there problems are surmountable. Further, in some areas, futures have beneficial effects, such as the potential to improve the functioning of credit markets discussed in Section 3.

An interesting question is whether futures markets are required in each country in the region, or whether agents in Eastern Europe should simply use international exchanges in Paris, London or the USA. Without full convertibility of the relevant currencies, this remains a hypothetical question. However, ignoring this problem, the value of a futures contract to a hedger is dependent on how closely the relevant futures price tracks the price of the physical commodity to be hedged. Alternatively, it depends in an inverse fashion on the variability of the difference between these two prices, this difference being known as the basis. In turn, the basis variability depends on exchange rate fluctuations, variations in transport costs, variations in qualities of the physical good and on shifts in trade policies.[17] Our view is that for grains, where the Chicago market is more relevant, the basis between Chicago futures and Eastern Europe grain prices is likely to be highly variable. Chicago futures may thus not provide a good hedge. However, there may be a stronger case for a single, regional exchange within Eastern Europe, especially as the economies within the region become more integrated.

5 Risk management in the grain sectors of Hungary and Poland

The agricultural sectors are of great importance for both Hungary and Poland. Agriculture and food production accounts for about 20 per cent of Hungary's GDP and about 20 per cent of total employment.[18] Much of Hungarian agriculture is organised within large state farms or cooperatives. In Poland, agriculture accounts for about 12 per cent of GDP and

28 per cent of employment. Private farms remained very significant throughout the period of central planning and as much as 40 per cent of the population still resides in rural areas.[19]

Hungary produces about 14 million tonnes of grain with about 6 million tonnes of this being relatively hard wheat and about 8 million tonnes being coarse grains, mostly maize. The coarse grains and about 2.5 million tonnes of the wheat are used for feeding animals. Hungary has been a regular exporter of wheat, with exports exceeding 2 million tonnes in recent years. The Soviet Union has been by far the largest purchaser of Hungarian wheat, followed by Czechoslovakia, Poland, and Eastern Germany.

Polish grain production has varied between 25 and 30 million tonnes. Soft wheat is the principal grain product, followed by barley, rye and triticale. Most grains are produced for livestock feeding, and are either consumed on the farm where they are produced or are exchanged only through local markets. The commercial grain business merchandises about 5 or 6 million tonnes of Polish grain. During the 1980s Poland imported as much as 2 million tonnes of wheat per year, most of which was of relatively harder varieties. An excellent harvest in 1990 combined with a reduction in consumption gave rise to some exports of rye and barley.

The Hungarian trade regime has been liberalised for a number of products, but throughout 1990 quantitative restrictions were in place for both grain imports and exports. Export licences, which formerly had been awarded only to the state grain export monopoly (AGRIMPEX) were extended to only one additional firm. In contrast, Poland adopted a very liberal trade regime. Quantitative import restrictions were eliminated in early 1990 and were replaced by tariffs. Subsequently, many tariffs were eliminated or reduced. Similarly, exports were liberalised; however, grains for human consumption are still subject to export licensing.

Under central planning, in Hungary and Poland, the procurement, storage and processing of the grain harvest was managed by a state grain monopoly although prices were set by government. In each case, the company was organised by province. There was a limited trade in grains among the cooperatives, state farms and (particularly in Poland) private farms. In both countries, liberalisation has implied that the former grain monopoly was broken up into separate provincial grain companies, but they continue to be state owned. Producers can now sell to anyone, and the provincial grain companies are free to determine their purchase prices for most grains independently.

The regional grain companies have inherited a great deal of monopsony power. Their main competition comes from grain companies in neighbouring provinces, but this is hampered by lack of good transport. Poland has passed an anti-monopoly law, and has created an aggressive anti-monopoly office. One of the first targets of this office has been the state grain companies. In the name of reducing the regional concentration, it is dividing some of the provincial companies and at the same time privatising them. In the case of Hungary, however, there is no general anti-monopoly law in operation.

Since the approaches to liberalisation have been different in Hungary and Poland, it is not surprising that different types of pressures have emerged. We now describe briefly the different experiences of these two countries, commencing with Poland.

In Poland the sudden liberalisation of almost all prices in 1989 translated into an immediate burst of inflation. The response by government was to maintain high interest rates, credit controls, an excess wage tax and a stable exchange rate. The effects on the grain economy were severe, with consumption and demand falling. Further, in 1990 Poland received food aid from the EC and elsewhere. The result of these factors was that wheat prices relative to the consumer price index dropped by 40 per cent in the first six months of 1990.

There was a political outcry against the devastation of the agricultural sector, and there was a widespread demand that the government should be set guaranteed minimum prices for major agricultural products and that these prices be based on average costs. The response to these demands was twofold. Credits were extended to agriculture at subsidised rates and the Polish parliament created a new, semi-independent Agency for Agricultural Markets (Agencja Rynku Rolnego). Parliament was vague as to the specific functions of this Agency; however, it did charge it with the task of 'stabilising the farm products markets and protecting farm incomes'.[20]

The debate that followed was a graphic illustration of the apparently conflicting objectives of liberalisation and stabilisation. A unique compromise was struck. A policy for the Agency was conceived whereby the Agency would make deferred delivery (forward) contracts. The Agency thus acts as a type of dealer-cum-market maker, although it remains under state control. Default risks are controlled as the forward contracts are signed only with agents possessing accredited storage facilities, and grains in store are used as collateral. Prices are set by the Agency, such that (i) the Agency does not hold large quantities of grains, (ii) forward prices rise to reflect the cost of storage, and (iii) the cost to the Agency of hedging its book by selling to large commercial users (or, in the future, by hedging on foreign futures markets conforms to the available budget). By the supply of forward contracts, the Agency was designed to allow price-fixing in advance and to encourage private storage.

In 1990, the Agency signed contracts for the delivery of about 600,000 tonnes of grain, about 10 per cent of the commercialised harvest in Poland, and was thus perceived as an extremely successful enterprise. However, there were drawbacks. First of all, it was deemed necessary for the Council of Ministers to approve the price schedules, and this made it virtually impossible for the Agency to change prices according to market conditions. Secondly, the forward contracts could be cancelled by mutual consent, and in practice the Agency agreed to cancel some contracts without penalty when sellers would have lost by their hedging operation. In effect, this turned the forward contracts into put options granted by the Agency for no premium. In brief, it implies that the hedgers received the minimum price that the government initially refused to grant. Finally, the Agency took no steps to hedge its position, and was forced to sell grains at considerable loss.

We now turn to the case of Hungary. Prior to the Second World War, Hungary was a major grain supplier throughout central Europe and the Budapest Grain Exchange played a prominent role in that grain economy. In 1989, the Hungarian Agricultural Commodity Exchange (Termeny-tozsde Kft) was founded in the hopes of eventually restoring Budapest to its former position of prominence in the region. The initiative for the exchange came from the two leading agricultural banks and AGRIMPEX. One reason that commodity trading emerged so rapidly after liberalisation was that AGRIMPEX had regularly used the Chicago Board of Trade (CBOT) soybean meal contract for hedging Hungary's protein meal imports. This familiarity, and the personal contacts so established, were important in setting the initial direction.

The model for the Budapest exchange is clearly the grain market at the CBOT. There are two futures contracts traded, one for wheat and one for maize. The contracts call for physical delivery at a location south of Budapest. Prices are determined by open outcry in a pit which is open to exchange members only. Membership is gained by buying a seat on the exchange, and is open to individuals only. This restriction is in the hope of avoiding domination by the state-owned companies and of creating a core group of local floor traders who will provide liquidity. All trades pass through a clearing house. There is a system of initial and variation margins, the latter being assessed after the close of every trading session (weekly).

Trading began in early 1990. By June weekly trading was up to 1000 tonnes of wheat and maize combined. Weekly volumes during the September harvest rose to about 3600 tonnes. However, this represented less than 3/100 of a per cent of the total harvest: that is, although the level of activity was non-negligible commercially it represented only a tiny fraction of the commercial grain trade.

The experience of the Budapest exchange can be deemed a qualified success in two respects. First, its prices quickly became established as the best indicators of market conditions; they are now used regularly by the government and also as references for off-exchange transactions. Second, there are indications that new private merchandisers are using the futures market and that it is already facilitating the process of entry into the business of storing and shipping grain.

The main shortcoming of the market is that encountered by most new futures contracts. It does not, at the time of writing, provide enough liquidity to be of practical use to large commercial users and thus cannot fulfil a large-scale hedging function. At some stage it will be vital for large commercials to enter, in order for the market to achieve a critical mass, and to become a dominant factor in merchandising.

6 Conclusions

In our introduction, we emphasised that the countries of Eastern Europe could be considered as moving from a disequilibrium position with quantity rationing to a more market-orientated position where prices are given more freedom to bring supply and demand into equality. The consensus is that this adjustment is required. Instability is therefore necessary, even desirable. The trade tools and stabilisation measures discussed in Sections 2 and 3 appear to hinder this process. They tend to upset market signals and preserve the status quo. It is possible that they may reduce uncertainty, but at the same time they stifle change.

On the other hand, futures markets can reduce uncertainty and – importantly – can encourage the adjustment process. The hedging role allows uncertainty reduction and the price discovery role allows expectations of future changes to be readily observed by all the relevant actors. Furthermore, by reducing uncertainty they can lower the cost of entry in agricultural production and merchandising, promoting competition.

In adopting a gradual approach to liberalisation, Hungary has allowed inertia to slow the pace of transformation. The result has been relatively small swings in relative prices and relatively moderate political reaction to the liberalisation of agriculture. In this environment, some enterprising organisations have initiated a futures market closely following the CBOT. The market has made a promising beginning. However, it remains to be seen whether this institution will become the effective hedging vehicle that will be needed if and when the Hungarian agricultural sector is exposed to more substantial supply and demand shocks.

The Polish approach has been to liberalise more radically and then to proceed to develop the necessary market institutions. This has prompted dissatisfaction with the consequences of liberalisation for the agricultural sector and the government has responded to calls for stabilisation by creating a specialised agency with significant powers. This agency has implemented an original forward contracting mechanism which has the potential to promote private merchandising.

The Polish experiment shows that governments can provide short-cuts to supply risk-sharing contracts. However, a public status appears to invite pressures from producer groups to use what funds are available to protect incumbent agricultural enterprises. In Hungary, this problem has been avoided but here a learning phase is required before the market can fulfil the full hedging role.

NOTES

We have benefited from discussions with a very great number of people in Budapest and Warsaw. We also would like to thank Stefan Tangermann of the University of Göttingen for the clarification of a number of trade issues. The views expressed in this paper are entirely our own and do not reflect those of any other individual or organisation.

The current paper is a drastically shortened version of Discussion Paper 9107 of IRES (Université Catholique de Louvain, 3 Place Montesquieu, B-1348 Louvain-la-Neuve, Belgium).

1 The 1990 presidential election results in Poland were widely interpreted as demonstrating growing discontent with the liberalisation process on the part of rural populations. The return to power of the revamped Communist Parties in elections in Rumania, Bulgaria and Albania can be credited to the success of these parties in rural areas. This experience is not unique to Eastern or Central Europe, thus much of this discussion pertains to other countries undergoing transformation.

2 For a political discussion of this problem, see Lesourne and Lecomte (1990).

3 See Gilbert (1990a) for a survey.

4 See Knudsen and Nash (1990), Gilbert (1990a) and many examples in UNCTAD (1987).

5 See Gilbert (1990a) for a discussion.

6 See Knudsen and Nash (1990).

7 See Walters (1987) for a discussion.

8 See Knudsen and Nash (1990) for a survey and Helleiner (1964) for a case study.

9 Note that there are often problems in defining the correct 'world price'. For example, in the case of grains, there are problems associated with variable concessions, variable and large transport costs, variable qualities and fluctuating exchange rates. For an expanded discussion, see Anderson and Powell (1991).

10 For example, Gilbert (1990a) and Knudsen and Nash (1990).

11 See, for instance, Deaton and Laroque (1990), Cuddington and Urzúa (1990) and Powell (1991).

12 See Anderson and Powell (1991, Appendix 1) for empirical results for maize.
13 See the simulation experiment detailed in Anderson and Powell (1991, Appendix 2), for an analysis.
14 We leave aside the slippery concept of the convenience yield, see Brennan (1958).
15 This perspective is consistent with the analysis presented by Arrow and Lind (1970).
16 See Black and Scholes (1973) for an analysis of the hedging strategy, and thus the evaluation of simple option contracts.
17 In the simplest case, if Chicago wheat were exported to Warsaw, say, the Chicago–Warsaw basis in zlotys would equal the dollar transport costs, handling fees, all converted to zlotys plus tariffs and domestic transport. Uncertainty about any of these contributes to basis risk.
18 See World Bank (1989).
19 See the joint Polish, EC, World Bank Task Force Report (1990).
20 The Law of 7 June 1990.

REFERENCES

Anderson, R. W. (1984) 'The Industrial Organization of Futures Markets: A Survey', in R. W. Anderson, *The Industrial Organization of Futures Markets*, Lexington: D. C. Heath.

Anderson, R. W. and A. Powell (1991) 'Markets, Stabilisation and Structural Adjustment in Eastern European Agriculture', **DP 9107** Université Catholique de Louvain, Belgium.

Arrow, K. J. and R. C. Lind (1970) 'Uncertainty and the Evaluation of Public Investment Decisions', *American Economic Review*, **60**: 364–78.

Black, F. and M. Scholes (1973) 'The Pricing of Options and Corporate Liabilities', *Journal of Political Economy*, May: 637–59.

Brennan, M. K. (1958) 'The Supply of Storage', *American Economic Review*, **68**: 316–404.

Cuddington, J. T. and C. M. Urzúa (1990) 'Trends and Cycles in the Net Barter Terms of Trade: A New Approach', *Economic Journal*, **99**: 426–42.

Deaton, A. and G. Laroque (1990) 'On the behaviour of commodity prices', Princeton University (mimeo); (1992) *Review of Economic Studies*, **59**.

Gilbert, C. L. (1990a) 'Domestic Price Stabilization Schemes for LDC's, May (mimeo).

(1990b) 'Futures Trading, Storage and Price Stabilization', *Working Paper*, **204**, Department of Economics, London: Queen Mary and Westfield College.

Helleiner, G. K. (1964) 'The Fiscal Role of the Marketing Boards in Nigerian Economic Development', *Economic Journal*, **64**: 582–610.

Knudsen, O. and J. Nash (1990) 'Domestic Price Stabilisation Schemes in Developing Countries', *Economic Development and Cultural Change*, **38**: 539–58.

Lesourne, J. and B. Lecomte (1990) *L'Après-Communisme*, Paris: Laffont.

Polish, EC, World Bank Task Force Report (1990) *An Agricultural Strategy for Poland*, Washington, D.C.: World Bank.

Powell, A. (1991) 'Commodity and Developing Country Terms of Trade: what *does* the long run show?', *Economic Journal*, November.

Salant, S. (1983) 'The Vulnerability of Price Stabilisation Schemes to Speculative Attack', *Journal of Political Economy*, **91**: 1–38.

Townsend, R. M. (1977) 'The Eventual Failure of Price Fixing Schemes', *Journal of Economic Theory*, **14**: 190–9.

UNCTAD (1987) 'Handbook of Trade and Control Measures', UNCTAD, **ISBN 92/1/112231–7**.

Walters, A. A. (1987) 'The Mischief of Moving Average Pricing', Washington D.C.: World Bank (mimeo).

World Bank (1989) 'Agricultural Policy Analysis: A Position Paper on Selected Issues' (mimeo).

Discussion

F. GERARD ADAMS

Chapter 9 begins with a clear, objective perspective on the problem of agricultural adjustment in Eastern Europe. The authors describe the need to move from massive disequilibrium under planning toward a market economy while, at the same time, satisfying desires for stability. The path is uncertain in ways that are external to the participants and very different from the ones usually encountered in agricultural markets. The destination – the ultimate level of equilibrium market prices and outputs – is not known.

The authors attempt to evaluate various approaches to stabilizing agricultural prices and incomes by:

- trade tools, such as variable import and export tariffs
- domestic stabilisation programmes, and
- market-based risk contracts – futures markets.

Their evaluation is based on three criteria:

- effectiveness as stabilisers
- facilitating (or impeding) the adjustment
- creation of new private enterprise institutions.

I remain uncertain which of these objectives comes first. The authors make many judgements which imply that the last criterion plays a most important role in their appraisals.

Sometimes a look at the real world is exceedingly revealing. That is certainly true in this case. This study includes a comparison of what happened in Hungary and in Poland: the contrast is striking. Whereas Hungary has developed a futures market, like that in Chicago, it accounts for only a very small fraction of trade, it does not do much to stabilise prices, and provides little hedging. In Poland, on the other hand, a government agency has been set up. It has provided a large volume of forward contracts, these are not hedged, and they do not appear to be enforced. In other words, as Anderson and Powell point out, they serve to guarantee minimum prices to farm producers. And, if market prices fall below the minima, the public sector bears the cost, the revealed preference is for minimum prices. The lack of hedging, like the low level of activity in the Hungarian market, suggests that there may not be anyone willing to take the other side of the market, risks may be too large and unpredictable, the need for cover for purchasers of agricultural products may be very different from the requirements of farmers to protect their incomes, and finally, the intent may be to subsidise agriculture, as in many other parts of the world.

What are the implications of this story? Economic and judgemental appraisals of different institutional approaches to risk reduction may not be very useful in the face of a desire by farmers with political clout for minimum prices rather than symmetric risk reduction.

One cannot but agree with the authors that a public institution setting minimum prices is likely to set them in a fixed way in relation to costs and/or political pressures, avoiding adjustment and discouraging the development of private trading institutions. Free market institutions allowed to operate with intervention could perhaps avoid this problem, though it is remarkable how few countries have allowed market forces to operate freely in agriculture. One is tempted to ask 'Why?'

In the absence of effective market mechanisms, it is essential to make an effort to see where the ultimate objective – the market price – might be. What is the destination of the adjustment process? This computation is a sort of planning exercise, looking first at agriculture and then at other relevant considerations – exchange rates and international competitiveness, for example. It may call for sophisticated modelling and forecasting studies. But it should be possible to get a fix on the longer-term outcome, an efficient price–output target. Once that has been established, minimum price provisions could be phased down and out gradually to develop eventual reliance on competitive private institutions operating in the market. Admittedly, until then the risk of continued government intervention in pricing remains very high. But such a gradualist approach may be more realistic than an overly quick reliance on futures markets.

NOTE

This comment was prepared while the author was a visiting researcher at the OECD Development Centre, Paris.

10 Should marketing boards stabilise prices through forward purchases?

CHRISTOPHER L. GILBERT

1 Stabilisation or hedging

The focus of discussion in international commodity policy in the decade immediately following the first OPEC price rise in 1973–4 was the negotiation of international commodity agreements (ICAs), in particular under the auspices of the UNCTAD Integrated Programme for Commodities. This process was almost totally unsuccessful, in part because the debate between the developed and the developing countries became politicised, and in part because the developed countries suspected, with some justice, that the so-called New International Economic Order (NIEO) would involve a move away from markets. The objective of stabilising prices at a level which was 'fair to consumers and remunerative to producers' suggested that these prices were likely to be higher on average than those which had prevailed under free market conditions.

Developed country suspicions about price stabilising agreements were enhanced by the performance of those agreements which were already operating. Five agreements were in place during this period, although not all were operational all the time. Two (cocoa and sugar) were completely ineffective. The coffee agreement was widely perceived as primarily a price-raising agreement – a coffee OPEC but both enforced and moderated by consumer representation. The tin agreement, which could claim a long history of successful stabilisation, was under-resourced in the 1980s and committed to defending what became (through the appreciation of the dollar) an absurdly high price – its spectacular collapse in 1985 was seen by many as the death knell of international stabilisation. Only the natural rubber agreement, the sole child of the UNCTAD programme, functioned reasonably efficiently.[1]

This undistinguished history, together with suspicions that stabilisation schemes would inhibit market mechanisms, lead agencies and governments in the developed economies to enquire whether stabilisation might be achieved through rather than against the market. The principal candidates for the performance of this function were futures and options markets. It was noted that the revenue of a farmer who sold his crop forward (equivalently, went short futures) would (in the absence of output and basis risk) be independent of the actual cash price out-turn. Alternatively, by purchasing an out-of-the-money put option, he could guarantee a minimum price level for his crop. This suggested that stabilisation might be obtained through greater use of futures and options markets where they existed, and through the growth of new markets where suitable markets were not already available.[2]

Two significant difficulties have emerged in relation to this suggestion. First, it has been found that while the use of futures markets does to some extent reduce price variability, it nevertheless does not in general give substantially more stable prices than are obtained from trading on cash markets. This is because, for storable commodities, cash and futures prices tend to move together.[3] Although liquid futures markets exist only a matter of 6–18 months ahead, producers could in principle hedge a long way forward by rolling over a succession of short-dated hedges. However, there is risk (basis risk) associated with the rolling over procedure, and in any case the reduction in uncertainty at the delivery date is achieved at the expense of some increase in cash flow variability at intermediate dates. This implies that futures and options markets have important functions to perform, but that stabilisation is not one of them.

Second, by changing farmers' behaviour, access to forward or futures markets will alter the overall price distribution. The direction of this effect will depend on how farmers respond to the reduced riskiness of production. Newbery and Stiglitz (1981) show that if farmers have constant relative risk aversion, a reduction in riskiness will result in lower production if the coefficient of risk aversion is greater than unity, and higher production in the converse case. This is because very risk averse producers are anxious to avoid very bad out-turns and therefore respond to increased risk through increased effort. In this case, price stabilisation will shift the supply function upwards and give producers the double benefit of higher prices on average, and lower price variability. However, the converse result is also possible, either because producers are not very risk averse, or if increased effort is not the principal cost of increased output. An alternative model is that increased output can be obtained through an increase in inputs, so that the producer faces a rising cost curve. I show that in this case a reduction in risk will raise planned output levels. Here, a reduction in price variability will generate lower average prices to producers.

A second focus of the commodity policy debate in the post-ICA period has been the policies which LDC governments have themselves adopted in attempting to stabilise commodity prices. On the one hand, it is suggested that by driving a wedge between border prices and the local producer (and possibly also consumer) price, governments can offer effective stability to their own citizens. On the other hand, there is concern that in setting domestic producer and consumer prices governments may fail to provide appropriate incentives. This raises the question of when it is sensible for governments to set domestic prices away from border prices, and how increased stability is to be balanced against loss of efficiency. Is it possible to design schemes which provide some benefits without imposing efficiency costs?[4]

Typically, marketing boards have set producer prices on an administrative rather than an economic basis, and these prices have been adjusted only relatively slowly in response to external market conditions. Taxation has been an important element in many schemes. The result has been that agricultural producers have not been offered the incentives required for them to respond to changes in world market conditions, and in certain cases producer prices have been squeezed to such an extent as to precipitate a major economic decline. The decline in cocoa production in Ghana provides the clearest example of this; there is evidence that over this period the Ghana Cocoa Marketing Board, or its employees, managed to extract much of the rent in the industry (see Loxley, 1988).

A major element in structural adjustment policy has been the perceived need to align domestic with border prices. Within this approach, traditionally conceived marketing boards appear to have little to offer. In its structural adjustment lending to Ghana, the World Bank has, for example, been anxious to achieve privatisation of the Ghana Cocoa Marketing Board's functions. Toye (1991) reports that although there has been some retrenchment in the Board's activities, the government has resisted privatisation and a compromise appears to have emerged to the effect that the Board should do only 'those things which the private sector cannot do more efficiently' (Toye, 1991, p. 190).

That may be considered to beg rather than answer the question. Nevertheless, it may be argued that there is a considerable educational element in crop marketing, particularly where export crops are concerned. This extends from crop quality through packaging and transportation to pricing. Governmental marketing boards have been concerned with these activities which the private sector might not find directly profitable. Specifically, in relation to pricing, I wish in this paper to explore the suggestion that marketing boards might be well advised simply to offer farmers the ability to sell their produce forward. In doing this, an LDC marketing board would play the same sort of role as elevator companies in North America in intermediating futures markets and farmers. Farmers would not be compelled to sell to the marketing board and, if the commodity was internationally traded, the board could offset its position in an international market. Once these functions became established, the marketing board might then become a candidate for privatisation.

The appeal of this proposal is that it appears to square the circle by providing continuity in the institutional arrangements for commodity marketing already present in many commodity exporting countries, while at the same time strengthening market incentives by providing indirect access to international forward and futures markets. The proposal would appear to offer producers better incentives, and in addition afford a degree of risk reduction – and, perhaps, revenue stabilisation.

I do not wish to oppose these arguments, except to note that the scale of these benefits might be relatively small; this is in line with previous findings that producer benefits from risk reduction may be relatively low (Kanbur, 1984). But I also show that it is possible that if access to forward or futures markets in production of a particular commodity becomes general, the supply responses to reduced riskiness may in aggregate outweigh the benefits from risk reduction. This is similar to the finding that although a particular country may benefit from World Bank funding to aid expansion of a particular commodity, the overall market effects of general expansion may be negative.

In the remainder of this paper, I set out a simple model to explore the benefits from a marketing board offering to purchase forward. The results are dramatically negative. Individually, farmers gain by only a small amount; collectively, they are considerably worse off. These results are certainly both parameter-specific and model-specific, but they do serve to warn against the easy equation of individual and collective benefits, and against the easy assumption that price stabilisation is always welfare-raising.

2 Producer behaviour under different pricing regimes

A farmer produces a stochastic output x_1 in period 1 subject to an additive disturbance ϵ_1:

$$x_1 = \xi_0 + \epsilon_1 \tag{1}$$

where ξ_0 is planned production (i.e., the period 0 plan for period 1 production) and ϵ_1 is a disturbance satisfying $E_0 \epsilon_1 = 0$.

The cash price in period 1 is p_1 but it is also possible to sell forward in period 0 for delivery in period 1 at the price f_0. The farmer has a concave period 1 utility function $u(y_1)$ where y_1 is his period 1 income.[5]

If the farmer does not have access to a forward or futures market, his problem is

$$\max_{\xi_0} E_0 u(y_1) = \max_{\xi_0} E_0 u(p_1 x_1 - c(\xi_0)) \tag{2}$$

The first order condition for this problem gives

$$E_0(u'(y_1)p_1) = c'(\xi_0) E_0 u'(y_1) \tag{3}$$

where a prime indicates a derivative.

Taking a first order approximation[6] to marginal utility u', one obtains

$$c'(\xi_0) = \frac{\lambda - \rho(\sigma_p^2 + 2\sigma_{\epsilon p})}{\lambda - \rho\sigma_{\epsilon p}} E_0 p_1 \tag{4}$$

where

$$\sigma_p^2 = \frac{E_0(p_1 - E_0 p_1)^2}{(E_0 p_1)^2}$$

$$\sigma_{\epsilon p} = \frac{E_0[(p_1 - E_0 p_1)\epsilon_1]}{\xi_0 E_0 p_1}$$

$$\rho = -\frac{\bar{y}u''(\bar{y})}{u'(\bar{y})}$$

$$\lambda = \frac{\bar{y}}{E_0 p_1 \xi_0}$$

and

$$\bar{y} = E_0 p_1 \xi_0 - c(\xi_0)$$

ρ (> 0) is the farmer's coefficient of relative risk aversion and σ_p^2 is the squared coefficient of variation of the price.

For the standard case of $0 > \sigma_{\epsilon p} > -1$, the covariance of the farmer's revenue and the commodity price is positive, and price variability leads him to plan a lower level of output ξ_0 than he would choose under certainty. The second term in the numerator of equation (4) may be interpreted as a risk premium.

Now suppose that the farmer sells the quantity h_0 forward at time 0 for delivery in time 1. His income y_1 now becomes

$$\begin{aligned} y_1 &= f_0 h_0 + (x_1 - h_0)p_1 - c(\xi_0) \\ &= p_1 x_1 + (f_0 - p_1)h_0 - c(\xi_0) \end{aligned} \tag{5}$$

He now maximises his expected utility with respect to both ξ_0 and h_0. In the additive case, the first order condition with respect to h_0 is

$$E_0(u'(y_1)p_1) = f_0 E_0 u'(y_1) \tag{6}$$

Combining equations (3) and (6) we obtain the separation result[7]

$$c'(\xi_0) = f_0 \tag{7}$$

so that when he can hedge, the farmer simply sets marginal cost equal to the forward price. The price uncertainty no longer affects his output.

It is useful also to have an approximation to the hedge h_0. Taking a first order expansion of the marginal utility of hedged income and substituting into equation (6) gives

$$h_0 = \left(1 + \frac{\sigma_{\epsilon p}}{\sigma_p^2}\right)\xi_0 + \frac{\lambda - \rho\sigma_{\epsilon p}}{\rho\sigma_p^2}\frac{f_0 - E_0 p_1}{E_0 p_1}\xi_0 \tag{8}$$

This expression gives the familiar decomposition of the farmer's forward position into a pure hedge and a speculative term which depends on the bias in the forward price. In the standard case in which the forward price is downward biased the farmer will wish to buy forward in order to capture this bias, and this will offset his pure hedge. In the remainder of this paper I shall simplify by assuming an unbiased forward price, so that equation (8) becomes

$$h_0 = \left(1 + \frac{\sigma_{\epsilon p}}{\sigma_p^2}\right)\xi_0 \tag{9}$$

In agricultural markets it is generally more realistic to suppose that disturbances are multiplicative (Newbery and Stiglitz, 1981, p. 65). In this case, equation (1) is replaced by

$$x_1 = \xi_0(1 + \epsilon_1) \tag{10}$$

and the first order condition (3) becomes

$$E_0(u'(y_1)p_1(1 + \epsilon_1)) = c'(\xi_0) E_0 u'(y_1) \tag{11}$$

First order approximation of this expression gives

$$c'(\xi_0) = \left\{1 - \frac{\lambda\sigma_{\epsilon p}}{\lambda - \rho\sigma_{\epsilon p}} - \frac{\rho(\sigma_p^2 + 2\sigma_{\epsilon p} + \sigma_\epsilon^2)}{\lambda - \rho\sigma_{\epsilon p}}\right\} E_0 p_1 \tag{12}$$

Comparing equations (4) and (12) one sees an additional term in $\sigma_{\epsilon p}$ which reflects the fact that positive supply disturbances are on average associated with lower prices. In addition, the final risk premium term is more complicated than in equation (4).

With multiplicative output disturbances we lose the separation result in equation (7). Combination of the first order condition with respect to h_0, which is unchanged from equation (6), and the first order condition with respect to output in equation (11) gives

$$c'(\xi_0) = f_0 + \frac{E_0[u'(y_1)p_1\epsilon_1]}{E_0u'(y_1)} \tag{13}$$

First order approximation of equation (13) gives

$$c'(\xi_0) = f_0 + \frac{\lambda\sigma_{\epsilon p}}{\lambda - \rho\sigma_{\epsilon p}} E_0 p_1 - \frac{\rho\left(\frac{\xi_0 - h_0}{\xi_0}\sigma_{\epsilon p} + \sigma_\epsilon^2\right)}{\lambda - \rho\sigma_{\epsilon p}} E_0 p_1 \tag{14}$$

This equation has the same general form as (12) but it is apparent that a number of terms from equation (12) are absent. The optimal hedge h_0 is given by equation (8) as in the additive case. Substitution into equation (14) shows

$$c'(\xi_0) = f_0 + \frac{\lambda\sigma_{\epsilon p} - \rho(1 - r_{\epsilon p}^2)\sigma_\epsilon^2}{\lambda - \rho\sigma_{\epsilon p}} E_0 p_1 \tag{15}$$

where

$$r_{\epsilon p}^2 = \frac{\sigma_{\epsilon p}^2}{\sigma_\epsilon^2 \sigma_p^2}$$

We are now in a position to approach the question of how hedging affects the farmer's production decisions. At this stage, we consider the decision of an individual farmer to use the forward market, holding the decision of all other farmers constant. It follows that the price distributions will be unaffected and we may simply compare his decisions given by equation (15) when he hedges with that given by equation (12) when he sells cash. Write the difference in marginal costs as $\Delta c'(\xi_0)$ (equation (15) – equation (12)). Then

$$\frac{\Delta c'(\xi_0)}{E_0 p_1} = \frac{\rho\sigma_p^2}{\lambda - \rho\sigma_{\epsilon p}}\left(1 - \frac{\sigma_{\epsilon p}}{\sigma_p^2}\right)^2 \tag{16}$$

Provided $\sigma_{\epsilon p} < \lambda/\rho$, which we will suppose to be the case, it follows that given the same price distributions, forward market sales on an unbiased market will result in unambiguously higher planned output levels than those associated with cash market sales.[8]

Equation (16) gives one possible comparison. The other comparison arises if we consider the introduction of a forward market with a significant number of farmers taking advantage of this opportunity. The result of this is that, in general, the price distributions will change and the comparison given by equation (16) will no longer be appropriate. In order to investigate this question we need to resort to simulation analysis.

3 A simulation model

One may evaluate the welfare gains from hedging by examination of historical experience,[9] by simulating hedging using an empirically estimated model,[10] or by the use of a theoretically-based simulation model. Each procedure has its advantages. Theoretical models necessarily simplify, whereas empirical models may give results which are specific to particular periods, and can give misleading results if the empirical relations are poorly or incorrectly determined.

Theoretical work by Wright and Williams (1982), Williams and Wright (1991) and Deaton and Laroque (1992) has emphasised the non-linear character of commodity price cycles. Private sector storage reduces the negative price impact of a good harvest by more than it can, on average, offset the positive price impact of a poor harvest, since stockout limits the ability of stockholders to sell into rising prices. The result is that even if yields are symmetrically distributed, price distributions will exhibit positive skewness. Good harvests result in a run of low (but not very low) prices as the surplus is carried over into successive years, whereas poor harvests can result in sharp peaks in the cash price. This results in cycles which have long flat bottoms and occasional sharp peaks. This is illustrated in Figure 10.1, which shows a Monte Carlo simulation over 200 years of the model which is developed in this section.

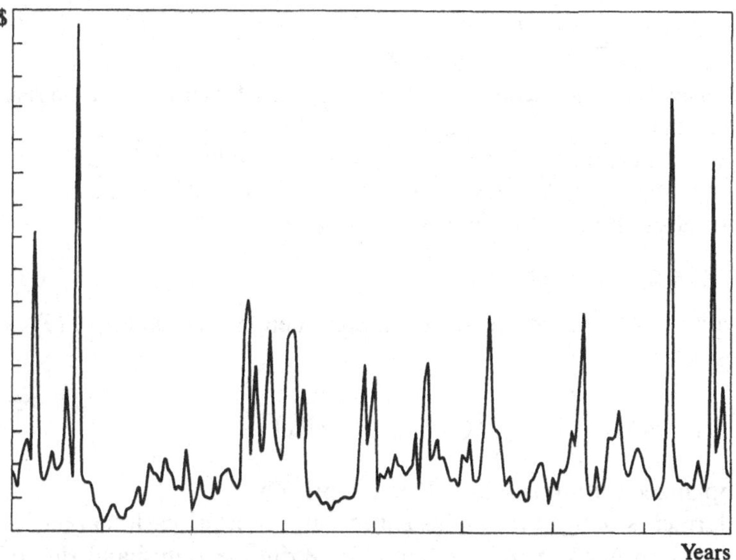

Figure 10.1 A price simulation

The model is an extension of the basic model used by Deaton and Laroque (1992). It differs from their model in two respects. First, farmers set their production levels in relation to expected prices, whereas in the Deaton and Laroque model production is completely random. Second, the model explicitly links aggregate market behaviour to the behaviour of the individual farmers.

The market consists of n identical farmers producing a crop with cost function

$$c(\xi_0) = \frac{\eta}{1+\eta} a^{-(1/\eta)} \xi_0^{1+(1/\eta)} \tag{17}$$

where ξ_0 is again the farmer's planned output.

I suppose that the production disturbances are multiplicative, so that actual supply x_1 is related to planned supply by equation (10). In the absence of any uncertainty, equation (16) would imply planned supply function

$$\xi_0 = ap_0^{\eta} \tag{18}$$

so that η may be interpreted as the supply elasticity.

We shall normalise such that under certainty the price p will be unity so that a becomes the farmer's planned output under certainty. In what follows $a = 10$ and $\eta = 0.25$.

I suppose that the farmer's utility function is

$$u(y_1) = \frac{1}{1-\gamma} y_1^{1-\gamma} \tag{19}$$

where y is his net farm income. γ is the farmer's coefficient of relative risk aversion. I take $\gamma = 2.5$ throughout.

Using the chosen parameter values one obtains a value for $\lambda = 0.8$ when $p = 1$. The effective risk aversion parameter $\rho/\lambda = 3.125$. In the case of cash market sales, his net farm income y is given by

$$y_1 = p_1 x_1 - c(\xi_0) \tag{20}$$

If instead he sells on the forward market then, using equation (9), y becomes

$$y_1 = p_1 x_1 + \left(1 + \frac{\sigma_{\epsilon p}}{\sigma_p^2}\right)(f_0 - p_1)\xi_0 - c(\xi_0) \tag{21}$$

since unplanned output is sold at the cash price.

If the farmer is obliged to sell his entire output on the cash market his output decision is given by equation (12). Write the right-hand side of equation (12) as the certainty equivalent price p_0^*. It follows that his planned production ξ_0 is given by equation (18), with this certainty equivalent price p_0^* replacing p_0; and that his net income is given by equation (20). If it is open to him to sell on the forward market, he will take the short forward position of h_0 given by equation (9). His planned production is now given by equation (15). Write the right-hand side of equation (15) as the certainty equivalent p_0^+. It follows that planned production now satisfies equation (18), with p_0^+ replacing p_0. In either case, therefore, the farmer's decision may be represented in terms of a response to a certainty equivalent price, but this price will depend (through equations (12) or (15)) on the moments of the price distribution – specifically the mean E_0p_1 of the price distribution, and the covariance $\sigma_{\epsilon p}$ of the price and the firm's production disturbance. However, the moments of the price distribution themselves result from the outcomes of individual decisions, and if farmers in general decide to sell forward rather than use the cash market, this will alter these moments.

In order to investigate this dependency we need to turn to the aggregate market-level relationships. Aggregate market production X is obtained by summing over the n identical supply functions. The form of the supply function is therefore unchanged. I take $n = 1000$, and output at the aggregate level in units of thousands, allowing me to use the same expressions at the individual and the market level. Under certainty, aggregate output would now be $1000a = 10{,}000$ units or 10 aggregate units. I suppose that the production disturbance ϵ_1 may be split into two independent components – u_1, which is common to all n farmers, and v_1, which is specific to the farmer in question. I assume

$$\begin{pmatrix} u_1 \\ v_1 \end{pmatrix} \sim \begin{pmatrix} \sigma_u^2 & 0 \\ 0 & \sigma_v^2 \end{pmatrix} \tag{22}$$

I take $\sigma_u = 0.1$ and $\sigma v = 0.2$ implying $\sigma_\epsilon = 0.23$. At the aggregate level the disturbance $\epsilon = \Sigma\epsilon$ has variance σ_ϵ^2 given by

$$\sigma_\epsilon^2 = \sigma_u^2 + \frac{1}{n}\sigma_v^2 \tag{23}$$

With $n = 1000$, we may safely ignore the second term so that $\sigma_\epsilon = 0.1$.

The demand side of the market is very simple. I adopt the standard specification in Deaton and Laroque (1992) of a non-stochastic constant elasticity demand function written in inverse form as

$$p_1 = D^{-1}(C_1) = \left(\frac{C_1}{a}\right)^{-(1/a)} \tag{24}$$

where C_1 is consumption demand. This implies that a is the price elasticity of demand. I take $a = 0.33$. Market clearing requires that

$$C_1 + S_1 = X_1 + S_0 \tag{25}$$

where S_0 is the carry-over from the previous period (I neglect depreciation for simplicity) and S_1 is the current period stock demand. The market is closed by the stock demand equation. If stockholders are risk-neutral this is given by the Kuhn–Tucker condition

$$p_0 \geq \frac{E_0 p_1}{1 + r} \quad : \quad S_0 \geq 0 \tag{26}$$

where r is the rate of interest which I take to be constant at 3 per cent.

Equation (26) asserts that if positive stocks are held, they must earn the riskless interest rate r, whereas if stock levels are zero, the current cash price can be above the expected price in the next period.

The model I have outlined contains rationally formed forward expectations in both the production and storage relationships. Solution must therefore be by dynamic programming methods, and this may be conveniently implemented by adopting a recursive formulation of the problem. This was the procedure adopted by Deaton and Laroque (1992). Despite the additional complexity arising from the dependence of production on the lagged expected price, this model maintains the feature of a single state variable, availability, which characterises the basic Deaton and Laroque model. Deaton and Laroque prove uniqueness of the solution to their model and, under weak conditions, convexity of the storage function. Although I am not in a position to make these claims about the modified model, I proceed on the basis that the solution is unique. However, the dependence on variances and covariances appears in certain circumstances to result in non-convexity – see also Gilbert (1989).

Availability Z_0 is defined as current production plus the lagged carry-over

$$Z_0 = Q_0 + S_{-1} \tag{27}$$

Dropping time subscripts, we may write the solutions to the model in the form

$$\begin{aligned} p &= P(Z) \\ f &= F(Z) \\ S &= S(Z) \\ \sigma_p^2 &= V(Z) \\ \sigma_{\epsilon p} &= W(Z) \end{aligned} \tag{28}$$

Explicit representations of these functions are as follows. The spot price function $P(Z)$ gives price as a function of availability *less* current storage

$$P(Z) = D^{-1}(Z - S(Z)) \tag{29}$$

The forward price function $F(Z)$ evaluates the current expectation of next period's spot price. This will depend on production next period plus the current carry-over *less* anticipated carry-over next period.

$$G(Z) = \int_{-\infty}^{\infty} D^{-1}(Q(F(Z), \epsilon) + S(Z) - S(Q(F(Z), \epsilon) + S(Z)))\varphi(\epsilon)\,d\epsilon \tag{30}$$

where $\phi(\cdot)$ is the standard normal density function. Current storage, $S(Z)$, is given as current availability *less* current consumption, where consumption is represented in terms of the discounted forward price.

$$S(Z) = \max\left[Z - D\left(\frac{F(Z)}{1+r}\right), 0\right] \tag{31}$$

The variance function $V(Z)$ is defined analogously with the forward price:

$$V(Z) = \int_{-\infty}^{\infty} \{D^{-1}(Q(F(Z), \epsilon) + S(Z) - S(Q(F(Z), \epsilon) + S(Z)) - F(Z))\}^2 \varphi(\epsilon)\,d\epsilon \tag{32}$$

The definition of the covariance process $W(Z)$ is similar:

$$W(Z) = \int_{-\infty}^{\infty} \{[D^{-1}(Q(F(Z), \epsilon) + S(Z) - S(Q(F(Z), \epsilon) + S(Z)) - F(Z))]\epsilon\}\varphi(\epsilon)\,d\epsilon \tag{33}$$

In the case that farmers sell only on the cash market, the supply function $Q(F(Z), \epsilon)$ is given by

$$Q(F(Z), \epsilon) = a\left[\left(1 + \frac{\lambda W(Z) - \rho(V(Z) + 2W(Z) + \sigma_\epsilon^2)}{\lambda - \rho W(Z)}\right)F(Z)\right]^\eta (1 + \epsilon) \tag{34}$$

(from equations (12) and (18)), while if farmers all sell forward the corresponding function (from equations (15) and (18)) is

$$Q(F(Z), \epsilon) = a\left[\left(1 + \frac{\lambda W(Z) - \rho\left(1 - \frac{W(Z)^2}{V(Z)}\right)\sigma_\epsilon^2}{\lambda - \rho W(Z)}\right)F(Z)\right]^\eta (1 + \epsilon) \tag{35}$$

These functions may be computed iteratively, although convergence is not guaranteed.

Figure 10.2 illustrates the computed spot price function $P(Z)$ and the forward price $G(Z)$.[11] At low availability the spot price is above the forward price which is independent of current market conditions. This is a

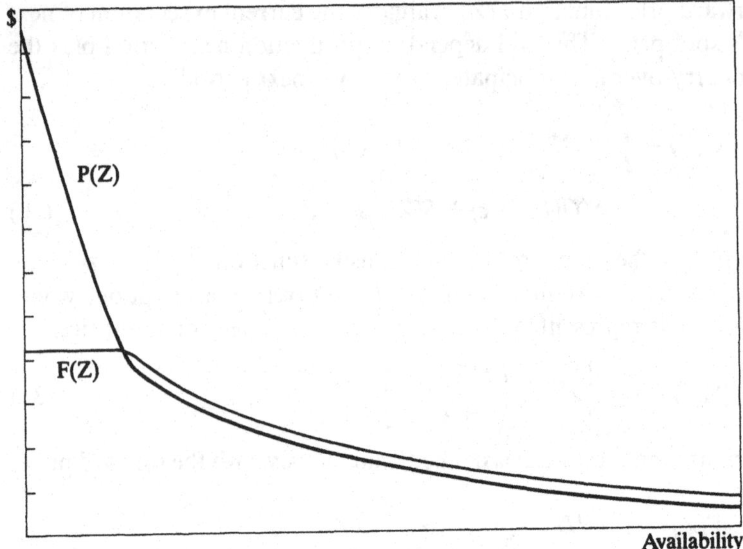

Figure 10.2 *P(Z)* and *F(Z)*

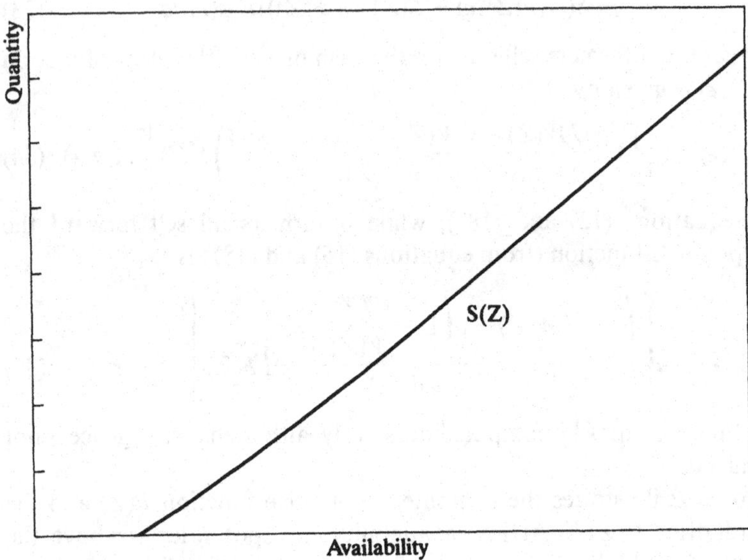

Figure 10.3 *S(Z)*

market backwardation. When availability is high the market is in contango with the forward price above the spot price. The computed storage function $S(Z)$ is shown in Figure 10.3. It is near-piecewise linear with zero storage at low availability followed by a slowly rising marginal storage propensity after the kink; the latter is at the same availability level as that in Figure 10.2 and covariance functions $V(Z)$ and $W(Z)$ respectively are shown in Figure 10.4. The variance drops sharply and the covariance rises towards zero to the right of the kink.

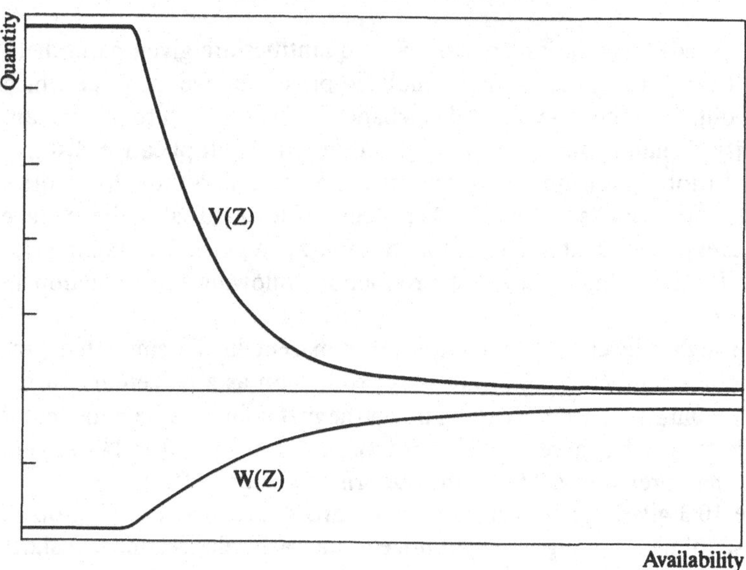

Figure 10.4 $V(Z)$ and $W(Z)$

4 Simulation results

I consider two regimes. In the first, the farmer sells only on the cash market, while in the second he has access to the forward market. There are also two market regimes, one with and one without a forward market. I distinguish two polar cases: in the spot market regime, I ask how much a single producer would gain from the ability to make forward transactions while all other producers remain confined to the cash market; and conversely, in the forward trading regime, I ask how much a particular producer benefits from the ability to sell forward in the situation that all other producers already do so. This gives a matrix of four possibilities.

In Table 10.1, I give the means and standard deviations of the price distributions averaged over 100 simulations. (In this and the succeeding

Table 10.1 *Price means and standard deviations*

	Mean	s.d.
Cash sales	108.92 (1.87)	20.64 (3.45)
Forward sales	107.12 (1.66)	15.48 (2.88)

tables, standard deviations of estimated quantities are given parenthetically.) In each case, the average simulated price is above the price which would obtain in the absence of disturbances. This is a feature of constant elasticity demand functions in conjunction with multiplicative disturbances.[12] More interesting, therefore, is the result that although the price standard deviation is reduced by $4\frac{1}{2}$ per cent by forward sales, the average price level is 1 per cent higher in the cash market regime. This fall in price results from the higher level of production following the reduction in price risk.[13]

These higher levels of production are apparent in the simulated production levels in Table 10.2 (given as production as a percentage of the certainty output of 100). Reading down the first column, one finds that if a single farmer has access to forward markets, his output is $1\frac{1}{2}$ per cent higher than previously. This is the pure risk reduction effect.

Table 10.3 gives the farmer's simulated gross revenues. Looking down the first column, the higher mean price in the cash sales regime translates to higher revenue levels. Indeed, in each of the regimes the farmer obtains a higher revenue by making use of the forward market. However, comparison of the two diagonal entries indicates that if all farmers use the forward market the increase in revenue is very small. Furthermore,

Table 10.2 *Production levels*

Farmer's regime	Market regime			
	Cash sales mean	s.d.	Forward sales mean	s.d.
Cash sales	96.5 (1.3)	1.8 (0.8)	96.6 (1.1)	1.8 (0.9)
Forward sales	98.0 (1.3)	1.8 (0.8)	97.9 (1.1)	1.8 (0.9)

Table 10.3 *Simulated gross revenues*

Farmer's regime	Market regime			
	Cash sales mean	s.d.	Forward sales mean	s.d.
Cash sales	104.6 (2.4)	21.7 (2.7)	103.1 (1.9)	22.1 (1.8)
Forward sales	105.6 (2.2)	20.2 (1.4)	104.7 (1.9)	21.0 (1.1)

forward trading is seen as doing little to reduce revenue variability despite the clear reduction in price variability.

In order to evaluate the trade-offs between increased expected revenues and reduced revenue variability, we need to look at expected utility levels. The results of this comparison are given in Table 10.4, where, without loss of generality, comparisons are made relative to the case in which all farmers sell on the cash market. In Table 10.4, the utility gains are translated into a money metric as the maximum amount of money which the farmer would be prepared to pay, as a percentage of mean income in the base case, in order to exercise the regime choice in question (where negative, this is the amount of money by which he must be bribed to accept this regime). I approximate this sum as

$$g = 100\frac{EU(y^*) - U(Ey_0)}{Ey_0 U'(EY_0)} \tag{36}$$

where y_0 is his income in the base case and y^* that in the regime under consideration.

Reading down the columns of Table 10.4, the results of this comparison show that the farmer does better by selling on the forward than on the cash market. Access to the forward market is worth 0.24 per cent of his

Table 10.4. *Utility comparisons*

Farmer's regime	Market regime	
	Cash sales	Forward sales
Cash sales	Base case	− 1.41
Forward sales	0.24	− 0.49

expected income in the case that other farmers sell cash, but this rises to 0.92 per cent if all other farmers sell forward. It is not obvious what lies behind this difference. By contrast, reading across the rows of Table 10.4 one finds that in both cases the farmer is better off if other farmers are obliged to sell cash – by between $\frac{1}{2}$ per cent and $1\frac{1}{2}$ per cent of his expected income. This matrix has the familiar prisoner's dilemma structure. Individually, farmers gain from use of forward markets, but collectively the risk reduction they obtain drives down the commodity price and makes them all worse off. The reduction in riskiness is offset by the lower average price.

These results are derived from a specific model and it may be possible to obtain quite different results from different choices of parameters. Nevertheless, two conclusions stand out: marketing boards can offer farmers a greater degree of income stability than is obtainable from forward market sales; but the effects of this risk reduction may, in the aggregate, not be beneficial to farmers since the consequential higher production levels in conjunction with inelastic demand reduces farm incomes.

5 Conclusion

The results reported in this paper are illustrative rather than conclusive. I have assumed a special, and perhaps implausible, functional form for producers' utility functions, and the results relate in the first instance to farmers who hire additional labour at the margin rather than expending additional effort at the margin. I have also simulated the model assuming values for parameters which produce an emphatic result; this result may not generalise very widely. Within this model, however, it appears that individual farmers benefit only marginally from access to forward markets, while collectively they are made significantly worse off through this access. The beneficiaries are the consumers who enjoy lower expected prices.

These results should not be taken as arguing against structural adjustment policies aimed at aligning domestic prices with prices prevailing internationally. But they do suggest that these policies are likely to offer very little by way of stabilisation or risk reduction benefits, so to the extent that these remain priorities they need to be addressed explicitly. Access to international futures markets offers very little to developing country agricultural producers, and may even affect them adversely in aggregate. As a result, the conflict between efficacy and risk reduction inherent in traditional marketing board schemes remains, and must be confronted directly.

NOTES

I am grateful to Ron Anderson, Antonella Mori and Alan Winters for helpful comments on the initial draft. All errors remain my own responsibility.

1 See Gilbert (1987) and, on the collapse of the tin agreement, Anderson and Gilbert (1988).
2 I advanced this view in Gilbert (1985). The comparison between band stabilisation and hedging using options is made in Gilbert (1988).
3 Newbery and Stiglitz (1981) cite this as demonstrating that futures markets usefully stabilise only for non-storable commodities. I criticise this argument in Gilbert (1989). The argument in Gilbert (1985) which suggests that futures markets will stabilise revenues implicitly assumes non-storability by taking the futures price to be equal to the unconditional cash price mean in every period.
4 See Walters (1987), Mirrlees (1988) and Gilbert (1991).
5 Newbery and Stiglitz (1981) assume a utility function of the form $u(p_1 x_1) - c(\xi_0)$. This is appropriate to a subsistence farmer, while my assumption is preferable for a farmer who can hire additional labour at the margin.
6 The first order approximation is strictly valid only if the producer has constant absolute risk aversion. In that case, the relative risk aversion parameter ρ should be interpreted as relative risk aversion at the mean income level. On the accuracy of these approximations see Newbery and Stiglitz (1981, pp. 90–2).
7 See Danthine (1978).
8 This result is not general. Newbery and Stiglitz (1981, pp. 81–2) show, in a slightly different model, that a reduction in risk increases supply of the risky crop if $\rho < 1$, but increases supply if $\rho > 1$.
9 See, for example, Badillo and Daloz (1985).
10 See, for example, Gemmill (1985).
11 These functions are all illustrated for the case in which producers have no access to forward markets. I am grateful to Angus Deaton for the original software used in computing these functions. Needless to say, I am responsible for any errors.
12 See Turnovsky (1976) and Gilbert (1986).
13 If we take risk aversion in the storage activity in account, we should also find an additional stabilising effect from this source (see Gilbert, 1989).

REFERENCES

Anderson, R.W. and C.L. Gilbert (1988) 'Commodity Agreements and Commodity Markets: Lessons From Tin', *Economic Journal*, **98**, 1—15.

Badillo, D. and J.-P. Daloz (1985) *Marché, Spéculation, Stabilisation*, Paris: Economica.

Danthine, J.-P. (1978) 'Information Futures Prices and Stabilizing Speculation', *Journal of Economic Theory*, **17**, 79–98.

Deaton, A.S. and G. Laroque (1992) 'On the Behavior of Commodity Prices', *Review of Economic Studies*, **59**.

Gemmill, G. (1985) 'Forward Contracts or International Buffer Stocks? A Study of Their Relative Efficiency in Stabilising Commodity Export Earnings', *Economic Journal*, **95**, 400–17.

Gilbert, C.L. (1985) 'Futures Trading and the Welfare Evaluation of Commodity Price Stabilisation', *Economic Journal*, **95**, 637–61.
(1986) 'Commodity Price Stabilization: the Massell Model and Multiplicative Disturbances', *Quarterly Journal of Economics*, **100**, 635–40.
(1987) 'International Commodity Agreements: Design and Performance', *World Development*, **15**, 591–616.
(1988) 'Buffer Stocks, Hedging and Risk Reduction', *Bulletin of Economic Research*, **40**, 271–86.
(1989) 'Futures Trading, Storage and Price Stabilization', *Review of Futures Markets*, **8**, 152–76.
(1991) 'Domestic Price Stabilization Schemes for Developing Countries', *QMW Discussion Paper*, **231**, London: Queen Mary and Westfield College.
Kanbur, S.M.R. (1984) 'How to Analyze Commodity Price Stabilization: a Review Article', *Oxford Economic Papers*, **36**, 336–58.
Loxley, J. (1988) *Ghana: Economic Crisis and the Long Road to Recovery*, Ottawa: The North–South Institute.
Mirrlees, J.A. (1988) 'Optimal Commodity Price Intervention', Washington, D.C.: World Bank (mimeo).
Newbery, D.M.G. and J.E. Stiglitz (1981) *The Theory of Commodity Price Stabilization*, Oxford: Oxford University Press.
Toye, J. (1991) 'Ghana', Chapter 14 in P. Mosley, J. Harrigan and J. Toye (eds), *Aid and Power: the World Bank and Policy-Based Lending*, vol. 2, London: Routledge: pp. 150–200.
Turnovsky, S.J. (1976) 'The distribution of welfare gains from price stabilization: the case of multiplicative disturbances', *International Economic Review*, **17**, 133–48.
Walters, A.A. (1987) 'The mischief of moving average pricing', Washington, D.C.: World Bank (mimeo).
Williams, J. C. and Wright, B. D. (1991) *Storage and Commodity Markets*, Cambridge: Cambridge University Press.
Wright, B.D. and J.C. Williams (1982) 'The economic role of commodity storage', *Economic Journal*, **92**, 596–614.

Discussion

WALTER C. LABYS

Chapter 10 is a well conceived paper which presents many interesting ideas and results. Much consideration has been given to the use of forward purchases and futures market to stabilise prices. The paper shows that the results for farmers of such stabilisation effects would be minimal at best. Most of us are aware that drawing policy conclusions using a theoretically-based simulation model may be risky. However, the present paper does offer insights which could provide the basis for a more in-depth study.

The model itself is cleverly structured and the policy simulations are informative. An essential step of any modelling procedure is to provide some indication of a model's validity so that the validity of the results obtained can be assessed. In this case, the simulation results have been transformed to yield the standard deviations in addition to the means of the solved endogenous variables. In all cases, the means are large relative to the standard deviations, which lends credence to the results. In further work on models of this type, some encouragement should be given to performing simulations in the context of experimental design (parameter testing). This could very well require the production of a version of the model which is more conventionally econometric in character.

Part Four
Government's role

11 Infrastructure, relative prices and agricultural adjustment

RICCARDO FAINI

1 Introduction

Contrary to initial optimistic expectations, adjustment by developing countries to the new international economic environment in the wake of the debt crisis has typically proved to be a lengthy and taxing process. As a matter of fact, since 1982 developing countries have been forced to transfer a sizeable share of domestic resources to foreign creditors in order to service their external debt. Under these circumstances, it soon became clear that exclusive reliance on aggregate demand policy was totally inadequate to cope with the economic emergency. For the adjustment effort to be sustainable, aggregate demand management had to be supplemented by supply-enhancing measures. This fact has been fully recognised by international organisations like the World Bank and the International Monetary Fund (IMF). It has prompted these organisations to supplement their lending programmes with policy loans aimed at introducing far-reaching economic reforms in developing countries' economies with a view of enhancing the efficiency in resource use and improving their long-run growth perspectives.

The agricultural sector was bound to play a major role in this context for several reasons. First, it still represents a substantial component of aggregate domestic production: supply response in agriculture will always be a crucial factor in determining the overall response of the economy to changing economic incentives. Second, there is widespread agreement among both economists and policy makers that previous trade and sectoral policies have discriminated against agriculture. Redressing such a bias represents an indisputable priority on the structural reform agenda. It is not altogether surprising, therefore, to find that agricultural reform was included as a key element in the great majority of structural adjustment programmes supported by the World Bank. Third, as shown in a recent FAO policy review (FAO, 1990), it appears that a 'healthy' pattern of adjustment (i.e., based on export and income expansion rather than on import and demand compression) was typically associated with a strong performance of agriculture. These considerations underscore the need for a careful analysis of the determinants of agricultural growth, particularly in the context of adjustment programmes. Yet, the impact of standard IMF–World Bank policy packages on agriculture is far from being unambiguous. Whereas price reforms should normally stimulate agricultural production, especially if production of tradable commodities is sufficiently large, other components of adjustment packages – such as aggregate demand restraint and cuts in government expenditure, particularly if concentrated on public investment – may have a contractionary effect on agricultural output. The net impact is therefore ambiguous, and will depend on the relative strength of price versus non-price factors in affecting agricultural performance. The fact that the price elasticities of aggregate agricultural supply appear to be fairly low, even for developed countries, does not bode well for the success of adjustment programmes.

In this paper, I focus on two issues. First, I attempt to assess the overall impact of adjustment lending on a set of key economic indicators, including agricultural growth, in the context of a simple reduced form approach. Second, I rely on a production theory approach to evaluate in a more detailed fashion the impact on agricultural output of price policies and public investment. Overall, I find that adjustment programmes were typically associated with a relatively buoyant performance of agriculture. Both prices and infrastructure availability seem also to play a positive role in affecting agricultural production. Sustained growth in agriculture will require that the brunt of adjustment does not fall, as it has done in the past, on public investment.

2 Economic performance under adjustment lending

The evaluation of adjustment programmes is fraught with difficulties. First, economic performance in adjustment lending recipient countries depends on a host of factors besides the programme itself. It is necessary to control as carefully as possible for these other factors to isolate the impact of the programme. Second, adjustment programmes typically include several components with possibly opposing impacts on key indicators of macroeconomic performance. The mix of the various components is likely to differ depending, for instance, on whether the programme has been undertaken with the support of the IMF, the World Bank or both organisations. Third, initial economic conditions will most probably determine whether a given country will need to resort to a comprehensive adjustment package supported by international financial organisations. Participation in an adjustment lending programme is likely therefore to be endogenous, a fact which, by itself, may severely bias the overall evaluation.

Some of these problems are even more acute when one tries to identify the performance of the agricultural sector under adjustment lending. As mentioned earlier, the multifaceted nature of adjustment programmes precludes the possibility of identifying their impact on agriculture in an unambiguous manner. Even the effect of price measures is not unequivocal. Price reforms will usually include higher prices for agricultural commodities (particularly of tradable ones), but will also require the elimination (or, at least, a substantial reduction) of producer subsidies on crucial inputs such as fertiliser, water and credit. If the share of tradable goods in total agricultural production is sufficiently small, this set of measures may well end up having a contractionary impact on the supply side. This negative effect will most probably be reinforced both by contractionary aggregate demand policies, which will depress domestic demand for agricultural commodities, and by the severe cuts in vital rural infrastructures undertaken in the name of fiscal restraint. Overall, therefore, there is no way to predict *a priori* what the net impact of an adjustment programme on the agricultural sector will be.

In what follows, I attempt to address some of these issues in the context of a simple statistical model designed to evaluate the effectiveness of adjustment lending. I draw on the work by Goldstein and Montiel (1986) and Khan (1990) (and subsequent applications by Faini *et al.*, 1991 and World Bank, 1990a). The crucial assumption is that changes in the macroeconomic performance of a given country, as measured by a set of indicators ΔY_{ij} (where subscripts i and j refer to the country and the performance indicator respectively), can be expressed as a function of changes in the international environment (SH_i), policy changes ($\Delta \chi_i$) and participation in IMF–World Bank adjustment programmes (D_i), where D_i is a dummy variable which takes a value of one for countries which received some form of adjustment lending:

$$\Delta Y_{ij} = a_0 + a_1 \Delta \chi_i + a_2 SH_i + a_3 D_i + \epsilon_{ij} \tag{1}$$

It is also assumed that the vector of autonomous policy changes ($\Delta \chi_i$) i.e., those policy measures which would have been undertaken anyway even in the absence of an adjustment programme is a function of initial pre-programme conditions ($Y_{i,t-1}$). By substituting this relationship into equation (1), we obtain the final equation for estimation:

$$\Delta Y_{ij} = a_0 + a_1 \gamma Y_{i,t-1} + a_2 SH_i + a_3 D_i + \eta_{ij} \tag{2}$$

As mentioned earlier, it is also necessary to allow for the possibility that participation in an IMF–World Bank programme i.e., the dummy variable D may be endogenous. Indeed, in such a case, our estimates would suffer from a sample selection bias which would affect all coefficients, in particular a_3. For instance, suppose that countries with unsatisfactory performance at time t − 1 (i.e., with low values of $Y_{i,t-1}$) are more likely to request an adjustment loan. If economic performances exhibit a mean-reverting trend (i.e., if negative shocks tend to be reversed in a later period the consequent improvement could be mistakenly attributed to the effects of the adjustment programme). Similarly, if countries had previously embarked on overly ambitious investment programmes, the subsequent investment retrenchment should not be ascribed to the effect of the adjustment programme itself. To control for these possibilities, I first estimate a Probit participation equation. This yields for each country an estimate of the probability of participating in an adjustment programme. I then use this probability as an instrument for D_i in equation (2).

For the purpose of empirical analysis, I rely on a large sample of 59 developing countries. The data are taken from the World Bank (1990b). Changes in international environment are measured as the sum of terms of trade and interest rate shocks after 1982 (see Faini *et al.* (1991) for details of the calculations). As performance indicators, I use the growth rate of GDP, the current account balance, the ratio of investment to GDP and the growth rate of agricultural value-added. In the econometric estimation, ΔY_{ij} measures the difference between the average value of the relevant indicator in the 1982–6 and the 1977–81 periods. I do not allow, therefore, for the possibility that adjustment programmes may have been undertaken at different times by different countries. Table 11.1 provides a glance at the behaviour of these indicators before and after 1982, both for adjustment lending (AL) and non-adjustment lending (NAL) countries.

Table 11.1 *Performance indicators for adjustment lending (AL) and non-adjustment lending (NAL) countries*

	AL countries		NAL countries	
	Pre-1982	Post-1982	Pre-1982	Post-1982
CA	−5.8	−3.7	−4.2	−5.5
GY	3.8	2.1	6.4	3.6
I/Y	20.3	16.9	25.5	25.0
GYA	2.3	2.8	4.0	2.3

CA: current account balance (in % of GDP)
GY: growth rate of GDP
I/Y: investment rate
GYA: growth rate of agricultural value-added

By comparing changes in performance between AL and NAL countries, one would be tempted to conclude that adjustment programmes were effective in rising agricultural growth and improving the current account balance, although at the expense of the investment rate. This temptation should, however, be resisted to the extent that the pattern of performance changes may be predicted on the different evolution of the international economic environment between AL and NAL countries or, as mentioned before, may simply reflect the fact that AL countries featured initially large current account deficits, a lagging agricultural performance and excessive investment.

Table 11.2 presents our econometric results based on equation (2) where account is taken of the possible endogeneity of the participation variable.[1] The results basically confirm the findings of previous research. Adjustment programmes appear to be effective in raising agricultural growth, but are associated with a lower investment rate. There is no significant impact of adjustment lending either on the growth rate of the economy or on the current account. Interestingly enough, had we not allowed for the endogeneity of D_{ij} the estimates would have suggested a positive and highly significant impact of adjustment lending on the current account. With respect to the other variables, external shocks have a negative (albeit weak) effect on both investment and agricultural production. All performance indicators, except agricultural output, are significantly affected by their lagged value. A good current account performance in the past also leads to more sustained GDP growth afterwards. These results should be taken as mostly indicative to the extent that, as noticed earlier, they abstract from the numerous aspects which comprise an adjustment

Table 11.2 *The impact of adjustment lending*

Eq.	SH	I/Y(−1)	CA(−1)	GY(−1)	GYA(−1)	D	F(6,51)
CA	0.002	−0.03	0.68	0.51	−0.35	−0.01	5.8
	(0.01)	(0.25)	(3.4)	(1.3)	(1.44)	(0.16)	
GY	−0.008	0.04	0.16	0.46	−0.42	−0.01	4.2
	(0.24)	(0.67)	(2.1)	(3.4)	(3.0)	(0.61)	
I/Y	−0.13	0.64	−0.05	0.10	0.12	−0.06	20.2
	(1.69)	(5.59)	(0.38)	(0.41)	(0.56)	(2.1)	
GYA	−0.06	0.14	0.08	0.01	–	0.04	
	(1.11)	(1.66)	(0.78)	(0.07)	–	(1.73)	

See Table 11.1.
t-statistic in parenthesis. A White procedure has been used to yield a consistent estimate of the variance–covariance matrix.

programme. Perhaps more crucially, they do not allow for differences in design and/or implementation between adjustment programmes. They seem to suggest, however, that overall, adjustment lending has led to more sustained agricultural growth.[2]

3 Public investment and relative prices: an econometric analysis

The analysis in the previous paragraph does not permit a separate identification of the impact of the various components of an adjustment package on the relevant performance indicators. This is a serious shortcoming, especially when, as in the case of agriculture, different policy measures are likely to exert opposing effects on the selected indicator. Our results, for instance, suggest that adjustment programmes are associated with a relatively better performance of the agricultural sector. Presumably, this indicates that the impact of price reforms was substantial and, in any case, was not negated by the offsetting decline in vital infrastructure (or, more generally, by a deterioration in non-price factors). But it is difficult, in this context, to go much beyond these fairly imprecise statements. Yet the relative contribution of price versus non-price factors is at the heart of a long-standing controversy, with substantial implications for the design of adjustment programmes.

In this section, I rely on a simple production theory approach to present a more detailed analysis of the determinants of agricultural production levels. The starting point is a revenue function, which indicates the maximum revenue associated with given factor endowments (V) and fixed output prices (p). This is a familiar analytical tool, especially in international trade theory. Formally, the revenue function is a solution to the following problem:

$$\max_{y_i} \sum_i p_i y_i \tag{3}$$

subject to the condition that the vector of production levels y_i is feasible given existing technology and factor endowments V. The revenue function can be written as:

$$R = R(V,p) \tag{4}$$

For our purposes, a most useful property of the revenue function is summarised by the Samuelson–McFadden lemma:[3]

$$\partial R/\partial p = y(V,p) \tag{5}$$

where y denotes output supply. In other words, the gradient of the revenue function with respect to the price vector is equal to the vector of output supplies. Note also that the revenue function is not-decreasing, homogenous of degree one and convex in prices. The last two properties imply respectively that the supply function $y(\rho,V)$ is homogeneous of degree zero in prices, while the own-price derivitive:

$$\partial y_i/\partial \rho_i = \partial^2 R/\partial \rho^2$$

is positive.

For the purpose of empirical analysis, I consider a three-sector model, with agriculture, industry (inclusive of the mining sector) and services. On the factor side, I distinguish three factors labour, private and public capital stock. The empirical model used in this paper relies on a translog specification of the revenue function:

$$\ln R = a_0 + \sum_i a_i \ln \rho_i + \sum_k \beta_k \ln V_k + \tag{6}$$

$$+ \sum_i \sum_j a_{ij} \ln \rho_i \ln \rho_j + \sum_k \sum_v \beta_{vk} \ln V_k \ln V_v +$$

$$+ \sum_k \sum_i \eta_{ki} \ln V_k \ln \rho_i$$

where, in the empirical application, $i, j = A, I, S$ denoting respectively agriculture, industry and service and $k, v = L, K, P$ indicating respectively labour, private capital and public capital stock. Symmetry requires that $a_{ij} = a_{ji}$ and $\beta_{kv} = \beta_{vk}$. The following restrictions reflect the condition of linear homogeneity in prices:

$$\sum_i a_i = 1 \tag{7}$$

$$\sum_i a_{ij} = \sum_j a_{ji} = 0$$

$$\sum_i \eta_{ki} = 0$$

Equation (5) implies that the log derivative of the revenue function (equation (6)) is equal to the output share of sector i:

$$\partial \ln R/\partial \ln \rho_i = (\partial R/\partial \rho_i)\,(\rho_i/R) = \rho_i\, y_i/R =$$

$$a_i + \sum_k \eta_{ik} \ln V_k + \sum_j a_{ij} \ln \rho_j \tag{8}$$

Equation (8) will be applied to a time-series cross-section of 26 developing countries. Data on output prices and production levels are taken from World Bank (1990b). One major difficulty in applying standard production theory, particularly to the case of developing countries, stems from the lack of data on both private and public capital stock. To circumvent this problem, it is possible to rely on the following transformation. Let us first lag equation (8) by one period and multiply the resulting expression by $1 - \delta$, where δ denotes the depreciation rate of both private and capital stock. The assumption of a common depreciation rate for both types of capital stock is undoubtedly strong, but is implicitly made in most of the applied literature. We can then subtract the resulting equation for $(-\delta)\ (\rho_i y_i/R)_{t-1}$ from equation (8). It is easy to show that, if one uses a logarithmic approximation to the identity which relates the capital stock at time to investment and the capital stock at time t – 1, then the capital stock terms disappear, and one is left only with the levels of public and private investments. Data on total investment are taken again from World Bank (1990b). Data on public investment come from Faini and de Melo (1990). Finally, given that employment data for developing countries are either not available or fairly unreliable, I rely on life expectancy as a proxy for the quality of the labour force.

The quasi-difference transformation of equation (8) is very handy to the extent that it does not require data on the capital stock. It leads, however, to several econometric problems. The first one is obvious. If the error term in equation (8) was white noise to begin with, it has now, after the transformation, a moving average structure with root $1 - \delta$. This in turn would lead, given the presence of a lagged dependent variable, to inconsistent estimates. Only if the error term in equation (8) followed from the outset an autoregressive process with parameter equal to $1 - \delta$, would ordinary least squares estimation be appropriate. There is a further, equally relevant, problem. The data set consists, as mentioned earlier, of a time-series cross-section of 26 developing countries. The explanatory variables also include a lagged dependent variable. It is well-known, however, that, in a dynamic panel data context, the speed of convergence of the fixed effect estimator is a function of the number of observations per unit (i.e., per country) rather than of the total number of observations (Nickell, 1981). Following Anderson and Hsiao (1982), it is necessary to take first differences in the estimating equation to remove this source of bias. Once again, however, even if the error term was white noise after the first quasi-difference transformation – it has now been transformed into a unit-root moving average error, which is correlated with the lagged dependent variable. I therefore use an (efficient) instrumental variable procedure by exploiting all the restrictions between the error term and the lagged dependent variable $(\rho_i y_i/R)_{t-i}$ where $i > 1$. This generalised method of moments estimator was implemented in the DPD programme developed by Arellano and Bond (1988b). Note that, if the error term in the first-difference equation follows a first-order moving average process, all endogenous variables lagged at least two periods constitute valid instruments. If, however, the error term was already autocorrelated before taking first differences (presumably because the original error term in equation (8) did not follow an autoregressive process with parameter $1 - \delta$), even instruments dated at time $t - 1$ would no longer be valid.[4] It is therefore essential to check, both the validity of the instrument set and the absence of second-order serial correlation in the final equation. I rely, for this purpose, on the Sargan test and the autocorrelation test for dynamic panel data estimation (Arellano and Bond, 1988a).

There is a final econometric problem that must be dealt with. Eq. (8) implicitly defines a system of equations, one for each sector. The equations, however, are not independent given that the sum of the output shares must be equal to one. In the estimation, I therefore drop the share equation for the service sector and focus only on industry and agriculture. Cross-equation constraints should still be imposed; I refrain from doing so for two main reasons. First, there are good reasons to be sceptical that imposing the system constraints at this level of aggregation would be altogether meaningful. The problem is even more relevant in the context of an application to cross-country data. Second, there is not, to the best of my knowledge, a well-developed theory of system estimation for dynamic panel data. There is, therefore, some justification for relying on consistent single-equation methods, even though one foregoes efficiency by not imposing the cross-equation restrictions.

The transformed version of the system of equation (8) has been applied to a panel of 26 developing countries over the period 1976–85. The panel is unbalanced, given that for a few countries some observations are not available for the whole period. It is instructive to examine beforehand the evolution of some of the variables. From Table 11.3, three facts stand out. First, there was a general and substantial fall in sectoral output growth rates in the 1982–7 period which hit both primary and manufacturing exporting countries. Second, the decline in the growth rate of industry was substantially higher in primary exporting countries. As argued in Faini and de Melo (1990), adjustment policies were less effective in eliciting a significant response and in inducing a reallocation of resources for this group of countries. It was instead relatively easier for manufacturing exporting counties to shift resources toward manufacturing exports, whose demand was still growing relatively fast. Third, after 1982 the agriculture sector outperformed the industrial sector. As noticed by FAO (1990), this was the first time in the postwar period where the secular decline in the GDP share of agriculture was reversed. The declining, but still sustained, growth rate of agriculture

Table 11.3 *Production indicators for primary exporting (PE) and manufacturing exporting (ME) countries*

	ME countries		PE countries	
	Pre-1982	Post-1982	Pre-1982	Post-1982
GYI	4.1	1.6	8.8	1.2
GYA	2.8	1.9	3.8	2.7
GPA	−2.6	−2.1	−1.2	−1.0

GYI: average annual growth rate of industrial value-added
GYA: average annual growth rate of agricultural value-added
GPA: average annual growth rate of the relative price of agriculture (measured by the ratio of the implicit deflators of agriculture to industry)

was instrumental in cushioning developing countries from the disruption caused by the external shocks.

Table 11.4 presents the results of the econometric estimation for industry and agriculture, based on the full sample of 26 countries. Price homogeneity has been imposed throughout by normalising the supply equations with respect to the price of services. Notice that both equations include a constant, despite the fact that they have been estimated in first differences, to allow for the presence of (non-neutral) technological progress. Consider first the equation for industry. Both private and public investment play a positive and significant role in determining industrial production. The quality of the labour force, as measured by the indicator of life expectancy, displays instead a negative coefficient. This may seem surprising at first sight, but reflects only some of the constraints which tie together the various share equations. Recall that price homogeneity requires that

$$\sum_i \eta_{ki} = 0$$

where η_{ki} measures the impact of factor k on the revenue share of good i. Therefore, for given k, η_{ki} will be negative for at least one i.

This is simply a restatement of the Rybczynski theorem, according to which an increase in the endowment of one factor of production will lead to a contraction in the output of the sector which uses that factor in a relatively less intensive way. The previous results, in other words, simply suggest that the industrial sector is not relatively labour-intensive. This conjecture is supported also by the fact that the coefficients on investment and the labour proxy in the agricultural share equation are respectively

Table 11.4 *The supply function for agriculture and industry, full sample*

	Industry	Agriculture
Constant	0.004	−0.0004
	(2.46)	(0.66)
Lagged share	0.31	0.39
	(10.1)	(6.81)
Investment	0.014	−0.015
	(2.41)	(1.79)
LE	−1.84	0.15
	(2.08)	(0.32)
Lagged LE	1.40	−0.14
	(1.61)	(0.31)
p_a/p_s	−0.01	0.12
	(0.72)	(10.41)
Lagged p_a/p_s	0.06	−0.05
	(4.5)	(8.05)
p_i/p_s	0.17	−0.09
	(24.8)	(9.54)
Lagged p_i/p_s	−0.05	0.04
	(5.3)	(11.3)
IPUB	0.019	0.00001
	(4.91)	(0.004)
Sargan test (15)	18.5	15.4
Wald test (9)	39407	1825
Autocorrelation test	0.382	1.123

p_i: price of good *i*
LE: life expectancy
IPUB: public investment

The Sargan and the Wald tests are distributed as χ^2. The degrees of freedom are indicated by the number in brackets . The autocorrelation test checks for second-order autocorrelation. It is distributed as a standard normal variable.

negative and positive, contrary to what was found for industry. Again, this indicates that agriculture is relatively labour-intensive.[5]

For policy analysis, the sign (and the size) of the coefficients on prices and public investment are particularly important. Consider first the impact of prices. The own-price effects (i.e., the coefficients a_{ii}) have the correct sign and are quite well determined for both agriculture and industry. This fact, however, does not guarantee that the own-price elasticities will also have the correct sign and will be statistically different from zero. The issue is taken up below. The cross-price effect is also statistically different from zero for agriculture, but not for industry. Had we normalised the equation with respect to the price of agriculture, the cross-price effect between industry and services would have been highly significant. Incidentally, recall that the symmetry conditions have not been imposed. With respect to public investment, it is found that this variable bears a positive and well-determined coefficient in the equation for industry, but is not statistically different from zero for agriculture.

Any conclusions would at this point be at best premature. The results in Table 11.4 may indeed suffer from an aggregation bias. As a matter of fact, existing econometric evidence (Faini and de Melo, 1990) suggests that price responsiveness differs quite significantly between primary and manufacturing-oriented countries. To account for this possibility, the share equations have been estimated only for the subset of manufacturing-oriented countries.[6] The results are presented in Table 11.5. The comparison with the findings based on the full sample suggests some significant differences. First, for both agriculture and industry, the point estimates of the price coefficients are substantially larger. Again, the implications for the estimates of price elasticities should be explored. As is well-known, in a translog model elasticities are a non-linear function of the price coefficients and the output shares. Confidence intervals for price elasticities can be computed by relying on the approximation derived by Anderson and Thursby (1986). They are presented in Table 11.6, together with price elasticities measured at sample mean values. For both agriculture and industry, price elasticities appear to be low and not particularly well determined, given that the 5 per cent confidence interval spans both positive and negative values. As noticed by Anderson and Thursby (1986), this is however a common finding if one applies their procedure to previous translog studies. Moreover, the fact remains that both price elasticities are positive. Also, if measured at the final sample year's values, the point estimate of the own-price elasticity for agriculture would rise to 0.09. In this latter case, however, there is no way to be sure that the Anderson–Thursby approximation is appropriate.

A further interesting result relates to the impact of the two types of capital. Contrary to the findings in Table 11.4, the results for manufacturing-oriented countries indicate that public capital stock exerts a negative impact on agriculture. Moreover, a higher capital stock is no longer associated with a smaller share of agriculture. For industry, though, the impact of both private and public capital stock remains positive. Overall, therefore, the results indicate that, while the industrial sector continues to benefit from capital accumulation (be it private or public), the impact on agriculture is less clear cut. First, the factor intensity gap between industry and agriculture seems less pronounced for manufacturing-oriented countries. Second, public investment has either no effect (for the full

Table 11.5 *The supply function for agriculture and industry, manufacturing countries*

	Industry	Agriculture
Constant	0.004	–
	(2.19)	–
Lagged share	0.11	0.21
	(2.16)	(2.49)
Investment	0.043	0.001
	(3.43)	(0.52)
LE	−2.34	0.46
	(3.94)	(0.70)
Lagged LE	1.75	−0.40
	(3.26)	(0.65)
p_a/p_s	−0.04	0.14
	(2.60)	(7.72)
Lagged p_a/p_s	0.034	−0.03
	(2.13)	(1.82)
p_i/p_s	0.27	−0.03
	(12.6)	(1.07)
Lagged p_i/p_s	−0.07	−0.02
	(2.68)	(1.0)
IPUB	0.014	−0.019
	(2.45)	(2.98)
Sargan test (36)	86.9	36.9
Wald test (9)	287.2	247.5
Autocorrelation test	0.86	1.47

p_i: price of good *i*
LE: life expectancy
IPUB: public investment

Table 11.6 *Price elasticities and confidence intervals, manufacturing countries*

	Industry	Agriculture
Elasticity	0.055	0.011
Confidence interval	0.055 ± 0.12	0.011 ± 0.22

Own calculations using the Anderson–Thursby (1986) methodology.

sample) or a negative impact (for manufacturing-oriented countries) on the GDP share of agriculture. This is a somewhat surprising result. Most econometric analyses (see Binswanger, 1989 for a review) indicate that shift variables, including publicly-provided capital stock, account for a substantial portion of agricultural growth. Our results are at variance with such findings. There are several possible explanations. First, notice that the results for the full sample should not be interpreted as saying that higher public investment will not lead to higher agricultural output.[7] On the contrary, they indicate that, following an increase in public capital stock, agricultural growth will not differ significantly from overall GDP growth.[8] Second, contrary to other studies, I rely on an aggregate measure of public capital stock.[9] Perhaps public investment in our sample countries (particularly in manufacturing-oriented countries!) was unduly biased toward industrial infrastructure, and therefore did not provide a significant contribution to agriculture. Finally, a perhaps more palatable conjecture is that the impact of public investment on agriculture works both directly by increasing the availability of vital infrastructures, and indirectly by facilitating the supply response to changes in relative prices. Formally, this would imply that the supply response to prices, measured by the set of coefficients a_{ij}, is not fixed but depends also on the availability of infrastructure. This is a somewhat empirically appealing supposition. The translog second-order approximation to the revenue function, however, does not allow for this kind of effect. This neglect may bias our estimates – provided, of course, that such effects are important. To test for this possibility, I follow Stevenson (1980) in using a truncated third-order Taylor-series expansion instead of the normal translog second-order form. It is then possible to write the revenue function as follows:

$$\ln R^* = \ln R + \sum_i \sum_j \gamma_{ij} \ln K^p \ln p_i \ln p_j + \\ + \sum_i \sum_k \phi_{ik} \ln K^p \ln p_i \ln V_k + \sum_v \sum_k \psi_{vk} \ln K^p \ln V_v \ln V_k \quad (9)$$

where ln R is given by equation (6) and K^p denotes the public capital stock. Only third-order terms in K^p have been considered. In the empirical application, the coefficients ϕ_{ik} are assumed to be identically equal to zero. We can now follow the same procedure as before. First, we take the logarithmic derivative of equation (9) with respect to output prices. This yields the sectoral output shares. Because of lack of data on the capital stock, we then take the first-quasi-difference of the new supply equations. Some care needs to be taken, when using the approximation to the capital stock identity, because of the presence now of a number of interaction terms. If we are willing to rely on a further approximation, it can then be shown that the estimating equation for a generic sector i includes the following new term:

$$\sum_j \{y_{ij} I^p \ln p_j(t) + y_{ij} I^p (\ln p_j(t) - \ln p_j(t-1))\} \tag{10}$$

where I^p denotes public investment.

The results of the estimation of the new specification are not too encouraging (Table 11.7).[10] The gist of our previous results is basically unchanged. The coefficients of factor inputs in the two equations bear the same sign as before. Similarly, the pattern of price responses does not register any noticeable change. The interaction terms, however, are not statistically different from zero. This yields little support to the contention

Table 11.7 *The supply function for agriculture and industry with interaction terms, manufacturing countries*

	Industry	Agriculture
Constant	0.005	−0.003
	(2.68)	(1.47)
Lagged share	0.11	0.15
	(2.09)	(1.56)
Investment	0.041	0.001
	(3.14)	(0.07)
LE	−2.32	0.98
	(3.40)	(1.28)
Lagged L	1.64	−0.47
	(2.67)	(0.74)
p_a/p_s	−0.03	0.13
	(1.54)	(5.91)
Lagged p_a/p_s	0.06	−0.03
	(2.58)	(1.27)
p_i/p_s	0.24	−0.02
	(10.18)	(0.71)
Lagged p_i/p_s	−0.09	0.03
	(2.70)	(0.69)
IPUB	0.012	−0.023
	(2.04)	(2.61)
IPUB × p_a	−0.001	0.0001
	(1.41)	(0.20)
IPUB × p_i	0.001	0.0001
	(1.11)	(0.47)
Sargan test (36)	84.9	32.9
Wald test (11)	265.1	178.9
Autocorrelation test	0.961	1.68

See Table 11.4.
IPUB × p_j: see equation 10 in the text.

that public investment may affect agriculture also in an indirect way – that is, by facilitating the supply response to price variations.

A call for further research on the importance of interaction effects between price responses and the availability of infrastructure is probably warranted. This research should surely benefit from relying on microeconomic data, rather than on aggregated information which have been used throughout this paper. Notice, though, that even microeconomic data are not free from problems. Indeed, they often suffer from an embarrassment of riches. The multitude of capital stock variables, none of which can be excluded from the equation on *a priori* grounds, leads to serious multicollinearity problems, which would only be compounded by any attempt to assess the importance of interaction effects.

4 Conclusions

The secular declining trend of the GDP share of agriculture has been halted during the 1980s in developing countries. It is much too early to say whether the new trend will soon subside; in any case, the events of the 1980s have highlighted the importance of the agricultural sector in cushioning developing countries' economies from the disruptive impact of external shocks. The fact, furthermore, that a 'healthy' pattern of adjustment (that is, based on supply expansion rather than on demand contraction) was typically associated with a buoyant performance on agriculture further reinforces the belief about the crucial role played by this sector.

Overall, the results in this paper indicate that adjustment programmes had a positive effect in stimulating agricultural production. At a more detailed level, it was found that both price factors and the availability of infrastructures are likely to play a positive role in determining the performance of the agricultural sector. It was not possible, however, to identify an indirect impact of public infrastructures on agriculture through their effects on the supply response to prices. The results in this paper, nonetheless, indicate that the long-standing controversy between 'pricism' and 'structuralism' in the analysis of agricultural supply is perhaps less relevant than it has sometimes been thought. More specifically, our findings suggest that the relative importance of price versus non-price factors is, to a significant extent, a function of the level of development. The impact of relative prices on agricultural supply was found to be much more pronounced for manufacturing countries. Conversely, for the same group of countries, the effect of public investment was significantly weaker. It is perhaps safe to argue that any policy package which relies only, or mostly, on one of these two sets of factors will severely undermine its chances of success.

NOTES

I am very grateful to Paul Seabright for his stimulating comments, to Angelo Cardini and Marzio Galeotti for helpful discussions and for providing me with their computer program, and to Carlo Maggi for skilful research assistance. The responsibility for any errors is, of course, solely my own.

1 The Probit equation indicates that the probability of a country's undertaking an adjustment programme with the support of the World Bank and/or the IMF is negatively related to its investment rate (I/Y) in the pre-shock period. Similarly, the GDP growth rate (GY) exerts a negative (albeit statistically weak) effect on the participation probability. These results seem to indicate that high investment rates are not, *per se*, a cause of economic distress. The estimated coefficients are as follows (standard errors in parenthesis):

I/Y: -7.19 (3.29), GY: -10.24 (6.95),
$CA/Y = -2.18$ (3.77), $GYA = 0.52$ (7.09)

where CA and GYA denote respectively the current account surplus (as a share of GDP) and the growth rate of agricultural production.

2 The results about agriculture may be picking up its countercyclical behaviour. For instance, Contré and Goldin (1991) show that, in the course of adjustment, the decline in agricultural growth is less pronounced than the fall in GDP growth. The results in Table 11.2, however, show something else (i.e., that, after controlling for other factors, agricultural growth is higher in adjustment lending countries).

3 The properties of the revenue function are fully analysed in Chambers (1988).

4 The whole issue can be expressed, perhaps more simply, in the following terms. Suppose that equation (8) is written as follows:

$$y(t) = b\,X(t) + u(t).$$

Take

$$(1-\delta)\,y(t-1) = (1-\delta)\,(b\,X(t-1) + u(t-1))$$

and subtract it from the expression for $Y(t)$. We get:

$$\begin{aligned} y(t) &= (1-\delta)\,y(t-1) + b\,X(t) - (1-\delta)\,b\,X(t-1) + u(t) - (1-\delta)\,u(t-1) \\ &= (1-\delta y(t-1) + b\,X(t) - (1-\delta)\,b\,X(t-1) + v(t) \end{aligned}$$

If $u(t)$ followed an autoregressive process with parameter $(1-\delta)$, the error term in the transformed equation $v(t)$ would be white noise. This is not, however, the end of the story. Panel data estimation of the transformed equation would still be inconsistent, for the reasons explained in the text. We must then take first differences of such an equation. The new error term will be $v(t) - v(t-1)$. If $v(t)$ is white noise, all endogenous variables dated $t-i$ with $i > 1$ will be valid instruments, as claimed in the text.

5 The reader may wonder why in estimating the equations LE and the price variables appear twice, dated at time t and at time $t-1$. This specification is the results of the first-quasi-difference transformation of equation (8) (see n.4 above). There are some additional non-linear restrictions because of this transformation (which, however, we do not impose).

6 The choice was dictated by the desire to rely on a sufficiently large sample of relatively homogeneous countries. Still, the smaller sample precluded the possibility of robust estimation.

7 I am grateful to Paul Seabright for his comments on this point.

8 With respect to manufacturing countries, notice that the negative value of η_{ap} does not imply that a higher stock of public capital leads to lower agricultural output. In fact, it can be shown that the elasticity of agricultural output with respect to public capital stock is equal to:

$$\eta_{ap}/S_a + S_p$$

where S_a and S_p denote respectively the GDP share of agriculture and public investment. We lack an estimate for S_p but, for plausible parameter values, the above elasticity (with S_a evaluated at the sample mean) is likely to be positive.

9 The following reasons add to suspicion about the public investment variable. First, it neglects changes in capacity utilisation and/or productivity (induced, for instance, by varying maintenance). Second, it assumes a fixed one-year installation lag. None of these assumptions, while common to many production studies, constitutes a valid approximation to reality. I am grateful to Ajay Chhibber, Christian Morrisson and Vito Tanzi for their comments on this point.

10 The specification with the interaction terms was also estimated for the full sample, but again it did not lead to any remarkable change. In Table 11.7, we report only the estimation for manufacturing countries.

REFERENCES

Anderson, T. and C. Hsiao (1982) 'Formulation and Estimation of Dynamic Models Using Panel Data', *Journal of Econometrics*, **18**: 47–82.

Anderson, R. and J. Thursby (1986) 'Confidence Intervals for Elasticity Estimators in Translog Models', *Review of Economics and Statistics*, **58**: 647–56.

Antle, J. (1983), 'Infrastructure and Aggregate Agricultural Productivity: International Evidence', *Economic Development and Cultural Change*, **31 (3)**: 609–20.

Arellano, M. and S. Bond (1988a) 'Some Tests of Specification for Panel Data: Montecarlo Evidence and an Application to an Employment Equation', *IFS Discussion Paper*, **88–4**.

Arellano, M. and S. Bond (1988b) 'Dynamic Panel Data Estimation using DPD', *IFS Discussion Paper*, **88–10**.

Binswanger, H. (1989) 'The Policy Response of Agriculture', in Proceedings of the World Bank Annual Conference on Development Economics, supplement to the *World Bank Economic Review and the World Bank Research Observer*: 231–58.

Binswanger, H., Y Mundlak, M. Chang and A. Bowers (1987) 'On the Determinants of Cross-country Aggregate Agricultural Supply', *Journal of Econometrics*, **36**: 111–31.

Bond, M. (1983) 'Agricultural Responses to Prices in Sub-Saharan Africa', *IMF Staff Papers*, **30 (4)**: 703–26.

Chambers, R. (1988) *Applied Production Analysis. A Dual Approach*, Cambridge: Cambridge University Press.

Chhibber, A. (1988) 'The Aggregate Supply Response in Agriculture: A Survey', in S. Commander (ed.), *Structural Adjustment in Agriculture: Theory and Practice in Africa and Latin America*, London: James Curry.
Contré F. and Ian Goldin (1991) 'L'Agriculture en period d'adjustment au Brésil', *Revue Tiers Monde*, **32 (126)**: 271–302.
Cornia, G. A. and R. Strickland (1990) 'Rural Differentiation, Poverty and Agricultural Crisis in Sub-Saharan Africa: Toward an Appropriate Policy Response', *UNICEF Innocenti Occasional Papers*, **4**, Florence.
Faini, R. and J. de Melo (1990) 'Adjustment, Investment and the Real Exchange Rate in Developing Countries', *Economic Policy*, **11**: 492–519.
Faini, R., J. de Melo, A. Senhadji-Semlali and J. Stanton (1991) 'Growth-oriented Adjustment Programs: a Statistical Analysis', *World Development*, forthcoming.
FAO (1990) 'The State of Food and Agriculture 1990: Structural Adjustment and Agriculture', Rome (mimeo).
Goldstein, M. and P. Montiel (1986) 'Evaluating Fund Stabilization Programmes with Multicountry Data: some Methodological Pitfalls', *IMF Staff Papers*, **33 (2)**: 304–44.
Khan, M. (1990) 'The Macroeconomic Effects of Fund-supported Adjustment Programmes', *IMF Staff Papers*, **37 (2)**: 195–231.
Nickell, S. (1981) 'Biases in Dynamic Models with Fixed Effects', *Econometrica*, **49**: 1417–26.
Smith, L. D. (1989) 'Structural Adjustment, Price Reform and Agricultural Performance in Sub-Saharan Africa', *Journal of Agricultural Economics*, **40 (1)**: 21–31.
Stevenson, R. (1980) 'Measuring Technological Bias', *American Economic Review*, **70 (1)**: 162–173.
World Bank (1990a) 'Adjustment Lending Policies for Sustainable Growth', *Country Economics Department, Policy and Research Series*, **14**, Washington, D.C.: World Bank.
World Bank (1990b) *World Development Tables 1989–90*, Washington, D.C.: World Bank.

Discussion

PAUL SEABRIGHT

Riccardo Faini's interesting paper does valuable work in summarising what can be said using aggregate cross-country data about the impact of structural adjustment programmes on developing country agriculture. It turns out that what we can say is more limited than might be hoped, but this in itself is an important lesson, and draws attention to the need for more country- and sector-specific studies. I shall deal with the two parts of his paper in turn, drawing attention first to econometric and then to interpretational issues.

First of all, does the evidence reveal that adjustment programmes have a beneficial effect on agricultural growth? Table 11.2 suggests they do. In interpreting Table 11.2, it is important to note that it is expressed in terms of the impact of independent variables on the *levels* of the performance indicators (not their first differences as Equation 11.2 would lead us to expect). One implication of this is that the insignificance of the coefficient on the lagged agricultural growth rate means that improvements in GYA between the two periods were on average equal and opposite in sign to deviations of GYA from the sample men in the first period (controlling for other effects). So none of the factors explaining the dispersion of GYA between countries in the first period has any explanatory power left in the second, which is surprising given the ingrained character of the structural rigidities that adjustment programmes have sought to reform.

Table 11.2 suggests that participation in adjustment programmes raised agricultural growth by 4 percentage points in this sample. This is a large effect, though its t-ratio is only 1.73; it is unsurprising that the coefficient is not well determined when one considers what it is trying to measure.[1] 'Adjustment' has meant different things in different countries; there have been different programmes, implemented to different degrees and at different dates. At this level of aggregation there is not much one can do about this diversity, except with regard to the problem of dates. It is a pity Faini did not take his performance indicators in the five-year periods before and after each programme was implemented, rather than in the same period regardless of programme date.

Nevertheless, the diversity means that Faini is right to caution us about drawing policy conclusions. First, the programmes under consideration are adjustment *lending* programmes: how can we separate the effect of adjustment from the effect of lending (which we should expect to be positive, at least in the short term)? Secondly, agricultural growth rates are not themselves an adequate welfare indicator if achieved at the cost of growth elsewhere in the economy. The EC's CAP shows that it is not hard to raise agricultural growth rates if we are not too fussy about the overall welfare costs. I am therefore more disturbed by the lack of impact of participation on GNP growth rates in Table 11.2 than I am encouraged by their positive impact on agricultural growth.

The paper's most significant contribution comes in Section 3. The use of first-quasi-differencing is an ingenious way to solve the problem of inadequate data on capital stocks; it essentially allows us to look at the impact of investment instead of total capital, and to let the data determine how much of that investment is gross and how much is net. However, the assumption of a common depreciation rate for private and public capital stock is not very satisfactory, and will bias the coefficient estimates. If countries with high proportions of public investment in total investment also have high output shares for a particular sector (which is certainly true for industry in Tables 11.4 and 11.5), then coefficient estimates on public investment will be biased away from zero; conversely for sectors in which high public investment implies low output shares. Though there is not much the author can do about this, it would be useful for the direction of bias to be acknowledged.

The results of this estimation are certainly not as much at variance as they seem with theories about the importance of infrastructure in determining agricultural growth. In the full sample, increases in public capital stock contribute no less to agricultural growth than they do to GDP growth overall. When one considers that 'industry' in these tables includes construction, for which there is a substantial demand-side effect from public investment on output, it is hardly surprising that the supply-side response of agricultural output is comparatively muted. In this kind of estimation demand-side effects will tend to dominate supply-side effects: the demand-side impact of an increase in public investment will be concentrated into the period during which that investment takes place (except for multiplier effects), while its supply-side impact will be spread over the life of the capital thereby created (which for infrastructure can be many years). This does not mean that supply-side effects are unimportant, rather that their importance is difficult conclusively to measure. It requires a more microeconomic focus, and more precise data, so that it is unlikely to be possible to reach cross-country conclusions. Faini's paper has shown us how far we can go with this kind of aggregative study; it has also provided a welcome antidote to the sterile debates about the importance of prices versus structural factors, as though these explanations were incompatible with each other.

NOTE

1 High standard errors on a number of coefficients mean that interpretation needs special caution here. For example, the coefficient on *SH* is 50 per cent higher than on *GYA*(−1) though its t-ratio is only a little above unity. Again, it is curious that allowing for the endogeneity of participation reduces the estimated impact on the current account from positive and highly significant to insignificantly negative, when the impact of the current account on the participation probability in the Probit equation in n.1 is itself insignificant. These and

other factors suggest that there is a lot going on in this data set that is hard to explain, as well as significant multicollinearity between the performance indicators and participation in the programmes: performance is both a cause and an effect of participation, and it is even harder than usual to sort out which is which.

12 Structural factors and tax revenue in developing countries: a decade of evidence

VITO TANZI

1 Introduction

The decade of the 1980s was not an easy one for the majority of the developing countries. Many of them experienced high rates of inflation, difficulties with their balance of payments, slow growth rates, and other problems. These problems caused significant structural changes in the economies of the developing countries. In some cases, countries became more open; in others, they restricted imports to generate trade account surpluses to service the debt. The importance of agriculture was recognised and policies that tended to retard its development began to be changed. The import substitution model began to be replaced by a model that attached more importance to international market forces.

A common element in adjustment programmes was the perceived need to bring public finances under control. Since political (and, at times, administrative–institutional) reasons make expenditure control difficult, many adjustment programmes have come to rely on tax increases. Another factor causing tax increases during the 1980s was the need for many countries to mobilize resources to service their public debt. As far as foreign debt is concerned its servicing requires two surpluses, one in the trade account and the other in the primary budgetary account (see Reisen and van Trotsenburg, 1988).[1] The higher is the servicing, the larger must be the primary surplus. The debt situation itself thus created calls for tax increases.

Finally, some well-intentioned, but not well-informed, individuals called for large tax increases in developing countries on the grounds that their level of taxation was much lower than in OECD countries. The realisation that the average tax level in the former was only about half the average tax level in the latter led these individuals to believe that tax increases in developing countries should be feasible – and, perhaps, even easy.

Unfortunately, anyone who has been seriously involved in the reform of tax systems in developing countries should be aware of the great difficulties encountered by attempts to raise tax levels. These difficulties increase when structural changes are taking place, and especially when countries are undergoing major macroeconomic problems. The author has shown elsewhere how macroeconomic developments can have major effects on tax levels (Tanzi, 1989). *A priori*, one would expect that the macroeconomic developments in the 1980s would have put downward pressures on tax levels. For example, excluding China and India, imports of low-income economies in the 1980–8 period fell at an annual rate of 3.2 per cent; those for low middle-income economies fell at an annual rate of 0.2 per cent; and those for highly-indebted countries fell at an annual rate of 2.3 per cent (see World Bank, 1990). Since imports provide countries with a very important tax base, the fall in imports cannot fail to put downward pressure on tax levels.[2] The inflation that characterised many of these countries and that accelerated over the decade, especially in Latin America and Africa, must also have negatively affected tax revenue.

The aim of this paper is largely empirical. It sets itself three objectives. The first is to assemble relatively updated basic tax data for as large a number of developing countries as possible for the 1978–88 period. The initial year, 1978, was still a relatively good one for developing countries. Commodity prices were high; industrial countries were in the middle of a boom; world real interest rates were very low; and foreign credit was abundant. The final year, 1988, was the latest for which data are now available for many countries. It was a very different year from 1978. Commodity prices had fallen; world real interest rates were high; credit to developing countries remained very scarce; and the effects of the debt crisis continued to reverberate throughout the developing world. In many developing countries, growth had stopped. This is likely to be the most comprehensive collection of tax data available for such a *large number* of countries (88) and for a decade.[3] The data came from the IMF's *Government Finance Statistics* (*GFS*) and from national sources, which were used to fill many gaps in the *GFS*.

The second objective is to use the cross-section, time-series data to estimate what has happened to the level and the structure of taxation (a) for all developing countries; (b) for different regions; and (c) for groups of countries with different economic characteristics. To my knowledge this has been done before for such a large group of countries, only for a point in time (see Tanzi, 1987; World Bank, 1988; Burgess and Stern, 1991).

A third objective is to use the new data to re-estimate some basic relationships between tax variables and economic variables. Although the paper does not focus on agricultural taxation, it will pay particular attention to the relationship between taxation and agriculture.

2 The level of taxation

2.1 Descriptive elements in the level of taxation

Tax levels and structures differ from country to country. These differences are considered in subsections 2.1 and 2.2.

As a reference point, let us look at the tax performance of the OECD. The level of taxation for all OECD countries rose from 34.5 per cent of GDP in 1978 to 38.4 per cent in 1988. For the members of the EC, the increase was from 35.1 per cent in 1978 to 40.8 per cent in 1988. The taxes that increased the most were those on general sales (VAT, etc.) and the social security contributions.

Table 12.1 is a summary table for the 88 developing countries for which data could be obtained over the 1978–88 period. To reduce the effects of extraordinary shocks in any one year, a moving three-year average has

Table 12.1 *All countries: tax revenue by major tax, 1978–88, per cent of GDP*

	1978–80	1980–2	1983–5	1986–8
Total tax revenue	17.2	17.5	18.0	17.9
Income taxes	5.2	5.6	5.6	5.3
Individual	1.9	2.0	2.1	2.1
Corporate	2.9	3.3	3.2	2.8
Other	0.4	0.3	0.4	0.4
Domestic taxes on goods and services	4.3	4.6	5.0	5.2
General sales taxes	1.9	2.1	2.3	2.5
Excise taxes	1.7	1.8	1.9	2.0
Other	0.7	0.7	0.8	0.7
Foreign trade taxes	5.3	5.0	5.1	5.0
Import duties	4.3	4.2	4.2	4.2
Export duties	0.8	0.7	0.6	0.5
Other	0.1	0.1	0.2	0.3
Social security contributions	1.4	1.4	1.5	1.5
Taxes on wealth	0.3	0.3	0.4	0.3
Other taxes	0.7	0.5	0.5	0.6

Sources: IMF *Government Finance Statistics*, and country sources.

been used. Table 12.1 shows that (a) the level of taxation in developing countries, at 17 to 18 per cent of GDP, was about half as high as that of OECD countries; and (b) that it remained relatively constant over the decade, increasing by somewhat less than 1 percentage point. During the 1980s the distance in the average level of taxation between developed and developing countries thus widened.

It should be mentioned here that these averages, as well as those given for the OECD countries, are simple averages for the countries in the groups; they are not weighted for the size of the economies. They suffer from what some economists may consider the shortcoming of, say, giving the same weight to China and to Chad.

The highest ratio of taxes to GDP was experienced by African countries which also showed some increase in the tax level over the period.[4] This is somewhat surprising, since the general impression was that African countries were unsuccessful in raising tax revenue. Another surprise is to find that, next to the African countries, the Latin American countries had the highest tax levels. Furthermore, these countries also showed some significant increases in their average tax levels over the 1978–88 period.

The Asian economies – and even more so those of the Middle East and North Africa – averaged the lowest tax ratios; their ratios were a few percentage points lower than the average for all the developing countries. Furthermore, the tax level for the Middle Eastern and African countries declined by about 1 percentage point over the period. One who believed that high taxes were inimical to growth would see this result as supporting such a thesis, since the Asian countries and the Middle Eastern and North African countries experienced faster rates of growth than the rest during the period under consideration.

Table 12.2 presents the tax revenue data for the 17 highly-indebted countries.[5] *A priori*, one would expect Table 12.2 to reflect the effect of two macroeconomic developments affecting the level of taxation in these countries over the 1978–88 decade. First, the considerable macroeconomic difficulties (inflation, balance of payments disequilibria, etc.) after 1982 should have had some immediate *negative* impact on tax revenue. Second, because of the need to raise additional tax revenue to generate the primary surplus necessary to service the debt, there should have been in later years a greater effort in these countries than elsewhere to raise the average tax ratio. To a limited extent both of these expectations seem to be supported by the data in Table 12.2. The highly-indebted countries did experience a fall of about 1 percentage point after 1980–2, which was fully recovered in the later years.

Table 12.3 introduces another common classification, namely that between low-income countries (*per capita* income below $400) and

Table 12.2 *High-debt countries: tax revenue by major tax, 1978–88, per cent of GDP*

	1978–80	1980–2	1983–5	1986–8
Total tax revenue	17.7	17.6	16.7	17.6
Income taxes	4.6	5.1	4.4	4.6
Individual	1.2	1.3	1.2	1.2
Corporate	3.2	3.6	2.8	2.7
Other	0.1	0.2	0.3	0.5
Domestic taxes on goods and services	5.5	5.8	6.1	6.3
General sales taxes	3.1	3.3	3.0	3.2
Excise taxes	2.0	2.0	2.3	2.4
Other	0.4	0.4	0.8	0.7
Foreign trade taxes	3.0	3.0	2.9	3.1
Import duties	2.4	2.3	2.1	2.4
Export duties	0.6	0.7	0.5	0.3
Other	–	–	0.3	0.3
Social security contributions	3.1	2.8	2.6	2.9
Taxes on wealth	0.3	0.2	0.3	0.3
Other taxes	1.2	0.6	0.4	0.4

Sources: IMF *Government Finance Statistics*, and country sources.

high-income countries (*per capita* income over $2000). A general assumption by specialists working in developing countries is that richer countries find it easier (and perhaps more necessary, as argued by Wagner's Law) to raise a larger share of taxes in GDP. Table 12.3 lends support to this view: the richer countries show, on average, much higher tax ratios. The difference between the two groups ranged between 4 and 8 percentage points over the period; by the end of the period it had been reduced by 3 percentage points, due both to an increase in the poorest developing countries and to a decrease in the richest developing countries.

2.2 *Analytical issues*

This section reviews some major factors determining the level of taxation across countries. Traditionally, the point of departure for this analysis has been an assessment of the relationship between the tax level and *per capita* income.

Table 12.3 *Tax revenue breakdown for low-income and high-income developing countries, 1978–1988[1], per cent of GDP*

	1978–80		1980–2		1983–5		1986–8	
	L	H	L	H	L	H	L	H
Total tax revenue	13.7	21.7	12.3	20.7	13.7	20.2	14.9	20.2
Income taxes	3.1	7.6	2.7	7.4	3.1	6.9	3.4	6.1
Individual	1.0	2.5	1.0	2.5	1.1	2.6	1.2	2.6
Corporate	1.9	4.4	1.6	4.5	1.9	3.8	2.7	3.4
Other	0.2	0.7	0.1	0.4	0.1	0.5	0.1	0.6
Domestic taxes on goods and services	3.4	5.0	3.8	5.2	4.4	5.5	4.5	5.5
General sales taxes	1.7	2.3	1.9	2.7	2.5	2.6	2.4	3.0
Excise taxes	1.4	1.4	1.6	1.5	1.5	1.7	1.7	2.4
Other	0.3	1.2	0.3	1.0	0.4	1.2	0.5	0.8
Foreign trade taxes	6.6	4.1	5.1	3.5	5.4	3.4	6.3	3.4
Import duties	4.7	3.9	3.9	3.2	4.1	2.9	5.3	3.0
Export duties	1.6	0.1	0.9	0.2	1.1	0.2	0.9	0.1
Other	0.3	0.1	0.3	0.1	0.2	0.3	0.2	0.3
Social security contributions	0.2	3.7	0.2	3.6	0.2	3.4	0.2	3.9
Taxes on wealth	0.2	0.6	0.2	0.5	0.2	0.5	0.2	0.5
Other taxes	0.3	0.8	0.3	0.6	0.3	0.5	0.3	0.7

Sources: IMF *Government Finance Statistics*, and country sources.
[1] L: *Per capita* income below $400; H: *Per capita* income above $2000.

The power of *per capita* income in determining the level of taxation is striking when the poorest and the richest developing countries are compared (as in Table 12.3). However, it is much less obvious when two intermediate groups (those with *per capita* incomes between $400 and $900 and those with *per capita* income between $900 and $2000) are compared. Interestingly enough, while the level of taxation for these two other groups is much higher than for the poorest countries, the richer group (with *per capita* income between $900 and $2000) has the lower tax level.

A more formal analysis below will try to assess the impact of *per capita* income and other factors in determining the tax level. At this point, the results of a very simple statistical test are reported. The share of tax to GDP was regressed against the logs of *per capita* income for 83 developing countries and for several years starting in 1978 and ending in 1988. The method of estimation was ordinary least squares. The results were as follows:

1978	$T/GDP=$	-1.541	$+\ 6.645$	Y	$\bar{R}^2 = 0.149$
		(-0.317)	(3.922)		
1981	$T/GDP=$	-0.870	$+\ 6.181$	Y	$\bar{R}^2 = 0.128$
		(-0.167)	(3.606)		
1983	$T/GDP=$	6.326	$+\ 3.827$	Y	$\bar{R}^2 = 0.042$
		$(\ 1.175)$	(2.151)		
1985	$T/GDP=$	9.734	$+\ 2.931$	Y	$\bar{R}^2 = 0.021$
		$(\ 1.845)$	(1.661)		
1988	$T/GDP=$	9.634	$+\ 2.739$	Y	$\bar{R}^2 = 0.015$
		$(\ 1.745)$	(1.501)		

The figures in parenthesis are $t-$values.

What is immediately obvious from these results is the declining importance over time of *per capita* income as a major determinant of the level of taxation.[6] While in 1978 and in 1981, *per capita* income seems to have played an important role (a relatively high $\bar{R}^2$ for a cross-section analysis, and a statistical coefficient significant at the 1 per cent level for *per capita* income, Y), it loses its importance after the beginning of the debt crisis. *Per capita* income, therefore, represents only a partial, and increasingly unimportant, factor in explaining the variation in the level of taxation across countries. Other factors (such as macroeconomic instability, the need to service the high debt, and the changing structure of the economy) became more important determinants.

A country's economic structure is another factor that could be expected to influence the level of explicit taxation. A salient feature in this regard is the share of agriculture in GDP. This influence may come from both demand and supply considerations. On the demand side, it seems reasonable to assume that the more agricultural is a country, the less it will have to spend for governmental activities and services. Many public sector activities are largely city-oriented: in other words they are associated with correcting for the costs of urbanisation. As the share of agriculture in GDP rises, the need for total public spending and so for tax revenue must thus fall.[7] On the supply side, it is well-known that it is very difficult to tax the agricultural sector *explicitly*. As several authors (Bird, 1974; Ahmad and Stern, 1991) have pointed out, although the agricultural sector is often *very heavily* taxed in many implicit ways (through import quotas, tariffs, controlled prices for output, overvalued exchange rates), explicit taxes (normally export duties and land taxes) on this sector are very limited. The difficulty of raising the tax level tends therefore to rise with the increase in the share of agriculture in GDP.

The data bear out the above conclusion to a surprising degree (see Table 12.4). Furthermore, the fall in the level of taxation is continuous as the

Table 12.4 *Tax revenue breakdown for countries with low and high agricultural share, 1978–88*[1], *per cent of GDP*

	1978–80		1980–2		1983–5		1986–8	
	L	H	L	H	L	H	L	H
Total tax revenue	20.4	11.0	20.5	11.1	21.1	11.2	19.9	9.9
Income taxes	8.4	2.1	8.2	2.6	8.1	2.3	6.8	1.8
Individual	2.8	0.9	2.4	1.1	2.5	0.9	2.6	0.8
Corporate	5.0	1.0	5.1	1.3	4.7	1.2	3.3	0.9
Other	0.6	0.1	0.7	0.1	0.9	0.1	0.8	0.1
Domestic taxes on goods and services	5.1	3.2	5.4	4.1	5.5	4.4	5.8	3.9
General sales taxes	2.6	1.7	2.7	2.4	2.6	2.8	2.7	2.3
Excise taxes	1.5	1.3	1.8	1.6	1.7	1.4	1.9	1.3
Other	1.0	0.2	0.9	0.2	1.1	0.2	1.2	0.3
Foreign trade taxes	3.0	5.0	3.1	3.7	3.9	3.7	3.5	3.3
Import duties	2.8	3.3	2.7	2.9	3.5	2.0	3.2	2.1
Export duties	0.2	1.6	0.3	0.8	0.2	1.4	–	1.2
Other	0.1	0.1	0.1	0.1	0.2	0.3	0.3	–
Social security contributions	2.0	0.1	2.6	–	2.3	0.1	2.5	0.1
Taxes on wealth	0.5	0.3	0.5	0.3	0.6	0.4	0.5	0.4
Other taxes	1.4	0.4	0.8	0.3	0.8	0.3	0.8	0.4

Sources: IMF *Government Finance Statistics*, and country sources.
[1] L: Share of agriculture in GDP less than 10 per cent; H: Share of agriculture in GDP above 40 per cent.

share of agriculture in GDP rises. For countries with an agricultural share of zero to 10 per cent of GDP, the level of taxation is around 20 per cent. That level falls to 10–11 per cent for countries with an agricultural share of more than 40 per cent.

A more formal test confirms the existence of a relationship between the tax level and the share of agriculture in GDP. For 77 countries for which the information is available, the share of tax to GDP has been regressed against the share of agricultural output in total GDP. This is done for 1978, 1981, and 1988. The results are as follows:

$$1978 \quad T/GDP = \underset{(16.759)}{22.994} - \underset{(4.293)}{0.216} \quad A/GDP \qquad \bar{R}^2 = 0.187$$

$$1981 \quad T/GDP = \underset{(16.138)}{22.884} - \underset{(4.168)}{0.212} \; A/GDP \qquad \bar{R}^2 = 0.173$$

$$1988 \quad T/GDP = \underset{(14.000)}{20.684} - \underset{(3.190)}{0.177} \; A/GDP \qquad \bar{R}^2 = 0.112$$

The figures in parenthesis are t-values.

The results show the explanatory power of the share of agriculture in GDP in determining the level of taxation; it performs far better than *per capita* income and has the correct (i.e., negative) sign. Furthermore, although the power of this independent variable was also reduced by the events of the 1980s, it remained highly significant (at the 1 per cent level) in 1988. This leads to the conclusion that any multiple regression analysis that aims at statistically explaining the behaviour of the tax level must include the agricultural share among the explanatory variables.

In past years many papers have tried to explain statistically the factors that determine tax levels. See, in particular, Chelliah, Baas and Kelly (1975); Tait, Grätz and Eichengreen (1979); Tabellini (1985); and Tanzi (1987). Generally this literature has not been too successful in explaining differences in tax levels and the $\bar{R}^2$s obtained from cross-section statistical regressions have been relatively low. Before closing this section, I will perform a simple statistical experiment based on an eclectic underlying model that combines demand and supply considerations among the determinants of the tax levels.

The reasons why the ratio of agricultural output in GDP should affect the tax level have already been discussed. For this variable supply and demand factors act jointly and in the same direction: a highly agricultural country has greater difficulty in raising explicit taxes and, not having to cope with the high costs of urbanisation, it may also have less need for a high level of taxation. We have also discussed the reason why a high public debt requires a higher tax level. However, the high debt burden can also create macroeconomic imbalances that may tend to reduce the tax level, as argued in Tanzi (1989). In general, however, we would expect that, on balance, a high debt burden would tend to raise the tax level, *ceteris paribus*. Because of the unavailability of data on domestic debt and because of the large scope of foreign debt in many of the countries in the sample, we will focus on foreign debt.

Another variable that should be introduced into the analysis is the share of imports in GDP. *Ceteris paribus*, a higher share of imports in GDP should facilitate the maintenance of a higher tax level. This is a pure supply factor since imports provide a significant tax base for various taxes such as import duties, a large part of general sales taxes, a large part of excise taxes, and so forth (see Tanzi, 1989).

Taking all the factors discussed above into account, we will estimate a simple equation.

If *A*, *M*, and *D* are respectively the shares of agricultural output, imports, and foreign debt in GDP, and *Y* is *per capita* income, we shall assume that

$$T/GDP = f(A, M, D, Y)$$

The above equation was estimated for 1978, 1981, and 1988, using the ordinary least squares method. The results are shown in Table 12.5. Some of the equations shown in the table include all the variables. Some exclude either *per capita* income, *Y*, or the share of agriculture, *A*. The reason for this is the high correlation between *A* and *Y*. In general, the equations that include both of these variables do much less well than those which include only one. And those that exclude *Y* do better than those that exclude *A*.

It is indeed remarkable that such good results could be obtained from such a simple model. When *per capita* income is excluded the coefficients for the agricultural and the imports variables are consistently significant at the 1 per cent level, while the debt variable is generally significant at the 5 per cent level. For all three variables, the signs are the expected ones. The model explains a full 52 per cent of the variance in 1988, a high percentage for a cross-sectional sample. It should not be surprising if the debt variable does not perform better. For the reasons outlined above, this variable could be expected to perform poorly. The same debt/GDP ratio could require different service payments, and thus different tax requirements, if in one country the debt was obtained on concessional terms while in another it was obtained from commercial sources. Furthermore, some countries may find it easier to go into arrears in their debt

Table 12.5 *Tax revenue to GDP ratio, regression summary table*

Year	a	A	Y	M	D	$\bar{R}^2$	Observations
1978							
Coefficient	22.99	−0.22				0.187	77
t-Statistic	16.76	−4.29					
Coefficient	−1.54		6.65			0.149	83
t-Statistic	−0.32		3.92				
Coefficient	25.32	−0.23	−0.68			0.176	76
t-Statistic	2.42	−2.60	−0.22				

Year	a	A	Y	M	D	$\bar{R}^2$	Observations
Coefficient	15.46	−0.17		0.13	0.19	0.393	66
t-Statistic	6.10	−3.14		3.77	1.84		
Coefficient	−10.13		7.20	0.12	0.27	0.424	72
t-Statistic	−2.21		4.37	3.65	2.68		
Coefficient	−6.75	−0.10	6.25	0.14	0.23	0.427	65
t-Statistic	−0.58	−0.27	1.94	4.05	2.23		
1981							
Coefficient	22.88	−0.23				0.173	79
t-Statistic	16.14	−4.17					
Coefficient	−0.87		6.18			0.127	83
t-Statistic	−0.17		3.61				
Coefficient	36.68	−0.36	−3.61			0.226	76
t-Statistic	3.20	−3.53	−1.14				
Coefficient	16.80	−0.25		0.12	0.19	0.459	68
t-Statistic	7.99	−4.84		3.89	2.27		
Coefficient	−13.40		8.19	0.33	0.26	0.411	74
t-Statistic	−2.76		5.21	3.25	3.15		
Coefficient	0.33	−0.12	4.49	0.12	0.21	0.472	67
t-Statistic	0.11	−1.25	1.46	4.07	2.46		
1988							
Coefficient	20.68	−0.18				0.112	74
t-Statistic	13.99	−3.19					
Coefficient	9.63		2.74			0.015	82
t-Statistic	1.74		1.50				
Coefficient	50.55	−0.39	−8.60			0.208	72
t-Statistic	5.32	−4.52	−3.20				
Coefficient	13.34	−0.15		0.16	0.07	0.523	66
t-Statistic	7.57	−3.28		5.35	1.97		
Coefficient	−3.71		4.69	0.16	0.08	0.433	75
t-Statistic	−0.74		2.86	5.56	2.01		
Coefficient	14.94	−0.16	−0.45	0.16	0.07	0.515	66
t-Statistic	1.61	−2.15	−0.18	5.27	1.83		

a = Constant
A = Agriculture to GDP ratio
Y = Log of *per capita* income ($)
M = Import to GDP ratio
D = Debt to GDP ratio
$\bar{R}^2$ = Adjusted R^2

obligations than to increase the tax burden. Finally, as mentioned earlier, domestic debt has not been accounted for.

3 The structure of taxation

In this section we turn our attention away from the *level* and toward the *structure* of taxation in developing countries. In other words, we discuss the relative use of different tax sources across the regional–economic groupings described above and over the 1978–88 period. We shall once again use the tables for reference, starting with Table 12.1, which refers to the whole sample of 88 developing countries.

Broadly speaking, and on the average, the developing countries raise about one-third of their tax revenue from income taxes, one-third from foreign trade taxes, and the remaining third from all other taxes. These proportions did not change much in 1980s.

The contrast with OECD countries is striking. First, the OECD countries do not raise much revenue from foreign trade taxes. Second, while developing countries raise about the same proportion from general sales taxes and from excises, the OECD countries raise much more from the former than from the latter. Third, developing countries raise more revenue from corporate income taxes than from individual income taxes while the reverse, to a significant extent, is the case for industrial countries. Finally, social security contributions and wealth taxes are much more important in industrial countries.

Table 12.1 indicates a remarkable stability in the structure of taxation in developing countries over the 1978-88 period. The main changes were: (a) a significant increase in domestic taxes on goods and services, and especially in general sales taxes; and (b) a significant fall in export duties, which are predominantly imposed on agricultural products. The first of these changes was probably associated with the introduction of the value-added tax in many countries, and with the fact that these taxes are less affected than other taxes by major macroeconomic shocks (inflation, balance of payments crises, etc.). The second change probably resulted from the strong criticism in recent years directed against export taxes. This is one area where economists probably have had a major impact.

Table 12.1 averages the tax structures of all the 88 developing countries. Substantial differences are likely to be found when different groupings are taken and, of course, individual countries diverge considerably from the averages of Table 12.1. While we cannot discuss individual countries, we can consider various geographical or economically-oriented groupings.

The high-debt countries have characteristics somewhat different from the average. They have a higher, and increasing, share of taxes on goods and services, and a lower share of foreign trade taxes; individual income taxes are also very low for these countries. The post-1982 debt crisis seems to have had a major impact on revenue from corporate income taxes, which fell sharply after 1982; this loss was partly compensated by increases in domestic taxes on goods and services.

The different tax structures, and the changes in those structures over the 1978–88 period, for low-income and high-income developing countries, can be seen from Table 12.3. The major differences were: (a) in the income taxes, which are much higher for the high-income developing countries; (b) in the foreign trade taxes, which are much higher for the low-income countries; (c) in the social security taxes, which are much higher in the high-income countries – in fact, these taxes generate insignificant revenues in low-income countries; and (d) (to a much lesser extent) in the domestic taxes on goods and services, which are somewhat higher in high-income countries.

Over the decade the most significant changes observed in low-income developing countries were: (a) the substantial increase in the share of corporate income taxes and of domestic taxes on goods and services, and (b) the fall in export duties. With respect to high-income developing countries the most significant changes were: (a) the fall in corporate income taxes, and (b) the increases in general sales and excise taxes.

Table 12.4 also shows the remarkable impact on the tax structure of the agricultural share in GDP. That impact is most evident in income taxes and in social security contributions. These taxes, combined, account for 50 per cent of total tax revenue for the countries with a low agricultural share, while they account for only about 20 per cent of total tax revenue in countries with a high agricultural share. As one would expect, foreign trade taxes (and especially export duties) contribute a much higher tax revenue share in agricultural countries.

As far as major trends are concerned, a very significant change over the decade is the fall in the share of corporate income taxes and the increase in import duties for the countries with a low agricultural share, and the sharp fall in import duties and the increase in general sales taxes in the highly agricultural countries. These trends are difficult to explain.

4 Concluding remarks

The decade of the 1980s witnessed major economic crises in many developing countries, followed by more or less successful attempts at stabilisation and structural adjustment. Adjustment programmes have often required major tax reforms to raise more revenue and to make the tax systems more efficient. What was the impact of these changes on the tax systems? Did the level of taxation rise? Did it rise more in some regions or in some groups of countries than in others? And what about the structure of taxation? Was it much changed by these developments? These are some of the questions addressed in this paper. In order to deal with them a major effort at data gathering was carried out. It produced a set of basic tables which should be useful to those who deal with these issues.[8]

In the process of dealing with these questions, the paper also addressed a few analytical issues such as the determinants of the level of taxation and the role of agriculture in revenue generation. Some interesting results were obtained. Four factors that seem to have a substantial impact on the level of taxation are: (a) the share of imports in GDP, (b) the share of agriculture in GDP, (c) the share of foreign debt in GDP; and (d) *per capita* income. These factors explained statistically almost half of the variation in the level of taxation among countries; the share of agriculture in GDP proved to be much more important than *per capita* income.

An interesting conclusion of the paper was that in spite of all the attention paid to taxation, the average tax level for the developing countries changed little over the decade. But, then, this may be seen as a favourable result since the structural difficulties faced by many developing countries must have put downward pressures on tax levels. As far as the structure of taxation is concerned, there were several significant changes among the groups of countries but the major developments for the whole sample were: (a) the increasing importance of domestic taxes on goods and services, and (b) the gradual disappearance of export duties. Both of these changes should be welcomed by economists.

NOTES

The views expressed in this paper are strictly personal. They do not necessarily reflect Fund positions. The author wishes to thank John Brondolo for the invaluable statistical assistance he provided and for comments. This paper could not have been written without his help. Thanks are also due to Chris Wu for earlier statistical assistance. The paper was much improved by comments received from Professor Nicholas Stern, Ian Goldin and from other participants at the OECD–CEPR conference (April 1991).

1 The surplus in the primary budgetary account is also needed to service the domestic portion of the debt.
2 The external sector may account directly or indirectly for about 50 per cent of the total tax revenue of developing countries. Thus what happens to imports and exports is particularly significant (see Tanzi, 1986).
3 In a way, this paper should be seen as a logical sequence to my paper in Newbery and Stern (1987). My earlier paper focused exclusively on cross-sectional analysis; this paper, *inter alia*, adds a time dimension to that analysis.

4 Background regional tables are available on request from the author.
5 These are: Argentina, Bolivia, Brazil, Chile, Colombia, Costa Rica, Côte d'Ivoire, Ecuador, Jamaica, Mexico, Morocco, Nigeria, Peru, the Philippines, Uruguay, Venezuela, and Yugoslavia.
6 These results should be compared with those in Tanzi (1987: 218–22) and in Burgess and Stern (1991: 19). The differences are due to data revisions and the inclusion of different countries.
7 This conclusion may, however, reflect not just the relative need for public services by the agricultural and the urban sectors but also the relative political power of agricultural and urban populations.
8 Detailed tax data for 1988 are shown in Statistical Appendixes 1 and 2.

REFERENCES

Ahmad, Etisham and Nicholas Stern (1991) *The Theory and Practice of Tax Reform in Developing Countries*, Cambridge: Cambridge University Press.

Bird, Richard M. (1974) *Taxing Agricultural Land in Developing Countries*, Cambridge, MA: Harvard University Press.

Burgess, Robin and Nicholas Stern (1991) 'Taxation and Development', *Journal of Economic Literature*, **29**.

Chelliah, Raja J., Hessel J. Baas and Margaret R. Kelly (1975) 'Tax Ratios and Tax Effort in Developing Countries, 1969–71', *IMF Staff Papers*, **22**, March: 187–205.

Newbery, David and Nicholas Stern (1987) *The Theory of Taxation for Developing Countries*, Oxford: Oxford University Press for the World Bank.

Reisen, Helmut and Axel van Trotsenburg (1988) *Developing Country Debt: The Budgetary and Transfer Problem*, Paris: OECD.

Tabellini, Guido (1985) 'International Tax Comparisons Reconsidered', unpublished paper, Washington, D.C.: IMF.

Tait, Alan A., Wilfrid M. Grätz and Barry J. Eichengreen (1979) 'International Comparisons of Taxation for Selected Developing Countries, 1972–76', *IMF Staff Papers*, **26**, March: 123–56.

Tanzi, Vito (1986) 'Fiscal Policy Responses to Exogenous Shocks in Developing Countries', *The American Economic Review*, **76**, May: 88–91, Chapter 5 in Tanzi (1991) pp. 85–103.

(1987) 'Quantitative Characteristics of the Tax Systems of Developing Countries', Chapter 8 in Newbery and Stern (1987): 205–41.

(1989) 'The Impact of Macroeconomic Policies on the Level of Taxation and on the Fiscal Balance in Developing Countries', *IMF Staff Papers*, **36**, September: 633–56, Chapter 8 in Tanzi (1991).

(1991) *Public Finance in Developing Countries*, London: Edward Elgar.

World Bank (1988) *World Development Report 1988*, Oxford: Oxford University Press.

(1990) *World Development Report 1990*, Oxford: Oxford University Press.

Statistical Appendix 1. *Tax to GDP ratios in 1988: Africa and Asia*

	Total revenue	Tax revenue	Individual income tax	Corporate income tax	Other income tax	General sales tax	Excise taxes	Other domestic indirect taxes	Import taxes	Export taxes	Other foreign trade taxes	Social security taxes	Property taxes	Other taxes
AFRICA														
Botswana	52.9	28.5	1.6	17.9	2.0	0.4	0.0	0.1	6.4	0.0	−0.0	0.0	0.0	−0.0
Burkina Faso	15.5	12.7	1.5	0.6	0.3	2.5	1.1	0.0	3.6	NA	NA	1.2	0.9	0.6
Burundi	16.3	14.5	1.5	1.6	0.3	0.0	3.4	2.4	3.4	1.7	0.2	0.0	0.8	−0.8
Cameroon	16.8	14.7	1.8	5.3	0.0	1.1	1.2	0.1	2.3	0.4	0.0	1.1	0.3	1.0
Comoros	15.0	11.3	0.3	2.9	0.1	1.1	0.0	0.2	5.3	1.4	−0.0	0.0	0.1	−0.2
Congo	19.5	12.7	2.1	1.2	0.0	2.9	0.1	0.0	3.9	0.2	0.0	0.6	0.0	1.6
Côte D'Ivoire	NA	22.0	2.3	1.4	0.0	1.4	4.3	1.7	7.4	1.9	0.0	1.5	NA	NA
Djibouti	27.1	24.8	3.0	1.4	0.0	9.4	4.6	2.3	1.6	0.0	0.0	0.0	1.4	1.0
Ethiopia	29.3	20.4	2.1	NA	NA	2.0	4.0	0.3	4.2	1.2	0.0	0.0	0.4	0.0
Gabon	24.4	17.9	1.9	3.8	0.5	4.1	0.0	0.5	6.1	0.3	0.0	0.0	0.2	0.4
Gambia	22.3	21.3	0.9	1.8	0.3	0.0	0.6	1.0	15.9	0.6	0.1	0.0	0.0	0.1
Ghana	13.4	12.4	1.2	2.6	0.0	1.2	2.6	0.1	2.4	2.3	0.0	0.0	0.0	0.0
Kenya	22.8	20.8	NA	NA	NA	7.4	1.8	0.7	3.9	0.2	0.0	0.0	0.0	0.2
Lesotho	36.8	31.0	1.6	1.4	0.1	6.7	1.2	0.0	19.9	0.0	0.0	0.0	0.0	0.0
Liberia	NA	NA	NA	NA	NA	NA	NA	NA	NA	NA	NA	NA	NA	NA
Malawi	19.2	17.4	2.4	5.0	0.1	6.0	0.6	0.3	3.1	−0.1	−0.0	0.0	0.0	0.1
Maldives	40.8	26.0	0.0	0.7	−0.0	0.0	0.0	5.8	17.8	0.0	1.3	0.0	0.0	0.3
Mali	18.3	11.7	0.5	1.4	0.1	2.3	2.5	0.4	1.9	0.2	0.1	0.8	0.3	1.3
Nigeria	14.2	13.7	0.0	10.5	0.0	0.0	0.6	0.0	2.4	0.0	0.0	0.0	0.0	0.1
Senegal	18.1	13.8	2.4	0.9	0.3	3.4	0.4	0.3	5.2	0.0	0.0	0.3	0.3	0.3

Sierra Leone	9.1	7.3	0.7	2.0	0.0	0.0	1.4	0.4	2.6	0.0	0.1	0.0	0.0	0.0
South Africa	28.2	26.1	7.7	5.6	0.0	6.6	1.7	0.5	1.1	0.0	0.0	0.5	0.5	1.9
Swaziland	30.5	27.5	3.7	6.0	0.7	3.7	0.0	0.2	11.7	1.3	−0.0	0.0	0.0	0.1
Tanzania	14.9	13.7	0.9	2.4	0.2	7.3	0.0	0.1	1.8	0.0	−0.0	0.0	0.0	0.9
Togo	26.8	20.2	3.9	3.6	0.3	2.1	0.3	0.2	6.6	0.0	2.0	1.8	0.2	−0.8
Uganda	6.6	6.0	0.0	0.5	0.0	1.9	0.5	0.1	1.0	1.8	0.0	0.0	0.0	0.2
Zaire	26.5	25.6	6.3	3.2	0.0	1.9	0.9	0.3	8.1	3.9	0.0	0.2	0.1	0.5
Zambia	22.9	20.9	1.8	6.4	0.6	5.4	3.0	0.1	3.6	0.0	0.0	0.0	0.0	0.1
Zimbabwe	35.1	31.0	9.5	6.6	0.5	5.5	3.2	0.1	5.1	0.0	0.2	0.0	0.1	0.3
ASIA														
Bangladesh	8.7	7.3	0.2	0.8	0.0	0.9	2.0	0.0	2.7	0.0	0.0	0.0	0.2	0.4
Fiji	23.9	19.6	5.8	2.9	0.2	0.0	2.5	0.9	6.8	0.0	−0.0	0.0	0.0	0.3
India	14.2	11.1	0.9	1.1	0.0	0.1	4.8	0.0	4.0	0.0	0.0	0.0	0.0	0.0
Indonesia	16.8	14.9	0.8	8.5	0.1	3.1	1.0	0.0	0.8	0.1	0.0	0.0	0.3	0.2
Korea	17.9	15.9	2.9	2.5	0.0	3.3	2.0	1.2	2.5	0.0	0.0	0.7	0.3	0.5
Malaysia	25.7	17.5	2.0	5.9	0.0	1.6	1.7	1.3	2.7	1.6	0.0	0.2	0.1	0.5
Mauritius	25.2	22.5	1.2	1.5	−0.0	1.8	1.5	1.4	10.3	2.4	0.1	1.0	1.2	0.1
Myanmar	9.1	4.8	0.9	0.0	0.0	2.0	0.0	0.5	1.4	0.0	0.0	0.0	0.0	0.0
Nepal	10.5	8.5	0.6	0.3	0.0	1.9	1.2	0.7	3.1	0.2	0.0	0.0	0.6	0.0
Pakistan	17.5	NA	NA	NA	NA	NA	NA	NA	NA	NA	NA	NA	NA	NA
Papua New Guinea	22.7	18.5	5.3	4.7	0.1	0.0	2.2	0.2	5.1	0.5	0.0	0.0	0.0	0.4
Philippines	13.5	10.9	1.0	1.6	0.7	1.1	2.4	0.7	2.8	0.0	0.1	0.0	0.0	0.5
Singapore	28.4	14.8	1.7	4.0	0.0	0.0	1.1	4.2	0.7	0.0	0.0	0.0	1.8	1.3
Solomon Islands	22.5	19.8	5.0	1.4	−0.0	0.0	0.1	0.4	9.6	3.2	−0.0	0.0	0.0	0.1
Sri Lanka	18.8	16.2	0.7	1.4	0.0	5.6	2.0	0.1	4.8	0.8	0.0	0.0	0.8	0.0
Thailand	17.4	16.0	1.6	1.8	0.0	3.3	4.2	0.6	3.8	0.2	0.0	0.0	0.4	0.1
Western Samoa	44.8	30.8	NA	NA	NA	0.0	5.4	0.0	1.6	0.3	15.6	0.0	0.0	0.7

Source: IMF, *Government Finance Statistics*, and unpublished national sources.

Statistical Appendix 2. *Tax to GDP ratios in 1988: Europe, Latin America and Middle East/North Africa*

	Total revenue	Tax revenue	Individual income tax	Corporate income tax	Other income tax	General sales tax	Excise taxes	Other domestic indirect taxes	Import taxes	Export taxes	Other foreign trade taxes	Social security taxes	Property taxes	Other taxes
EUROPE														
Cyprus	26.8	22.0	3.6	1.1	0.6	0.0	3.3	1.4	4.7	0.0	0.0	4.4	0.6	2.2
Greece	38.6	32.5	4.9	1.4	0.4	9.9	4.0	0.0	0.1	0.0	0.0	11.2	0.8	−0.1
Israel	41.9	36.8	12.4	3.4	1.7	12.4	1.0	0.3	1.0	0.0	0.6	2.9	0.3	0.9
Malta	36.2	24.8	3.9	3.8	0.1	0.0	1.0	0.9	8.1	0.0	0.6	5.4	1.0	0.1
Portugal	35.3	33.2	2.9	1.8	2.3	6.9	5.3	1.5	1.3	0.0	0.0	9.5	0.2	1.3
Turkey	17.5	14.2	4.8	2.1	0.0	4.2	0.4	1.0	1.2	0.0	0.0	0.0	0.0	0.6
Yugoslavia	32.6	31.5	3.8	2.5	0.0	7.9	0.0	0.0	3.4	0.0	0.0	13.8	0.1	0.0
LATIN AMERICA														
Argentina	13.1	12.0	0.0	0.0	0.5	0.8	1.9	0.2	1.0	0.3	0.2	5.7	0.8	0.6
Bahamas	21.5	19.2	0.0	0.0	0.0	0.0	0.0	1.6	12.8	0.2	0.8	1.7	0.7	1.4
Barbados	32.1	29.8	5.0	3.6	0.2	5.7	0.2	2.1	3.7	0.0	0.0	4.8	1.6	2.9
Belize	32.9	26.9	4.0	1.1	−0.0	0.0	2.2	0.6	13.2	0.4	1.9	0.0	0.4	3.2
Bolivia	13.0	7.8	0.1	0.2	0.0	2.7	1.7	0.0	1.3	0.1	0.0	0.3	1.0	0.3
Brazil	40.5	13.8	0.3	1.4	2.4	0.7	2.4	0.7	0.4	0.2	0.0	4.6	0.0	0.8
Chile	28.7	21.5	1.0	5.6	0.0	8.2	2.3	0.0	2.4	0.0	0.4	1.7	0.1	−0.2
Colombia	13.2	11.8	1.6	NA	NA	2.8	0.7	0.1	2.3	0.1	0.1	1.1	0.0	1.3
Costa Rica	25.1	21.5	1.9	0.4	0.0	2.0	1.9	0.6	5.9	2.6	0.1	6.8	0.1	−0.8
Dominican Rep.	16.4	14.2	1.4	1.5	0.0	0.0	2.7	0.8	5.8	0.6	0.4	0.6	0.1	0.2
Ecuador	13.2	12.8	0.0	5.3	1.2	2.7	0.5	0.1	2.3	0.0	0.1	0.0	0.3	0.3
El Salvador	10.3	9.6	0.8	1.3	−0.0	2.6	1.6	0.3	0.8	1.4	0.0	0.0	0.7	0.0

Guatemala	10.1	9.3	0.5	1.6	0.0	1.2	1.3	0.3	3.2	0.5	0.1	0.0	0.2	0.5
Guyana	47.4	40.2	5.0	9.5	0.1	8.4	1.7	0.5	2.2	0.4	1.2	3.6	0.5	7.1
Haiti	10.1	9.1	0.7	0.6	0.0	1.8	2.5	−0.8	2.3	0.0	0.4	0.0	0.2	1.4
Jamaica	37.6	29.1	5.2	3.2	2.9	6.3	2.3	3.0	2.9	0.0	0.0	0.5	0.3	2.4
Mexico	17.0	14.3	2.3	2.8	0.0	3.4	2.6	3.7	0.6	0.0	0.0	1.9	0.0	−3.0
Netherlands Ant.	NA	NA	NA	NA	NA	NA	NA	NA	NA	NA	NA	NA	NA	NA
Nicaragua	23.7	19.0	NA	NA	NA	2.2	9.2	0.8	2.4	0.0	0.0	0.0	0.2	0.8
Panama	25.1	18.0	0.3	1.7	2.3	1.1	1.7	0.9	1.5	0.0	0.0	7.6	0.4	0.4
Paraguay	9.4	8.2	0.0	1.2	0.0	0.8	1.5	0.1	1.0	0.0	0.1	1.2	0.8	1.5
Peru	9.2	8.5	NA	NA	NA	2.0	2.5	0.1	1.2	0.1	0.0	0.0	0.5	0.0
Suriname	27.8	22.0	5.7	4.4	−0.0	0.0	3.3	0.7	5.7	0.1	0.8	1.6	0.0	−0.2
Uruguay	23.4	21.9	0.5	1.3	0.2	7.0	3.1	0.0	1.9	0.1	0.4	6.2	1.0	0.1
Venezuela	NA	NA	NA	NA	NA	NA	NA	NA	NA	NA	NA	NA	NA	NA
MIDDLE EAST/ NORTH AFRICA														
Bahrain	28.6	8.0	0.0	1.2	0.0	0.0	0.1	1.1	2.7	0.0	0.0	2.6	0.1	0.2
Egypt	35.9	21.0	0.5	3.9	0.6	0.0	3.6	0.2	4.4	0.1	0.0	4.8	0.3	2.4
Iran	11.1	6.2	0.4	1.8	0.0	0.1	0.3	0.5	0.6	0.0	0.1	1.6	0.4	0.5
Jordan	21.7	14.7	1.0	0.9	0.1	0.0	2.8	0.7	7.1	0.0	0.5	0.0	0.7	0.9
Kuwait	60.7	1.2	0.0	0.2	0.0	0.0	0.0	0.0	0.9	0.0	0.0	0.0	0.0	0.0
Morocco	22.7	21.5	2.6	2.1	0.2	5.3	5.2	0.5	4.0	0.1	0.0	1.2	0.4	0.0
Oman	34.2	8.0	0.0	6.4	0.1	0.0	0.0	0.3	1.0	0.0	0.0	0.0	0.1	0.2
Syria	21.6	17.0	0.9	6.7	0.4	0.0	0.4	1.4	1.1	0.0	0.0	0.0	0.3	5.9
Tunisia	31.6	23.2	1.6	1.4	0.7	2.8	3.0	0.9	8.2	0.1	0.1	2.6	0.6	1.0
Yemen	22.6	13.5	1.4	3.1	0.0	0.0	2.0	0.3	4.7	0.0	0.0	0.0	0.2	1.9

Source: IMF, *Government Finance Statistics*, and unpublished national sources.

Discussion

NICHOLAS STERN

It is always instructive and a pleasure to discuss a paper by Vito Tanzi. He and his Fiscal Affairs Department at the IMF possess a unique body of experience and wisdom in the analysis of taxation in developing countries. My comments will be organised as follows: (1) the general approach; (2) the data; (3) the econometrics; (4) the problems of agricultural taxation; (5) structural adjustment and agricultural taxation; (6) concluding remarks.

1 The general approach

The analysis of data from a cross-section of countries at a given point in time is one way of structuring comparative work, and one which can provide helpful lessons. There are, however, always problems in method and in interpretation. When we fit a relationship to a cross-section of countries explaining, for example, tax structure or tax levels in terms of variables such as income *per capita* or the share of agriculture in income, we have to ask what our fitted regression line or surface represents. Should we think of it as a description of structure or what people can do; or as a theory of policy, where we think of the successful as revealed by the regression line as showing what the unsuccessful should do; or do we regard it as a model of behaviour of the body politic of different countries? We find that we are in practice tempted to use all three of these interpretations.

A second question arises from seeing the relationship as a deterministic socioeconomic model. If we follow this approach literally we are essentially saying that the figures for each country arise from a statistical drawing from an underlying process which is common to all the countries. We would indeed like to think that basic economic relationships are common to all countries, but nevertheless we should be a little uncomfortable about seeing India and Lesotho as simply two different drawings from the same underlying distribution. And I would argue here that in this kind of analysis we should present China and India separately. They are both so large that thinking of them as observations r and s in a collection of n sample points is surely to suppress crucial information and understanding.

Thirdly, in interpretation or prescription we should think carefully about the problems of direction of causation. At this level of aggregation, the problems of endogeneity are, in my judgement, probably insuperable, so that policy prescriptions based on such regressions should be avoided. There are many, for example, who would think of tax rates determining income in addition to any possible relationship going from income to tax revenue.

Given these problems, it is perhaps better to see this kind of approach as one of data description, where we might hope to find ideas and suggestions, rather than a formal exercise in model estimation and hypotheses testing.

2 The data

Obtaining comparable cross-country data on taxation is an exercise fraught with difficulty, and I know of no group that could do it better than the Fiscal Affairs Department. There remain, however, many grounds for unease. If I understand it correctly, the figures mostly exclude local taxation and the difficulties of collecting comparable information are entirely understandable. The problems do not stop here. There are many different treatments of nomenclature and legal process which mean that some sources of revenue are called 'tax revenue' in some countries, but 'non-tax revenue' in others (petroleum revenue is a particularly important example, and similarly surpluses of marketing boards). We also have to worry about where to put subsidies. In many ways these are simply negative taxes and thus analytically close or identical to taxes, but they are generally treated on the expenditure side. However, if they come in terms of remittances of taxation or special tax allowances, they will appear on the tax side. Having said this, I do think that the data carry important information, and let me re-emphasise that I do not believe there is a source superior to this.

3 The econometrics

In my remarks above, I have already mentioned the problems of endogeneity and errors in variables. Most applied econometrics exercises must come to grips with these problems, but in this case they are particularly severe.

The special interest of this paper is in its presentation of a time-series of cross-sections – that is, it provides cross-sectional estimates for up to five different years over the 10-year period, 1978–88. In this important sense the paper is a real advance on earlier work since it allows us to examine how relationships have changed over time. It would therefore have been interesting to see more detailed econometric analysis of structural change – for example, by pooling all the data and conducting Chow or likelihood ratio tests to examine whether the differences in the relationships for different years were statistically significant. Looking at the results one would expect that such differences would indeed be significant, but a more formal analysis would help. One could also examine more explicitly just how the relationships changed.

4 Agricultural taxation

Most countries have found extreme difficulty in taxing agriculture, for reasons which are largely political and administrative. Because of these difficulties taxation of agriculture is usually carried out in a somewhat concealed manner by a manipulation of prices faced by producers and prices faced by rural consumers. This is in contrast to a method of taxation which is very attractive from the point of view of equity, efficiency and administration – that is, the land tax. The disincentive effects of land taxation are probably less than for other taxes; in many developing countries there is an unequal distribution of land and it could be a highly equitable tax. Further, the measurement of the basis is in many respects easier than other possible bases such as income, production or various forms of indirect taxation. Notwithstanding its advantages, the importance of land taxation has declined in most developing countries so that whereas it was, in a number of countries, the central contributor to tax revenue in the nineteenth century it is now, in most developing countries, negligible in terms of revenue. The reasons for this would seem to be largely political opposition, and here we have an illustration not only of the power of the landed classes but also of a basic catch in tax theory in relation to tax practice. In theory, the most attractive taxes are those which are unavoidable in the sense that economic actions by individuals cannot change the amount of tax that they pay. It is precisely these taxes which are the most obvious (and, legally, most difficult to avoid). They therefore tend to generate the most active and vociferous opposition. There is, it seems, a collective irrationality here in that those taxes which are most efficient in the sense of imposing least economic losses on the community are those which are most vigorously and effectively opposed.

5 Agricultural taxation and structural adjustment

Here I would simply like to suggest some possibilities or hypotheses which might be investigated in applied research, concerning how we would expect agriculture to fare in relation to taxation in the process of structural adjustment. Our expectations would obviously depend on how the adjustment took place. One could imagine various ways in which it might turn out. An optimistic pattern from the point of view of economic efficiency could be the following: in structural adjustment output prices were raised and input subsidies were cut or abolished. This would raise the relative price of agricultural labour and, as well as increasing efficiency, benefit poorer workers and those farmers who were intensively using their own labour. Urban consumers would be worse off and compensation to them might be considered. A second scenario would be where the budgetary pressures led to a cut in subsidies to agriculture but not an increase in the output price. The same pressures might generate cuts in infrastructure and investment. Taken together, the consequence could be a very depressing effect on agriculture.

These are just two possibilities, and one could generate many more, and it would be interesting to see which different kinds of responses were adopted in different countries and what effects there were.

6 Concluding remarks

The paper provides a number of important contributions. First it is innovative in presenting a time-series of cross-sectional analyses so that we can examine the ways in which the cross-sectional relationships changed over the late 1970s and the 1980s. Second, it provides an unusually good fit in that the proportion of agriculture in income and the share of imports in income together explain much of the variation in tax revenue and tax structure across countries. Third, it reminds us of the possible conflicts in the process of adjustment between revenue and efficiency. It used to be common for one World Bank team concerned with industrial reform to press a developing country to reduce tariffs, and thereby protection, on the grounds of economic efficiency and the requirements of structural change, to be followed soon after by an IMF or World Bank team arguing strongly for macrostability, including the raising of tax revenue. In other words one team would have asked them to lower tariffs and the other asked them to tax more heavily. These positions are not necessarily contradictory, but where tax handles were limited there was sometimes insufficient understanding by those arguing for tariff reductions of the constraints facing developing countries in raising revenue. An advantage of this paper, therefore, is that the analysis illustrates, even if it does not establish, the possibility of important relationships between economic structure and taxation possibilities. Finally, I would agree with Vito Tanzi that in some respects the tax performance by developing countries in very strained circumstances in the 1980s was surprisingly good. What was much less admirable was their ability to control expenditure, and we might regard this as the main culprit in their macroeconomic difficulties.

13 International dimensions of the political economy of distortionary price and trade policies

KYM ANDERSON

One of the most important influences on structural adjustment is the trend in the terms of trade. This in turn is influenced by evolutionary changes in government distortions to incentives at home and abroad. Research on the differences in distortionary policies across countries and over time suggests that as economies grow, they tend gradually to change from taxing to subsidising farmers relative to other producers and from effectively subsidising to taxing food relative to other consumption. With global economic growth, the aggregate effect of this changing pattern of domestic distortions is thus to turn the international terms of trade increasingly against agriculture. For those countries with a potential comparative advantage in farm production – which includes many developing countries that are currently net food importers – this is clearly an undesirable policy trend.

Will we continue to see agricultural protectionism increase in advanced industrial economies and spread to newly industrialising economies as they grow, thereby worsening welfare in the vast majority of poorer economies by putting downward pressure on the relative price of farm products in international markets? Recent studies of the political economy of agricultural policies seem to suggest so (e.g., Anderson, Hayami *et al.*, 1986). However, those studies of vested interest group behaviour tend to focus on domestic political forces at work, and scarcely mention the prospect of additional international forces which may offset (or intensify) these domestic forces.

The neoclassical economists' approach to seeking to understand why governments intervene in agricultural and other markets follows Stigler (1971) and Peltzman (1976), and begins with the assumption that a country's political leadership behaves so as to maximise its chances of remaining in office. The government need not be democratically elected, but it is assumed that the leadership is contestable. One way for the government to obtain political support is to supply policies which assist particular groups. Such policies, however, typically harm other groups and the overall national economy. Hence the amount of assistance or protection provided by a government (positive or negative) is limited to the point where the marginal gain in positive support from the group being assisted is just equal to the marginal political cost in terms of the reduced support from other groups.

In adopting this concept of a political market in which interest groups demand policies and the government supplies them, analysts have to date focused almost exclusively on domestic factors affecting these demand and supply curves. The purpose of the present paper is to argue (a) that there are also influences from abroad which affect national political markets for agricultural and other price and trade policies, (b) that those international influences have become increasingly more important determinants of policy outcomes in recent years, and (c) that even though they may never be as large as domestic influences, there is scope for them to become more influential than in the past in improving world agricultural production and consumption in general and the primary sector's contribution to the economic growth of developing countries in particular.

The first section of the paper provides a brief interpretation of the modern neoclassical political economy approach to understanding sectoral policy formation. The second section shows how this 'closed' political market approach needs to be 'opened' to international influences, mentions some instances where these have been important in affecting sectoral assistance/taxation policies in the past, and then discusses several new and emerging international influences on these policies. The paper concludes by drawing out the implications of the analysis for future policy developments in both advanced and developing economies and the effects of such development on the structural adjustment of developing country agriculture.

1 A simple model of the political market for agricultural policy

Perhaps the simplest model of the political market for agricultural policy is a partial equilibrium one, in which the government supplies (positive or negative) assistance policies for the sector in response to demands for assistance by vested interests (mainly farmers). The marginal preparedness of farmers to pay for increased assistance via, say, a price-support policy is likely to decline as the amount of assistance increases. This is because more assistance encourages new firms to enter the sector and this spreads the benefits to new entrants and worsens the free-rider problem of collective lobbying action by the group. The marginal political cost to the government of assisting that group, on the other hand, is likely to increase with the amount of assistance because at higher levels of intervention the government loses support from more and more groups for whom the adverse effects of the policy exceed the costs of getting members together to voice their opposition. It is thus possible to conceptualise this political market with a downward-sloping demand curve and an upward-sloping supply curve. The currency of payment is political support for the government, which includes – but is not limited to – cash contributions to electoral campaigns.

This simple political market is illustrated in Figure 13.1. The vertical axis measures the 'price', in terms of political support, of a unit of assistance to agriculture, while the horizontal axis measures the 'quantity' of assistance in terms of the effective protection coefficient (EPC, the percentage by which policy has raised value-added) for this sector relative to the average EPC for other sectors of the economy. Given the levels of assistance to other sectors, if this index exceeds unity it indicates that government policy is assisting agriculture relative to other sectors, as is the case in most rich industrial economies. By contrast, an index value of less than unity indicates that agriculture relative to other production is being discouraged, as in many poor agrarian and developing economies. As shown in Figure 13.1, the demand and supply curves intersect to the right of unity for the former type, and to the left of unity for the latter type, of economy.

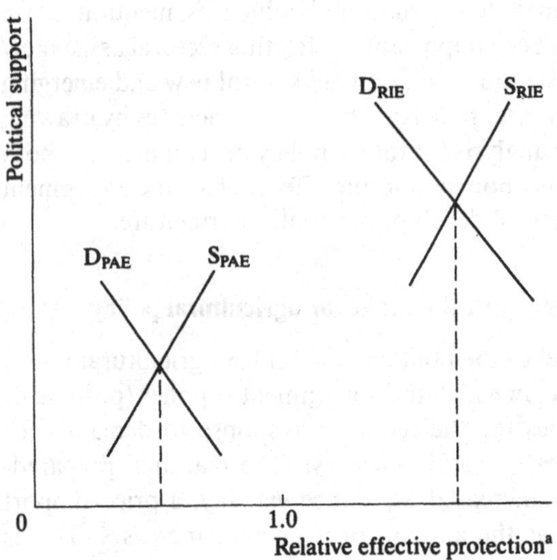

Figure 13.1 The political market for government assistance to agriculture
a D and S refer to the assistance demand and supply curves: PAE and RIE refer to a poor agrarian economy and a rich industrial economy. The quantity of assistance index on the horizontal axis is defined as the effective protection coefficient (EPC) for agriculture relative to the given average EPC for other sectors.

There are good politico-economic reasons for expecting this difference in policies between rich and poor countries. They have to do with the income distributional effects of policy intervention in these two different types of economies, as well as differences in the relative costs of collective action by interest groups and in the preferences of society. On preferences, it is not difficult to understand why a poor agrarian society may wish to encourage the infant industrial sector to 'modernise', while in a rich industrial society people will be sympathetic to the small farm sector as it comes under pressure to shed labour. Citizens may even believe that farm subsidy increases are worthwhile simply to ensure adequate political stability and food security. But the distributional effects of policy choices and the relative costs of collective action by lobby groups in the two different types of economies are no doubt the main driving forces behind the observed pattern of distortions, for the following reasons.

In an extreme situation in which capital (including land) is sector-specific and labour is the only mobile resource, the distributional effects of altering the relative price of farm products depend importantly on the latter's impacts on wage costs and on the share of the community's expenditure on food. In a poor economy where most people work in the relatively labour-intensive agricultural sector, raising the relative price of agricultural products had a large impact on the demand for labour, thereby substantially rising wage rates. This erodes much of the gain in the value-added to landholders, and yet could be insufficient to offset the increase in the cost of living for labourers. Even more importantly, it reduces very substantially the income of industrial capitalists. These effects, plus the fact that farmers have much greater free-rider and other costs of getting together to lobby collectively than do urban groups, ensure that there is both a relatively weak demand for agricultural assistance policies relative to demand for industrial-sector assistance in poor agrarian economies, and relatively high marginal political costs of supplying support policies for farmers – that is, the demand and supply curves in the political market for agricultural assistance intersect close to the origin in Figure 13.1.

In rich industrial economies, on the other hand, agriculture is a small employer and not very labour-intensive, so raising the relative price of farm products has little impact on the demand for labour, and hence wages and the cost of producing non-farm products. And since people spend much less of their income on farm products in these as compared with poor economies, the product price change affects the demand for non-tradables and the cost of living less. Hence other groups, including industrial capitalists, have little incentive to oppose agricultural support policies in advanced economies – that is, the supply curve in rich industrial economies is well to the right in Figure 13.1. Moreover, so too is the demand curve. Farmers are much stronger demanders of support policies in rich industrial economies than in poor agrarian ones for at least two reasons. First, their use of intermediate inputs is far greater than in poor economies, both in absolute terms and relative to other sectors. Hence a given price increase boosts farm income net of input costs proportionately much more in rich than in poor economies. And, second, the costs of collective lobbying action by farmers relative to urban groups is much lower in rich than in poor countries. This is partly because of smaller differences in the private costs of urban versus rural education, transport and communication services, and partly because the commercialisation of agriculture breeds farmer cooperatives, thereby reducing the free-rider problem for farmers seeking to lobby collectively.

When typical values for these and other parameters for a poor agrarian economy and a rich industrial one are included in a computable general equilibrium model, the income distributional effects of policy intervention in the two archetype economies markedly contrast. A simulation exercise by Anderson (1991) suggests that an increase in the relative price of farm products would raise farm owner-operators' real incomes in the 'typical' poor country by only one-tenth as much as it would reduce the real incomes of industrial capitalists, while a similar price policy shock in the 'typical' rich country raises farmers' real incomes substantially more than it reduces the incomes of industrial capitalists. Moreover, the real incomes of non-farm workers would be lowered by four times as much in the poor as in the rich country, hence they too would be more inclined to join industrialists in opposing an increase in the relative price of food in a poor than in a rich country. Even poor countries with a wealthy landed aristocracy are likely to adopt policies which discriminate against agriculture, since landowners typically are also to some extent industrial capitalists. Anderson's simulation exercise suggests that if landlords earned as little as one-sixth of their income from industrial capital they would prefer policies which lowered the domestic price of farm relative to industrial products. This helps explain why Krueger (1990b) found agriculture to be only slightly less discriminated against in those developing countries with concentrated land ownership as compared with those with a more even distribution of land.

While this is far from the full story, it goes some way towards explaining why we observe farm subsidies in rich countries but disincentives for agriculture in poor ones. It suggests that the tendency observed in Western Europe and Northeast Asia, for policies gradually to change from discouraging to excessively encouraging agriculture in the course of economic development (see Anderson, Hayami *et al.*, 1986 and

Lindert, 1989), may occur in subsequent generations of newly industrialising economies too. Moreover, there tends also to be a strong negative correlation between agricultural protection and agricultural comparative advantage.[1] This suggests that densely populated countries are likely to switch from being more to being less than fully self-sufficient in farm products at a slower rate than might be expected from looking just at the theory of changing comparative advantage, as outlined by, for example, Krueger (1977) and Leamer (1987).

Is it inevitable that agricultural protectionism will continue to grow in currently protected countries and to spread to more and more developing countries as they industrialise?[2] Consider first the factors affecting the distribution of gains and losses from a policy bias towards agriculture. In the course of economic growth at home and abroad, the *per capita* benefits to farmers will continue to grow relative to the *per capita* losses to other groups. This is because economic growth is likely to continue to be characterised by declines in agriculture's shares of GDP and employment, in the relative labour-intensity of farming and in the share of farm products in household expenditure. The costs of collective action by farmers relative to those costs for other groups are also likely to keep falling as farmers' associations become firmly established and as the numbers of farmers decline (assuming that assistance only slows rather than reverses that decline, as predicted by Hillman, 1982 and Long and Vousden, 1991). Moreover, supply and demand conditions are such that even without increases in agricultural protection the real price of agricultural products in international markets is likely to continue to gyrate around a declining long-run trend (Anderson, 1987). In this environment, politicians are understandably reluctant to deregulate and thereby reduce, and in some cases destabilise, producer returns: that can always be done after the next election when the inefficiency of present policies will be even more obvious. Should the cost of protection become more evident, as with the emergence of surplus farm products in Western Europe during the 1980s, the inclination of politicians and bureaucrats is to 'do something' rather than 'undo something' (Winters, 1987). So rather than reduce domestic-to-border price ratios, the tendency is to introduce a quantitative limit on production; this maintains existing farmers' incomes and ensures more bureaucrats are needed, but reduces the visibility of the policy (thereby keeping down the marginal political cost) and prevents potential newcomers from enjoying the benefits of protection.

There is, however, the possibility that the rightward shift in the *aggregate* (as distinct from the *per capita*) demand for farm support policies will slow down, given the decline in the proportion of employment and GDP from farming. The downward shift in the aggregate supply curve in this market may also eventually reverse, for at least three reasons. One is that where high domestic food prices generate an exportable surplus of agricultural products which can be disposed of in international markets only with the help of explicit subsidies, taxpayer opposition to these overt payments is added to the general opposition associated with the import restrictions. With the growing demand for smaller government and an ageing population which requires a reallocation of funds to pensions, tolerance for additional cash handouts to farmers is diminishing – especially as the inefficiency of that mechanism for transforming welfare is becoming more widely recognised. The second and related reason is that once export subsidies, production quotas and cropland set-asides are being used, the food security justification for further assistance to agriculture begins to look hollow. Finally, high food prices encourage farmers to use greater volumes of chemical fertilisers and pesticides, animal growth hormones and more irrigation than would otherwise be the case. The consequent adverse effects of intensified input use on food safety and the environment, especially in densely populated countries, is reducing the preparedness of urban people to continue to tolerate agricultural price supports. Cassing and Hillman (1986) have shown that there are conditions under which, with the aggregate demand for an assistance policy shrinking relative to the opposition to that policy, a point can be reached when it becomes in the government's interest fully to withdraw its support policy. Indeed, such action has already been taken in a number of notable non-farm sectors such as US footwear and Swedish shipbuilding and textiles and clothing.

Over and above all these domestic influences on a nation's political market for government assistance to agriculture, there are also a number of international influences on such markets. As the next section will show, some have been around for a long time, but others have been added more recently and these are becoming increasingly important with the decline in the real costs of international travel and other means of communication.

2 Opening the political market to international influences

Pressures from abroad on a nation's domestic political markets can take several forms. A sudden decline in the international competitiveness of a domestic sector due to economic developments abroad can trigger an outward shift in the domestic demand for protection (Bhagwati, 1982), but such impersonal effects of economic forces are not the focus of attention here; rather, we are concerned with the effects of direct action by foreign interest groups and governments and by international institutions on the demand for, and supply of, a country's sectoral policies.

Some of those are influences forced on a country, others are voluntarily taken on board (presumably because they serve broader domestic political goals).

Prior to the Second World War, many developing countries' policies were influenced heavily by an imperial power which sought uninhibited supplies of raw materials and other primary products from its colonies. Investments in mines and plantations were made in the periphery by the centre, and vested interests in the centre ensured that the price and trade policies adopted by the developing country government were favourable to the imperialist: that is, trade taxes on agricultural exports and on imports of manufactures were kept close to zero. This often had a reciprocal effect on the imperial nation's own trade policy. Agricultural protection lobbyists in Britain, for example, were less able than their colleagues in some continental European countries to argue that protecting farmers from import competition (as real transport costs fell) was necessary to ensure security of supply. This is because Britain had access to ample and secure sources of food and fibre from its colonies in the southern hemisphere. During the first half of this century, too, Japan's rice producers were less successful in seeking increases in protection from import competition than they would have been if Japan had not had secure access to rice supplies from its colonies of Korea and Taiwan, while rice production in Korea and Taiwan was assisted more than it would otherwise have been (Hayami, 1972). During this period Japan adopted an imperial rather than a national rice self-sufficiency policy.[3]

In terms of the political market outlined in Section 1 above, the political cost of protecting agriculture in an advanced industrial economy is higher when there are colonial sources of farm products. This is partly because there is less of a security of supply excuse for protection by the centre, but probably more importantly because much of the agricultural investment in the periphery originates from the centre whose landed capitalists have a strong vested interest in joining with the centre's industrial capitalists to lobby for the maintenance of open trade between the two economies. These same interest groups affect the policy imposed by the centre on the agrarian colonial economy as well, leading it to have policies less skewed against agriculture than would be the case in a similar but independent agrarian economy.[4]

At a broader international level has been the institution of the General Agreement on Tariffs and Trade (GATT). Drawn up after the Second World War, the GATT aimed to reduce the trade barriers that had been erected during – and which contributed to – the Depression of the 1930s. The contracting parties recognised that the phasing out of protectionist trade policies was likely to involve less change to relative international prices, and hence less structural adjustment, when other countries also reformed their policies at the same time. Multilateral liberalisation is thus less costly politically for a country than an equivalent unilateral liberalisation. In addition, being a signatory to the GATT places obligations on a contracting party's government which provide it with an additional reason to resist future domestic demands for economically costly protectionist policies: to refuse protection to an import-competing industry on the grounds of an international obligation under the GATT is less costly politically than to refuse it on the grounds of not wanting to harm export industries. While it had not been in the political interests of enough GATT contracting parties until recently to bring agricultural policies onto the negotiations agenda (see below), significant progress has been made in reducing tariffs on manufactured imports during the past four decades. Insofar as those tariff reductions have been less than fully offset by increases in non-tariff barriers to trade in manufactures, they have contributed to the further distortion of incentives in favour of agriculture in industrial countries.

There are several new and emerging international influences on domestic political markets for farm policy which, in combination, are likely to lead to a more efficient use of the world's agricultural resources, and in particular to benefit developing country agriculture. The following are discussed in turn: the US–EC food export subsidy war and the Uruguay Round of trade negotiations; US–Northeast Asian trade frictions; reforms in Eastern Europe and expanding European Community (EC) membership; the 'greening' of world politics; new initiatives by international institutions; and the resurgence of tensions between nationalism, regionalism and globalism.

2.1 The US–EC subsidy war, the Cairns Group and the Uruguay Round

The protection-induced growth in subsidised farm exports from the EC put downward pressure on international food prices in the first half of the 1980s. With US presidential and congressional elections scheduled for November 1984, it is not surprising that the USA responded by boosting assistance for its own farmers. As a result, the estimated US agricultural producer subsidy equivalent during 1985–8 was double that of the early 1980s (Table 13.1). The marginal political cost of this extra assistance fell in the mid-1980s because it was perceived in the USA that the drop in farmers' returns was in large part due to EC farm policies and would be remedied by retaliating in kind and thereby raising the budgetary, and hence political, cost of the EC continuing its export subsidies. Even though the EC showed no sign of reducing its subsidies during the latter

1980s, the greater US subsidies continued in part to keep the pressure on EC policy makers and in part to create a higher base from which to reduce assistance in the event of a Uruguay Round agreement in the early 1990s which involved liberalising farm policies.

The US export subsidies put even further downward pressure on international food prices. Canadian farmers responded by successfully demanding an assistance boost (see Table 13.1). By contrast, in Australia and New Zealand, where a much larger proportion of output is exported, such overt subsidies would have created proportionately much larger pressures on government budgets than in North America, and so were perceived by the reform-oriented labour governments there to be politically too costly. Instead, those governments sought to take the high moral ground in two ways. One was to seek an effective way directly to combat the escalating farm protection in the northern hemisphere: Australia and New Zealand helped to form a group of 14 agricultural-exporting nations (the Cairns Group) whose key goals were (a) to ensure that agricultural trade liberalisation remained high on the agenda of the Uruguay Round of multilateral trade negotiations and (b) to encourage non-farm groups in countries with protected agricultural sectors to voice their concern at the high domestic costs of farm-support programmes.

Table 13.1 *Producer subsidy equivalents of food policies in industrial market economies, 1979–88*

	OECD estimates				USDA estimates	
	1979–81	1982–4	1985–6	1987–8	1982–4	1985–7
Australia	9	14	15	11	10	10
Canada	24	29	42	50	26	41
EC-10	37	33	45	46[a]	29	46
EFTA	n.a.	53[b]	67[c]	68	n.a.	n.a.
Japan	57	63	71	76	68	76
New Zealand	18	27	26	11	25	13
United States	16	22	34	38	21	31
Weighted average	29	31	43	47	31[d]	44[d]

[a]EC-12.
[b]1979–85. EFTA's weighted average is derived using as weights the value added by agriculture in each of the five member countries.
[c]1986 only.
[d]Weights based on value of agricultural production at domestic prices.
n.a. not available.
Sources: OECD (1988; 1990); Webb, Lopez and Penn (1990).

How successful they ultimately will be is yet to be seen but, unless they indulge in what turns out to be misjudged brinkmanship, they are likely to be more successful as a group than if the member countries had continued to negotiate individually (Higgott and Cooper, 1990). The other way was to assist farmers indirectly by heeding their (and other exporters') calls for a lowering of assistance to the highly protected manufacturing sectors in Australia and New Zealand. This was done by lowering agricultural assistance but then reducing manufacturing protection even more.[5] This also served to placate their East Asian neighbours, who are the suppliers of manufactured imports, and to make Australia and New Zealand look less hypocritical in demanding through the Cairns Group that other countries reduce protection. Since the Uruguay Round was underway it was possible to ward off industrial protection lobbyists by claiming that such reforms would inevitably in any case be demanded of them in the early 1990s.

2.2 *US-Northeast Asian trade frictions*

The growth in current account surpluses in Japan, South Korea and Taiwan during the 1980s, the not unrelated deficit in the US current account, and in particular the widening bilateral trade imbalance between the USA and Northeast Asia, increased suspicions in the USA of unfair trading practices in Northeast Asia. The USA responded in part by threatening to raise barriers to manufactured imports from Northeast Asia unless agricultural import barriers in Northeast Asia were lowered. This threat – made credible via the Super 301 provisions in US trade law (see Bhagwati and Patrick, 1990) – caused manufacturers in Northeast Asia to voice their opposition to protectionist farm policies more loudly, thereby raising the political cost of maintaining high barriers to farm imports. As a result, beef and citrus trade has begun to be liberalised, and discussions on rice policy are now much less dismissive of calls for import liberalisation. These changes almost certainly would not have occurred as soon as they did, nor been as large, had it not been for pressure from the USA.[6] The fact that the Uruguay Round was underway helped, however, because in the event that Japan and Korea have to liberalise their farm policies as a result of that round, the present liberalisation will probably be counted by GATT Contracting Parties as part of such liberalisations.

2.3 *East European reforms and expanding EC membership*

The dramatic reforms that have begun to transform the economies of Eastern Europe and the USSR away from central planning are likely to put additional pressure on the EC to liberalise its Common Agricultural Policy (CAP) during the 1990s. Since the usable industrial capital stock per worker in those former centrally planned economies is very low relative to the stock of agricultural land per worker, their initial export specialisation as market forces come into play is likely to be in primary products (and perhaps labour-intensive simple manufactures – see CEPR, 1990). This will especially be the case if agricultural markets are reformed first, as was done in China. As those countries seek hard currency markets for their agricultural exports, they will necessarily come into conflict with the EC, and take a position similar to the Cairns Group, over EC export subsidies. It is ironic that their movements towards freer markets – and their imports of manufactures and services from the EC – are being hampered by foreign exchange shortages caused in part by EC agricultural policies. By stressing this irony, these countries will increase opposition to the CAP, both directly and via non-farm producers within EC member countries.

The likely expansion of EC membership from the mid-1990s could add to these pressures for CAP liberalisation. It is already clear that the absorption of eastern Germany into the EC helped increase the projected budgetary cost of the CAP for 1991 above the ceiling set by member countries. The publicity this causes increases awareness of the cost of that farm policy to EC taxpayers, and thereby raises the political cost of maintaining that policy. Should Czechoslovakia, Hungary, Poland and perhaps other East European countries join the EC – not to mention Turkey – the budgetary cost of current rates of farm protection would escalate dramatically, forcing a new political market equilibrium at a lower rate of protection. Note, however, that the new lower average rate of farm protection for such an enlarged EC would not necessarily mean lower average protection than currently for the EC-12 plus the would-be East European members. This is because today the latter's protection rates are very much lower than that of the EC-12 countries.

There is one caveat to the above, however. Some EFTA countries in Western Europe also are actively seeking EC membership. Since they are considerably more protectionist toward their farmers than the EC (see Table 13.1), and since only part of the cost of their protection will be borne by their nationals should they become full EC members, their membership is likely to add to the demand for agricultural support policies. At the same time, their membership will add to the budgetary, and hence political, cost of the CAP, so the assistance supply curve will shift up. What the net effect will be on the protection level for Western Europe as a whole is unclear. However, Sweden's recent decision to lower unilaterally the level of its agricultural protection to that in the EC during the next five years suggests that it believes the EC will not be able to supply much higher levels of farm support.

2.4 *The 'greening' of world politics*

Another substantial international development in recent years has been the surge in interest in the environment, including the global commons. Attention is focusing not only on activities which pollute or otherwise degrade the global environment, but also on policies which promote such activities. Brazil's agricultural development policies have thus come under pressure from abroad because they encourage the felling of trees in the Amazonian rainforest (Binswanger, 1989). Another example is in the EC, where member governments with relatively weak environmental policies are arguing with those with stricter standards over the level at which to harmonise those standards, particularly on activities which produce transfrontier pollution. The pressure for stricter standards would intensify if EFTA countries were to join the EC, given EFTA's 'greener' attitudes and policies.

There is a considerable risk that import-competing industries will embrace the green movement and use it to serve their own protectionist ends. In the case of agriculture, farm lobbies have begun to play on the concerns of consumers regarding food safety and of environmentalists worried that food trade liberalisation will stimulate more felling of tropical rainforests. Whether these domestic protectionist pressures will affect agriculture more than other sectors is not easy to discern. But even if they do, there is the possibility of an offsetting effect, because the view that agricultural production is more environmentally friendly than non-farm production is under serious challenge in advanced economies. More than that, the use of chemicals in farming is highly correlated with the extent of agricultural price supports (OECD, 1989). As this becomes more widely recognised, environmental groups will become opponents of agricultural protection policies in densely populated countries, especially if they also realise that the alternative location of food production in the absence of those policies will be in more scarcely populated southern hemisphere and developing countries (Anderson and Tyers, 1986; 1990a), where use of farm chemicals and damage to the global environment by farmers is far less intense.

2.5 *New initiatives by international institutions*

A number of international institutions have traditionally had a role in providing comparative information on the economic costs of distortionary policies, which has the effect of raising the domestic political cost of supplying those policies. In the 1970s, studies by the OECD and the World Bank focused mainly on industrial protection policies (e.g., Little, Scitovsky and Scott, 1970; Balassa and associates, 1971). More recently, however, detailed empirical analyses of policies affecting agriculture in developing countries also have appeared (see, for example, the summaries in World Bank, 1986; Krueger, Schiff and Valdes, 1988; and Goldin and Knudsen, 1990). These, together with numerous studies on the positive effects of liberalising trade (e.g., the major series of studies summarised in Krueger, 1978; World Bank, 1987; and Michaely, Papageorgiou and Choksi, 1991, have encouraged the World Bank, the IMF, regional development banks and even individual industrial countries' aid agencies (through cross-conditionality) to tie their developing country lending to structural adjustment programmes. Such conditionality involves price, trade, exchange rate and environmental policy reforms, acceptance of which generally reduces the distortions against agriculture in those countries.

The OECD (1988; 1990) and the World Bank (1986) have also been involved, together with the US Department of Agriculture (e.g., Webb, Lopez and Penn, 1990), in generating and disseminating information on the extent and global costs of agricultural protection in industrial economies. By appearing during the Uruguay Round of multilateral trade negotiations, these and other similar empirical studies helped considerably in capturing the attention of the mass media, thereby raising permanently the political cost of agricultural protection as consumers, taxpayers and non-farm exporters in the countries concerned became better informed. In addition, the GATT Secretariat has recently implemented a trade policy review mechanism aimed at further improving the transparency of agricultural (and other) trade policies of GATT contracting parties.

2.6 Tensions between nationalism, regionalism and globalism

The slow economic growth of the 1980s encouraged an increase in nationalism, notably in the USA. There has also been an increased emphasis on regionalism, largely in response to the increasing economic integration associated with the 'Europe 1992' programme in Western Europe. This has manifested itself most notably in the USA's bilateral trade agreements with Canada, Israel, the Caribbean and prospectively Mexico and other Latin American countries. It is also evident in negotiations between North American and Western Pacific countries (the latest acronym for which is APEC – Asian–Pacific Economic Cooperation) and more recently among the East Asian economies themselves. While such bilateral and regional arrangements run the risk of diverting rather than expanding trade, and thereby harming excluded countries, some of them at least are likely to expand trade. Indeed the APEC initiative is specifically aimed at encouraging trade and investment on a non-discriminatory, most-favoured-nation basis and supporting multilateralism through the global GATT trade system (Drysdale and Garnaut, 1989).

Moreover, these nationalist and regionalist tendencies are being offset – and perhaps will be more than offset in the 1990s – by a countervailing tendency towards internationalism. This results from at least two sources. One is the growth of the intra-firm international trade of multinational corporations (capitalists who develop lower-cost export-oriented operations abroad are likely to lobby for lower import barriers in their former country of operation, for example). The other is the blossoming of specialised service industries, such as international banking and insurance, whose growth is tied to the expansion in international trade. Both of these groups of producers are becoming ever-stronger advocates for the strengthening and extending of global GATT rules and disciplines. Their emergence increases the prospects for liberalising world trade, including that in farm products. Traditional agricultural-exporting countries would obviously gain if the relative price of farm products rose as a consequence of such liberalisation. But, in addition, recent research suggests that many developing countries that are net food importers would also gain, particularly if agricultural innovation is price-responsive (Anderson and Tyers, 1990a; Goldin and Knudsen, 1990; Tyers and Anderson, 1992).

3 Implications for future policies and structural adjustments

Clearly, there are some important international influences affecting the domestic political markets for policies which affect agricultural incentives. Prior to the middle of this century, imperial–colonial relationships probably generated freer trade than would otherwise have been the case.[7] Whether the formation of customs unions such as the EC has added to or reduced distortions in agricultural incentives is less obvious: the growth of agricultural protection in some EC member countries might have been even faster without the formation of the EC, and prices received for some farm products are higher than they otherwise would have been in those African, Caribbean and Pacific countries that are signatories with the EC to the Lomé Convention. But the more recent international influences examined above are likely to slow, if not reverse, the growth in agricultural protection in industrial countries,[8] and to reduce more rapidly the disincentives to agriculture in developing countries.

The Cairns Group's efforts in the Uruguay Round and beyond, in conjunction with US pressure, are likely to be more successful in bringing about policy reform as the following points are integrated into their message. First, reducing agricultural protection rates is not synonymous with reducing farm production levels. Indeed, even if OECD farm protection levels were as much as halved over the course of the 1990s, agricultural production levels would still expand somewhat in virtually all OECD countries, according to recent simulation results (Anderson and Tyers, 1992). Second, not just a few but the vast majority of developing countries are likely to gain from such a liberalisation, including many that are currently net food importers (Anderson and Tyers, 1990a). If non-Cairns Group developing countries can be convinced of this, they will be more inclined to lend their support to the Cairns Group's cause. Third, large farmers receive most of the benefits from current protection policies. Disseminating information on this and the previous point could increase domestic political opposition to current policies from community groups concerned with equity, and might even cause small farmers in protected countries to form separate lobby groups and seek alternative policies, such as direct income supports, which would give them a larger share of the benefits at less cost to consumers/taxpayers. Finally, current farm policies are being seen increasingly by conservationists as contributing to national and global environmental damage and increasing the chemical residues in the food consumed in protectionist economies. Given the rapid 'greening' of community attitudes in middle- and upper-income countries, it is possible that analyses of the environmental cost of agricultural protection may be even more effective in prompting reform in the 1990s than were studies in the 1980s of the conventional economic costs of those policies.

NOTES

The author is grateful for helpful comments from David Blandford, Bernard Hoekman, Michael Leidy, Richard Snape and Alan Winters. The views expressed are the author's alone and are not intended to represent the views of the GATT Secretariat or GATT Contracting Parties.

1 For a discussion of various politico–economic reasons for expecting exporting industries to be assisted less than import-competing ones, see Krueger (1990a). Anderson and Tyers (1986) estimate the following regression equation for 30 countries/country groups spanning the world (t-values in parentheses):

$$\underset{(8.7)}{NPC = 0.22} + \underset{(5.6)}{0.11\ YPC} - \underset{(-10.7)}{0.51\ CA} \qquad \bar{R}^2 = 0.83$$

where NPC is the log of the weighted average nominal agricultural protection coefficient in 1980–2, YPC is the log of the ratio of an economy's *per capita* income to the global average *per capita* income in 1982, and CA is the log of the food self-sufficiency ratio at global free trade prices as estimated by the author's model of world food markets.

The main exceptions to the rule that rich countries subsidise agriculture are the slowly growing agricultural-exporting economies of Australia and New Zealand, while import exceptions to the opposite rule for developing countries are rapidly growing food-importing economies of Korea and Taiwan. All four economies have extreme values for CA, and so are not inconsistent with the above political economy theory when the points raised by Krueger (1990a) are incorporated. The fact that they are at extreme ends of the spectrum of economic growth rates also helps to explain the slow decline in policy discrimination against agriculture in Australasia and its fast decline in Northeast Asia. See also n. 3 below.

2 On the extent of nominal agricultural protection growth in the various West European countries, see, for example, Gulbrandsen and Lindbeck (1973) for the 1950s and 1960s and OECD (1988; 1990) and Webb, Lopez and Penn (1990) for the past decade or so. Effective rates of assistance to value-added have risen even more than the nominal rates of protection on output, because over time the value-added share of output has been falling (Anderson, 1987, Table 1).

3 As it happened, despite large investments in agricultural development in those two colonies and free trade between them and Japan, Northeast Asia's rice self-sufficiency was able to be maintained only at the expense of an ever-more protective common external barrier to rice imports by the three economies (Anderson, Hayami *et al.* 1986, Ch. 2; Anderson and Tyers, 1990b).

4 Another historically important case where international influences have affected the extent of a nation's agricultural protection is in the formation and subsequent enlargement of the EC. By adopting common external trade barriers and reasonably free trade within the EC, agricultural protection initially rose in some of the original six member countries but probably fell for the previously most-protectionist members. In the latter countries the political cost of supplying agricultural protection increased as non-agricultural export interests sought a more liberal farm policy at home toward food imports from elsewhere in the EC, in return for greater access for their non-farm products in other EC member country markets. In the previously less-protected food-exporting EC countries, on the other hand, the government's marginal cost of supplying assistance to farmers fell. This was partly because of the improvement in the terms of trade associated with this new preferential access to previously higher-priced markets within the EC. But another contributing factor was that the budgetary cost of disposing of any export surplus was borne by all EC taxpayers, not just nationals (von Witzke, 1986; Ardy, 1988). Furthermore, recall that there is increasing politico–economic pressure on governments, as non-farm incomes increase over time, to increase assistance to farmers (as discussed in Section 1). It is thus perhaps not entirely coincidental that the newer entrants to the EC (Denmark, Ireland and the UK in the 1970s; Greece, Portugal and Spain in the 1980s) are countries whose pre-membership agricultural protection levels were below those of the EC, while the West European countries yet to become EC members (that is, the EFTA countries) continue to

be more agricultural protectionist than the EC. See Gulbrandsen and Lindbeck (1973) for the 1950s and 1960s and Table 13.1 below for the 1980s.

5 The large decline in the 1980s in direct assistance to farmers in New Zealand, reported in Table 13.1, was from a temporary, unsustainably high level, and was accompanied by a decline in assistance to other sectors of that economy as part of a general reform of economic policy. The net effect of the package of reforms on agricultural incentives over the decade was therefore probably positive, rather than negative as suggested by the decline in agricultural producer subsidy equivalent estimates. According to a recent report, the effective rate of assistance to New Zealand agriculture was 8 per cent in 1970 and 12 per cent in 1980, before it rose to more than 100 per cent in 1982 and 1983 in the last days of the conservative government. The subsequent reforms by the new labour government brought the rate back to 15 per cent by 1988. Meanwhile, the effective rate of assistance to New Zealand manufacturing was brought down from around 40 per cent in the early 1980s to less than 25 per cent by the late 1980s (GATT, 1990, pp. 203, 221). The decline in agricultural assistance in Australia, too, is being accompanied by even larger reductions in assistance to manufacturing: the effective rate of assistance fell between 1985–6 and 1988–9 from 12 to 9 per cent for agriculture, while for manufacturing it fell from 19 to 16 per cent between 1987–7 and 1989–90 and is expected to be below 12 per cent (compared with agriculture's 10 per cent) by the mid-1990s (Industry Commission, 1990, pp. 136, 138, 182). Both countries are thus following the policy trend of other industrial economies in shifting incentives in favour of agriculture, even though the sector is still indirectly discriminated against.

6 See Lee, Hadwinger and Lee (1990) for further discussion of this point. There is a double irony here. First, liberalisation of farm imports by Northeast Asia will *strengthen* those economies and may thereby increase rather than decrease the bilateral imbalance in their commodity trade with the USA. And, second, should Northeast Asia or other countries not heed US threats, the invoking of Super 301 provisions could be more costly to the USA than to its trading partners.

7 Once developing countries gained their independence, however, the new rulers often reflected people's socialist tendencies, which included inclinations to reduce their economy's dependence on trade with rich industrial countries, to provide urban households with cheap food and housing, and to develop state-financed, import-substituting industrial projects (Bates, 1981). Funds for the latter were often raised most cheaply by trade taxes which, for countries with a comparative advantage in agriculture, also contributed to the goals of being less agrarian and less trade-dependent. The larger these 'non-economic' social benefits of taxing manufactured imports and agricultural exports are perceived to be relative to the perceived costs of trade taxes, the lower is the political cost of such a trade policy regime.

8 One other international influence not mentioned above, because it has mainly affected manufacturing rather than agriculture, has to do with the sharing of protectionist rents between exporting and importing countries, as occurs with voluntary export restraints. These have sprung up as an alternative to tariffs now that tariffs are mostly bound under the GATT. See, for example, Hillman and Ursprung (1988) and Hillman (1990).

REFERENCES

Anderson, K. (1987) 'On Why Agriculture Declines with Economic Growth', *Agricultural Economics*, **1 (3)** June: 195–207.

(1991) 'Lobbying Incentives and the Pattern of Protection in Rich and Poor Countries', paper presented to the annual economics conference of the Association of French-speaking Swiss Universities (Champéry, 17–22 March).

Anderson, K., Y. Hayami *et al.* (1986) *The Political Economy of Agricultural Protection: East Asia in International Perspective*, Boston, London and Sydney: Allen & Unwin.

Anderson, K. and R. Tyers (1986) 'Agricultural Policies of Industrial Countries and Their Effects on Traditional Food Exporters', *Economic Record*, **62 (170)** December: 385–99.

(1990a) 'Welfare Gains to Developing Countries from Food Trade Liberalization Following the Uruguay Round', Centre for International Economic Studies, University of Adelaide, July (mimeo).

(1990b) 'Japanese Rice Policy in the Interwar Period: Some Consequences of Imperial Self-Sufficiency, Centre for International Economic Studies, University of Adelaide, July (mimeo).

(1992) 'Effects of Gradual Food Policy Reforms in the 1990s', *European Review of Agricultural Economics*, **19 (1)**, January.

Ardy, B. (1988) 'The National Incidence of the European Community Budget', *Journal of Common Market Studies*, **26 (4)**: 401–30.

Balassa, B. and associates (1971) *The Structure of Protection in Developing Countries*, Baltimore: Johns Hopkins University Press.

Bates, R. H. (1981) *Markets and States in Tropical Africa: The Political Basis of Agricultural Policies*, Berkeley: University of California Press.

Bhagwati, J. N. (ed.) (1982) *Import Competition and Response*, Chicago: University of Chicago Press.

Bhagwati, J. N. and H. T. Patrick (eds) (1990) *Aggressive Unilateralism: America's 301 Trade Policy and the World Trading System*, London: Harvester Wheatsheaf.

Binswanger, H. (1989) 'Brazilian Policies that Encourage Deforestation in the Amazon', *Environment Department Working Paper*, **16**, Washington, D.C.: World Bank.

Cassing, J. H. and A. L. Hillman (1986) 'Shifting Comparative Advantage and Senescent Industry Collapse', *American Economic Review*, **76 (3)** June: 516–23.

CEPR (1990) *Monitoring European Integration: The Impact of Eastern Europe*, London: Centre for Economic Policy Research.

Drysdale, P. and R. Garnaut (1989) 'A Pacific Free Trade Area?', in J. Schott (ed.), *Free Trade Areas and US Trade Policy*, Washington, D.C.: Institute for International Economics.

GATT (1990) *Trade Policy Review: New Zealand 1990*, Geneva: GATT Secretariat.

Goldin, I. and O. Knudsen (eds) (1990) *Agricultural Trade Liberalization: Implications for Developing Countries*, Paris and Washington, D.C.: OECD and World Bank.

Gulbrandsen, O. and A. Lindbeck (1973) *The Economics of the Agricultural Sector*, Stockholm: Almqvist & Wicksell.

Hayami, Y. (1972) 'Rice Policy in Japan's Economic Development', *American Journal of Agricultural Economics*, **54 (1)** February: 19–31.

Higgott, R. A. and A. F. Cooper (1990) 'Middle Power Leadership and Coalition Building: Australia, the Cairns Group, and the Uruguay Rounds of Trade Negotiations', *International Organisation*, **44 (4)**, Autumn: 589–632.

Hillman, A. L. (1982) 'Declining Industries and Political-Support Protectionist Motives', *American Economic Review*, **72 (5)** December: 1180–7.

(1990) 'Protectionist Policies as the Regulation of International Industry', *Public Choice*, **67 (2)**: 101–10.

Hillman, A. L. and H. W. Ursprung (1988) 'Domestic Politics, Foreign Interests, and International Trade Policy', *American Economic Review*, **78 (4)** September: 729–45.

Industry Commission (1990) *Annual Report 1989–90*, Canberra: Australian Government Publishing Service.

Johnson, H. G. (1968) *Comparative Cost and Commercial Policy Theory for a Developing World Economy*, Stockholm: Almqvist & Wicksell.

Krueger, A. (1977) *Growth, Distortions and Patterns of Trade Among Many Countries*, Princeton: International Finance Section.

Krueger, A. O. (1978) *Foreign Trade Regimes and Economic Development: Liberalization Attempts and Consequences*, Cambridge, MA: Ballinger for the NBER.

(1990a) 'Asymmetries in Policy Between Exportables and Import-Competing Goods', Chapter 10 in R. W. Jones and A. O. Krueger (eds), *The Political Economy of International Trade*, Oxford: Basil Blackwell.

(1990b) 'Some Preliminary Findings from the World Bank's Project on the Political Economy of Agricultural Pricing', in A. Maunder and A. Valdes (eds), *Agriculture and Governments in an Interdependent World*, London: Dartmouth for the IAAE.

Krueger, A. O., M. Schiff and A. Valdes (1988) 'Measuring the Impact of Sector-Specific and Economy-Wide Policies on Agricultural Incentives in LDC's, *World Bank Economic Review*, **2 (3)** September: 255–72.

Leamer, E. E. (1987) 'Paths of Development in the Three-Factor, *n*-Good General Equilibrium Model', *Journal of Political Economy*, **95(5)** October: 961–99.

Lee, Y. S., D. F. Hadwinger and C. B. Lee (1990) 'Agricultural Policy Making Under International Pressures', *Food Policy*, **15(5)** October: 418–33.

Lindert, P. H. (1989) 'Economic Influences on the History of Agricultural Policy', Working Paper, **58**, Agricultural History Center, University of California, Davis, November.

Little, I., T. Scitovsky and M. Scott (1970) *Industry and Trade in Some Developing Countries: A Comparative Study*, London: Oxford University Press for the OECD.

Long, N. V. and N. Vousden (1991) 'Protectionist Responses and Declining Industries', *Journal of International Economics*, **30**: 87–103.

Michaely, M., D. Papageorgiou and A. M. Choksi (eds) (1991) *Liberalizing Foreign Trade: The Lessons of Experience in the Developing World*, Oxford: Basil Blackwell.

OECD (1988; 1990) *Monitoring and Outlook of Agricultural Policies, Markets and Trade*, Paris: OECD.

(1989) *Agricultural and Environmental Policies: Opportunities for Integration*, Paris: OECD.

Peltzman, S. (1976) 'Toward a More General Theory of Regulation', *Journal of Law and Economics*, **19(2)** August: 211–40.

Stigler, G. J. (1971) 'The Theory of Economic Regulation', *Bell Journal of Economics*, **2(1)**: 3–21.
Tyers, R. and K. Anderson (1992) *Disarray in World Food Markets*, Cambridge: Cambridge University Press, forthcoming.
Webb, A. J., M. Lopez and R. Penn (eds) (1990) *Estimates of Producer and Consumer Subsidy Equivalents: Government Intervention in Agriculture 1982–87*, Statistical Bulletin, **803**, Washington, D.C.: US Department of Agriculture.
Winters, L. A. (1987) 'The Political Economy of the Agricultural Policy of Industrial Countries', *European Review of Agricultural Economics*, **14**: 285–304.
Von Witzke, H. (1986) 'Endogenous Supranational Policy Decisions: The Common Agricultural Policy of the European Community', *Public Choice*, **48(2)**: 157–74.
World Bank (1986) *World Development Report 1986*, New York: Oxford University Press.
(1987) *World Development Report 1987*, New York: Oxford University Press.

Discussion

DAVID BLANDFORD[1]

Kym Anderson's thesis is that international factors are becoming increasingly important in influencing domestic agricultural policies. In chapter 13, he focuses primarily on the reform of policies in richer countries. This is legitimate given the central role of these countries in world agricultural markets, and by implication the significance of their policies for developing country exporters or importers.

Anderson argues that it is necessary to make the transition from a closed to an open economy model of the political market for protection. Such a transition would parallel recent developments in some other areas of economic theory (e.g., macroeconomics). In this regard, I am in full agreement with him. It has long seemed to me that the political economy approach has been unnecessarily simplistic in focusing almost exclusively on the role of domestic interest groups in determining the supply and demand for protection. It is time for the concept of the open economy to find its place in this branch of the literature.

The political market model for government assistance is useful for characterising the broad difference between rich and poor countries in their approach to agricultural policy. The model posits that in poor countries both the demand for and supply of agricultural protection is weak, consequently effective protection is low relative to other sectors. The opposite conditions hold in richer countries.

Anderson identifies the principal cause of the position of the relevant curves in poorer countries as one of weak demand for agricultural assistance. In these countries, political power is often urban-centred; consequently, the supply of protection for agriculture is also relatively weak. This tends to result in discrimination, particularly against domestic food-crop or smallholder export agriculture. Numerous African countries provide examples of this phenomenon. However, it does not necessarily lead to significant discrimination against non-food or large-scale export agriculture, particularly when these are dominated by large landowners. Such a group may have sufficient political influence to ensure that even if not highly supported, it is not a victim of undue discrimination. There are examples in Latin America and Asia which appear to conform to this typology.

Selective discrimination against the producers of primary export commodities is likely to have distributional consequences in developing countries, but will not necessarily lower national income. The implicit taxation of exports, which have low price and income elasticities of demand in international markets and a high potential for supply-expanding technological change, can lead to higher domestic welfare; it may also complement efforts to stimulate exports of value-added processed products. These may have better market prospects than the primary commodities from which they are derived, providing that processed imports are not restricted or discouraged by industrial countries. This being said, the historical record of most primary commodity exporters does not inspire confidence in their ability to determine and implement an optimal export tax, to use the revenues derived from commodity taxes wisely, or to diversify successfully into higher-valued processed exports.

In moving from the static to the dynamic, Anderson seeks to explore the factors that cause the supply and demand curves for protection to shift. Several plausible long-term forces are identified which, it is argued, will lead to smooth and predictable changes in the position of these curves. There are indeed historical examples to which one can point of smooth transitions from one equilibrium to another (Anderson, Hayami *et al.*, 1986). However, the assumptions of stable dynamic processes and marginalism, with which neoclassical economists have been so comfortable, increasingly seem to be in question: perhaps alternative paradigms, such as chaos theory, deserve close scrutiny! How else can one deal with the radical shifts in economic policies in some advanced market economies in recent years, let alone those in developing countries and economies of the former Eastern bloc! Some economists would be reticent about predicting the relative position of the supply and demand curves for agricultural protection in Australia and New Zealand over the next five years, and would not even hazard a guess for Argentina or Brazil. I know of few economists who are eager to predict where these curves will be in Hungary or Poland next month, let alone next year.

Anderson seems to be relatively optimistic that international influences will be consistently and universally favourable to the reform of domestic agricultural policies, and to the opening up of domestic markets. I would like to believe this, but find somewhat less cause for optimism. As an example, take one of the factors he cites, the 'greening' of agriculture. There is increasing concern about the environmental implications of agricultural production, and growing recognition that agriculture may have an important role as the supplier of public goods, such as rural amenity. However, there often seems to be a strong protectionist thread in the policy debate on the agriculture–environment linkage. Environmental concerns may result in moves to restrict trade and raise domestic prices in order to prevent 'environmental dumping' or to protect food safety, rather than to lower support prices. Farmers themselves may use environmental arguments to justify high support prices as a means of safeguarding current agricultural structure and protecting the rural fabric. There is a risk that pressure for 'environmentally sensitive' agriculture will result in more, rather than less, agricultural protection.

Similarly, the view is presented in Anderson's paper that economic conflicts among large nations or blocs (the United States and the European Community, the United States and Japan, and in the future perhaps Western and Eastern Europe) have, and will continue to have, a positive effect on agricultural policy and policy reform. I am not convinced that this is the case. Despite some positive short-run effects, regionalism may present a threat to the world economy in the longer term. The interests of developing countries in particular will probably be less protected under a system in which bilateral relationships between the large and the small become more important than multilateral disciplines. Furthermore, there is no guarantee that the short-run pressures on domestic agricultural programmes generated by trade conflicts will have positive or lasting results. Despite nagging and persistent imperfections in the global economy, multilateralism and cooperation have been central to world economic progress since the end of the Second World War. There is a clear danger that were polarisation, confrontation and economic brinkmanship to become the norm, this would have a negative rather than a positive impact on the trend towards agricultural reform.

Finally, I am less sanguine than Anderson about the effects of budgetary pressures and trade concerns on reform. Efforts to control the taxpayer costs of support can simply perpetuate a situation in which the majority of support is hidden in high food prices created by import barriers. Taxpayer costs and the effects of support on trade may be reduced by constraining production through quotas, rather than through lowering domestic support prices. There are strong domestic welfare arguments for reducing the support for agriculture in industrial countries and for adopting more market-oriented policies; these imply that reforms should extend beyond the confines of policy adjustments designed solely to meet budgetary or trade concerns.

Despite these reservations, Anderson's final arguments about the need for reform are well taken. I agree fully with his view that current agricultural policies may not be effective in achieving their aims, and that the distributional effects of policy choices are a major force behind the pattern of distortions. I would, however, add redistributive inefficiency to the list of the negative features of existing policies which need to be brought to public attention: the perception that policy bias towards agriculture leads to significant gains to farmers, which is noted in the paper, may itself be seriously distorted. The substantial costs of current agricultural policies in richer countries to consumers and taxpayers are well known (OECD, 1990a). The efficiency of current policies in transferring income to farmers may be extremely low (Blandford, 1990). The replacement of price supports by other measures, such as direct payments delinked from production, could contribute both to greater transparency and greater efficiency in achieving policy objectives (OECD, 1990b). These issues should also be explored further in order to contribute to the momentum for the reform of agricultural policies in industrial countries.

NOTE

1 The opinions expressed in this comment are those of the author and do not necessarily correspond to those of the Organisation for Economic Cooperation and Development.

REFERENCES

Anderson, K., Y. Hayami *et al.* (1986) *The Political Economy of Agricultural Protection: East Asia in International Perspective*, Boston, London and Sydney: Allen & Unwin.

Blandford, D. (1990) 'The Costs of Agricultural Protection and the Difference Free Trade Would Make', in F. H. Sanderson (ed.), *Agricultural Protec-*

tionism in the Industrialized World, Washington, D.C.: Resources for the Future.

OECD (1990a) *Agricultural Policies, Markets and Trade: Monitoring and Outlook*, Paris: OECD.

(1990b) *Reforming Agricultural Policies: Quantitative Restrictions on Production and Direct Income Support*, Paris: OECD.

Index

Printed in the United States
By Bookmasters